THE GANG BOOK

A detailed overview of street gangs in the Chicago metropolitan area.

chicago crime commission

J.R. Davis
Chairman and President
Chicago Crime Commission

Andrew Henning
Vice President and General Counsel
Chicago Crime Commission

Principal Editor & Researcher:

Franco Domma
Inspector
Cook County Sheriff's Department

Co-Editors:

Charito Romero
Chicago Crime Commission

Elisabeth Saffell
Chicago Crime Commission

A special thank you to Chicago Police Department Gang Investigations Division Sergeant Charles Daly, Cook County Sheriff's Department officers, Chicago Crime Commission Research Analyst Anthony Buccola, Chicago Crime Commission Intern Emma Maxwell and Chicago Crime Commission Volunteer Lauren Cantine

ACKNOWLEDGEMENTS

The Chicago Crime Commission recognizes the following individuals and agencies have been especially valuable in providing information and their expertise for this report. The production of this report is an excellent example of the strong partnerships among law enforcement and other community organizations in the Chicago Metropolitan area.

Thank you to:

Cook County Sheriff's Office . . . . Sheriff Thomas J. Dart

Chicago Police Department . . . . Superintendent Eddie Johnson

Federal Bureau of Investigation . . . . Special Agent in Charge Michael Anderson

Drug Enforcement Administration . . . . Special Agent in Charge Dennis Wichern

Bureau of Alcohol, Tobacco, Firearms and Explosives . . . . Special Agent in Charge Celinez Nunez

High Intensity Drug Trafficking Agency . . . . Executive Director Nicholas Roti

Illinois Attorney General . . . . Attorney General Lisa Madigan
Assistant Attorney General Shannon O'Brien

Cook County State's Attorney's Office . . . . State's Attorney Kimberly M. Foxx

Cicero Police Department . . . . Commander Vincent Acevez

Maywood Police Department . . . . Lieutenant Dennis Diaz

Skokie Police Department . . . . Officer Sabih Khan

Suburban Police Departments

Cook County

Barrington Hills Police Department	Cicero Police Department	Homewood Police Department
Bartlett Police Department	Crestwood Police Department	Inverness Police Department
Bedford Park Police Department	Des Plaines Police Department	Kenilworth Police Department
Bellwood Police Department	East Hazel Crest Police Department	La Grange Police Department
Berkeley Police Department	Elgin Police Department	La Grange Park Police Department
Berwyn Police Department	Elk Grove Police Department	Lemont Police Department
Blue Island Police Department	Evanston Police Department	Lincolnwood Police Department
Bridgeview Police Department	Forest Park Police Department	Lynwood Police Department
Broadview Police Department	Franklin Park Police Department	Matteson Police Department
Burnham Police Department	Glencoe Police Department	Maywood Police Department
Calumet Park Police Department	Hanover Park Police Department	Morton Grove Police Department
Chicago Ridge Police Department	Hodgins Police Department	Mount Prospect Police Department
	Hoffman Estates Police Department	Niles Police Department

Northbrook Police Department
Northfield Police Department
Northlake Police Department
North Riverside Police Department
Oak Forest Police Department
Oak Park Police Department
Orland Park Police Department
Palatine Police Department
Palos Heights Police Department
Park Ridge Police Department
Prospect Heights Police Department
Richton Park Police Department
Riverdale Police Department
River Forest Police Department
River Grove Police Department
Riverside Police Department
Rolling Meadows Police Department
Schiller Park Police Department
Skokie Police Department
South Barrington Police Department
South Holland Police Department
Steger Police Department
Streamwood Police Department
Western Springs Police Department
Wheeling Police Department
Winnetka Police Department

DuPage County

Darien Police Department
Downers Grove Police Department
Elmhurst Police Department
Glen Ellyn Police Department
Glendale Heights Police Department
Itasca Police Department
Lisle Police Department
Naperville Police Department
Oakbrook Terrace Police Department
Warrenville Police Department
West Chicago Police Department
Wood Dale Police Department

Kane County

Aurora Police Department
Batavia Police Department
Carpentersville Police Department
East Dundee Police Department
Geneva Police Department
Gilberts Police Department
North Aurora Police Department
Pingree Police Department
Sleepy Hollow Police Department
St. Charles Police Department
Sugar Grove Police Department

Lake County

Bannockburn Police Department
Buffalo Grove Police Department
Fox Lake Police Department
Hawthorn Police Department
Highland Park Police Department
Highwood Police Department
Lake Forest Police Department
Lake Villa Police Department
Lakemoor Police Department
Libertyville Police Department
Lindenhurst Police Department
Mundelein Police Department
Park City Police Department
Riverwoods Police Department
Tower Lakes Police Department
Wauconda Police Department
Waukegan Police Department
Winthrop Police Department

McHenry County

Algonquin Police Department
Crystal Lake Police Department
Harvard Police Department
Hebron Police Department
Johnsburg Police Department
Lake in the Hills Police Department

Marengo Police Department
Spring Grove Police Department
Union Village Police Department
Woodstock Police Department

Will County

Channahon Police Department
Village of Crete Police Department
Lockport Police Department
Joliet Police Department
Mokena Police Department
New Lenox Police Department
Plainfield Police Department

chicago crime commission

Combating Crime Since 1919

Dear Residents:

Public safety is – and should always be – an expectation of the general public. It sustains the quality of life for everyone and is necessary for the welfare of society. When public safety is jeopardized, so too is the wellbeing of our citizens, the health of our economy and the development of our communities. The Chicago Crime Commission's *Gang Book* was created in an effort to address the direct threat gangs pose to the public safety so vital to the livelihood of our families, coworkers and neighbors.

The City of Chicago, local, state, and federal agencies make consistent, positive strides effectively addressing the criminal activity of gangs. However, gangs remain active and continue to plague our institutions and endanger the places we call home. Violence, guns, and drugs continue to demand our attention, and the increasingly sophisticated and nefarious activities of gangs require our immediate awareness too.

True, lasting solutions involve partnering with all parts of the community, from schools and businesses, to churches and government agencies. It is imperative that we work together to address the issue of gangs and deliver positive solutions protecting and expanding our shared public safety. This publication endeavors to do exactly that.

The *Gang Book* is a well-researched resource and training guide designed to assist and inform law enforcement and the broader community. It has been an honor working with the wide range of agencies and departments that contributed to the development of the *Gang Book*. Its publication would not have been possible without their support and the Chicago Crime Commission extends its sincere gratitude to all who assisted in producing the new *Gang Book*.

As a non-profit organization, we depend on citizens like you to grow and improve our initiatives, and are grateful for your support. We hope you explore learning more about the Chicago Crime Commission and consider making a contribution to assist our efforts making Chicago a safer and vibrant city for all.

Most sincerely,

J.R. Davis
Chairman and President

Andrew Henning
Vice President and General Counsel

U.S. Department of Justice

Federal Bureau of Investigation

In Reply, Please Refer to
File No.

2111 West Roosevelt Road
Chicago, Illinois 60608

August 30, 2017

Mr. J.R. Davis
President
Chicago Crime Commission
P.O. Box 8021
Chicago, Illinois 60680

Dear Mr. Davis:

Given the alarming and escalating rise in violence in the Chicagoland area in recent years, both shootings and homicides, FBI Chicago's highest priority is to target the most violent of the violent in our city. Specifically, these individuals are the leaders (shot callers) and trigger pullers who are terrorizing numerous neighborhoods on a regular basis.

There are some individuals and violent criminal gangs whom, as a result of their actions and threats, not only inflict serious bodily harm and death upon citizens, but directly interfere with community members' rights to safe housing, schools, health care, employment, and a criminal justice system free of witness retaliation, intimidation and tampering. Consequently, the environment of fear created by these individuals and gangs pose the greatest challenge to law enforcement officials in securing cooperation from the community to reclaim so many neighborhoods in Chicago.

The law enforcement/private sector partnership, including the tireless and dedicated efforts of the Chicago Crime Commission, is vital to our collective success in eradicating the gang violence in our city. The publication of the Commission's *Gang Book* and collaboration in its assembly, greatly furthers these objectives.

Thank you and your entire team for all the significant contributions the Chicago Crime Commission has made over the years to make Chicago a safe and thriving community.

Sincerely,

Michael J. Anderson
Special Agent in Charge

U. S. Department of Justice

Drug Enforcement Administration

Chicago Field Division
230 South Dearborn, Suite 1200
Chicago, Il 60604

www.dea.gov

Chairman and President J.R. Davis   JUN 27 2017
Chicago Crime Commission
P.O. Box 8021
Chicago, Illinois 60680-8021

Dear Chairman Davis:

On behalf of the Drug Enforcement Administration (DEA), Chicago Field Division, thank you for this opportunity to contribute to the Chicago Crime Commission's new "Gang Book". The Chicagoland area is in the midst of a heroin and fentanyl epidemic - driven by Mexican drug cartel traffickers and our cities numerous street gang members which control street level sales in our great city. For these reasons, the gangs and cartel members who traffic in heroin and fentanyl will continue to be my office's number one priority.

According to the Illinois Department of Health, approximately three people die every day in the Chicago area due to a heroin or fentanyl overdose. A recent Roosevelt University study indicates that 80% of the State's heroin treatment admissions occurred in the Chicago Metro Area with 79% of the Illinois hospitalizations for opioids, including heroin occurring in Cook County. Tragically, the average age of death of a heroin user is 30 causing untold scarring and pain to their family members.

On behalf of the DEA, I want to thank the Chicago Crime Commission for their leadership and vision in the publication of the "Gang Book". The Chicago Field Division of the DEA commits their full support to partner with your agency and others willing to battle the gangs and the cartels that fuel death and violence in our great city.

Sincerely,

Dennis A. Wichern
Special Agent in Charge

U.S. Department of Justice

Bureau of Alcohol, Tobacco,
Firearms and Explosives

June 22, 2017
www.atf.gov

CN:772000
2400

JR Davis, Chairman & President
Chicago Crime Commission
Post Office Box 8021
Chicago, Illinois 60680

Dear Mr. Davis:

On behalf of the Bureau of Alcohol, Tobacco, Firearms and Explosives' (ATF), Chicago Field Division, I want to commend the extraordinary efforts put forth by the Chicago Crime Commission in producing the latest edition of "The Gang Book," which is a very valuable investigative tool for law enforcement at all levels. As practitioners, we are constantly reviewing new trends and patterns associated with gang and other criminal organizations, and this resourceful publication has proven to be quite beneficial in furtherance of these efforts.

In addition, I also want to applaud the Chicago Crime Commission for the continued support and assistance provided to law enforcement through your research and practical application.
As we know, the criminal activities associated with street gangs and street gang members including firearms-related violence, pose a significant threat to our communities, and we must address these issues to ensure public safety. The forging of partnerships and collaborative engagement are paramount in our quest to combat the senseless violence perpetrated by this criminal element.

ATF takes great pride in our close working relationship with our Federal, State, and local law enforcement partners and we are equally proud of our continued partnership with the Chicago Crime Commission. Thank you for allowing us to once again be a contributor to this very important endeavor as we all strive to make our communities a better, and safer place.

Sincerely yours,

Celinez Nunez
Special Agent in Charge

OFFICE OF THE ATTORNEY GENERAL
STATE OF ILLINOIS

Lisa Madigan
ATTORNEY GENERAL

September 29, 2017

Mr. J.R. Davis
Chicago Crime Commission
P.O. Box 8021
Chicago, IL 60680

Dear Chairman Davis and friends,

As Illinois Attorney General, I want to thank and congratulate the Chicago Crime Commission on the publication of its newest edition of the Gang Book. This comprehensive and indispensable publication aimed at informing law enforcement, civic leaders and concerned residents about the scourge of violent street gangs is an invaluable resource in the fight against organized crime.

We know all too well the violence that has plagued Chicago, and gangs are a major part of that intolerable situation. Some estimates put Chicago area's gang membership as high as 150,000, the most gang members of any city in America. The commission's Gang Book helps us understand this problem – from the violent history of these organizations in Chicago to the relatively new influence of social media on gang violence. This information and insight is vital in order to combat gang crime.

The Gang Book is just one example of the Chicago Crime Commission bringing together and supporting law enforcement all across Illinois to help make our communities safer. I am proud to be a part of this effort, and I am very appreciative of the hard work that goes into this tremendous resource.

Very truly yours,

Lisa Madigan
ATTORNEY GENERAL

500 South Second Street, Springfield, Illinois 62706 • (217) 782-1090 • TTY: (877) 844-5461 • Fax: (217) 782-7046
100 West Randolph Street, Chicago, Illinois 60601 • (312) 814-3000 • TTY: (800) 964-3013 • Fax: (312) 814-3806
601 South University Avenue, Suite 102, Carbondale, Illinois 62901 • (618) 529-6400 • TTY: (877) 675-9339 • Fax: (618) 529-6416

OFFICE OF THE SHERIFF

RICHARD J. DALEY CENTER
COOK COUNTY
CHICAGO, ILLINOIS 60602

THOMAS J. DART
SHERIFF

Mr. J.R. Davis
President
Chicago Crime Commission
P.O. Box 8021
Chicago, IL 60680

Dear Mr. Davis,

Having served as the Sheriff of Cook County for over eleven years now, I have seen first-hand the degradation of our communities by the activities of the street gangs that populate Cook County. These gangs are pervasive, populating both the streets of Chicago and the surrounding suburbs, and are a continuing presence in the Cook County Jail.

The consequences of gang life are devastating and far-reaching. One cannot turn on the news without hearing of another innocent child murdered in the cross-fire of gang violence, or of entire neighborhoods turned into active war zones where no one can leave their residence without fear of accidentally getting caught in any number of the retaliatory shootings. I find it simply unacceptable for any more innocent lives to be lost in this seemingly never-ending cycle of gang violence.

That is why the annual publication of *The Gang Book* continues to be so crucial in combating this violence. When people are properly educated on an issue, particularly an issue with such a complicated breadth as the Chicago gang violence, it becomes far easier to come up with solutions. *The Gang Book* is written by premier law enforcement experts on gangs and gang activities. Their expertise and years of valuable knowledge gained by being on the frontlines set this book apart from other academic literature. I have the pleasure of knowing some of the contributors to this book. They are among the best and brightest members of the Sheriff's Office, and I am proud that law enforcement agencies throughout Cook County, including our own dedicated staff, continue to use the information in this book to identify and combat Chicagoland gang activity.

This book is also an invaluable resource for social workers, community educators, and all citizens who are keen to educate themselves on the subject of gangs so that they can contribute to the ridding their communities of gang violence. Having dedicated community members who can recognize gang graffiti or other suspicious activities and report it to law enforcement is imperative in rebuilding their communities and preventing potentially horrendous crimes.

It is an honor to partner with the Chicago Crime Commission in producing this book. Their continued dedication to educate the community on gang violence in this city is inspiring, and I hope that law enforcement officers and citizens alike will utilize this book to work towards making the great city of Chicago free of all gang violence.

Sincerely,

Thomas J. Dart
Sheriff of Cook County

Department of Police · City of Chicago
3510 South Michigan Avenue · Chicago, Illinois 60653

September 21, 2017

J.R. Davis, Chairman & President
P.O. Box 8021
Chicago, IL 60680

Dear Chairman Davis:

As the Superintendent of the Chicago Police Department, I am writing to express my support of the Chicago Crime Commission's Gang Book.

This compilation of Chicago area gang information is a resource for law enforcement and community groups alike to keep abreast of what is happening in the neighborhoods of Chicago and throughout Cook County. Gangs and guns are two of the biggest threats to our communities. The more the public can be informed about the prevalence of gangs and their impact on communities, the better equipped we are to counteract their effects on neighborhoods. Most gang activity revolves around the selling of drugs, and the damage caused by these gangs isn't just measured by the loss of lives to the community but by the loss of resources expended in efforts to repair the damages gangs have caused in the neighborhoods.

On behalf of the Chicago Police Department I would, once again, like to express our support to the Chicago Crime Commission on another edition of their Gang Book. As Thomas Jefferson once stated "an informed citizenry is at the heart of a dynamic democracy."

Sincerely,

K. B. Navano For

Eddie T. Johnson
Superintendent of Police

Emergency and TTY: 9-1-1 • Non Emergency and TTY: (within City limits) 3-1-1 • Non-Emergency and TTY: (outside City limits) (312) 746-6000
E-mail: clearpath@chicagopolice.org • Website: www.chicagopolice.org

10

OFFICE OF THE STATE'S ATTORNEY

KIMBERLY M. FOXX
STATE'S ATTORNEY

69 WEST WASHINGTON, SUITE 3200
CHICAGO, ILLINOIS 60602
(312) 603-1880

Dear Concerned Citizens,

The Cook County State's Attorney's Office values the opportunity to collaborate with other law enforcement agencies to develop creative strategies to address gang crimes and violence in our communities.

We applaud the efforts of the Chicago Crime Commission and their commitment to addressing public corruption and violent crime, through the publication of the Gang Book. This detailed guide on combating and understanding violent street gangs provides schools, businesses and law enforcement agencies with a valuable resource.

The Cook County State's Attorney's Office is proud to work in partnership with the Chicago Crime Commission in helping to provide this comprehensive and useful tool for all citizens.

Sincerely,

Kimberly M. Foxx
Cook County State's Attorney

TABLE OF CONTENTS

Section III – Social Media 311

Section IV – Suburban Gang Activity 321

Section V – Cartels, Gangs and Drugs 331

Section VI – Gun Trafficking 357

Section VII – Directories For Assistance 367

Section VIII – Gang Book References 381

During the 1990s Chicago gangs designed patches for sweaters and jackets used to self-identify.

Introduction

Chicago is no stranger to the criminal element in its almost 200-year existence. From saloons filled with pickpockets and thieves of the 1800s, to infamous mobsters such as Al Capone and Tony Accardo, to super gangs like the Vice Lords, Gangster Disciples, and Latin Kings. Chicago has had long history with organized crime and gangs. Modern times have given rise to factions and break-offs of these super gangs. The type of gang activity being displayed now is a far cry from the hierarchical business model of gangs in the past. The hyper-violent and indiscriminate violence is terrorizing the streets of Chicago with innocent civilians getting caught in the crossfire.

History

From the 1960s to the early 2000s, gangs in Chicago were well organized and followed a strict command structure. In the 1970s the main African-American, Latin, and Caucasian gangs were divided into two main groups: People and Folks. There were also Independents, or gangs that did not choose to align with either of the two groups. In the 1960s many of these gangs dabbled in pseudo-social and political activity as a means of diverting attention from law enforcement and trying to restructure their public image. However, in the 1970s, profits from criminal activities superseded social issues.

During this time Jeff Fort, leader of the Stone Rangers, united nearly 50 street gangs under the Black P Stone Nation. The newly formed Black P Stone Nation was highly organized and structured; taking part in multiple criminal enterprises such as drug trafficking, prostitution, extortion, robbery, etc. Other gangs followed Fort's example and began to form alliances with one another. Arguably the most famous was the union between David Barksdale of the Black Disciples and Larry Hoover of the Gangster Disciples forming the Black Gangster Disciples. Following the creation of the Black P Stone Nation and the Black Gangster Disciples came one of the bloodiest gang wars in Chicago's history. Members of the Black P Stones and the Black Gangster Disciples fought each other for territory to expand their criminal enterprises which led to many members from both sides losing their lives and ending up in both state and federal prison.

The fallout of the gang wars led to new dividing lines and alliances, many of them made while members were in incarcerated. Within the prison system came the new alignment of People and Folks. While in prison, gang members could not represent their individual gangs, only People or Folks. Members who aligned with People displayed their affiliation by turning their hat to the left, wearing earrings in their left ear, rolled their left pant leg up, etc. Folks did the same thing only to the right. Both members of the Folks and People employed various symbols and graphics to identify their affiliation. Members and gangs that identify with People use a five-pointed star. The Latin Kings,

one of Chicago's largest gangs, is affiliated with People and demonstrates their alliance by displaying a five-pointed crown in many of their graphics and graffiti. Contrary to the People gangs, a commonly displayed Folks symbol is a six-pointed star. The six-pointed star is most often seen in reference to the Gangster Disciples. The People and Folks alliances were strictly maintained up until the early 2000s. However, the old alliances have not held up through the years.

The razing of public housing led to a breakdown in infrastructure which was necessary for the gangs to operate the way they did in the past. In the days of public housing, structural hierarchy was promoted through a "big house" mentality, where members of specific gangs had to live together. With the fall of public housing, gangs and gang members were displaced and there were instances of rival gang members living in close proximity with one another. For example, Gangster Disciples living near Four Corner Hustlers.

Another explanation for the breakdown of the traditional street gang is gentrification and deconstruction of neighborhoods. Chicago's main tourist areas such as the North Side, the Loop and near South Lakefront are the safest they have been since the city started keeping records. Violence is concentrated in the west and south side, areas with high poverty levels and little employment opportunities.

In a recent study conducted by University of Illinois at Chicago's Great Cities Institute, 47% of African-American men between the ages of 20-24 are either

Alleged members of the Latin Dragons disrespecting Latin Kings

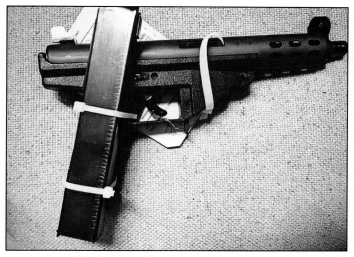

Seized firearm provided by the Bureau of Alcohol, Tobacco, Firearms and Explosives

unemployed or not attending colleges in Chicago. This decline in youth employment and youth education has been tied to Chicago's most racially segregated neighborhoods and the rise of crime and poverty.

Present Day

A noticeable difference between the super gangs of the past and the modern-day splinter groups is their presence online. Gangs "cyber-bang" on various social media platforms by insulting their opposition, praising their gang and fallen members, and selling illicit drugs. The use of social media and the instant accessibility for gangs to insult their rivals is believed by law enforcement to be a main catalyst for the violence plaguing Chicago's south and west sides.

In the same vein, Chicago-based "drill rap" is not only promoting violence but encouraging it. Drill rap glorifies the Chicago gangster life, with lyrics about guns, drugs, and murder. Many drill rappers are affiliated with Chicago gangs. Moreover, these drill rappers post videos on various social media platforms, often times insulting a rival gang or faction. The videos take place in the rapper's neighborhood and features gang members, many not older than teenagers, brandishing firearms, clouds of marijuana smoke, and throwing up gang signs with their hands.

Gangs and gang membership has always been fluid and is constantly changing. The frequent formation and dissolution of gangs and leadership makes it nearly impossible to compile a census with precision. The breakdown of hierarchy and leadership in conjunction with the emergence of factions has added a new dimension to gang life in Chicago. Currently, there are over 50 active gangs operating within the city of Chicago.

Factions make this issue more difficult because they can form overnight and can consist of as little as a dozen members. For example, the Gangster Disciples have over 200 break-offs from the original gang (All Bout Money, Money Over Bitches, Insane Cutthroat Gangsters). The commonality between factions is they all claim Gangster Disciples but represent different blocks. There has been evidence that factions within the same gang fight each other over territory and money. Loyalty has given way to income. For example, members of the Gangster

Alleged Chicago gang member uploads a video brandishing a firearm to Facebook

Disciples will work with members of the Black Disciples as long as it profitable for both sides.

The drug trade fuels violence. Narcotics being supplied by Mexican cartels flood the streets of Chicago, creating a viable drug market. The trafficking and distribution of heroin is of particular concern in Chicago. Heroin has caused significant harm to Chicago and the surrounding counties. Fentanyl, a synthetic opioid analgesic about 50 times more potent than heroin, adds a new health risk to Chicago's drug market. Fentanyl-laced heroin has hit Chicago's streets causing abusers to overdose because most are unaware of its potency.

While Chicago's gangs may be at war with one another, law enforcement remains active. Local, state, and federal law enforcement agencies are working individually as well as collaborating with one another to suppress gang activity and violence in the city. New strategies and policies are being applied citywide in order to ensure Chicago's streets are safe and free of gang violence and criminal activity.

Gang (Law Enforcement Definition): A gang is an organized group with a recognized leader whose activities are either criminal or, at the very least, threatening to the community. Although gang members are part of these organizations, they rarely acknowledge their own roles as contributing to the problems in that community. Gangs display their identity and unity in obvious ways such as jewelry, colored clothing, jargon, and signals. Members remain together in quiet times as well as in conflict. In response to this twisted loyalty, members are rewarded by being accepted and recognized as a gang member. The main source of income for most gangs is narcotics. Members of all ages are used by the gang in the illegal sale of narcotics and other unlawful activities. It is a mistaken belief that gangs only operate in less affluent neighborhoods. Gangs exist in virtually every community in Chicago. And while there are many individual street gangs in Chicago, most gangs also belong to one of two alliances, either "People" or "Folks." The alliances are not aligned along traditional racial boundaries, and both contain black, white, and Hispanic street gangs. Both alliances are alive and well on Chicago's streets, and in most cases are bitter rivals. The "People" gangs all wear their identifiers to the left side, while the "Folks" gangs wear their identifiers on the right. *(Source: CPD)*

Gang (Legal Definition): "Streetgang" or "gang" or "organized gang" or "criminal street gang" means any combination, confederation, alliance, network, conspiracy, understanding, or other similar conjoining, in law or in fact, of 3 or more persons with an established hierarchy that, through its membership or through the agency of any member engages in a course or pattern of criminal activity. *(Source: 740 ILCS 147/10)*

Gang-related Activity: "Streetgang related" or "gang-related" means any criminal activity, enterprise, pursuit, or undertaking directed by, ordered by, authorized by, consented to, agreed to, requested by, acquiesced in, or ratified by any gang leader, officer, or governing or policy-making person or authority, or by any agent, representative, or deputy of any such officer, person, or authority:

1. with the intent to increase the gang's size, membership, prestige, dominance, or control in any geographical area; or

2. with the intent to provide the gang with any advantage in, or any control or dominance over any criminal market sector, including but not limited to, the manufacture, delivery, or sale of controlled substances or cannabis; arson or arson-for-hire; traffic in stolen property or stolen credit cards; traffic in prostitution, obscenity, or pornography; or that involves robbery, burglary, or theft; or

3. with the intent to exact revenge or retribution for the gang or any member of the gang; or

4. with the intent to obstruct justice, or intimidate or eliminate any witness against the gang or any member of the gang; or

5. with the intent to otherwise directly or indirectly cause any benefit, aggrandizement, gain, profit or other advantage whatsoever to or for the gang, its reputation, influence, or membership. *(Source: P.A. 97-1150, eff. 1-25-13.)*

Gang Member Definition: "Streetgang member" or "gang member" means any person who actually and in fact belongs to a gang, and any person who knowingly acts in the capacity of an agent for or accessory to, or is legally accountable for, or voluntarily associates himself with a course or pattern of gang-related criminal activity, whether in a preparatory, executory, or cover-up phase of any activity, or who knowingly performs, aids, or abets any such activity. *(Source: P.A. 97-1150, eff. 1-25-13.)*

Faction Definition: A gang faction is a subsection or break-off of a larger gang. A faction will usually have its own name. The faction may change or alter its name as it matures, but the same individuals tend to remain in close association with each other. *(Source: CPD)*

Racketeer Influenced and Corrupt Organizations (RICO): The RICO statute was established with the purpose of eliminating infiltration of organized crime and racketeering into legitimate organizations operating in interstate commerce. The RICO statute makes it possible for syndicate leaders to be prosecuted for criminal acts they may have orchestrated but were not directly involved in. RICO is sufficiently broad to encompass illegal activities relating to any enterprise affecting interstate or foreign commerce. An "enterprise" includes:

1. any partnership, corporation, association, business or charitable trust, or other legal entity; and

2. any group of individuals or other legal entities, or any combination thereof, associated in fact although not itself a legal entity. An association in fact must be held together by a common purpose of engaging in a course of conduct, and it may be associated together for purposes that are both legal and illegal. An association in fact must:

   a. have an ongoing organization or structure, either formal or informal;

   b. the various members of the group must function as a continuing unit, even if the group changes membership by gaining or losing members over time; and

   c. have an ascertainable structure distinct from that inherent in the conduct of a pattern of predicate activity.

"Labor organization" includes any organization, labor union, craft union, or any voluntary unincorporated association designed to further the cause of the rights of union labor that is constituted for the purpose, in whole or in part, of collective bargaining or of dealing with employers concerning grievances, terms or conditions of employment, or apprenticeships or applications for apprenticeships, or of other mutual aid or protection in connection with employment, including apprenticeships or applications for apprenticeships.

"Operation or management" means directing or carrying out the enterprise's affairs and is limited to any person who knowingly serves as a leader, organizer, operator, manager, director, supervisor, financier, advisor, recruiter, supplier, or enforcer of an enterprise in violation of this Article.

"Predicate activity" means any act that is a Class 2 felony or higher and constitutes a violation or

violations of any of the following provisions of the laws of the State of Illinois (as amended or revised as of the date the activity occurred or, in the instance of a continuing offense, the date that charges under this Article are filed in a particular matter in the State of Illinois) or any act under the law of another jurisdiction for an offense that could be charged as a Class 2 felony or higher in this State.

"Pattern of predicate activity" means

1. at least 3 occurrences of predicate activity that are in some way related to each other and that have continuity between them, and that are separate acts. Acts are related to each other if they are not isolated events, including if they have similar purposes, or results, or participants, or victims, or are committed a similar way, or have other similar distinguishing characteristics, or are part of the affairs of the same enterprise. There is continuity between acts if they are ongoing over a substantial period, or if they are part of the regular way some entity does business or conducts its affairs; and

2. which occurs after the effective date of this Article, and the last of which falls within 3 years (excluding any period of imprisonment) after the first occurrence of predicate activity.

"Unlawful death" includes the following offenses: under the Code of 1961 or the Criminal Code of 2012: Sections 9-1 (first degree murder) or 9-2 (second degree murder). (*Source: P.A. 97-686, eff. 6-11-12; 97-1150, eff. 1-25-13.*)

SECTION I

Gang Profiles

chicago
crime
commission

Section One profiles, alphabetically, the 52 most prominent gangs in Chicago. Each profile contains the gang's history, in text, accompanied with illustrated identifiers.

The history of the gang examines traditional locations, alliances, known leadership and previous law enforcement operations.

Gang identifiers include gang graffiti, hand signs, tattoos, slogans and drawings.

In addition, the profiles include images of alleged gang membership from Chicago which were created in collaboration with the Cook County Sheriff's department. Although identified in this book, some individuals are currently incarcerated or deceased. All individuals are arranged alphabetically.

Immediately following the gang profiles is a detailed overview of Chicago factions. The history of the emergence of factions, membership structure, modes of operation, and how prosecutors can target factions is summarized. Further, a comprehensive list of Chicago factions is included with illustrations of faction hand signs and group images. Next, an examination of female gang membership in Chicago is explored. Reasons for joining, a female's role, and community resources available for young girls in Chicago is discussed. Finally, Section One identifies Chicago tagging Crews with a brief description of their tagging style and illustrations.

AMBROSE
(Alliance – Folks)

In the 1960s, Walouie Lemas founded Ambrose as a primarily Hispanic street gang around the West Side Pilsen area. Ambrose immediately allied with the Latin Counts. In the 1980s, they joined the Folks Alliance. At this point they were at odds with other Hispanic gangs allied with the People Alliance over turf in the south and southwest side. The two major rivalries were with the Party People and La Raza. In 1999, after an Ambrose member killed an undercover Chicago police officer, the Chicago Police Department and federal agents implemented "Operation Blue Water." This led to the arrest of 17 high-ranking members of the Ambrose gang. While this operation severely damaged their business, Ambrose continues to maintain a presence in several Chicago neighborhoods.

Identifiers:

- **Clothing:** sportswear in color scheme of light blue and black. Oakland A's athletic wear.

- **Gang Symbol:** Plumed helmet with spear; old English letter "A" and "Folks" alliance logos

TATTOOS, HAND SIGN AND COLORS

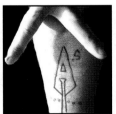

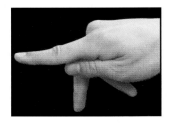

GANG COLORS

Light Blue   **Black**

ALLEGED AMBROSE GANG MEMBERS

Source: Cook County Sheriff's Department

CHICAGO

Jose Acosta
Ghost

CHICAGO

Michael Alenjandro
Juevo

CHICAGO

Rogelio Castañeda
No Love

CHICAGO

Ignacio Cruz
NuNu

CHICAGO

Edwin Diaz
Reckless

CHICAGO

Robert Dowdy
Bird

CHICAGO

Eduardo Gamez
Eddie aka "Caveman"

CHICAGO

Paul Gomez
Weasel

CHICAGO

Sergio Gomez
Sir G

CHICAGO

Rudy Gonzalez
Link

CHICAGO

Peter Guzman
Peter G

CHICAGO
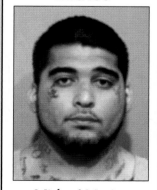
Michael Macias
Mikey

ALLEGED AMBROSE GANG MEMBERS

Source: Cook County Sheriff's Department

CHICAGO

Victor Martinez

Cerelo

CHICAGO

Eleno Meza

No Love

CHICAGO

Jose Negrete

Old Man

CHICAGO

Edgar Rendon

Lucky

CHICAGO

Phillip Sanchez

Lucky

CHICAGO

Candelario Saucedo

C-Murder

CHICAGO

Jonathan Thomas

Lil' Pita

CHICAGO

Paul Villagomez

Prince Paul

CHICAGO

Alejandro Villazana

Casper

AMBROSE IDENTIFIERS

Source: Cook County Sheriff's Department

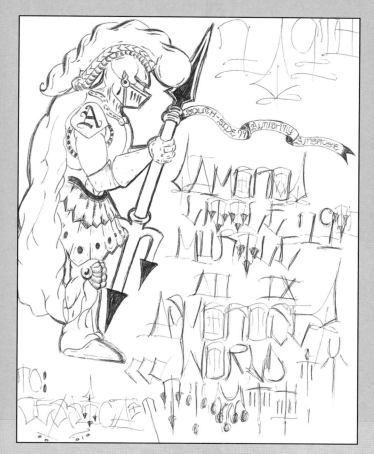

ASHLAND VIKINGS
(Alliance – Folks)

The Ashland Vikings are a predominately Hispanic gang that began in opposition to the Latin Kings in the early 1960s near the East Village area of Ashland and Augusta. They were originally part of the Insane Family under the Spanish Cobras and were often battling the Harrison Gents and the Satan Disciples for turf. These turf battles, mixed with constant police efforts, have since forced the Ashland Vikings from their original area of Ashland and Augusta and into the 24th District near Clark Street and the 25th District near North Avenue.

Identifiers:

- **Clothing:** Minnesota Vikings sportswear and Philadelphia Eagles (Green and Black) athletic wear

- **Gang Symbol:** Viking helmet, six-point star and "AVN" (Almighty Viking Nation)

TATTOOS, HAND SIGN AND COLORS

GANG COLORS

Green   Black

ALLEGED ASHLAND VIKINGS GANG MEMBERS

Source: Cook County Sheriff's Department

CHICAGO

Joaquin Degante
David

CHICAGO

Rafael Gonzalez
Rafa

CHICAGO

Alfredo Martinez
40

CHICAGO

Edwin Perez
Youngblood

CHICAGO

Jesus Perez
Chewy or Chuy

CHICAGO

Armando Valle
Big Bunks

BISHOPS
(Alliance – People)

The Bishops were founded in the early 1980s on 18th Street and Bishop Avenue as an offshoot of the Latin Counts and were one of the founding members of the People Alliance. Their territory has since expanded to cover the west area along 18th Street near Damen and even though the Bishops use a church Bishop as their symbol, it has no religious significance and merely represents the place where they were founded (Bishop Avenue). Although founded through the Latin Counts, both gangs have been at odds since the 1990s.

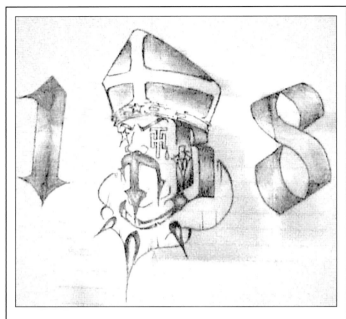

Identifiers:

- **Clothing:** Athletic clothing in the color scheme of their gang
- **Gang symbol:** The gothic letter "B", the Bishop's miter, and the Bishop's cross. There is no religious significance or connotation to these symbols.

TATTOOS, HAND SIGN AND COLORS

GANG COLORS

Copper (Brown)   Black

28

ALLEGED BISHOPS GANG MEMBERS

Source: Cook County Sheriff's Department

CHICAGO

Bernadetter Becera

Kilo

CHICAGO

Rene Perez

Smokey

CHICAGO

James Rodriguez

Negro

CHICAGO

Jose Rodriguez

Cat

CHICAGO

Martin Silva

Raton

BLACK DISCIPLES
(Alliance – Folks)

In the early 1980s, the Black Disciples (BDs) fought a bloody war with the Gangster Disciples over street turf and narcotics sales. In 1990, Jerome "Shorty" Freeman was sentenced to 28 years in prison following a narcotics conviction. Freeman was thought to have been the leader of the BD nation while in prison, but recent federal court testimony actually implies BDs on the streets claimed to be under the leadership of Marvel "King" Thompson. Law enforcement sources have said because of the arrest and indictment of many of the GD leaders, the BDs were able to expand under the leadership of Thompson, who expanded their territory on the South Side. On May 12, 1994, a joint FBI and CPD taskforce led to the arrest of Marvel Thompson. He and other top BD leaders and members were indicted in a federal court on conspiracy, as well as drug and money laundering charges. This was the result of many hours of investigations conducted by the FBI, CPD, and the IRS. With the arrest of Thompson, his second in command and Chairman of the Board, Melvin Herbert took charge. Soon after, the gangs hierarchy structure was a complete mess. According to law enforcement sources, Freeman was released from prison in March 2005 on active parole, and is considered to be a "person of interest."

Identifiers:

■ **Gang Symbol:** Six-Pointed Star (a point each for Love, Life, Loyalty, Unity, Knowledge, and Understanding), Heart (for love of nation), Crown (for King David), Star (for David Barksdale), Sword (for commitment to the nation unto death), Pitchfork (for the Nation's power and their struggle over oppression), Wings, 78 (for the year of their new teachings), Devil's Tail

■ **Gang Anniversary:** Jan 15, 1969 – Anniversary date. This was when the Black Gangster Disiple Nation was formed.

There are over 4,000 members of the BDs at least, within the Chicago area and they are predominantly African American. The BDs are active in 10 police districts in the City of Chicago, and have a presence in many of the same areas as the GDs.

One of the most infamous BD episodes was in 1994 when an 11-year old BD member was sent to kill a GD. He was unsuccessful in this attempt by only wounding the GD, and also killing an innocent female bystander. When news of the murder caused an uproar, the BDs had their own 11-year old assassin murdered.

TATTOOS, HAND SIGNS AND COLORS

GANG COLORS

Blue   Black

ALLEGED BLACK DISCIPLES GANG MEMBERS

Source: Cook County Sheriff's Department

CHICAGO

Dirk Acklin
Don Dirky

CHICAGO

Samuel Apata
Samo

CHICAGO

Durk Banks
Lil Durk

CHICAGO

Daiquan Bennet
Tray-5

CHICAGO

Dayvon Bennett
Von

CHICAGO

Archildress Byrd
Byrd

CHICAGO

Kendrick Carter
Big Folks

CHICAGO

Percy Coleman
Worm

CHICAGO

Ronald Crump
Crump

CHICAGO

Tyree Davis
Boss Top

CHICAGO

Cordai Ealy
Edai

CHICAGO

Latrall Eatman

ALLEGED BLACK DISCIPLES GANG MEMBERS

Source: Cook County Sheriff's Department

CHICAGO

Jerome Freeman
Shorty Freeman
DECEASED

CHICAGO

Tyrone Freeman
Lil Tye

CHICAGO

Denitra Harris
Dee

CHICAGO

David Henry
DK

CHICAGO

Clarence January
King BJ

CHICAGO

Kenneth Jefferson
Krazy

CHICAGO

David Johnson
Bobby

CHICAGO

Gregory Johnson
Freak

CHICAGO

Keenan Lee
Kemo

CHICAGO

Lawerence Lee
Lil Law

CHICAGO

Pierre Lewis
P

CHICAGO

Lawrence Loggins
Law

ALLEGED BLACK DISCIPLES GANG MEMBERS

Source: Cook County Sheriff's Department

CHICAGO

Carlos Mcgary
Los

CHICAGO

Darnell McMiller
Murder

CHICAGO

Deontae McMiller
D-Thang

CHICAGO

Phillip Miller
Hotdog

CHICAGO

Darrell Pittman
White Boy

CHICAGO

Randy Porter
Randy

CHICAGO

Michael Robinson
Mike

CHICAGO

Tavares Taylor
Lil' Reese

CHICAGO

Joseph Thompson
Juice

CHICAGO

Brian Vandolah
Freckles

CHICAGO

Doane Wade
Big Red

CHICAGO

Jardon Washington
Jay Jay

ALLEGED BLACK DISCIPLES GANG MEMBERS

Source: Cook County Sheriff's Department

CHICAGO

Addison Williams
Auto

CHICAGO

Alfred Withers
Law

BLACK DISCIPLES IDENTIFIERS

Source: Cook County Sheriff's Department

BLACK DISCIPLES IDENTIFIERS

Source: Cook County Sheriff's Department

BLACK P STONE NATION
(Alliance – People)

In 1959, Eugene "Bull" Hairston, along with other neighborhood friends, decided to form a neighborhood gang in the Woodlawn community on Chicago's South Side in an attempt to defend themselves and other neighborhood youth from being intimidated by other gangs in the area. Hairston and his group named themselves the Blackstones, in reference to the area the group thought be their territory (63rd - 67th and Blackstone). Soon after, the group's name was expanded to the "Blackstone Rangers."

The first core group of the Blackstone Rangers consisted of Hariston, Charles Edwards-Bey, Wesley Brown, Ernest Vaughn, Charles Knox, Henry "Mickey" Cogwell, and Jeff "Angel of Malik" Fort. Of this group Hairston, Cogwell, and Fort were considered to be the overall leaders of the gang; by the mid-to-

Chief Malik's Tattoo

late 1960s they had turned the small neighborhood gang into a mini-organized crime syndicate absorbing numerous surrounding gangs.

As the gang continued to grow rapidly in number, Hairston, Fort, and Cogwell decided to form the "Main 21", a governing group that consisted of the 21 most trusted and influential leaders within the Blackstones. The 21 men would rule the ever-expanding gang known as the Blackstone Rangers, and each of the 21 would receive their own branch or faction. This means that during this time, the

Blackstones were basically just 21 smaller gangs who had agreed upon a set of terms on how to work together. After an argument between Fort and Hairston erupted, the Main 21 disbanded and most of the members allied under the leadership of Fort. This occurred during the black revolution or "Black Power" movement, and Fort renamed his group the Black P Stone Nation (BPSN). Fort inserted the P into the original name to represent People, Power, Prosperity, Peace, Potential, and Progress – a subtle way for Fort to include the vocabulary and agenda of the "Black Power" movement in an attempt to further legitimize his group.

In the 1960s, Jeff Fort applied for, and received thousands of dollars in grants for inner-city development. To establish a guise of philanthropy, he promised to use taxpayer money for the education of children and in the expansion of jobs. Instead, the money helped finance organizational campaigns for gang recruitment, the purchase and sale of weapons, and a terror campaign aimed at the small businessmen of Chicago's Woodlawn community. In 1972, Fort was sent to the U.S. Penitentiary in Leavenworth, KS for misappropriation of federal funds.

While in prison, Fort converted to Islam, assumed the title of Prince Imam Malik, and instilled his gang with Islamic beliefs. It was during his incarceration that Fort, along with the leaders of the Latin Kings and the Vice Lords, joined to form the People Alliance. Fort emerged from prison as the leader of the gang; he directed that the Black P Stone Nation be called the El Rukns (Arabic for "The Foundation Stones"), and to further adopt the practices of Islam, with particular adherence to the practices from the Moorish Science Temple. The changing of doctrine was not as well received as Fort had hoped, and several Black P Stone leaders not only refused to become El Rukn but also questioned Fort as their overall leader. Mickey Cogwell and several other of these leaders openly voiced their objections to Fort, who only responded in anger: as a way of demonstrating his power of position and his intolerance to insubordination, Fort allegedly ordered Cogwell's murder.

During an investigation, the federal government learned that Fort ran his enterprise from a federal prison through the help of a three-way calling system and a coded language. Federal agents listened to his calls during the mid-to-late 1980s and uncovered Fort's plans to make money through extortion, government fraud, real estate schemes, murder, and the sale of cocaine and heroin. In 1986, Fort, along with other high ranking El Rukns, was indicted for the attempted purchase of high-powered weapons from Libya with the intent to

commit terrorist acts against the United States government in conjunction with Moammar Gadhafi. Fort's fellow Rukn and co-defendant, Melvin Mays, was among those indicted after attempting to buy an anti-tank weapon from an undercover FBI agent. Fort was sentenced to an additional 80 years in federal prison; Mays was sentenced to three life terms. In 2006, after 34 years in Leavenworth, Fort was transferred to the Florence, Colorado ADMAX prison and banned from all human contact.

The name Black P Stones has since resurfaced as El Rukns on the streets. There is evidence left over from their recent Islamic past in some of their original territories, where temples and Arabic advertisements can still be found. In 1999, several top BPS leaders were arrested during "Operation Mo-Down," a Chicago Police operation. The result was that other BPS branches began to feud with one another for positions of power and drug territory. A few small groups of Black P Stones remained loyal to Bull Hairston and did not recognize Jeff Fort as their leader; however, the majority of the Black P Stones identified Jeff Fort, or Chief Malik, as the overall leader of their organization, even though there were other defined leaders on the streets. The infighting and breakdown of power has influenced the way the gang operates today. With over 120 factions, there is a lot of disharmony.

The Black P Stone Nation is the third largest gang in Chicago, after the Gangster Disciples and the Latin Kings. The gang is largely African American, with an estimated membership of 20,000 on the streets of Chicago and over 3,000 in prison systems throughout the United States. BPS control a large portion of

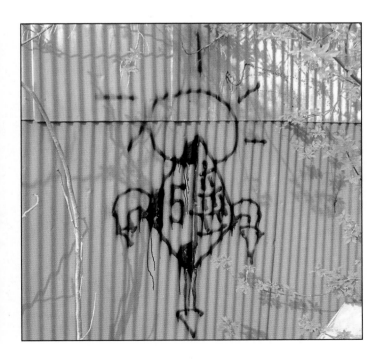

the north Englewood and South Shore communities, with strongholds in Halsted, Jeffrey, Cottage Grove, Stoney Island, 87th, and 79th streets (also known as the Auburn-Gresham, Calumet, Woodlawn, and Burnside neighborhoods). They have moved throughout the state and have strongholds in at least 25 suburbs.

August 8th is a BPSN feast day that commemorates the anniversary of the gang's plan to kill a Chicago Police Officer, which was executed successfully.

Identifiers:

■ **Gang Slogan:** "All's Well," "Stone to the Bone," "High Five, Six must Die"

■ **Gang Symbol:** Pyramid with five-pointed star, crescent moon with the five-pointed star, encircled 7

TATTOOS, HAND SIGNS AND COLORS

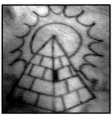

GANG COLORS

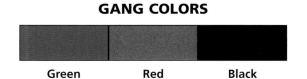

Green   Red   Black

ALLEGED BLACK P STONE NATION GANG MEMBERS

Source: Cook County Sheriff's Department

CHICAGO

Jeff Fort
Chief Malik

CHICAGO

Watkeeta Valenzuela
Prince Watkeeta

CHICAGO

Daryl Abney
Mosey or Moose

CHICAGO

Duante Anderson
Shawdee

CHICAGO

Donnell Ard
DB

CHICAGO

Jelani Bennett
Jaelain

CHICAGO

Teiwan Bergman
Ty

CHICAGO

Kenneth Bingham
KB

CHICAGO

Rufus Bingham
Rufus

CHICAGO

Dennis Booth
DB

CHICAGO

Henry Brown
June Bug

CHICAGO

Jason Brown
JT

ALLEGED BLACK P STONE NATION GANG MEMBERS

Source: Cook County Sheriff's Department

CHICAGO

Tommie Brown
Tommy

CHICAGO

Louis Clayborn
Homicide

CHICAGO

Otha Eagie
O

CHICAGO

Michael Flournoy
Bounce

CHICAGO

Antonio Fort
Tony

CHICAGO

Vozelle Franklin
Tank

CHICAGO

Eric Gauthreauz
E

CHICAGO

Raphael Hammond
Reg

CHICAGO

Cordell Hunter
Cold Steel

CHICAGO

Jerome Isom
Turk

CHICAGO

Kareem Jackson
PeeWee

CHICAGO

Michael Jenkins
Domino

ALLEGED BLACK P STONE NATION GANG MEMBERS

Source: Cook County Sheriff's Department

CHICAGO

Germond Johnson
Mal

CHICAGO

Antonio Jones
Boonie Mo

CHICAGO

Larry Jones
Lil' Larry

CHICAGO

Jackie Kelly
Captain Jack

CHICAGO

Samuel Knox
Little Gangs or Gaines

CHICAGO

Price Larone
Roni

CHICAGO

Johnny Martin
Jig

CHICAGO

Yaree Martin
Yaree

CHICAGO

Phillip McGhee
Phil

CHICAGO

Joseph McHaney
Jo-Jo

CHICAGO

Paris McKinley
Paris

CHICAGO

Tjuan Mitchell
T-Fly

ALLEGED BLACK P STONE NATION GANG MEMBERS

Source: Cook County Sheriff's Department

CHICAGO

Jermol Mixon
Yak

CHICAGO

Kenneth Preshon
Sly

CHICAGO

Ray Rico
Rico

CHICAGO

Donald Simpson
Don Don

CHICAGO

Marcus Simpson
MC

CHICAGO

Herman Smith
Curly

CHICAGO

Samson Smith
Kim Sam Sun

CHICAGO

Ernie Stewart
Kobe

CHICAGO

Jimmy Stewart
Jimbo

CHICAGO

Steven Suber
Lil' Sube

CHICAGO

Ezzittie Taylor
Big Man

CHICAGO

Michael Terrell
Big Mike

ALLEGED BLACK P STONE NATION GANG MEMBERS

ALLEGED BLACK P STONE NATION GANG MEMBERS

Source: Cook County Sheriff's Department

CHICAGO

Clifton Thomas
Wookie

CHICAGO

Donald Thomas
Big

CHICAGO

Justin Turner
TJ

CHICAGO

Allen Walker
Smoke

CHICAGO

Phillip Washington
Killer Phil

CHICAGO

Jamaal White
Aki

CHICAGO

Keith White
Kenyatta

CHICAGO

Kevin Williams
Kay Kay

CHICAGO

Aaron Wilson
Fat Boy

CHICAGO

Michael Woods
Ice

CHICAGO

Herbert Wright
Lil' Herb

BLACK SOULS
(Alliance – Folks)

William Earl Weaver AKA "King Wee" founded the Black Souls in the 1960s in the Garfield Park area near the streets of Madison and California after an internal struggle within the Black Gangster Disciples. There are roughly four major factions within the Black Souls, and twenty other smaller factions – each faction with their own leader. The major factions include the Mad Black Souls, the Gangster Black Souls, the New Life Black Souls, and the Outlaw Black Souls. Some factions may only have 25 members while others could have around 300. While factionalized, the Black Souls have still maintained their original tight-knit group dynamic which aids them in the sale of narcotics and distribution of firearms while maintaining a steady firearms cache. The Black Souls have a presence in the surrounding states of Indiana, Missouri, Ohio, and Wisconsin.

Identifiers:

■ **Gang Symbol**: Cross with two slashes, numbers 440, heart with wings, diamond

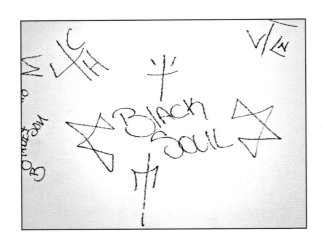

TATTOOS, HAND SIGN AND COLORS

GANG COLORS

Black   White

ALLEGED BLACK SOULS GANG MEMBERS

Source: Cook County Sheriff's Department

CHICAGO

Andrew Brown
Buck

CHICAGO

Booker Brown
T-Man

44

ALLEGED BLACK SOULS GANG MEMBERS

Source: Cook County Sheriff's Department

CHICAGO

Antwan Davis
Twilla

CHICAGO

Cornel Dawson
Corn

CHICAGO

Darryl Edwards
Flap

CHICAGO

Marquez Holmes
Lion King

CHICAGO

Cliffton Lemon
Big Daddy

CHICAGO

Marchello McGee
Chollo

CHICAGO

Johnny Newby
6-0

CHICAGO

Teron Odum
Ty

CHICAGO

Ulysses Polk
Fresh

CHICAGO

Wilson Rogers
Freck

CHICAGO

Terry Scott
Soul Man

CHICAGO

William Weaver
Old Man

C-NOTES
(Alliance – Folks)

The C-Notes street gang consists of primarily Caucasian and Hispanic youth. They first formed as a purely Italian organization and appropriated the colors of the Italian flag as one of their identifiers. During the 1970s, they loosened their Italian loyalty and switched their colors to black and green. They maintained an attitude of white supremacy, however, and only recruited white members, staying firm to their status as Independents. In the 1980s, to avoid extinction, they further loosened their racist mentality, allowing Hispanics moving into their territory to join. The C-Notes finally joined the Folks alliance and the Insane Familia of the Spanish Cobras. Today, its primary concentration of operations is in the area of Ohio and Leavitt and in Jefferson Park. Principal criminal activities include drug sales, armed robbery, auto theft, racketeering, and assault.

Identifiers:

- Dollar sign, Money bag with dollar sign

TATTOOS, HAND SIGN AND COLORS

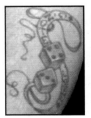

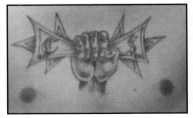

GANG COLORS

Green   Black

46

ALLEGED C-NOTES GANG MEMBERS

Source: Cook County Sheriff's Department

CHICAGO

Miguel Arellano
Capitan

CHICAGO

John Brock
J-Bee

CHICAGO

Stanley Brock
Lil Stan

CHICAGO

Josue Hernandez
Sway

CHICAGO

George Kasp
Stank

CHICAGO

Paul Koroluk
Peanut

CHICAGO

Fernando Martinez
Animal

CHICAGO

Gerrard Racasi
Big G

CHICAGO

Steve Renteria
Munchkin

CHICAGO

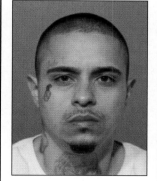

Carlos Rodriguez
T-Bone

CHICAGO

Edward Stiglich
Lil' Ed

CHICAGO

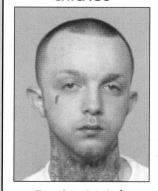

Frankie Stiglich
Googs

CULLERTON DEUCES
(Alliance – Folks)

The Cullerton Deuces were established in the 1970s on the south west side of Chicago. The gang's membership primarily consists of Mexican and Puerto Rican individuals. During their early days, the Cullerton Deuces joined the People Alliance. By aligning with another neighborhood gang in the 1980s, the Cullerton Deuces grew immensely in number. Despite their People Alliance, the Cullerton Deuces fought with the Latin Kings. Following several verbal disputes, the Latin Kings shot a member of the Cullerton Deuces. As a result, a series of retaliatory violence ensued. In the 1990s, the Cullerton Deuces joined the Folks Alliance with the Insane Deuces. Today, Cullerton and Insane Deuces fall under the same umbrella gang. They are currently active at 21st and Washtenaw and Washtenaw and Cullerton.

INSANE DEUCES
(Alliance – Folks)

In the 1960s, the Barons and the Blackhawks, two north side gangs, joined together to create the Insane Deuces. The name "Deuce" was used to illustrate a combination of their power. Because of this gang merger the Deuces were able to control their original territories in both Hamlin and Lathrop Park. However, maintaining these areas resulted in turf wars with the Simon City Royals and the Latin Kings. During this time, the Insane Deuces belonged to the People alliance and were more hesitant to fight with the Latin Kings (also in the People alliance). However, in the 1990's after a series of altercations between the Latin Kings and Deuces war between the two gangs emerged. As a result, the Deuces switched from the People alliance to the Folks alliance, and they joined the "Insane Familia" under the Spanish Cobras.

In 2001, the Insane Deuces incurred many arrests on weapons charges as a result of "Operation Stacked Deck," which was launched by the Chicago Police Department; shortly after, there were even more arrests with "Operation Double Down." They still have a major presence in Portage Park as well as in several Chicago Suburbs. The gang is mostly made up of Caucasian and Hispanic youth in these areas.

Identifiers:

- Playing card (2 of Spades), a spade with two dots, dice showing two, the number 2 with a spear and letters "ID"

TATTOOS, HAND SIGN AND COLORS

CULLERTON DEUCES TRADITIONAL COLORS	CULLERTON DEUCES ALTERNATE COLORS	INSANE DEUCES GANG COLORS
Gray / Black	White / Black	Green / Black

ALLEGED CULLERTON/INSANE DEUCES GANG MEMBERS

Source: Cook County Sheriff's Department

CHICAGO

Jesus Arevalos
Lil Mexico

CHICAGO

Sergio Beloufa
Juice

CHICAGO

Eric Carmolinga
Goon

CHICAGO

Carl Childers
Wizard

CHICAGO

Jose Contreras
Shorty

CHICAGO

Alfredo Lopez
Freddie

CHICAGO

Nelson Muniz
One Eyed Nelson

CHICAGO

Roberto Prieto
Mousey

CHICAGO

Hugo Rayo
Malo or Magic

CHICAGO

Anthony Watts
Scarface

CHICAGO

Luis Zapata
Luigi

FAMILIA STONES
(Alliance – People)

La Familia Stones is a predominantly Puerto Rican gang that began in the late 1970s near Logan Square. While they were originally allied with the Latin Kings, they later split off to establish themselves in a new area near Kedzie and Lawrence, where they have managed to keep a strong foothold today. They have fought wars with the Simon City Royals, the Maniac Latin Disciples, and the Latin Eagles, but as they maintain a position within the People alliance they have had no problem fighting turf wars with fellow alliance members. While remaining mostly Puerto Rican, membership has expanded to include individuals of African American and Caucasian descent. Though their numbers are still very small, Familia Stone members are known for being extremely vicious and as such have been able to maintain their power in the Albany Park area as well as along Kedzie. They have been known to engage in graffiti, drug sales, murder, assault, and "ramming" (purposely running one vehicle into another).

Originally called the Puerto Rican Stones or P.R. Stones

Identifiers:

- **Clothing:** San Francisco Giants sportswear
- **Gang Symbol:** Pyramid with the letters "F" and "S" or "P" and "S"

TATTOOS, HAND SIGN AND COLORS

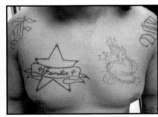

GANG COLORS

Orange   Black

ALLEGED FAMILIA STONES GANG MEMBERS

Source: Cook County Sheriff's Department

CHICAGO

Salomon Bernal

Salomon

CHICAGO

Angel Cardona

Macho

CHICAGO

Miguel Colon

Dirt

CHICAGO

Eduart Hoxha

Finn

CHICAGO

Damien Lay

Papo

CHICAGO

Marcos Martinez

Bebe

FOUR CORNER HUSTLERS
(Alliance – People)

Originally established as neighborhood protection, the Four Corner Hustlers are considered one of Chicago's largest street gangs. During the 1960s, a young Walter "King" Wheat (Al-Bahdee Hodari) and Marvin Evans organized a group of individuals to defend territory in the West Garfield Park area from people threatening the neighborhood with drugs and violence. With the help of Freddy Gauge, Jr. (Al-Malik Hodari), Monroe "Money" Banks, Jr. (Al-Ghandi) and Richard "Lefthand" Goodwin maintained control over Pulaski Road and Jackson Boulevard, Pulaski and Madison Street, Madison and Independence Boulevard, and Jackson and Independence.

During the 1970s, while Walter "King" Wheat and Freddy Gage were incarcerated, they formed an alliance with the Vice Lord Nation to gain better protection. Meanwhile, the operations of the Four Corner Hustlers shifted, and members began engaging in more and more drug dealings.

Following the death of Freddy Gauge in 1983(??), Monroe "Money" Banks rose to power organizing a complex drug operation and expanding the Four Corner Hustlers territory into the northern part of the Austin neighborhood. At this time, Banks added the black diamond to the Four Corner Hustlers logo to represent new found profits.

After Banks was murdered, young hustler Angelo Roberts became the new leader of the organization. Similar to Banks, Roberts expanded Four Corner Hustlers territory and drug markets thereby attracting the attention of law enforcement. In 1990, after a crackdown on Roberts' operations, he masterminded a plot to blow up a Chicago Police Department's Area 4 Headquarters located at Harrison and Kedzie, using machine guns and an anti-tank rocket weapon. Several Hustlers were arrested in connection with this bomb plot. Roberts, however, remained at large until January 1995, when his frozen body was found in the trunk of a car with a slashed throat.

After Angelo Roberts' death, Ray Longstreet took control of the Four Corner Hustlers. Ray Longstreet (along with 33 other defendants) was arrested in the federal investigation titled "Operation Street Sweeper" for conspiring in the sale of narcotics with ranking members of the New Breeds.

Identifiers:

- **Clothing:** Athletic wear in gang colors of gold and black and red and black
- **Gang Symbol:** Pyramid with a crescent moon, the letters "VL", top hat with cane and gloves, pair of dice, champagne glass, playboy bunny head with straight ears, crescent moon with 5-point star, dollar sign and globes

---

In 2017, nine alleged members of the Four Corner Hustlers were indicted in the Northern District of Illinois under federal Racketeering Conspiracy charges involving multiple murders. The indictment alleged Four Corner Hustlers engaged in drug-trafficking, armed robbery, violence and intimidation and extortion.

Today, the Four Corner Hustlers are regarded as one of Chicago's largest street gangs with documented membership in Chicago suburbs and neighboring states.

TATTOOS, HAND SIGN AND COLORS

TRADITIONAL COLORS

Gold	Black

ALTERNATE COLORS

Red	Black

ALLEGED FOUR CORNER HUSTLERS GANG MEMBERS

Source: Cook County Sheriff's Department

CHICAGO

Taurean Allen
T-Mac

CHICAGO

Anthony Anderson
Twin

CHICAGO

Pierre Arrington
Smiley

CHICAGO

Antonio Bell
Pooch

CHICAGO

Shawn Betts
Shakey Shawn or Shaky

CHICAGO

James Blue
Blue

CHICAGO

Roland Boyce
Gino

CHICAGO

Terrance Briggs
Big T

CHICAGO

Jeffery Brown
Lil Jeff

CHICAGO

Quincy Butler
Booty 4

CHICAGO

Rudolph Callaso
Big Lord

CHICAGO

Lionel Coles
Big Ride

ALLEGED FOUR CORNER HUSTLERS GANG MEMBERS

Source: Cook County Sheriff's Department

CHICAGO

Khari Cunningham
Khari

CHICAGO

Martiz Curtis
Poochie

CHICAGO

George Davis
June Bug

CHICAGO

Landis Dillard
Black

CHICAGO

Dennis Goodman
Den Den

CHICAGO

Felan Goodman
Felan

CHICAGO

Samuel Goodman
Red

CHICAGO

Domique Harris

CHICAGO

Timothy Hester
Lil Tim

CHICAGO

Terrell Houston
Relish

CHICAGO

Tellie Howard
Fly

CHICAGO

Ishman Jackson
Ish

ALLEGED FOUR CORNER HUSTLERS GANG MEMBERS

Source: Cook County Sheriff's Department

CHICAGO

Tremain Jackson
Droopy

CHICAGO

Demonte Johnson
Monte

CHICAGO

Dennis Johnson
Den Den

CHICAGO

Steve Lares
Lil Steve

CHICAGO

Charles Lee
Chuck

CHICAGO

Aaron Marshall
10-4

CHICAGO

Robert McClendon
Fella

CHICAGO

Rufus McGee
Rufus

CHICAGO

Willie McGee
Illy

CHICAGO

Tyrell Middleton
Shorty Cool

CHICAGO

Marshune Miller
Stach

CHICAGO

Carlos Moore
Lo-So

ALLEGED FOUR CORNER HUSTLERS GANG MEMBERS

Source: Cook County Sheriff's Department

CHICAGO

Jerome Murray
Head

CHICAGO

Jerry Partee
Greezy

CHICAGO

Tirece Reed
Fresh

CHICAGO

Everette Rice
Ghost

CHICAGO

Angelo Roberts
Lo

CHICAGO

Darrow Searcy
Woo-Thang

CHICAGO

Anthony Sipp
Big Ant

CHICAGO

Dwayne Sipp
Big Wayne

CHICAGO

Pervis Shields
Pervis

CHICAGO

Phillip Smith
Shakey

CHICAGO

Labar Spann
Broman

CHICAGO

James Starr

ALLEGED FOUR CORNER HUSTLERS GANG MEMBERS

Source: Cook County Sheriff's Department

CHICAGO

William Thomas
Burpee

CHICAGO

Rolandis Weathers
Ro-Ro

CHICAGO

Terrance Woods
T-Wood

CHICAGO

Demitrius Wyatt
Meter Man

FOUR CORNER HUSTLERS IDENTIFIERS

Source: Cook County Sheriff's Department

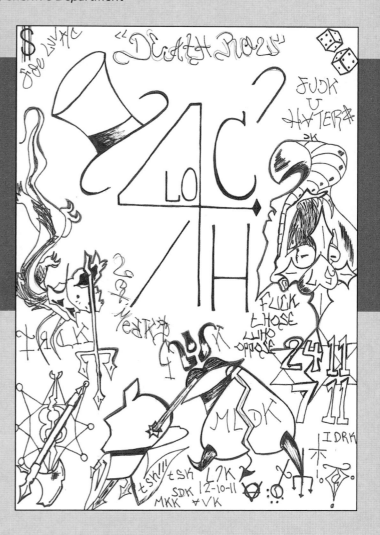

GANGSTER DISCIPLES
(Alliance – Folks)

In the early 1960s The Gangster Disciple Nation (GDN) was founded when the Black Disciples (BDs), under the leadership of David Barksdale, united with the Gangster Nation, led by Larry Hoover. Barksdale became the supreme leader with Hoover as his second in command. In addition, a third group, the Black Gangsters, known as a the New Breeds emerged from this split right after the GDN later split into two factions in 1974 with the death of David Barksdale.

Because of federal indictments and the following convictions of most of Hoover's board members, the hierarchical structure of the GDs is thought to be in shambles due to the large number of factions, each with its own leader.

The GDs main gang rivals include the Latin Kings, Black Disciples, Black P Stones, and the Vice Lords. Even though these traditional rivalries exist, the GDs are now willing to work with other African American gangs within nearby territory in order to make the most money possible. Their operations cover a very large area which includes Englewood, Roseland, Morgan Park, Garfield Park, Lawndale, the Near West Side, Bronzeville, Washington Park, Calumet Heights, Avalon Park, South Chicago, many of Chicago's suburbs, and an estimated 30 other states throughout the country.

Most of the highrise projects where they used to operate (Robert Taylor Homes, Cabrini-Green, Stateway Gardens, Henry Horner Homes, and Rockwell Gardens) have been demolished. This

Identifiers:

- **Gang Slogan:** "All is One" and "What up, G?"

- **Gang Symbols:** Six-point star with crossed pitchforks and the letters GD, six-point star, upward crossed pitchforks, BOS (brothers of the struggle), Heart with Wings

displacement has limited activity by forcing the gang to relocate to different areas in the city and into the suburbs. Some of these new areas already had a strong presence of rival gangs which lead to conflict and violence.

The scattering of members, along with the large size of this gang, is what is currently causing most of the problems within the GDs. Some of the members think there may be more conflict between factions within the gang itself than with any rival gang.

Most of the major sources of income for the GDs include narcotics sales, trafficking, armed robbery, auto theft, theft, extortion (street taxes on independent dealers), kidnapping, money laundering, and mortgage fraud. They have also been involved in homicide, arson, aggravated battery, and assault.

TATTOOS, HAND SIGN AND COLORS

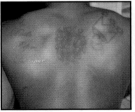

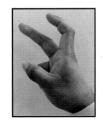

GANG COLORS

Blue   Black

58

ALLEGED GANGSTER DISCIPLES GANG MEMBERS

Source: Cook County Sheriff's Department

CHICAGO

Larry Hoover
Chairman

CHICAGO

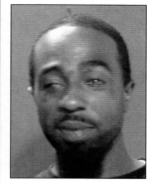

Kirk Williams
Big T OR Big Tony

CHICAGO

Tortantae Agee
Stone

CHICAGO

Winfield Agee
Money

CHICAGO

Walter Allen
Butta

CHICAGO

Dedrick Baker
Lil Dude

CHICAGO

Carl Bates
Poo OR T-Love

CHICAGO

Michael Bell
Fat Black

CHICAGO

Cedric Benjamin
C-100

CHICAGO

Jamal Bivens
Mall

CHICAGO

Michael Booker
Mike Mike

CHICAGO

Tremaine Brent
Bud

ALLEGED GANGSTER DISCIPLES GANG MEMBERS

Source: Cook County Sheriff's Department

CHICAGO

Julian Brooks

Ju-ju

CHICAGO

Dwan Brown

Big Money Mook

CHICAGO

Aaron Burns

Insane

CHICAGO

Deandre Butler

Lil D

CHICAGO

Robert Butler

Old Man

CHICAGO

Deshaun Carpenter

Hardknock

CHICAGO

Rodrick Carroll

Lil Roger OR Rod

CHICAGO

David Chambers

Lil Dave

CHICAGO

Derrick Claiborne

Baller

CHICAGO

Tevin Clark

Boosie

CHICAGO

Kenneth Cobb

Dirty

CHICAGO

Michael Colyar

Geezy

ALLEGED GANGSTER DISCIPLES GANG MEMBERS

Source: Cook County Sheriff's Department

CHICAGO

Wesley Cooke

Wesley

CHICAGO

Cleophus Cooks

Boo Man

CHICAGO

Jermaine Cozart

Main-Main

CHICAGO

Jerome Craft

Rome

CHICAGO

Hasan Cunningham

Jay

CHICAGO

Akeem Dillon

Keemo

CHICAGO

Richard Duerson

Rich

CHICAGO

Johnny Felder

J-Dilla

CHICAGO

Standford Foster

Stan

CHICAGO

Desmond Freeman

Dribble

CHICAGO

Kriston Gordon

So Icey

CHICAGO

Brandon Green

Big B

ALLEGED GANGSTER DISCIPLES GANG MEMBERS

Source: Cook County Sheriff's Department

CHICAGO

Bernard Harrison
Fats

CHICAGO

Michael Harvest
Keeta

CHICAGO

Keith Hayer
Bang Da Hitter

CHICAGO

Shermtat Holiday
40

CHICAGO

Corey Holmes
Corkie

CHICAGO

Lawrence Howard
Law

CHICAGO

Christopher Hughes
Dome

CHICAGO

Hayes Jackson
Fella

CHICAGO

Rico Jackson
Rico

CHICAGO

Thuran James
T-Baby

CHICAGO

Johnson Javon
Psycho

CHICAGO

Jermond Jenkins
Mano

ALLEGED GANGSTER DISCIPLES GANG MEMBERS

Source: Cook County Sheriff's Department

CHICAGO

Cordell Johnson
P-D

CHICAGO

Pierre Johnson
Pistol

CHICAGO

Marquise Jones
Quise

CHICAGO

Vern Jones
Marco

CHICAGO

Maurice Knighten
Don

CHICAGO

Tawan Langston
Julio

CHICAGO

Cordarius Lawrence
King Tall

CHICAGO

Gordon Lee
Lee-Lee

CHICAGO

Julius Lee
Juice

CHICAGO

Kevin Lenoir
Baby Kev

CHICAGO

Deandre Loveless
Shorty Red

CHICAGO

Kristan Mack
C-Mac

ALLEGED GANGSTER DISCIPLES GANG MEMBERS

Source: Cook County Sheriff's Department

CHICAGO

Stephon Mack
Youngin

CHICAGO

Randy Manuel
Five

CHICAGO

Dion Matthews
Don

CHICAGO

Byron McComb
Jug

CHICAGO

Reginald McDonald
Bull

CHICAGO

Darryl Moore
Squeak

CHICAGO

Eugene Moore
Jack

CHICAGO

Kenneth Moore
PK

CHICAGO

Erick Morgan
Erick

CHICAGO

Maurice Nesbitt
Monk

CHICAGO

Deandre Ollie
Super G

CHICAGO

Damon Parker
Dame Dash

ALLEGED GANGSTER DISCIPLES GANG MEMBERS

Source: Cook County Sheriff's Department

CHICAGO

Jimmie Perkins
Woo

CHICAGO

David Polk
D.O."

CHICAGO

Anderson Potts
Don Juan

CHICAGO

Elvin Prince
E-Dubb

CHICAGO

Michael Pryor
Mike Larry

CHICAGO

Jarod Randolph
Rod

CHICAGO

Damien Rogers
Damo

CHICAGO

Kelvin Ross
Ross

CHICAGO

Jawson Seller
J-Dub

CHICAGO

Bruce Smith
Leno

CHICAGO

Carlos Soto
Los

CHICAGO

Damian Spraggins
Dam

ALLEGED GANGSTER DISCIPLES GANG MEMBERS

Source: Cook County Sheriff's Department

CHICAGO

Daryl Stewart
Big D

CHICAGO

Michael Suggs
Mike Mike

CHICAGO

Leon Sutton
Boo Man

CHICAGO

Kenneth Taylor
F

CHICAGO

Tremaine Taylor
Bam

CHICAGO

Quotangelo Temples
Shrek

CHICAGO

Levon Thigpen
Von

CHICAGO

Henry Thomas
Big Hen

CHICAGO

Andre Turner
Woogie

CHICAGO

Terry Walker
Tito

CHICAGO

Jarvis Wallace
Sweet Pea

CHICAGO

Jeremy Watts
K-Breezy

ALLEGED GANGSTER DISCIPLES GANG MEMBERS

Source: Cook County Sheriff's Department

CHICAGO

Marcus Whatley
Los

CHICAGO

Lorenzo Williams
Zo

CHICAGO

Maurice Williams
Dough Boy

CHICAGO

Marshall Wilson
Marhall

CHICAGO

Marlon Womack
O

CHICAGO

Adam Woods
Shy Hoover

CHICAGO

Shawn Yancey
Shawn

CHICAGO

Quintin Yates
DJ Fats

HARRISON GENTS
(Alliance – Folks)

The Harrison Gents started in the 1960s with some Hispanic students in Harrison High School, located at Harrison and Western. Because the school colors were purple and black and the gang formed at the school, the Harrison Gents adopted those colors. In the 1970s they relocated to the East Village where they still maintain a presence. Historically, they fought with the Ashland Vikings over turf, and more recently were at war with the Satan Disciples. Because of the war between Harrison Gents and the Satan Disciples, the police increased their presence in the East Village. This, combined with gentrification of the neighborhood, has slowed operations of the Harrison Gents within the city. They currently have a presence in Rogers Park, Cicero and Berwyn. Some of their main sources of income include auto theft, kidnapping, ramming, arson, assault, armed robbery, theft, and drug sales.

Identifiers:

- **Clothing:** Clothing with color scheme of purple and black. Colorado Rockies athletic wear
- **Gang Slogan:** "HG Love"
- **Gang Symbol:** Two crossed Canes with a top hat and the letters "H" and "G" on each side of the canes

TATTOOS, HAND SIGN AND COLORS

GANG COLORS

Purple   Black

ALLEGED HARRISON GENTS GANG MEMBERS

Source: Cook County Sheriff's Department

I — Gang Profiles

CHICAGO

Robert Favela
Lil Kong

CHICAGO

Luis Rivera
Spook

CHICAGO

Samuel Torres
Sammy

CHICAGO

Ignacio Villa
Nachito

CHICAGO

Antoine Wells
Glide

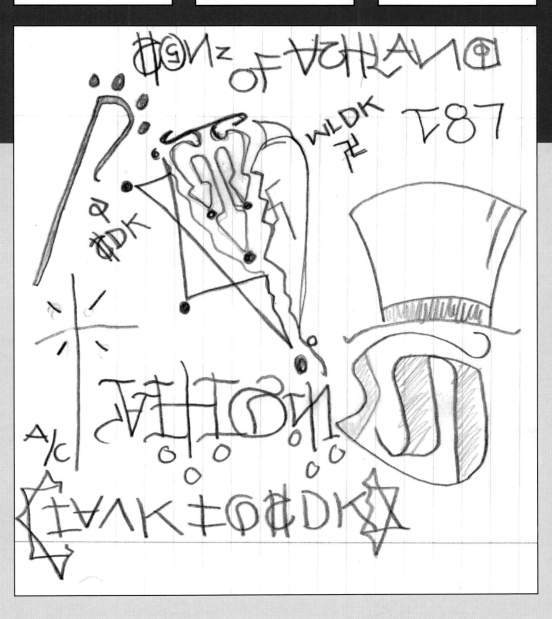

69

IMPERIAL GANGSTERS
(Alliance – Folks)

The Imperial Gangsters originated around the west Humboldt Park area of Palmer and Drake in the late 1960s. Since the 1970s, they have continually fought the Latin Kings over territory. As a result of this feud, they allied with the Spanish Cobras and helped form the United Latino Organization. Today, as members of the Folk alliance, this gang is an inter-racial mix of Latino, African American, and Caucasian youth.

Identifiers:

- 6-point crown with 7 dots, rounded crown, Pink Panther, number 197 (for 1st, 9th, and 7th letters of the alphabet — AIG)

TATTOOS, HAND SIGN AND COLORS

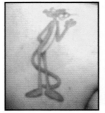

GANG COLORS

Pink	Black

70

ALLEGED IMPERIAL GANGSTERS GANG MEMBERS

Source: Cook County Sheriff's Department

CHICAGO

Victor Arroyo
Wicked & Vic

CHICAGO

Rafael Beltran
Ralphy

CHICAGO

Eddie Camacho
Ne-Ne

CHICAGO

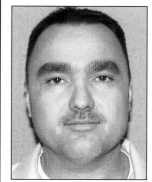

Ronald Carrasquillo
Mad Dog

CHICAGO

Oscar Delgado
Slick

CHICAGO

Angel Escobar
Shorty

CHICAGO

Daniel Flores
Kool Aid

CHICAGO

Arturo Galvez
Weto

CHICAGO

Michael Haley
Pow Wow

CHICAGO

Geraldo Iglesias
Snake

CHICAGO

Michael Johnson
Candyman

CHICAGO

Rogelio Perez
Popeye

ALLEGED IMPERIAL GANGSTERS GANG MEMBERS

Source: Cook County Sheriff's Department

CHICAGO

Jonathan Quesada
June Bug

CHICAGO

Joshua Ramos
Slim

CHICAGO

Freddy Rivas
F-Dog

CHICAGO

Alexander Rivera
Adolf

CHICAGO

Jonathan Santiago
Tank

CHICAGO

Guillermo Sinisterra
Memo

CHICAGO

Casean Tatum
Chippy

CHICAGO

David Trujillo
Rocco

CHICAGO

Osvaldo Velez
Oso

CHICAGO

Daniel Viviar
Kaos

IMPERIAL GANGSTERS IDENTIFIERS

Source: Cook County Sheriff's Department

IGN — Imperial Gangster Nation

INSANE DRAGONS
(Alliance – Folks)

The Insane Dragons are an Hispanic gang that began around the mid-1970s near Augusta Boulevard and Sacramento Avenue. The gang started as a way for Hispanic youths to protect themselves from the neighboring white gangs in the area. They maintain territory in the 12th Police District just east of Richmond Street to Western Avenue and north of Chicago Avenue to Augusta Boulevard. In the 25th Police District they usually operate near Palmer and Kilpatrick Streets. The Insane Dragons have no affiliation with the Latin Dragons in the 4th Police District.

Identifiers:

- **Clothing:** Morehouse Tigers, University of Alabama Crimson Tide, and Washington Redskins athletic wear
- **Gang Symbol:** A fire-breathing dragon and a six-pointed star

TATTOOS, HAND SIGN AND COLORS

    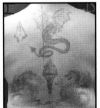

GANG COLORS

Maroon	Gray

ALLEGED INSANE DRAGONS GANG MEMBERS

Source: Cook County Sheriff's Department

CHICAGO

Carmelo Alicea
Bambi

CHICAGO

Edwin Almodovar
Lil Lee

CHICAGO

Octavius Dukes
Tay-Dog

CHICAGO

William Estrada
Sinbad

CHICAGO

Edgar Jimenez
E-Dog

CHICAGO

Luis Mejias
Weso

CHICAGO

Marco Pineda
Marco

CHICAGO

Juan Ruiz
Cocki

CHICAGO

Gabriel Serrano
Gambino

CHICAGO

Salvatore Suriano
Blue

CHICAGO

Manuel Velez
Big Pun

INSANE POPES (Alliance – Folks on the North Side; People on the South Side)

Popes is an acronym for Protect Our People Eliminate Spics/Scum. There are two Pope street gangs in Chicago: one on the North Side and one on the South Side. Originally formed by Caucasian youth who sought to protect their turf from Hispanics in the early 1970s, the North Side faction, or the Insane Popes, started in the Kolmar Park area. They later moved their factions further north into the 20th and 24th police districts and, subsequently, allied with the Simon City Royals. Upon joining the Folks alliance, the gang recruited members of many nationalities but was unable to maintain much of its former territory. The primary base of operation for the Insane Popes is in and around East Albany Park, where they are active in assaults, theft, and drug sales.

In the mid-1970s, another Pope street gang appeared on Chicago's South Side, in the area of Hoyne Park. There is disagreement about whether or not they formed as an offshoot of the North Side Popes. Eventually the South Side group took the name Almighty Popes and spread its influence through several areas. During the early 1990s, however, police pressure and internal disputes seriously disrupted gang activities and forced them out of much of their territory. Today, they are thought to be small in numbers, but still active in Archer Heights, Hoyne Park, and nearby southwest suburbs. Main activities consist of drug sales, armed robbery, theft, and assault. Unlike their North Side counterparts, they are members of the People alliance.

INSANE POPES – NORTH SIDE (Alliance – Folks)

Identifiers:

- Pitchfork, cloaked figure with cross, Grim Reaper

TATTOOS, HAND SIGN AND COLORS

     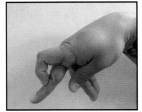

GANG COLORS

White	Black
Blue	Black

INSANE POPES – SOUTH SIDE (Alliance – People)

Identifiers:

- White t-shirts, black pants, and black Converse high-tops

TATTOOS, HAND SIGN AND COLORS

 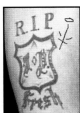  

GANG COLORS

White	Black
Blue	Black

ALLEGED NORTH SIDE INSANE POPES GANG MEMBERS

Source: Cook County Sheriff's Department

CHICAGO

James Reed

Casper

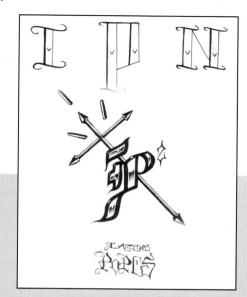

ALLEGED SOUTH SIDE INSANE POPES GANG MEMBERS

Source: Cook County Sheriff's Department

CHICAGO

Raymond Reyes

Sir Insanity

INSANE UNKNOWNS
(Alliance – People)

The Insane Unknowns are a predominantly Hispanic gang which began in the mid-1970s around Leavitt and Schiller. Early on they aligned themselves with the Latin Kings in a war between them and Maniac Latin Disciples. Their ranks were reduced after a war with the Spanish Cobras and the Simon City Royals, and as a result, the Insane Unknowns lost a lot of their credibility. Gentrification of their former turf has severely reduced their activities in the last few years, although they have maintained a foothold in the 25th Police District near Division and Pulaski. They continue to make money through drug and firearm sales, as well as through armed robberies, thefts, and assaults.

IIdentifiers:

- **Clothing:** Black and white athletic wear
- **Gang Symbol:** Ghosts with shotguns, five-pointed stars, candles and shields

TATTOOS, HAND SIGN AND COLORS

GANG COLORS

White	Black

ALLEGED INSANE UNKNOWNS GANG MEMBERS

Source: Cook County Sheriff's Department

CHICAGO

Hector Barreria
Rocco

CHICAGO

Terry Bencak
TJ

CHICAGO

Jesse Chagoya
Jess

CHICAGO

Reinaldo DeJesus
Butchie

CHICAGO

Carlos Garcia
Memo

CHICAGO

Valerio Gomez
Shorty

CHICAGO

Osvaldo Hernandez
Valdo

CHICAGO

John Mercado
Squirrel

CHICAGO

Robert Rodriguez
Mickey

CHICAGO

Eduardo Roman
Snoop

KRAZY GET DOWN BOYS
(Alliance – Folks)

The Krazy Get Down Boys (KGBs) emerged in the Marquette Park area in the early 1990s and quickly aligned with the Ambrose gang, which helped them join the Folks alliance. Membership is comprised mostly of Hispanic and Caucasian youth who battle continually with the Satan Disciples, Latin Kings, and La Raza. Primary criminal activities include drug trafficking, armed robbery, theft, and assault. When a member is arrested or confronted, he always claims to be only a member of a party crew; however, there are documented incidents of specifically KGB violence.

Identifiers:

- Sword, shield, six dots (usually around the sword), sword with ball and 6 slashes

- "Purple City" written in tattoos and graffiti

TATTOOS, HAND SIGN AND COLORS

GANG COLORS

Black   Purple   White

ALLEGED KRAZY GET DOWN BOYS GANG MEMBERS

Source: Cook County Sheriff's Department

CHICAGO

Mohammed Allen
Big Mo

CHICAGO

Diego Araujo
Diego

CHICAGO

Abdelrahma Ramandan
Shadow

CHICAGO

Carlos Soto
Big Mobster

KRAZY GET DOWN BOYS IDENTIFIERS

Source: Cook County Sheriff's Department

LA RAZA
(Alliance – Folks)

La Raza, which literally translates to "The Race", was formed in the early 1970s by Mexican immigrants in the Pilsen community, near 17th and Racine. La Raza began as a branch of the Party People and was meant to settle in new areas for the Party People; this lasted until they broke off and became their own gang. La Raza managed to gain control of the territory in the 48th corridor between Ashland and Racine in what is known as the Back of the Yards area. There are always new factions forming under the banner of La Raza. Because the gang rules and hierarchies are strictly enforced, the members of La Raza operate as a very tight-knit group. La Raza is also known to quickly resort to extreme violence in order to maintain turf.

Identifiers:

- **Clothing:** T-shirts with an image of the Mexican flag

- **Gang Symbol:** The letters LRZ usually written in script, the Mexican flag, the Mexican eagle, and logos associated with the "folks"

TATTOOS, HAND SIGN AND COLORS

     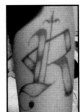

GANG COLORS

Red   Green   White

ALLEGED LA RAZA GANG MEMBERS

Source: Cook County Sheriff's Department

CHICAGO

Arturo Arroyo
Little Monster

CHICAGO

Santiago Arroyo
Monster

CHICAGO

Robert Billegas
Silent

CHICAGO

Edwin Calderon
Twin 8 OR Ocho

CHICAGO

Eric Calderon
Twin 4

CHICAGO

Steven Calderon
Steve OR Stevie

CHICAGO

Juan Campos
Jasper

CHICAGO

Rene Cardona
Cuba

CHICAGO

Ramiro Casis
Romero

CHICAGO

Freddy Corro
Choco

CHICAGO

Miguel Hernandez
Creeper

CHICAGO

Juan Jara
Fat Boy

ALLEGED LA RAZA GANG MEMBERS

Source: Cook County Sheriff's Department

CHICAGO

Vitaliano Jara
Buzz

CHICAGO

Darnell King
Bang Bang

CHICAGO

Albert Mareno
Birdman

CHICAGO

Orlando Medel
Big-O

CHICAGO

Andy Ojeda
T-Mac

CHICAGO

Alberto Pacheco
Beto

CHICAGO

Jamie Perez
Tito

CHICAGO

Marcelino Perez
Shorty G

CHICAGO

Rudy Reyes
Echo

CHICAGO

Rafael Ugarte
2 Short

CHICAGO

Jorge Vasquez
Lil Doughnut

ALLEGED LA RAZA GANG MEMBERS

Source: Cook County Sheriff's Department

CHICAGO

Luis Vasquez
Popeye

CHICAGO

Oziel Vella
Baby O

LA RAZA IDENTIFIERS

Source: Cook County Sheriff's Department

*La Raza artwork; 48 stands for their stronghold
at 48th and Bishop Streets*

85

LATIN BROTHERS ORGANIZATION
(Alliance – People)

The Latin Brothers formed in the 1970s in the Austin district. They are a very close-knit gang known for bursts of extreme violence, especially when battling for turf. Those most likely to be battling with them for an area would be the Maniac Latin Disciples, Imperial Gangsters, and certain factions of Four Corner Hustlers and Latin Kings. As the Hispanic population began to move out of the Austin neighborhood and into other parts of the city, the Latin Brothers have also moved. They have since relocated their operations to the Belmont and North Cicero Avenue area, better known as "Brother City." While historically they are a very small organization, the Latin Brothers Organization members have been known to ally themselves with the Insane Unknowns as a way to bolster their numbers. Their main sources of income include drug trafficking and assault.

Identifiers:

- **Gang Symbol:** Roman warrior helmet with "LBN" on it, also graffiti stating "Insane Latin Brothers Nation"

TATTOOS, HAND SIGN AND COLORS

TRADITIONAL COLORS

Black	Purple

ALTERNATE COLORS

Black	White

ALLEGED LATIN BROTHERS ORGANIZATION GANG MEMBERS

Source: Cook County Sheriff's Department

CHICAGO

Ibrahim Aysheh
Chaos

CHICAGO

Anthony Cuevas
Dittie

CHICAGO

Mario Garcia
Ears

CHICAGO

Carlos Gutierrez
Snoop OR Peanut

CHICAGO

Jose Hermosillo
Primo

CHICAGO

Rene Hermosillo
Rene

CHICAGO

Freddie Lopez

CHICAGO

Abraham Perez
Joker

CHICAGO

Carlos Rivera
Will Kill

CHICAGO

Marco Tavira-Sandoval
Shiesty

CHICAGO

Alejandro Torres
B Cool

LATIN COUNTS
(Alliance – People)

The Latin Counts formed in the 1950s in the Pilsen community near 18th and Loomis. Originally immigrants forming as a way to protect themselves from gangs already in place in those neighborhoods. They initially referred to themselves as the "Sons of Mexico City" and later, the Latin Counts. Two major things happened to the Latin Counts in the 1990s: first, because they were both fighting with the Latin Kings, the Latin Counts joined forces with the Vice Lords inside the prison system; second, a territory dispute with the 12th Street Players forced a drug turf war. The Latin Counts have maintained a presence in Chicago suburbs, especially in the areas of Cicero, Addison, and Chicago Heights. They also have a presence outside of Illinois in Detroit, Michigan. Because they have existed for so long, they have had turf wars with many groups, like Ambrose, Satan Disciples, and La Raza. In addition, they are responsible for the formation of the Bishops and the Latin Brothers, who are now gangs that run independently of the Latin Counts.

Identifiers:

- ■ **Clothing:** Sportswear in black and red
- ■ **Gang Symbol:** Knight's helmet with the letters "LC"

TATTOOS, HAND SIGN AND COLORS

GANG COLORS

Red	Black

ALLEGED LATIN COUNTS GANG MEMBERS

Source: Cook County Sheriff's Department

CHICAGO

Rafael Carrasco
Turtle

CHICAGO

Juan Castillo
Mouse OR Raton

CHICAGO

Eric Cedillo
Myrtle

CHICAGO

Julio Contreras
Rabbit

CHICAGO

John Duran
Casper

CHICAGO

Erik Galarza
Capone

CHICAGO

Carl Garibay
Red Dog

CHICAGO

Albert Magana
Shyster

CHICAGO

Gabriel Manzera
Demon

CHICAGO

Michael Mejia
Deadeye

CHICAGO

Manuel Rios
Big Nose OR MeMe

CHICAGO

David Rodriguez
Cee-low

ALLEGED LATIN COUNTS GANG MEMBERS

Source: Cook County Sheriff's Department

CHICAGO

Juan Rodriguez

Bam Bam

CHICAGO

Steven Rodriguez

Ruthless

CHICAGO

Larry Wilson

Rat

LATIN COUNTS IDENTIFIERS

Source: Cook County Sheriff's Department

I – Gang Profiles

90

LATIN COUNTS IDENTIFIERS

Source: Cook County Sheriff's Department

*A Latin Counts drawing disrespects Ambrose, Latin Kings, and Latin Stylers,
with a downward and broken spear, crown, and shield, respectively.*

LATIN DRAGONS
(Alliance – Folks)

The Latin Dragons started on the South Side in the early 1980s as a mostly Hispanic gang; at that time they were affiliated with the Latin Kings and the People alliance. They later broke ties with the Latin Kings in the 1990s and shortly after joined the Folks alliance instead. Ever since the split there have been turf wars between both the Latin Kings and the Latin Counts on the South Side. This results in their reputation being one of extreme violence. Their territory runs from East 83rd to East 87th between Colfax and Commercial. This is actually an area Latin Dragons shared with the Conservative Vice Lords. Additionally, they have territories in both Calumet City and Whiting, Indiana. Their main sources of income include drug sales, armed robbery, and assault.

Identifiers:

- **Clothing:** Black and white clothing such as black jogging suits with white stripes
- **Gang Symbol:** 5-pointed diamond

TATTOOS, HAND SIGN AND COLORS

GANG COLORS

White   Black

ALLEGED LATIN DRAGONS GANG MEMBERS

Source: Cook County Sheriff's Department

CHICAGO

Abraham Castellano
Rocko

CHICAGO

Joseph Diaz
He Man

CHICAGO

Manuel Diaz
Lucky

CHICAGO

Roberto Fernandez
Murder

CHICAGO

Miguel Garcia
Negro

CHICAGO

Rodolfo Guzman
Impact

CHICAGO

Francisco Herrera
Fat Frank

CHICAGO

Alberto Ortega
Al

CHICAGO

Alejandro Rodriguez
Squeaky

CHICAGO

Luciano Rubio
Chano

LATIN EAGLES
(Alliance – Folks)

In 1960s two militant political clubs from the area of Addison and Halsted came together and formed the Latin Eagles. By the 1970s the group moved away from their political roots and slowly became an actual street gang as they they joined and became part of the United Latino Organization with the Latin Disciples, Spanish Cobras, and Imperial Gangsters. When urban development began to expand its areas of interest, the Latin Eagles began to move toward Gill Park on Sheridan into an area known as "Ghost Town." They have also started up near Armitage and Kostner. Some of their main sources of income include drug sales, armed robbery, and auto theft.

Identifiers:

- **Clothing:** Black and gray clothing, Philadelphia Eagles sportswear

- **Gang Symbol:** Eagle, eagle head with the letters "L" and "E" on either side, or an eagle in flight

TATTOOS, HAND SIGN AND COLORS

GANG COLORS

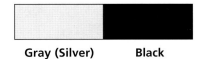

Gray (Silver)   Black

94

ALLEGED LATIN EAGLES GANG MEMBERS

Source: Cook County Sheriff's Department

CHICAGO

Tery Allen
Nephew

CHICAGO

Raul Chavez
Ringo

CHICAGO

Anthony DeJesus
Skeelo

CHICAGO

Thomas Jimenez
Pops

CHICAGO

Jeremy Koonce
Two Face

CHICAGO

Rafael Lopez
Munk

CHICAGO

Michael Rojano
Boo

CHICAGO

Glenn Watkin
Gray

CHICAGO

Dontae Wilson
Midnight

LATIN JIVERS
(Alliance – If any, Folks)

The Latin Jivers is an offshoot of the Maniac Latin Disciples born in the 1980s near Humbolt Park. After leaving the Maniac Latin Disciples and forming the Latin Jivers, they started their operations around Rockwell and Potomac. At one point the Latin Jivers attempted to join with both the Latin Kings and the Spanish Cobras, but disagreements have later caused them to go to war with both groups. Gentrification of their area of operations, as well as police actions, have slowed their activity, but their arrest numbers have been steadily increasing over the past few years. Some of the Latin Jivers main sources of income include narcotic drug sales, auto theft, and armed robbery.

Identifiers:

■ **Gang Symbol:** The letters "LJ"

TATTOOS, HAND SIGN AND COLORS

GANG COLORS

Brown   Black

96

ALLEGED LATIN JIVERS GANG MEMBERS

Source: Cook County Sheriff's Department

CHICAGO

Jonathan Feliciano
Tantu

CHICAGO

Alfredo Gonzalez
Freddy J

CHICAGO

Jason Gonzalez
Jay

CHICAGO

Alfonso Lebron
Junito

CHICAGO

Gary Lebron
Gary

CHICAGO

Orlando Matos
Orlay

CHICAGO

Mauricio Pantoja
Lil' Mex

CHICAGO

Floyd Urrutia
Bird

LATIN KINGS
(Alliance – People)

The Almighty Latin Kings, one of Chicago's oldest and largest Hispanic-led gangs, formed in the late 1960s in the Lower West Side. Initially, members of the Latin Kings joined together to defend themselves against the African-American gangs slowing invading their neighborhoods. Under a highly organized and structured leadership, the Latin King have expanded membership across the Chicago metropolitan area and the nation.

In the city of Chicago, the Latin Kings have three main networks, each with its own leader: southern, northern, and "Crown Town", located in the south west. All three have regional officers and supervisors (Incas) that are in charge of specific territories. Historically, the Latin Kings had two factions: Mexican and Puerto Rican. The Mexican factions were identified by a five-point crown symbol (which represents honor, obedience, sacrifice, righteousness, and love) with the colors of black (symbolizing knowledge of superiors past and present), red (symbolizing blood of brothers lost defending the crown of the Almighty Latin King Nation), and gold (symbolizing the sun shining on the Latin King crown). The Puerto Rican factions had a three-point crown but had other similar attributes.

Gustavo "Lord Gino" Colon was the most famous leader of the Northern/West Side Latin Kings, while Raul "Baby King" Gonzales ran the group in the south. Even after his arrest and confinement for a heroin charge, Lord Gino continued to run the gang from prison. In 1997, he was charged with running a drug ring within a state prison and is now serving a life sentence in the Florence Colorado ADMAX prison.

With the expansion of racial diversity within the Almighty Latin King Nation since its founding, the only colors recognized today are black and gold, with the five-point star as the primary symbol. The Latin King motto is "Once a King, always a King", and members pledge allegiance to the Almighty Latin King Nation and express "Amor de Rey", or King Love".

Membership in the Latin Kings is mostly Hispanic, but it also includes Caucasians, African-Americans, and Middle Easterners. Because they are active in

Identifiers:

- ■ **Clothing:** Black and gold sportswear, apparel featuring the Los Angeles Kings and the Sacramento Kings, members also wear yellow Converse All-Star and British Knight Brand gym shoes with black laces

- ■ **Gang Slogan:** : "Amor de Rey", "Kings Love", and "Behold Latin King"

- ■ **Gang Symbol:** 3- to 5-pointed crown, 5-pointed star, 5 dots, cross, lions, lion's head, the letters "L" and "K"

- ■ **Gang Anniversaries:** Kings Holy Day (January 6), Kings Week (starts March 1)

many parts of the Latin Kings retain great influence over the Hispanic populations, especially on the southwest side of Chicago. "Crown Town" is one of their most well-known strongholds and stretches from 51st to 58th between California and Central.

In February 2018, 34 alleged members of the Almighty Latin King street gang were charged with federal racketeering conspiracy for their participation in six murders, three attempted murders and three arsons.

Despite the arrests of many key leaders, the Latin Kings remain one of the largest street gangs in Chicago. Some of their major sources of income include: sale of narcotics, identity theft, auto theft, robbery, and extortion. They have also been known to be involved in drive-by shootings and murder and have used the threat of these things to enforce their desires to intimidate others.

ALLEGED LATIN KINGS GANG MEMBERS

Source: Cook County Sheriff's Department

CHICAGO

Gustavo Colon
Lord Gino

CHICAGO

Raul Gonzalez
BK

CHICAGO

Fernando Alvarado
Kane

CHICAGO

Felipe Avalos
Laser

CHICAGO

Juan Barajas
Evil

CHICAGO

Victor Bojorges
Chucho

CHICAGO

Luis Bravo
Diablo

CHICAGO

Arturo Cadena
Project Pat

TATTOOS, HAND SIGN AND COLORS

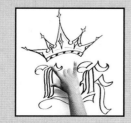

GANG COLORS

Gold   Black

ALLEGED LATIN KINGS GANG MEMBERS

Source: Cook County Sheriff's Department

CHICAGO

Raul Calvillo
Rah-Rah

CHICAGO

William Campos
Big Will

CHICAGO

Edulio Cano
Styles

CHICAGO

Carlos Cartagena
PR

CHICAGO

Arturo Cobus
AK

CHICAGO

Jose Colon
Smiley

CHICAGO

Ivan Corral
Evil

CHICAGO

Armando Cruz
Chucky

CHICAGO

Alfredo Diaz
Calfredo

CHICAGO

Jose Dominguez
Silent

CHICAGO

Patrick Dunai
Project Pat

CHICAGO

Omar Erazo
O Dog

ALLEGED LATIN KINGS GANG MEMBERS

Source: Cook County Sheriff's Department

CHICAGO

Ricky Fernandez
Tank

CHICAGO

Valentin Figueroa
Triste

CHICAGO

David Figuroa
Happy

CHICAGO

Eloy Fuentes
Sinister

CHICAGO

Jorge Galarza
G-Dog

CHICAGO

Bernadino Garcia
Green Eyes

CHICAGO

Isaac Garcia
Rambo

CHICAGO

Antonio Glenn
Spooky

CHICAGO

Mahdi Gomez
Indio

CHICAGO

Amilkar Gonzalez
Puppet

CHICAGO

Fausto Gonzalez
Fausto

CHICAGO

Paz Gonzalez
Markie

ALLEGED LATIN KINGS GANG MEMBERS

Source: Cook County Sheriff's Department

CHICAGO

Armando Gutierrez
Mundo

CHICAGO

Francisco Gutierrez
Puppet

CHICAGO

Jorge Guzman
Coco

CHICAGO

Kenneth Hernandez
Kenny Boy

CHICAGO

Oscar Hernandez
Stretch

CHICAGO

Rafael Hernandez
Shy

CHICAGO

Augustin Jarosz
Lil Tino

CHICAGO

Juan Jimenez
Big Chink

CHICAGO

Oran Jones
Boo

CHICAGO

Michael Juarez
Oso

CHICAGO

Julian Lindo
Silent

CHICAGO

Oscar Lopez
Trigger

ALLEGED LATIN KINGS GANG MEMBERS

Source: Cook County Sheriff's Department

CHICAGO

Jorge Marin
Biggie

CHICAGO

Adam Martinez
Minor

CHICAGO

Pedro Martinez
Reckless

CHICAGO

Alberto Martir
Moe

CHICAGO

Michael Medina
Fat Mike

CHICAGO

Ricardo Mendoza
Nacho

CHICAGO

Wayne Mitchell
Player

CHICAGO

William Moore
White Boy Willie

CHICAGO

Ethan Munoz
Brooklyn

CHICAGO

Victor Ochoa
Pigeon

CHICAGO

Carlos Ortega
Menace

CHICAGO

Alfredo Ortiz
Freddy

ALLEGED LATIN KINGS GANG MEMBERS

Source: Cook County Sheriff's Department

CHICAGO

Carlos Padilla
Poppie

CHICAGO

Oscar Paz
Hitman

CHICAGO

Jorge Perez
Tank

CHICAGO

Nicholas Pinto
BK

CHICAGO

Roberto Pintor
Panther

CHICAGO

Enrique Plata
Feo

CHICAGO

Octavio Posada
KG

CHICAGO

Juan Ramirez
Two-Third

CHICAGO

Cesar Ramos
Trouble

CHICAGO

Joseph Reyes
Bazooka Joe

CHICAGO

Damien Rivera
Spook

CHICAGO

Mario Robles
Oso

ALLEGED LATIN KINGS GANG MEMBERS

Source: Cook County Sheriff's Department

CHICAGO

Epifanio Rocha
Eppy

CHICAGO

Diego Rodriguez
Phantom

CHICAGO

Gildardo Rodriguez
Temper

CHICAGO

Luis Rodriguez
Dukey

CHICAGO

Oscar Rodriguez
Oso

CHICAGO

Jorge Romain
J-Dog

CHICAGO

Benjamin Rosario
Ninja

CHICAGO

Daniel Ruiz
D West

CHICAGO

Anthony Sanchez
Lil Man

CHICAGO

Jesus Sanchez
Spook

CHICAGO

Peter Serrano
Turtle

CHICAGO

Andre Smith
Q

ALLEGED LATIN KINGS GANG MEMBERS

Source: Cook County Sheriff's Department

CHICAGO

Christopher Stevenson
C-Mobb

CHICAGO

Favian Torres
Drac

CHICAGO

Jovan Torres
Black

CHICAGO

Noel Torres
Crazy

CHICAGO

Omar Torres
Chocolate

CHICAGO

Luis Vasquez
Casper

CHICAGO

Paul Vasquez
Garfield

CHICAGO

Rogelio Velasquez
Lucky

CHICAGO

Enrique Victor
Rascal

CHICAGO

Augustine Zambrano
Tino

CHICAGO

Tony Zaya
Lil' T

CHICAGO

Jose Zuno
Rican

LATIN KINGS IDENTIFIERS

Source: Cook County Sheriff's Department

LATIN LOVERS
(Alliance – Folks)

The Latin Lovers were put together around the mid-1970s by former members of both the Spanish Cobras and the Maniac Latin Disciples near the area of Palmer and Rockwell. In the 1990s, the Latin Lovers joined the Folk alliance, and shortly thereafter the Maniac family under the Maniac Latin Disciples. After a short while the Latin Lovers began to dispute the Maniac Latin Disciples over turf, and the Maniac family alliance ended. This turf war caused the Latin Lovers to seek out and join the Insane Familia under the Spanish Cobras. Their main sources of income are thought to be drug trafficking and assaults near Milwaukee and California Avenues.

Identifiers:

- **Clothing:** Kansas City Chiefs sportswear, other clothing featuring a red and yellow color scheme
- **Gang Slogan:** "Los Pocos Locos" ("the few but crazy")
- **Gang Symbol:** The letter "LL", pitchforks up, heart with wings, heart with horns, and the grim reaper

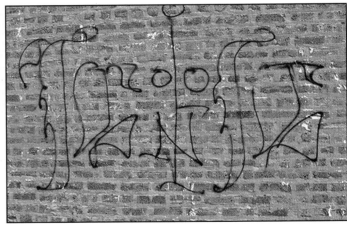

TATTOOS, HAND SIGN AND COLORS

GANG COLORS

Red   Yellow

ALLEGED LATIN LOVERS GANG MEMBERS

Source: Cook County Sheriff's Department

CHICAGO

Leroy Baron
Spot

CHICAGO

Pedro Hernandez
Cuba

CHICAGO

Pedro Hernandez
PJ

CHICAGO

Carmelo Munoz
Melo

CHICAGO

Mark Rosado
Rambo

CHICAGO

Cristobal Villareal
Fofi

LATIN LOVERS IDENTIFIERS

Source: Cook County Sheriff's Department

LATIN STYLERS
(Affiliation – Folks)

The Latin Stylers started in the late 1960s around the Logan Square area, near Diversey and Kedzie. For years they have maintained a presence in the Hermosa neighborhood, and during the 1990s expanded west near Blackhawk Park. They are still active in this 25th Police District. Members are primarily Hispanic and, at one point, allied with the Spanish Cobras under the "Insane Familia" Folks group. After a bitter dispute with the Cobras, they joined with the Maniac Latin Disciples under the "Maniac Family." Primary gang activities include graffiti, assault, armed robbery, auto theft, murder, and drug trafficking.

Identifiers:

■ Shield with letters LS

TATTOOS, HAND SIGN AND COLORS

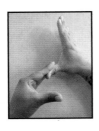

GANG COLORS

Maroon   **Gray**

110

ALLEGED LATIN STYLERS GANG MEMBERS

Source: Cook County Sheriff's Department

CHICAGO

Angel Alvarado
Quake

CHICAGO

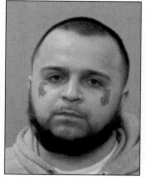

Victor Alvarez
Macho

CHICAGO

Jason Bergollo
Jay

CHICAGO

Danny Flores
Taco

CHICAGO

Arsenio Garcia
Sonio

CHICAGO

Johnny Rodriguez
Pee Wee

LATIN STYLERS IDENTIFIERS

Source: Cook County Sheriff's Department

MANIAC LATIN DISCIPLES
(Alliance – Folks)

The Maniac Latin Disciples, also known as the MLDs or Latin Disciples, originated sometime in the mid-1960s near Rockwell and Potomac in the 14th Police District. Their original leader was a man named Albert "Hitler" Hernandez, and because of this one of their more well-known symbols is a backward swastika. The MLDs joined the United Latin Organization with a few other smaller Latin gangs in an effort to fight the Latin Kings. After joining the Folks alliance, they also formed their own family, called the "Maniac Family," where they combined the efforts of several smaller Hispanic gangs under one banner to increase influence.

IPast MLD leaders met their fate in many different ways: some were killed, others incarcerated. First to meet death was "Hitler" Hernandez, killed in 1970 by a Latin King. His second in command, Fernando "Prince Ferne" Zayas was incarcerated on murder charges along with his own second in command, Johnny Almodovar. Zayas continued running the MLDs from prison until new leaders began to take control on the streets. After street leader Enrique "Rick Dog" Garcia was shot, the MLD hierarchy splintered. Between the years of 1998-1999 and again in 2004, many high-ranking MLD members were arrested on drug charges.

In the summer of 2011 the MLDs shot two girls near Humbolt Park, ages two and seven, while targeting the Latin Kings. The result was a massive police surge and the arrest of 120 MLDs within a two week time period. This was the beginning of a major crippling of the MLD gang.

The MLDs are a mix of Hispanics, Caucasians, and African Americans. Because the Latin Kings killed the MLD leader "Hitler" Hernandez, they became one of the biggest rivals of the Maniac Latin Disciples, who are currently led by Francisco "Pimp Daddy" Garcia, serving time with the Illinois Department of Corrections.

The MLDs still maintain a presence in the Humbolt Park and Logan Square areas in Chicago. They also have a presence in many of the cities just outside of the Chicago area such as Elgin, Joliet, and Rockford, as well as several other Midwest and Southern states. Their main source of income is through the sale of narcotics; in fact, they are better at this than many other gangs in the area. Some of their other activities and sources of income include armed robbery, kidnapping, auto theft, and extortion, and sometimes the MLDs use murder and violence to intimidate or control their rivals.

Identifiers:

- **Clothing:** Georgetown Hoyas, University of North Carolina Tar Heels, and Detroit Tigers athletic clothing

- **Gang Symbol:** Heart with tail of devil and horns, pitchforks, devil's head, 'MLD" or "FMLDN", "D" with backward swastika in the center and monks holding pitchforks and graffiti

---

TATTOOS, HAND SIGN AND COLORS

GANG COLORS

Light Blue	Black

ALLEGED MANIAC LATIN DISCIPLES GANG MEMBERS

Source: Cook County Sheriff's Department

CHICAGO

Mario Alicea
Lil' Rink

CHICAGO

Gustavo Barciaga
Nino

CHICAGO

Enrique Borjon
Oak

CHICAGO

Jonathan Brown
Johnny D

CHICAGO

Jonathan Burgos

CHICAGO

Angel Bustamante
Lil Angel

CHICAGO

Antonio Diaz
Slick

CHICAGO

Domingo Dominicci
Mingo

CHICAGO

Marquis Falls
Smiles

CHICAGO

Emmanuel Fernandez
Manny Fresh

CHICAGO

David Flores
Lil David

CHICAGO

Jesus Gama
Mex

ALLEGED MANIAC LATIN DISCIPLES GANG MEMBERS

Source: Cook County Sheriff's Department

CHICAGO

Francisco Garcia
Pimp Daddy

CHICAGO

James Harris
Romeo

CHICAGO

Richard Hernandez
RH

CHICAGO

Darrel Johnson
D

CHICAGO

Demetrius Johnson
DJ

CHICAGO

Angel Mendez
Big Spaulding

CHICAGO

Erik Miller
Wedo

CHICAGO

Mario Mora
Rio

CHICAGO

Milton Muntaner
Muppet

CHICAGO

Juan Perez
Fish

CHICAGO

Hector Rios
Green Eyes

CHICAGO

James Rios
Chocko

ALLEGED MANIAC LATIN DISCIPLES GANG MEMBERS

Source: Cook County Sheriff's Department

CHICAGO

Andres Rivera
Capone

CHICAGO

Luis Rodriguez
Gonzo

CHICAGO

Fabian Ruiz
Fable

CHICAGO

Jonathan Vallejo
Bam

CHICAGO

Alexander Varela
Flop

CHICAGO

Hector Vasquez
Hecdog

CHICAGO

Fernando Zayas
Fernie

MANIAC CAMPBELL BOYS

Moreando Lane
Q

MANIAC CAMPBELL BOYS

Alexander Lyon
Tre Deuce

MICKEY COBRAS
(Alliance – People)

The Mickey Cobras began as the Egyptian Cobras on Chicago's West Side in the mid-1950s led by a man named James Cogwell. They were forced to move into new territory on the South Side after being pushed out by the Vice Lords, and were then led by James' younger brother Mickey. Because Mickey was a friend of the Black P Stones leader Jeff Fort, ties were quickly established between groups. At this time they operated in the Robert Taylor homes and later they took control of a portion of Cabrini Green housing project. Mickey Cogwell was killed in the late 1970s, supposedly by his ally Jeff Fort, upset that Mickey did not agree with including the Islamic doctrine in the Black P Stone mindset. In honor of Mickey's death the Egyptian Cobras renamed themselves the Mickey Cobras, and began to slowly dissolve many of their ties with the Black P Stones. After the demolition of Cabrini Green and the arrests of both high level and street level leaders, the Mickey Cobras were crippled severely. They still maintain their operations in the Dearborn Homes, Washington Park, Fuller Park, and Roseland areas. They are currently led by Johnson "Dez" Preston and Otis "Red" McKenzie. Their primary sources of income are drug trafficking (especially in heroin), assault, armed robbery, auto theft, theft, and kidnapping. Their membership is made up mostly of African Americans.

Identifiers:

- **Clothing:** Chicago Bulls sports apparel, clothing with red and black color scheme

- **Gang Slogan:** "All is well", "MC love", "All is seen in the eye of the cobra" and "Snakebite"

- **Gang Symbol:** 5-point star, crescent moon, pyramid with an eye and "M/C", cobra snake, and MCN (Mickey Cobra Nation)

- **Gang Anniversaries:** Mick Day (July 27), the birthday of founder Henry "Mickey" Cogwell

The Mickey Cobras celebrate "Mick Day" every year on Henry "Mickey" Cogwell's birthday, July 27th. All members are required to attend the party held in his honor. The party is usually near Fuller Park, at 45th and Princeton.

TATTOOS, HAND SIGN AND COLORS

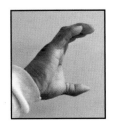

GANG COLORS

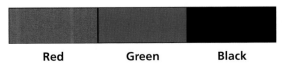

| Red | Green | Black |

ALLEGED MICKEY COBRAS GANG MEMBERS

Source: Cook County Sheriff's Department

CHICAGO

Hajji Adams
Hajji

CHICAGO

Rick Anderson
Pretty Rick

CHICAGO

Demetrio Brownridge
Mickey

CHICAGO

Devonshe Collier
Bay Zoo

CHICAGO

Aaron Collins
Arrow

CHICAGO

Mario Hancock
Ghost

CHICAGO

Devon Jackson
D-Bo

CHICAGO

Preston Johnson
Dez

CHICAGO

Angelo McCaskle
Low OR Bird

CHICAGO

Otis McKenzie
Red

CHICAGO

Terrell Phagan
T-Man

CHICAGO

Desmone Samuels
Little Dez

117

ALLEGED MICKEY COBRAS GANG MEMBERS

Source: Cook County Sheriff's Department

CHICAGO

Prentis Smith

Maniac

CHICAGO

Denard Stewart

Nardo

CHICAGO

Walter Tates

Dog

CHICAGO

William Tatum

D-Ack

CHICAGO

Yarmel Williams

Yarmel

MICKEY COBRAS IDENTIFIERS

Source: Cook County Sheriff's Department

MICKEY COBRAS IDENTIFIERS
Source: Cook County Sheriff's Department

Graffiti of the Mickey Cobra Nation disrespects Spanish Vice Lords with the downward cane, Latin Lovers with three downward dots under the N, and the Folks Nation with the downward pitchfork.

MILWAUKEE KINGS
(Alliance – Folks)

The Milwaukee Kings were founded as a branch of the Latin Kings in the early 1980s near North Milwaukee and West Grand Avenues. By 1992 they had allied themselves with the Maniac Latin Disciples (MLDs) and began to run their operation from the East Village Area. They had to move to Chicago's North Side Monte Clare neighborhood after wars with rival gangs as well as from pressure from the police and still maintain operations near Riis Park. The Milwaukee Kings parted ways with the MLDs after the MLDs murdered one of their high ranking members. They are usually involved in graffiti, murder, kidnapping, and assaults, and they generally use theft, robbery, and drug sales as a primary source of income.

Identifiers:

■ **Gang Symbol:** King with rounded crown, numbers 13 and 11 (13th and 11th letters in alphabet – M, K)

TATTOOS, HAND SIGN AND COLORS

GANG COLORS

Orange   Black

120

ALLEGED MILWAUKEE KINGS GANG MEMBERS

Source: Cook County Sheriff's Department

CHICAGO

Louis Bronge
Smurf

CHICAGO

Abraham Colon
AB

CHICAGO

Ricardo Cruz
Rick Dog

CHICAGO

Robert Edwards
Fat Baby

CHICAGO

Carlos Figueroa
Caritas

CHICAGO

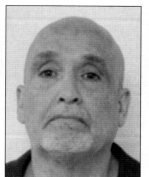

Ercilio Gonzalez
Big P

CHICAGO

Ercilio Gonzalez
Petey

CHICAGO

David Hernandez
Silent

CHICAGO

Raynard Hubbard
Bird

CHICAGO

Joseph Matos
Trouble

CHICAGO

Julio Mercado
Palma

CHICAGO

Alexis Olmo
Omo OR King Alex

ALLEGED MILWAUKEE KINGS GANG MEMBERS

Source: Cook County Sheriff's Department

CHICAGO

Jeramia Ortiz
Greeny

CHICAGO

Jose Ortiz
Jamie

CHICAGO

Darrell Plain
Bug

CHICAGO

Gary Roberson
Gotti

CHICAGO

Anthony Simble
KD

CHICAGO

Anthony Trevino
Tree-Tree

MILWAUKEE KINGS IDENTIFIERS

Source: Cook County Sheriff's Department

NEW BREEDS (aka BLACK GANGSTERS)
(Alliance – Folks or Independent)

The Black Gangsters emerged from within the Black Gangster Disciple Nation (BGDN) in the 1960s. Following the death of David Barksdale in 1972, the Black Gangster Disciple Nation split into three gangs. During this period of transition, many members strived for a leadership position. Those who were unsuccessful in securing leadership roles, often formed splinter groups; George Davis was one member, who went on to form the Black Gangsters.

George Davis, also known as Boonie Black, was the original leader of the Black Gangster Disciples on the West Side of the city in the early 1970s; he continued to serve as leader while incarcerated. In 1987, while in prison, Boonie Black was stabbed by members of the Black Souls. This incident was orchestrated by a former high-ranking member who had recently "flipped" and joined the Black Souls. Subsequently, Boonie Black dropped the "Disciples" from their name. Due to the closeness of the Gangster Disciples and the Black Souls, Boonie Black felt betrayed by his own gang. As a result, Boonie Black split away and began to call his group the Black Gangsters and the gang maintained three out of the six Folk Nation concepts; Love, Life, and Loyalty (LLL).

The LLL idea was adopted by Maurice "Baldy" Jackson, Samuel "King Ram" Lawrence, and George "Boonie Black" Davis/ Allegedly, Baldly represented "Love," King Ram represented "Life," and Boonie Black represented "Loyalty"

In the early 1990s, a group called the New Breeds splintered from the Black Gangsters. Shortly after, the two groups reunited establishing one gang. Today, most members refer themselves as New Breeds and consider the Black Gangsters name outdated.

The New Breeds maintain a hierarchical gang structure including a Don, King, Prince, General, Field Marshall, Commander, Lieutenant, and members. The largest source of income is derived from narcotic trafficking, but they are also involved in illegal firearms trafficking, homicide, extortion, armed robbery, theft and assault.

For nearly a decade, notorious New Breeds gang leader, Dana "Bird" Bostic, controlled a heroin trafficking operation on Chicago's West Side. Under Bostic's leadership, his organization established connections with Mexican Cartels and used violence maximize profits further advancing the gang's exploits. Dana Bostic was a career criminal, earning a reputation on the streets beginning when he was a teenager. At the age of 20, Bostic was arrested after police witnessed him selling a small bag of crack, two years later Bostic was charged for the murder of member of the gang's rivalry, Undertaker Vice Lords. Bostic was acquitted of the charge after numerous

witnesses recanted their testimonies. Furthermore, enhancing Bostic's reputation for using violence and intimation to evade prosecution. In 2012, Bostic was sentenced to 38 years in Federal Prison for drug conspiracy charges for controlling a major heroin operation centered around Pulaski Avenue and Van Buren Street on Chicago's West Side.

The main operations of the gang were originally located in the A.B.L.A homes along Roosevelt Road in the 12th Chicago Police District. A.B.L.A was an acronym for the four sets of housing projects that were situated on one large site: Grace Abbott Homes, Jane Addams Homes, Robert Brooks Homes (including Brooks extensions), and Loomis Courts. The housing project has since been demolished, but the New Breeds still operate in the area where those homes once were. They also have a presence in Garfield Park, Englewood, and in the K-Town area of Chicago's West Side.

Identifiers:

- **Gang Symbol:** 'COS' in a diamond, numbers 2 and 7 (2nd and 7th letters of the alphabet – BG), 3 dots, letters BG or LLL

TATTOOS, HAND SIGN AND COLORS

GANG COLORS

| Blue | Black |

ALLEGED NEW BREEDS GANG MEMBERS

Source: Cook County Sheriff's Department

CHICAGO

Dyre Almon
D-Ray

CHICAGO

Latonio Austin
Nook

CHICAGO

Dana Bostic
Bird

CHICAGO

Lamel Burns
Slim

CHICAGO

Levaughn Collins
Sweet Bobby

CHICAGO

Darrius Finley
Big Dez

CHICAGO

Larry Gambell
Bam

CHICAGO

Miguel Gore
Miguel

CHICAGO

Lanard Guider
Lil Lanard

CHICAGO

Curtis Jackson
G-Ball

CHICAGO

Mokomis Jefferson
Shooty Mac

CHICAGO

Melvin Martin
Ben Ben

ALLEGED NEW BREEDS GANG MEMBERS

Source: Cook County Sheriff's Department

CHICAGO

Floyd McWilliams
BS Floyd

CHICAGO

Dawon Meeks
Moochie

CHICAGO

Brian Robinson
B

CHICAGO

Brandy Schaffer
BMG

CHICAGO

Saunder Taylor
Birdman

CHICAGO

Markell Thomas
Twin

CHICAGO

Antonio Williams
T-Bone

CHICAGO

Edward Williams
Cousin Ed

NEW BREEDS IDENTIFIERS

Source: Cook County Sheriff's Department

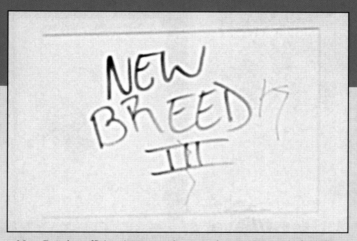

New Breed graffiti written over by a rival gang; K stands for killer

ORCHESTRA ALBANY
(Alliance – Folks)

When a Latin King killed a member of a salsa band on the North Side, the other members of that band formed the Orchestra Albany gang as a way to retaliate with a greater, and more organized force. The name of the gang comes from the word for band "orquestra," and the street where they hung out, Albany. They joined the Folks alliance in opposition to the Latin Kings and continue to be against them today. To make the rivalry stronger, Orchestra Albany allied themselves with the Spanish Cobras, with whom they share turf near Diversey and Harding. They also helped found the Insane Family, an umbrella organization which includes many Hispanic alliance groups. Currently, they claim the area along Milwaukee between Kedzie and California, near Albany.

Identifiers:

■ **Gang Symbol:** The letters "OA", "Insane OA", and a diamond

TATTOOS, HAND SIGN AND COLORS

GANG COLORS

| Brown | Yellow | Brown | Black |

ALLEGED ORCHESTRA ALBANY GANG MEMBERS

Source: Cook County Sheriff's Department

CHICAGO

Max Garcia

Malo

CHICAGO

Teddy Labron

OA Teddy

CHICAGO

Luis Lopez

Lil Jay

CHICAGO

Juan Martinez

Juan

CHICAGO

Raul Neris

Cool Raul

CHICAGO

Orlando Nunez

Nunez

CHICAGO

Daniel Roldan

Peanut

CHICAGO

Angel Rosado

Playboy

CHICAGO

Jonathan Sanchez

Lil Jay

*IOAN stands for Insane Orchestra Albany Nation; the
spearhead in the middle shows respect for the Spanish Cobras,
their fellow members in the Insane family.*

PACHUCOS
(Alliance – People)

The Pachucos started in the early 1980s and based their image on the zoot suit wearing, swing jazz character. In the 1990s the Pachucos established themselves in the Hanson Park area and eventually battled the Four Corner Hustlers, Spanish Cobras, and Maniac Latin Disciples for turf. They currently have operations in Kilbourn Park and Hanson Park. They are usually involved in drug trafficking, arson, assault, and ramming.

Identifiers:

■ **Clothing:** Brown fedoras with black bands

■ **Gang Symbol:** Rayed cross with the letter "p", a cartoon figure or "panama jack", the letter "p" with the pitchforks pointed downward, the letters "LP" for Latin Pachucos, and "ALPN" (Almighty Latin Pachuco Nation)

■ **Gang Hand Sign:** The middle finger extended down, index finger brought up and tucked in. This puts the pitchforks down and forms a "p" for pachucos.

TATTOOS, HAND SIGN AND COLORS

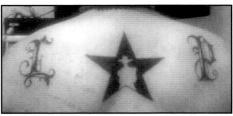

GANG COLORS

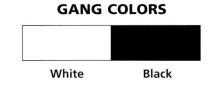

White · Black

ALLEGED PACHUCOS GANG MEMBERS

Source: Cook County Sheriff's Department

CHICAGO

Jose Almanza
Chavello

CHICAGO

Miguel Boyas
Flacko

CHICAGO

Manuel Chaidez
Horsie

CHICAGO

Omar Chaidez
Monkey

CHICAGO

Benjamin Forthye
Casper

CHICAGO

Jose Lucio
Cheeks

CHICAGO

Thomas Rodriguez
Gato

CHICAGO

Atvriel Salgado
Bam Bam

CHICAGO

Juan Salgado
Charlie

133

PARTY PEOPLE
(Alliance – Folks, if any)

The Party People are a mostly Hispanic gang that began in the late 1970s near Pilsen. As a way to protect the joining members from other existing street gangs like La Raza, Ambrose, Bishops, and the Latin Counts. Shortly after their formation, they took over the area of 18th and May, and extended their operations to Gage and Marquette Parks, frequently fighting with the Latin Kings, Black P Stones, Latin Souls, and Two Six Nation. They still have their operations in these areas, the largest of which runs from 16th to 19th, between Racine and Morgan. In the mid-1990s, gang member Geraldo Ferrer shot and wounded a Chicago Police Officer and was sentenced to eight years for attempted murder. After this, the Chicago Police Department were quick to take action against the Party People and initiated "Operation Just Cause" after a Party People member murdered a young child. Originally thought to be of the Folk alliance, some members reportedly prefer a Renegade street status.

Identifiers:

- **Clothing:** Clothing items in white and black
- **Gang Symbol:** playboy bunny, letters "PP" and the six-point star. "GPP" (Gangster Party People) and "PP/LRZ" symbolizing their close ties to the La Raza street gang.

TATTOOS, HAND SIGN AND COLORS

GANG COLORS

White | Black

ALLEGED PARTY PEOPLE GANG MEMBERS

Source: Cook County Sheriff's Department

CHICAGO

Jose Alcaraz
Joe

CHICAGO

Norberto Escobedo
Monstro

CHICAGO

Jose Gonzalez
Joey

CHICAGO

Jaret Ruiz
Lil Pelon

CHICAGO

Richardo Ruiz
Takua

CHICAGO

Jose Sanchez
Popotes

CHICAGO

Edgar Vazquez
Popeye

CHICAGO

Rafael Vieyra
Rafa

A Party People drawing disrespects (left to right, in the background) Latin Counts, Bishops, Latin Kings, and Ambrose, by drawing their emblems upside-down.

135

PARTY PLAYERS
(Alliance – People)

The roots of the Party Players trace to the Back of the Yards area near 24th and Washtenaw in the late 1970s to early 1980s. Mostly Hispanic, the Players originally allied with the Two Six street gang and adopted many of their same symbols. Both groups fought the Saints. During the 1990s, the Players formed bonds with the Latin Kings and expanded their presence from the Marquette Park area into the Chicago suburbs and Wisconsin. They still have a presence in the Back of the Yards, at 48th and Wolcott, and a small presence within Two Six territory in the 8th District. They consider their motherland the corner of 65th and Spaulding. Primary criminal activities include the sale of narcotics and assault.

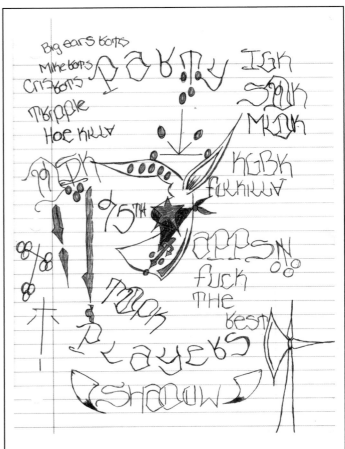

Identifiers:

■ Playboy bunny with bent right ear, hatchet, cross with 5 dots, 5 circles

TATTOOS, HAND SIGN AND COLORS

GANG COLORS

Maroon	White

136

ALLEGED PARTY PLAYERS GANG MEMBERS

Source: Cook County Sheriff's Department

CHICAGO

Miguel Cruz
Harpo

CHICAGO

Luis Galvan
Spook

CHICAGO

Tito Gamez
Demon

CHICAGO

Marcelo Gonzaga
Trigger

CHICAGO

Emmanuel Melendez
Beaver

CHICAGO

Leopold Sanchez
Bolo

CHICAGO

Marlo Warren
Shadow

SAINTS
(Alliance – People)

The Latin Saints began as a predominantly white gang in the late 1960s, and they are from the Back of the Yards community near 45th and Wood. As the neighborhood around them became more Hispanic, so did their membership. Throughout history, the Saints have been able to maintain their territory in the Back of the Yards area between 43rd – 47th streets from Damen to Ashland; this area is known as "Halo City." Although they were once a part of the Folks alliance, they switched to the People alliance after a serious rivalry with La Raza. Even though they are known as one of the most reclusive gangs, they are also known for being one of the most aggressive and violent street gangs in the Chicago area. The Saints are generally known to be involved in murder, assault, drug sales, armed robbery, auto theft, arson, and kidnapping. In early 2005, twenty-five Saints members were indicted on drug charges and gun trafficking as a result of the Chicago Police Department's "Operation Halo."

Identifiers:

- **Clothing:** Sports attire in a blue and black color scheme, especially sportswear of the North Carolina Tar Heels

- **Gang Symbol:** Stickman with a halo and three slashes

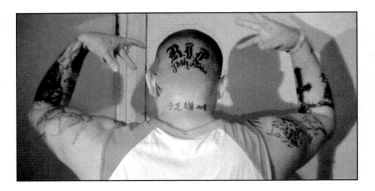

TATTOOS, HAND SIGN AND COLORS

GANG COLORS

Light Blue   Black

ALLEGED SAINTS GANG MEMBERS

Source: Cook County Sheriff's Department

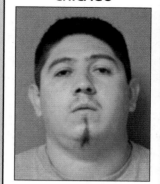

CHICAGO

Jorge Alvardo
Lizzard

CHICAGO

Victor Colosimo
Goofy

CHICAGO

Luis Contreras
Snoop

CHICAGO

Rodrigo Godinez
G-Man

CHICAGO

Joseph Krenstkowski
Butcher

CHICAGO

Evelio Lopez
Oso

CHICAGO

Jose Lopez
Baby J

CHICAGO

Martin Martinez
Lil Gonzo

CHICAGO

Darrell Mullins
Boy

CHICAGO

Daniel Nunez
Sly

CHICAGO

Carlos Padilla
Mally

CHICAGO

Lino Padilla
Chino

ALLEGED SAINTS GANG MEMBERS

Source: Cook County Sheriff's Department

CHICAGO

Jose Patino
Pat

CHICAGO

Esteban Rincon
T-Mac

CHICAGO

Richard Rincon
Suds

CHICAGO

Octavio Romero
Flaco

SAINTS IDENTIFIERS

Source: Cook County Sheriff's Department

Saints graffiti in black, written over in blue by the Latin Souls

SAINTS IDENTIFIERS

Source: Cook County Sheriff's Department

A Saints drawing shows their location at 45th and Wood, and disrespects Insane Unknowns, Latin Souls, Latin Kings, and Satan Disciples.

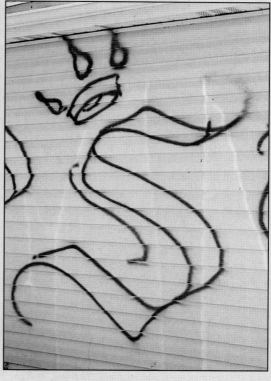

SATAN DISCIPLES
(Alliance – Folks)

The Satan Disciples formed in the area near West 24th Street and South California in the late 1960s. They managed to maintain that area throughout the 1980s and expanded into the neighborhoods of East Village, Gage Park, Brighton Park, and Bridgeport. There have also been factions found in Berwyn, Calumet City, Cicero, Joliet, and other Illinois suburbs. They have grown exponentially over the past few years that they are increasingly becoming one of Chicago's main gangs.

The Satan Disciples are known for being extremely violent when it comes to war with other gangs and are constantly at war with gangs in the People alliance. They are also known to battle with others within the Folks alliance, and even with fellow Satan Disciple members, for profit, turf, and respect. They are known to be involved in drug trafficking, armed robbery, theft, theft, ramming, kidnapping, and assault.

In 2005 the Satan Disciples began celebrating "Satan Disciple Days," which are celebrated May 4th and 6th. For both of these days, all of the members from the suburbs come to Chicago, wear the colors, and celebrate as a group in order to prove the gang's unified strength.

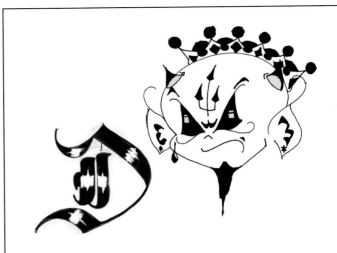

Identifiers:

- **Clothing:** Grambling University or Detroit Tigers athletic wear

- **Gang Symbol:** Pitchforks up, devil's logos associated with the folk's alliance, and the letters "SD"

- **Gang Anniversaries:** Satan Disciples or SD Days (May 04)

TATTOOS, HAND SIGN AND COLORS

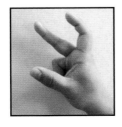

GANG COLORS

Canary Yellow   Black

ALLEGED SATAN DISCIPLES GANG MEMBERS

Source: Cook County Sheriff's Department

CHICAGO

Esteban Alvarez
Joker

CHICAGO

Jaime Andrade
Sin

CHICAGO

Eduardo Arias
4Eyes

CHICAGO

Jose Bijarro
Turtle

CHICAGO

Erick Calvillo
Shyster

CHICAGO

Luis Castaneda
Wedo

CHICAGO

Ricardo Correa
Wicked

CHICAGO

Carlos Cregan
Hammer

CHICAGO

Noel Cruz
Rocky

CHICAGO

Armando Diaz
Mando

CHICAGO

Daniel Diaz
Danny

CHICAGO

Gustavo Dirzo
Monster

ALLEGED SATAN DISCIPLES GANG MEMBERS

Source: Cook County Sheriff's Department

CHICAGO

Josue Dominguez
Zoko

CHICAGO

Rovel Fountain
Bay-Bay

CHICAGO

Michael Fox
Kaos

CHICAGO

Daniel Garza
Casper

CHICAGO

Kenneth Gayton
Biggie Rat

CHICAGO

Jouse Gurrola
Kato

CHICAGO

Efren Gutierrez
Chapo

CHICAGO

Paulo Hernandez
Rascal

CHICAGO

Raul Herrera
Capone

CHICAGO

David Juarez
Day Day

CHICAGO

Willie Kirkwood
Chocolate

CHICAGO

Sirerbnets Liles
Homie

ALLEGED SATAN DISCIPLES GANG MEMBERS
Source: Cook County Sheriff's Department

CHICAGO

Daniel Malave
Maniac

CHICAGO

Alberto Mangual
Psycho

CHICAGO

Alexander Marrero
Alpo

CHICAGO

Thomas Martinez
Lil Man

CHICAGO

Andrew Melaro
Chuckie

CHICAGO

Miguel Mendez
Slick

CHICAGO

Kenny Navejar
Diablo

CHICAGO

Carlos Padin
Bones

CHICAGO

Orlando Perez
Cuba

CHICAGO

Arturo Reveles
Spooky

CHICAGO

Emmanuel Roa
Mousey

CHICAGO

Serafin Rodriguez
Wedo

ALLEGED SATAN DISCIPLES GANG MEMBERS

Source: Cook County Sheriff's Department

CHICAGO

Stacey Salinas
Creeper

CHICAGO

Jessie Sanchez
Tiger

CHICAGO

Onyx Santana
O-Dog

CHICAGO

Jonathan Silva
Pacman

CHICAGO

Jose Soto
Trigger

CHICAGO

Tobias Orlando
Big O

CHICAGO

Jose Trejo
Vicious

CHICAGO

Ivan Valdez
Demon

CHICAGO

Dean Valera
Beast

CHICAGO

Agapito Villalobos
Aggie

CHICAGO

Juan Villanueva
Krazy

CHICAGO

Daniel Zizumbo
Joker

SATAN DISCIPLES IDENTIFIERS

Source: Cook County Sheriff's Department

SIMON CITY ROYALS
(Alliance – Folks)

One of the oldest Caucasian street gangs in the Chicago area, the Simon City Royals were formed in the late 1960s near Simon Park in the 14th Police District. They started as a way to defend themselves against rising Hispanic gangs moving into that area. When their area of operations became predominately Hispanic, they moved north and west into the 17th and 25th Police Districts. Since the 1980s their membership numbers have gone down due to tension within the group itself, wars with rival gangs, and arrests. For some time it has been suspected the Royals allied themselves with the Black Gangster Disciples within the prison system for protection, and make the alliance happen through an exchange for firearms. Although they are not as active now, the Royals still maintain their operations in the Albany Park area. They are generally linked to activities that include weapon sales, theft, armed robbery, extortion, kidnapping, and obtaining businesses to launder money.

Identifiers:

- **Clothing:** Kansas City Royals and Colorado Rockies athletic wear, black jackets over blue sweatshirts

- **Gang Symbol:** The letters "SCR", the letter "R", a rabbit head with a bent ear, a hat with crossed shotguns, and a cross

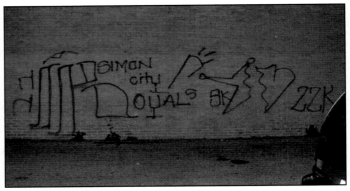

TATTOOS, HAND SIGN AND COLORS

GANG COLORS

Blue   Green   Blue   Black

148

ALLEGED SIMON CITY ROYALS GANG MEMBERS

Source: Cook County Sheriff's Department

CHICAGO

Luis Candelaria
Looney

CHICAGO

Sergio Candelaria
Serg/GQ

CHICAGO

Earl Casteel
Chief or Shorty

CHICAGO

Christian Godoy
Crush

CHICAGO

TJ Jimenez
TJ Batman

CHICAGO

Julio Lopez

CHICAGO

John Vazquez
Lil J or JJ

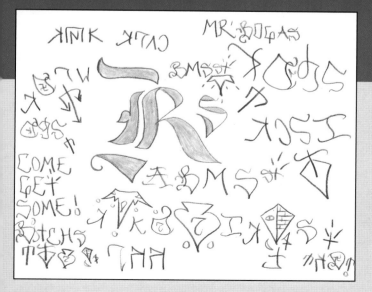

SPANISH COBRAS
(Alliance – Folks)

The Spanish Cobras are a large Hispanic gang that began in the early 1950s near Division and Maplewood under Richard "King Cobra" Medina. They began as part of the Maniac Latin Disciples with a mainly Puerto Rican membership. The Cobras broke away from the MLDs when both groups' escalating power forced them into competition over turf. After the break, the Spanish Cobras joined the United Latino Organization in an effort to fight the Latin Kings. The Cobras helped found the Insane Familia association in an effort to organize several smaller gangs to control how much influence MLDs have within the Folks alliance.

The Spanish Cobras have extended their influence to several different parts of the city – Logan Square, Kelvyn Park, Bucktown, and Albany Park – where they still operate today. They have also been identified in outlying areas of Illinois like Wisconsin, Indiana, Ohio, New York, and Connecticut. The Spanish Cobras are usually involved in narcotics sales, illegal firearms sales, murder, extortion, theft, armed robbery, kidnapping, assault, and arson. The founder of the Spanish Cobras was shot and killed by a member of the Insane Unknowns on April 13, 1979 and the gang still commemorates this day, often with acts of violence.

Identifiers:

- **Clothing:** Clothing in green and black, such as the New York Jets attire. Also "KOOL" baseball caps

- **Gang Symbol:** Coiled king cobra snake, the letters "S/C" and "ISC" (Insane Spanish Cobras)

- **Gang Anniversary:** 13-April-1979 The original founder of the Spanish cobra street gang was shot and killed on this date. Traditionally, members of the Spanish cobra street gang observe this date and pay homage to their fallen father (Richard "KC" Medina)

TATTOOS, HAND SIGN AND COLORS

  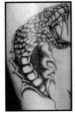    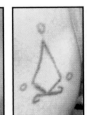

GANG COLORS

Green   Black

150

ALLEGED SPANISH COBRAS GANG MEMBERS
Source: Cook County Sheriff's Department

CHICAGO

Rafael Colon
Indio

CHICAGO

Vicente Guadarrama
Piasa

CHICAGO

Reinaldo Nieves
Funk

CHICAGO

Dwayne Payne
Taz

CHICAGO

Confessor Pizzaro
Big Cuzo

CHICAGO

Doel Pizzaro
Doogie

CHICAGO

Joar Reyes
Jo-R

CHICAGO

Miguel Rivera
MJ

CHICAGO

Adam Rodriguez
Peabody

CHICAGO

Adalberto Santiago
Sabu

CHICAGO

Alejandro Santiago
Flaco

CHICAGO

Anibal Santiago
Tuffy

ALLEGED SPANISH COBRAS GANG MEMBERS

Source: Cook County Sheriff's Department

CHICAGO

Melvin Santiago
Pollacko

CHICAGO

Reynal Valencia
B-Low

CHICAGO

Jose Velez
Chiefy

CHICAGO

Peter Venegas
Peter

SPANISH COBRAS IDENTIFIERS

Source: Cook County Sheriff's Department

SPANISH COBRAS IDENTIFIERS
Source: Cook County Sheriff's Department

A Spanish Cobra drawing shows disrespect to Latin Kings, Imperial Gangsters, La Raza, and Maniac Latin Disciples by breaking a 5-point crown, 7-point crown, Mexican flag, and a heart with horns, respectively.

153

SPANISH FOUR CORNER HUSTLERS
(Alliance – People)

Much like the original Four Corner Hustlers, the Spanish Four Corner Hustlers have many of the same identifiers and aliases. They mostly operate out of the 25th Police District from Fullerton to Diversey and Laramie to Central. They have also been known to have a presence in Schiller Park. Although small in numbers, it seems that they are getting larger each year as the number of arrests continues to increase.

Identifiers:

■ **Gang Symbol:** Top hat with cane and gloves, dice, Playboy bunny with straight ears

TATTOOS, HAND SIGN AND COLORS

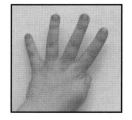

GANG COLORS

Red   Black

154

ALLEGED SPANISH FOUR CORNER HUSTLERS GANG MEMBERS

Source: Cook County Sheriff's Department

CHICAGO

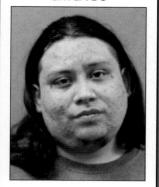

Alberto Garcia

Sleepy

CHICAGO

Javan Johnson

Jay

CHICAGO

Luis Medina

Cartoon

CHICAGO

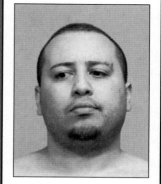

Daniel Ortiz

Shyster

CHICAGO

Arthur Presley

Lil' Black

CHICAGO

Jonathan Rivera

Weezy

CHICAGO

Benjamin Sida

Ben

SPANISH GANGSTER DISCIPLES
(Alliance – Folks)

The Spanish Gangster Disciples (SGDs) were founded in 1974 by a former Maniac Latin Disciple named Rudy Rios. While in prison, Rios helped to create the "Spanish Growth and Development" group. The goal of this group was uniting and settling any problems within the Latin Folk gangs. When released, he quickly turned this group into the Spanish Gangster Disciples after he received permission to adopt the name and identifiers of the Gangster Disciples from the South Side. Their territory once included Trumbull Park Homes at 106th and Bensley, and they expanded rapidly to overtake the eastern area of 87th to 90th between Baltimore and Commercial Avenue (85th and Houston was the center of this). They no longer have territory near Trumbull Park, but still maintain a faction at 88th and Houston.

A North Side faction of Spanish Gangster Disciples appeared around the same time the Hispanic members of the Gangster Disciples joined with the Maniac Latin Disciples. This new group adopted a creed that would combine Gangster Disciple and the Spanish "Growth and Development" principles, and gained recognition among fellow gangs as the main suppliers of marijuana in Rogers Park, Uptown, and Albany Park areas.

Any notion of ties between the North and South groups are extremely vague, but through the years, SGDs have fought many wars with other Hispanic

Identifiers:

- **Clothing:** Duke University Blue Devils sports apparel

- **Gang Symbol:** 6-pointed star with horns at the top and crossed pitchforks

gangs resulting in four ranking members, including founder Rudy Rios, being killed. The gang has little unity and the result has been a drop off in membership. The SGDs still have a presence in their original areas within Chicago as well as some outlying Illinois areas such as Algonquin, Crystal Lake, Elgin, Gurnee, and Prospect Heights. They are known to be involved in drug trafficking, armed robbery, auto theft, and assault.

TATTOOS, HAND SIGN AND COLORS

GANG COLORS

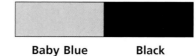

Baby Blue   Black

ALLEGED SPANISH GANGSTER DISCIPLES GANG MEMBERS

Source: Cook County Sheriff's Department

CHICAGO

Kevin Elia
Capone

CHICAGO

Victor Hernandez
Baby Silent

CHICAGO

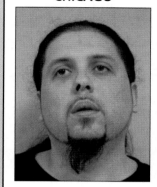

Jorge Jimenez
J-Folks OR Smiley

CHICAGO

Francisco Ramirez
Ghost

CHICAGO

Enrique Romero
Spike Rick

CHICAGO

Jose Serrano
Puppet

CHICAGO

Joe Uriostegui
Trouble

CHICAGO

William Vinet
Flacko

SPANISH GANGSTER DISCIPLES IDENTIFIERS

Source: Cook County Sheriff's Department

I – Gang Profiles

157

SPANISH LORDS
(Alliance – People)

The Lords began as a predominately Hispanic gang in the mid-1960s near Wicker Park, and for years have been closely tied with the Latin Kings. Because of the gentrification of their original territory, the Lords mostly operate in the Bucktown area (especially near Fullerton to Milwaukee and Oakley to Western), and their membership remains small but steady in numbers. The Lords tend to keep a low profile, but have been known to fight with the Insane Unknowns, Maniac Latin Disciples, and other Folks gangs for turf. They are usually involved in drug trafficking, ramming, and armed robbery.

Identifiers:

- **Clothing:** St. Louis Cardinals sportswear
- **Gang Symbol:** The Letters "S/L" and the Latin King crown emblem and a heart with a cross through it

TATTOOS, HAND SIGN AND COLORS

GANG COLORS

Red	Black

158

ALLEGED SPANISH LORDS GANG MEMBERS

Source: Cook County Sheriff's Department

CHICAGO

Miguel Chacon
Miguelito

CHICAGO

Jonathan Dejesus
Lucky

CHICAGO

Ramon DeValle
Ramon

CHICAGO

Steven Figueroa
Stevie

CHICAGO

Roberto Hernandez
Beto

CHICAGO

Silvino Molina
Shadow

CHICAGO

David Nieve
Chops

CHICAGO

Julio Reyes
Casper

CHICAGO

Dion Robinson
Flacka OR Slim

SPANISH VICE LORDS
(Alliance – People)

The Spanish Vice Lords were influenced by the original Vice Lords and have many of the same aliases and identifiers. They primarily operate in the 4th Police District from 106th to 110th Streets and from Buffalo to Avenue O in a faction called "Bukk City." They are also known to have a presence in Elgin.

Identifiers:

■ Top hat, cane, 5 dots, 5-point star, Playboy bunny with straight ears

TATTOOS, HAND SIGN AND COLORS

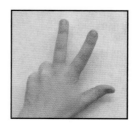

TRADITIONAL COLORS

Gold   Black

ALTERNATE COLORS

Red   Black

ALLEGED SPANISH VICE LORDS GANG MEMBERS

Source: Cook County Sheriff's Department

CHICAGO

Roy Abarca
Playboy

CHICAGO

Terrell Bradley
Tree

CHICAGO

Jimmy Fernandez

CHICAGO

Miguel Leon
Chucky

CHICAGO

Javier Mendez
Nuno

CHICAGO

Jamie Moreno
Jimmy

CHICAGO

Nicholas Ortega
Vicious

CHICAGO

Eric Rodriguez
E-Dog

TWO SIX
(Alliance – Folks)

The Gangster Two Six Nation started in the mid-1960s on 26th Street near Pulaski, and took their name "Two-Six" from 26th Street. Initially organized as a Caucasian and Hispanic gang, Two Six quickly became one of the most prominent Hispanic gangs in Chicago. As the Two Six Nation grew and began to get into drug sales on 26th Street, their rivalry with the Latin Kings also grew and still exists today.

The reputed Two Six leader throughout the 1970s, David Ayala, has been serving a life term in Tamms Correctional Facility since 1981 for murdering several Latin Kings, but the gang itself has a traditionally well-structured leadership. This leadership quickly developed into one of the most violent street gangs in Chicago. Since their founding, the Two Six have expanded their original operations from 26th Street and maintain operations in South Lawndale, Marquette Park, and Brighton Park. Recently, they have moved into many of the suburbs of Chicago as well as neighboring states such as Wisconsin and Indiana.

Identifiers:

- **Clothing:** Clothing in the color scheme of tan and black

- **Gang Symbol:** Playboy bunny head with a cocked ear, wearing a fedora and sunglasses. A pair of dice with two dots on one and six on the other. Tattoos using three dots, and the letters "TSN" (Two Six Nation)

TATTOOS, HAND SIGN AND COLORS

GANG COLORS

Tan   Black

ALLEGED TWO SIX GANG MEMBERS

Source: Cook County Sheriff's Department

CHICAGO

Michael Aguilar
Cartoon

CHICAGO

David Aguirre
Capers

CHICAGO

Anton Aseves
Suspect

CHICAGO

Efrain Atunez
Goofy

CHICAGO

Carlos Avila
Big Shorty

CHICAGO

Vincent Avila
Shorty

CHICAGO

David Ayala
Jehe

CHICAGO

Jose Batalla
Baby J

CHICAGO

Manuel Bobe
Hulk

CHICAGO

Javier Caballero
Smiley

CHICAGO

Daniel Camarena
Bozer

CHICAGO

Valentin Carbajal
Scarface

ALLEGED TWO SIX GANG MEMBERS

Source: Cook County Sheriff's Department

CHICAGO

Jose Carrillo
Nacho

CHICAGO

Ricardo Carrillo
Slim

CHICAGO

Richard Cisneros
Maniac

CHICAGO

Frank Coduto
Dago

CHICAGO

Josue De Alba
Loco

CHICAGO

Mauricio Espana
Modie

CHICAGO

Edwin Flores
Penguin

CHICAGO

Richard Gacho
Shorty

CHICAGO

Elio Galvez
Fly

CHICAGO

Jose Garcia
Negro

CHICAGO

Manuel Garnudo
Riddler

CHICAGO

Augustin Lopez
Silent

ALLEGED TWO SIX GANG MEMBERS

Source: Cook County Sheriff's Department

CHICAGO

Jessie Lopez

Lil Mobster

CHICAGO

Juan Lopez

Gordo

CHICAGO

Louis Lopez

Insane

CHICAGO

Luis Lopez

Buck

CHICAGO

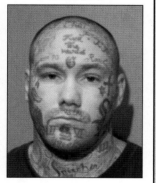

Richard Magnan

Roach

CHICAGO

Gregorio Medina

Baby Vicious

CHICAGO

Jose Morales

Maniac

CHICAGO

Eduardo Ramirez

Frosty

CHICAGO

Jose Reyes

Hoser

CHICAGO

Louis Rivera

Lucky Lou

CHICAGO

Francisco Sanchez

Smokey

CHICAGO

Jesus Santos

Villan

ALLEGED TWO SIX GANG MEMBERS

Source: Cook County Sheriff's Department

CHICAGO

Lorenzo Sauseda
Lolo

CHICAGO

Norman Steffanoni
Fester

CHICAGO

Raul Tamayo
Wedo

CHICAGO

Gabriel Trujillo
Playboy

CHICAGO

Michael Velasquez
Shadow

TWO SIX IDENTIFIERS

Source: Cook County Sheriff's Department

TWO SIX IDENTIFIERS

Source: Cook County Sheriff's Department

TWO TWO BOYS
(Alliance – Folks)

The Two Two Boys are a predominantly Hispanic and Caucasian gangformed in the 1970s at the corner of 22nd Street and California in the Pilsen area. They are also known as the 22nd Street Boys. While the Two Two Boys maintain close relations with the Ambrose Street gang, they are almost constantly at war with the Latin Kings over turf. They have started to move their influence into the suburbs of Chicago as well as into the states of Wisconsin, Kentucky, California, and Florida. While arrests of many of their members in the suburbs have slowed them down, they continue to be on the rise, evidenced by the number of arrests.

Identifiers:

- **Clothing:** Athletic wear with a blue and black color scheme
- **Gang Symbol:** 4-point crown, two dice with two dots showing on each side, a crest or shield with two lions guarding the dice reflecting the number two

TATTOOS, HAND SIGN AND COLORS

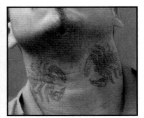

GANG COLORS

Blue   Black

ALLEGED TWO TWO BOYS GANG MEMBERS

Source: Cook County Sheriff's Department

CHICAGO

Rudy Cantu
Hitman

CHICAGO

Lionel Carlos
Malo

CHICAGO

Steve Gutierrez
Capone

CHICAGO

Eduardo Salazar
Silent OR DK

CHICAGO

Joaquin Salazar
Flacko

CHICAGO

Emma Serrano
Emma

CHICAGO

William Serrano
Joker

CHICAGO

Carlos Villagomez
Assassin

TWO TWO BOYS IDENTIFIERS

Source: Cook County Sheriff's Department

VICE LORDS
(Alliance – People)

At a reform school in St. Charles, Illinois in 1958, several young African American men from the area of North Lawndale formed a gang called the Vice Lords. Edward "Pepalo" Perry led this new gang, and was known for being both ruthless and intelligent. The demographic changes in Lawndale from a predominantly Caucasian to African American neighborhood caused delinquent youths to organize themselves with the purpose of fighting other organized groups of rival race. As the early members of the Vice Lords returned from the custody of St. Charles reform school, they came back to the Lawndale community, continued the fighting in a warped form of socialization, and eventually ended up recruiting other African Americans in the area to join their ranks. This resulted in a purge of Vice Lord members, who were constantly involved in conflicts with other neighborhood gangs. The Vice Lords quickly earned a reputation for violence and their use of extortion tactics, and the Vice Lords became known as a feared adversary throughout the Lawndale community.

By 1964, the Vice Lords became a main target for law enforcement. Their fighting with rival races escalated into more serious and rampant illegal activity including robberies, thefts, assaults, batteries, intimidation, and extortion. With all of this criminal activity, Vice Lords wanted to soften their image and change the public's perception of their organization. They added "Conservative" to the front of their name in order to make themselves look better. The Conservative Vice Lord faction of the Vice Lords is the foundation for the entire Vice Lord Nation or "VLN." The Conservative Vice Lords also adopted new identifiers such as the top hat, gloves, and cane to advertise this attempt at a new, more sophisticated cover. They went as far as to promote themselves as a community outreach group and petitioned for a new chapter under the name "Conservative Vice Lord Incorporated (CVL, Inc.)."

The Conservative Vice Lord, Inc. and its leaders were quite successful in their effort to change their public image. The Vice Lords began receiving positive responses from community leaders and politicians. They were able to establish various recreational areas for neighborhood youth, such as teen centers, that doubled as CVL meeting places after hours. They also forged a peace treaty with another rival gang, the Blackstone Rangers, and worked with them to repair the images of both groups.

Around 1970, CVL, Inc. and two of its leaders, Alfonso Alfred and Bobby Gore, applied for and received $270,000 in grant money from the Rockefeller Foundation under the false pretense of being a community outreach group. The Rockefeller Foundation was unaware this group would continue to grow away from being a community group, and into a more powerful and violent street gang. Also, by 1970, the Vice Lords were successful in converting all of the other neighborhood gangs (the Cherokees, the Morphines, the Commanchees, the Continental Pimps, the Imperial Chaplains, the Clovers, the Cobras, and the Braves) of the Lawndale area into the Vice Lord Nation. Although they had previously used CVL, Inc. to fool the public, it was becoming apparent they were still a criminal enterprise. Lawndale residents noticed the introduction of narcotics into their community and an increase in extortion, intimidation, and murders of business owners who refused to pay for protection. As these crimes surfaced, it erased what positive public image the Vice Lords had left, and caused community outrage. This public pressure caused local leaders and politicians to call for federal investigations of the apparent fraud/misuse of grant monies received by CVL, Inc. from the Rockefeller Foundation, which resulted in several CVL leaders being arrested and incarcerated.

In the early 1980s the leadership of the CVLs changed. Pepalo and Alphonso had passed away, and Bobby Gore was incarcerated for murder. Samuel "Mahdi" Smith and a younger CVL enforcer named Willie "Reico" Johnson (the Minister of Justice) assumed control over the Conservative Vice Lord Nation.

The 1990s saw the gang once again trying to change their image. Johnson attempted to hide their criminal practices by promoting his organization as a branch of Islam.

Willie "Reico" Johnson (aka "Ol' Man," "Rahim Justice El," "the Minister of Justice") is currently incarcerated in Tamms Correctional Center and is serving an indeterminate sentence for murder. Johnson is considered to be the national level leader of the Conservative Vice Lords, and continues to exert his influence on the streets from prison.

The headquarters of the Conservative Vice Lord Nation, which is also referred to as the "Holy City," is located near 16th and Pulaski.

The Vice Lord Nation actually includes many gangs in addition to the original Conservative Vice Lords faction, and they all use the title "Vice Lord" to describe themselves. Some examples: Cicero Insane Vice Lords, Imperial Insane Vice Lords, Mafia Insane Vice Lords, Renegade Vice Lords, Traveling Vice Lords, Undertaker Vice Lords, and the Unknown Vice Lords.

The VLN influence generally stays in low income neighborhoods as far west as Central Avenue, as far north as Lawrence Avenue, and as far South as Altgeld Gardens. Outside of Chicago, VLN influence has spread to many of the suburbs and other states.

The Vice Lord Nation has been involved in the sale of narcotics (with a street tax applied to independent dealers), robbery, auto theft, theft, and arson. They have been known to use murder and assault to enforce the territory and are sophisticated in their execution of mortgage fraud, credit card fraud, and money laundering.

Identifiers:

- **Clothing:** Athletic wear in gold and black or red and black color schemes

- **Gang Symbol:** 5-point star, the letters "VL" with a top hat, cane and gloves, a pair of dice, champagne glass, Playboy bunny with straight ears, dollar sign, globes, and a hand sign with the thumb, index and middle finger of the left hand extended to form a "V" and a "L"

VICE LORD TATTOOS

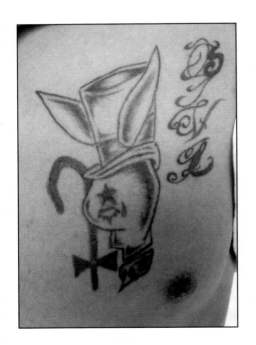

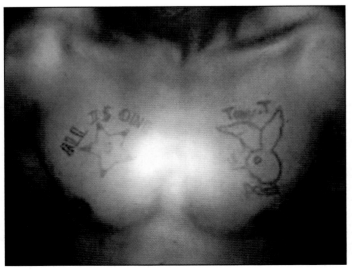

ALLEGED CONSERVATIVE VICE LORDS GANG MEMBERS

Source: Cook County Sheriff's Department

CHICAGO

Kwame Adeams

CHICAGO

Ramiro Brown

Heavy

CHICAGO

Dejuan Colon

Greek

CHICAGO

James Douthard

Mike Mike

CHICAGO

Raydell Flowers

Todd

CHICAGO

Jerry Gladden

Lil' Jerry

CHICAGO

Donald Harris Jr.

Big Snow

CHICAGO

Christopher Jackson

Chris

TATTOOS, HAND SIGN AND COLORS

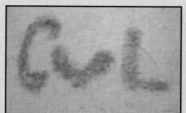

GANG COLORS

Gold   Black

173

ALLEGED CONSERVATIVE VICE LORDS GANG MEMBERS

Source: Cook County Sheriff's Department

CHICAGO

James Kenyata
Woodie

CHICAGO

Lamarn Johnson
Gucci

CHICAGO

Willie Johnson
Minister Rico

CHICAGO

Eric Mason
Slezzy

CHICAGO

Larry McDaniel
Lil' Ride

CHICAGO

Michael Page
MP

CHICAGO

Charles Pinkins
Lil' Charles

CHICAGO

Khalil Pugh
Killer

CHICAGO

Devonne Reed
Fifty

CHICAGO

Rickey Rhodes
Fonz

CHICAGO

Antonio Sanchez
Jesus

CHICAGO

Kenny Shannon
Shine

ALLEGED CONSERVATIVE VICE LORDS GANG MEMBERS

Source: Cook County Sheriff's Department

CHICAGO

Charles Smith
Lil Cuz

CHICAGO

Antonio Snell
Fatty

CHICAGO

Brandel Sutton
Money Rome

CHICAGO

Jonathan Tankson
Dollar

CHICAGO

Derrick Washington
D-Rock

CHICAGO

Jacquain Whittington
Qua-Qua

CHICAGO

Kenneth Williams
Lil' Kenny

ALLEGED MAFIA INSANE VICE LORDS GANG MEMBERS

Source: Cook County Sheriff's Department

CHICAGO

Javon Evans
Funny

CHICAGO

Wesley Hawkins
Ki-Ki

CHICAGO

Calvin Hunt
Chief Goo

CHICAGO

Diamond Lake
Diamond

CHICAGO

Darius Lewis
Lil' Rob

CHICAGO

Troy Martin
King Troy

CHICAGO

Anthony Morris
Tone Tone

CHICAGO

Mark Petties
Kadoffi

TATTOOS, HAND SIGN AND COLORS

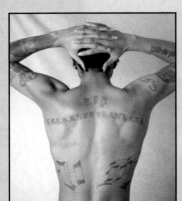

GANG COLORS

Red   Black

ALLEGED MAFIA INSANE VICE LORDS GANG MEMBERS

Source: Cook County Sheriff's Department

CHICAGO

Julius Rembert

Rose

CHICAGO

James Silas

Jello

CHICAGO

Terrance Smith

Kenya

CHICAGO

Darrell Thomas

Tippy

CHICAGO

Reginald Thompson

Reggie

CHICAGO

Kevin Watson

Tug

CHICAGO

Travanti Williams

Tay-Tay

CHICAGO

Cameron York

Cam

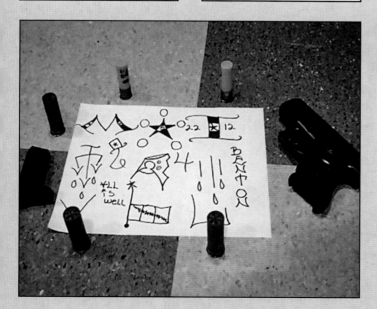

177

ALLEGED TRAVELING VICE LORDS GANG MEMBERS

Source: Cook County Sheriff's Department

CHICAGO

Elliot Allen
Lil' E

CHICAGO

Clarence Anderson
LC

CHICAGO

Jamual Baker
Big Jamaul

CHICAGO

Mardell Blount
Mardell

CHICAGO

Durwin Brooks
Weezy

CHICAGO

Darnell Brunt
Jun-Jun

CHICAGO

Donta Deloach
DT

CHICAGO

Dominic Eskridge
Fooly

TATTOOS, HAND SIGN AND COLORS

GANG COLORS

Gold   Black

178

ALLEGED TRAVELING VICE LORDS GANG MEMBERS

Source: Cook County Sheriff's Department

CHICAGO

Claudius Fincher
Scoop

CHICAGO

Shardell Green
Dale

CHICAGO

Jermaine Harris
Cat Daddy

CHICAGO

Leanthony Harris
Big Ant

CHICAGO

Brandon Harrison
Scummy

CHICAGO

Andrew Hawkins
Andy

CHICAGO

James Hawkins

CHICAGO

Antoine Heard
Phon-Phon

CHICAGO

Antonio Heard
Lil' Fred

CHICAGO

Robbie Horton
Wally

CHICAGO

Markley Jenkins

CHICAGO

Abraham Jewgrante
Ran Ran

ALLEGED TRAVELING VICE LORDS GANG MEMBERS

Source: Cook County Sheriff's Department

CHICAGO

Darren Jones

Fats

CHICAGO

Donald Lee

Don-Don

CHICAGO

Perry Luckett

P-Box

CHICAGO

Tremaine Mason

Cheesy

CHICAGO

Tyrone Moore

Cuddles

CHICAGO

Darnell Nelson

Jerry

CHICAGO

Charles Patton

Big Chill

CHICAGO

Curtis Roberts

Curto

CHICAGO

Lamont Ross

Ben Rich

CHICAGO

Joshua Sandifer

O Dog

CHICAGO

Tyrone Stallworth

Musch

CHICAGO

Ralph Starling

Ralph

ALLEGED TRAVELING VICE LORDS GANG MEMBERS

Source: Cook County Sheriff's Department

CHICAGO

Brian Thomas

Brian

CHICAGO

Joe Thomas

Lil Jo-Jo

CHICAGO

Maurice Tousant

Oily

CHICAGO

James Triplett

Tabell

CHICAGO

Brandon Williams

Lil' B

CHICAGO

Devante Williams

Vante

CHICAGO

Julius Wilson

Juby

CHICAGO

Keesler Wilson

Kee-Kee

CHICAGO

Quenton Wilson

Quint Man

ALLEGED UNDERTAKER VICE LORDS GANG MEMBERS

Source: Cook County Sheriff's Department

CHICAGO

Jason Anthony
Gio

CHICAGO

Duwante Branch
Lil Hurt

CHICAGO

Karry Dockery
Karo

CHICAGO

Darius Franklin
Foo Fap

CHICAGO

Darnell Howard
Red Bone

CHICAGO

Daniel Robinson
DB

HAND SIGN AND COLORS

GANG COLORS

Red   Black

182

ALLEGED UNKNOWN VICE LORDS GANG MEMBERS

Source: Cook County Sheriff's Department

CHICAGO

William Lloyd
Deceased

CHICAGO

Donovan Acker
Dirty Dirty

CHICAGO

Kendall Banks
Kilo

CHICAGO

Christopher Barbee
Chris

CHICAGO

Keith Barbee
Lemonhead

CHICAGO

Derrick Barnes
Squirt

CHICAGO

Laroy Battle
Baldy

CHICAGO

Bobby Boyd
Bobby Joe

HAND SIGN, TATTOOS AND COLORS

GANG COLORS

Gold   Black

ALLEGED UNKNOWN VICE LORDS GANG MEMBERS

Source: Cook County Sheriff's Department

CHICAGO

Fredrick Boyd
Fred

CHICAGO

Tremont Brewer
Tre-Tre

CHICAGO

Terrence Brown
Chuck

CHICAGO

Antoine Carter
Twon

CHICAGO

Sharrod Carter
Cooda

CHICAGO

Curtis Coffey
Neef

CHICAGO

Gregory Dockery
Old Dog

CHICAGO

Cornelius Ellison
Neil

CHICAGO

William Flynn
Worm

CHICAGO

Kenneth Gladney
Kenny

CHICAGO

Kevin Hager

CHICAGO

Conwell Hargrays
Bussie

ALLEGED UNKNOWN VICE LORDS GANG MEMBERS

Source: Cook County Sheriff's Department

CHICAGO

Alfonzo Hillard
Zoe

CHICAGO

Isaiah Ingram
Squirrel

CHICAGO

Lew Kimmons
Poo-Poo

CHICAGO

Samuel McGee
Sam

CHICAGO

Vincent Randall
Chico

CHICAGO

Lamont Tucker
Tap

CHICAGO

Anthony White
Ant Rat

CHICAGO

John Woodard
Dirty

CHICAGO

Maurio Young
Rio

YOUNG LATINO ORGANIZATION COBRAS & YOUNG LATIN ORGANIZATION DISCIPLES (Alliance – Folks)

The YLO Cobras and YLO Disciples are two distinct Hispanic street gangs operating along Armitage and North Avenues in Humboldt Park and west Bucktown. They were both originally part of the Young Latino Organization, a quasi-youth group used to disguise gang activity around the area of Yates School and help the young men for future membership in either the Spanish Cobras or Maniac Latin Disciples. In the early 80s, the two groups realized they could function independently, and instead of operating as feeder gangs became separate criminal entities. They coexisted peacefully within the Folks alliance but became enemies when the Folks broke up into the Insane and Maniac sub-groups: the YLOCs joined the Insane Family, established by the Spanish Cobras, and the YLODs joined the Maniac Family, established by the Maniac Latin Disciples. Both gangs operate in the 14th and 25th districts, often sharing turf boundaries with each other and their original parent gangs, the Cobras and MLDs.

YOUNG LATINO ORGANIZATION COBRAS (YLO COBRAS)

Identifiers:

- Diamond with 3 dots, cobra
- "Amor de Culebra"

YOUNG LATINO ORGANIZATION DISCIPLES (YLO DISCIPLES)

Identifiers:

- Pitchfork, horns, heart with horns and tail

ALLEGED YOUNG LATINO ORGANIZATION COBRAS GANG MEMBERS

Source: Cook County Sheriff's Department

CHICAGO

Rafael Alcantara
Rafael

CHICAGO

Richard Alcantara
Pac

CHICAGO

Jose Alvarez
Mikey

CHICAGO

Jovany Feliciano
Belushi

CHICAGO

Manuel Feliciano
Belushi

CHICAGO

Ivan Gomez
Negro

CHICAGO

Joseph Lopez
Jo Jo

CHICAGO

Nicholas Owens
Shaggy

CHICAGO

Elvis Roman
Elvis

TATTOOS, HAND SIGN AND COLORS

GANG COLORS

Green   Black

CHICAGO

Ricardo Santillanes
Chicano

ALLEGED YOUNG LATINO ORGANIZATION DISCIPLES GANG MEMBERS

Source: Cook County Sheriff's Department

CHICAGO

Gonzalo Acuna
Cuco

CHICAGO

Eduardo Castillo
Mush Mush

CHICAGO

Luis Cruz
Obie

CHICAGO

Rafael Cruz
Monkey

CHICAGO

Adrian Mendez
Powder

CHICAGO

Efrain Nunez
Easy E

CHICAGO

Wilfredo Ramos
Will Kill

CHICAGO

Beau Reyes
Bow

CHICAGO

Luis Rivas
Capone

CHICAGO

Roberto Rivera
Ki Ki

CHICAGO

Melvin Sykes
Cooch

TATTOO, HAND SIGN AND COLORS

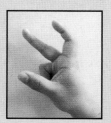 

GANG COLORS

Light Blue   **Black**

GANG FACTIONS

Factions

Modern day gang culture presents a new wave of gang membership. A significant and noticeable change in traditional gang hierarchy is the shift from strong structure into an assortment of cliques or sects. This change can be attributed to the arrest of gang leaders, dismantling of public housing and gentrification and deconstruction of Chicago neighborhoods. A faction is a subsection or break-off of a larger gang operating autonomously or in conjunction with the original gang, sometimes comprised of members from several different gangs. There is little to no central leadership governing factions and most are often disorganized.

History of Factions

There are several theories attributed to the evolution of factions. One theory ties the dismantling of public housing to a breakdown in the necessary infrastructure promoted through a "big house" mentality, requiring members of specific gangs to live together. As public housing decreased, rival gang members were sometimes forced to live within close proximity of one another, like a member of the Gangster Disciples living near a Four Corner Hustlers.

Another explanation for the rise in gang factions is gentrification and deconstruction of neighborhoods. Chicago's main tourist areas such as the North Side, the Loop and the south lakefront (high development) are the safest they have been since the city started keeping records. Areas with high poverty levels and few employment opportunities (low development) like the West and South Sides continue to see a high concentration in crime and a stronger gang presence than more well-developed areas.

Another theory suggests the arrest of gang leaders disrupted the traditional hierarchical gang structure. Without an organized leadership structure,

GANG FACTIONS

younger generations of gang members are not adhered to traditional gang territorial boundaries or rivalries. Without a chain-of-command, street-level members are establishing their own factions and becoming their own leaders. Consequently, this reformation of structure lead to more block-by-block gang sets and the chaotic violence observed in the media today. Members under the same umbrella gang have become rivals and fight over turf and drug markets.

Dividing Lines

Traditional gang loyalties are not the same as they have been in the past. Certain gangs such as the Latin Kings still maintain a traditional hierarchy, but what is being witnessed more and more is loyalty to money, not the gang. If members from separate gangs are making money together, they will maintain that partnership as long as it is mutually

beneficial. For example, high-ranking members of the Gangster Disciples and Black Disciples formed the Hobos in the early 2000s. The Hobos represent a new form of street gang affiliation, a membership mostly comprised of traditionally rival gang members. For a decade, the Hobos capitalized on Chicago's south side drug market through the use of violence and intimidation. This decentralization and breakdown of a once hierarchical structure makes factions and hybrid gangs even more dangerous because without leadership, more members are "putting in work" i.e. taking part in drugs deals and violence.

Faction violence is not solely motivated by money; familial bonds trump gang loyalty. For example, if an individual is a Gangster Disciple and his cousin is a Black P Stone and his cousin is killed by a fellow GD, that individual will work with the Stones to kill that GD who killed his cousin. This affirms the belief that traditional gang loyalties are beginning to be phased out and other variables are responsible for the gang violence within the city.

Another division among factions are drill rap crews. "Drill rap", a style of trap music, originated on Chicago's South Side and has gained notoriety for its graphic lyrics depicting and glorifying the gang lifestyle. A handful of drill rappers are nationally recognized for the music they've produced, such as Chief Keef, Lil' Durk, and Lil' Reese, despite ciminal affiliations. In addition, some Chicago music production companies are known to have gang ties.

For example, Super Savage Records, founded by Fredo Santana, is associated with the Frontstreet Black Disciples faction. Members of Frontstreet have associated the acronym 'SSR' with their gang names on their social media profiles.

Drill rap crews are comprised of gang members or gang affiliates and use their music as a way to insult rivals, often times on various social media platforms. One of the most recognized drill rap rivalries was between Black Disciple Keith Cozart, aka Chief Keef and Gangster Disciple Joseph Coleman aka Lil' Jojo.

The two drill rappers traded insults in tracks which ultimately ended with the death of Lil' Jojo. Chief Keef claimed he was not involved in the shooting but many believe Jojo's death was a result of his dispute with Keef and the BDs. Unlike a lot of rap beefs, drill rappers often follow through with their threats. Within drill rap crews there are shooters that sometimes have to make good on the threats proposed by the rappers. Some shooters look to move away from the violence and become rappers themselves.

More commonly factions divide based on historical residency and school enrollment. In most instances, factions will honor their fallen friend by naming a set after him. For example, after the death of Shondale "Tooka" Gregory, a Gangster Disciple from the St. Lawrence Boys (STL) set, STL adopted the nickname "Tooka Gang" that was meant to honor Gregory. Another example is after Lil' Jojo was killed, the 069 Bricksquad set of the Gangster Disciples adopted the nickname "Jojo World" in honor of their fallen member and rapper.

Violence

Factions carry out different brands of violence, sometimes sporadic and impulsive, other times calculated and well planned. In February 2017, a member of the Black Disciples opened fire on a car after the shooter suspected the occupants were members of a rival gang selling marijuana in BD territory. This shooting resulted in the death of

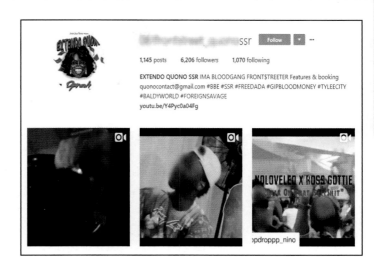

an 11-year-old girl after the shooter missed his intended target.

Although shootings can be reckless and impulsive, there are structural and practical barriers that preclude gang members from carrying out shootings. In his study, Dispatches from the Rap Wars, sociologist Forrest Stuart describes some of these barriers as individuals not having guns, cars, or someone with a license to drive the car. This is where the shootings shift from impulsive to calculated because while gang members wait to obtain a gun, car, or license, they can gather intelligence on rivals using various social media platforms (Facebook, YouTube, and Instagram), in search of rival gang members vehicles, houses frequented, and to track the membership of that gang. This information can be used to better coordinate their attacks against their opposition.

Gang members have begun engaging in more unorthodox criminal activities. Across the Chicago metropolitan area, juvenile gang members are committing more and more car-jackings. Frequently, the gang members steal a car and subsequently commit another crime such as drive-by, smash-and-grabs burglaries or transport of illegal narcotics. According to ATF Special Agent in Charge, Celinez Nunez, these juvenile offenders are committing these car-jackings at the instruction of adult gang members. At the beginning of 2018, the Chicago Police Department formed a joint task force with other federal agencies in response to this trend.

How to Combat Leaderless Gang Cliques

In Kings Only of Corners and Blocks: A primer on Using the Historical Conspiracy Strategy to Address the Violence of Non-traditional Leaderless Street gangs, Tate Chambers outlined how prosecutors tar-get and dismantle 'leaderless' organizations such as current gang factions in Chicago. The author argues the "Historical Conspiracy Strategy" is the most effective method against these smaller gang cliques. The historical conspiracy strategy theorizes gang members conspire together to maintain control over specific areas of the city. Every act committed by a gang member in furtherance of the gang or faction, whether the act is a crime or not, is an explicit act of the conspiracy. Below is an outline of seven steps in order to successfully prosecute and hold these individuals accountable for their criminal activities.

1. Build the Team (Federal, State, and local law enforcement)

2. Identify the targets (faction – 'Trigger pullers' members of the clique committing the violent crimes)

3. Pull the paper (retrieve all police reports on these individuals)

4. Organize the paper (categorize police reports in chronological order, write a summary synopsis of the reports, identify witnesses to testify against targets)

5. Review the paper for charges (possession of firearm by a felon and possession of a controlled substance with intent to distribute – all other charges will build off of these two)

6. Conduct the Grand Jury investigation (witnesses, electronic sources – social media, phone records, etc.)

7. Draft the indictment

On the following pages is a detailed list of known Chicago factions. The table includes faction name, gang affiliation, and location. Note: There can be multiple gang sets at one location; in addition, multiple variations for a faction name (i.e. Gangster Disciples Insane Cutthroat Gangsters are also known as Pooh Bear Gang).

GANG FACTIONS

There are many more factions that utilize the same hand signals depending on the areas they're located. These are just some examples.

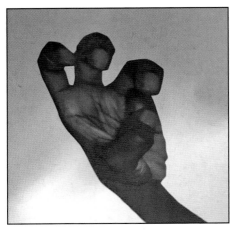

Cracking Treys: A sign of disrespect towards Black Disciples gang

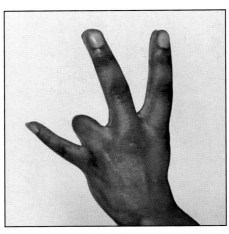

Gangster Disciples: MOB / Fly Boys / Deuce Life / Wuga World/ 50 Strong

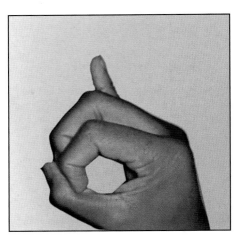

Black Disciples: O Block – Parkway Gardens

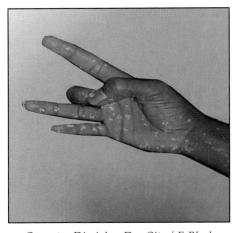

Gangster Disciples: Dro City / E Block

Black Disciples: Dog Pound

Gangster Disciples: Face World / Jig Dawg

Gangster Disciples: BOCA faction

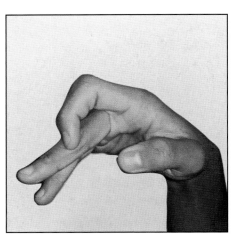

Black P Stones: REC City

YOUNG MONEY WELCH WORLD FACEWORLD HITSQUAD BOGUS BOGUS BOCO LAFLIN BOYS EBK JOJO WORLD 46 TERROR MO TOWN MOB
TUNECHIVILLE MIKE BLOCK DAMENVILLE BAD SIDE CALI ROCKWELL BOYS GUNNHEAD AIKIVILLE WUGA WORLD BRICKSQUAD D-VILLE BLOCK BURNERS
FOLLY BOYS O-BLOCK 600 BRICK CITY OBAMA WORLD TOUCH MONEY BOYS ZO LAND E-BLOCK 50 STRONG LOC CITY TERROR TOWN GLORY BOYZ FRONT
STREET WIIIC CITY 1017 DVG WENTWORTH BOYS FLY BOY GANG FOSTER PARK FLIPSIDE BASHVILLE BANG BANG GANG KILLA WARD SAC TOWN LOW BLOCK
WOODS AND BEYOND KDDG LIL HAITI LO CITY L-DUB KO-MAK K-TOWN 104 & L 3RD WARD ZONE 6IX 504 HOT BOYS SHAWTY WORLD ABERDEN BONE
CRUSHERS ALL BOUT MONEY 300 KETA WORLD LAFA TISKYVILLE ALLEY BOYS ANA BOYS AVENUE MONEY GANG BBB BANGOUT BOYS BARNONE
BEAST MOB BLA FLAG BLOCKHEADS BLACK MOB MAC TOWN MADVILLE GREEN MO BOYS SMASHVILLE MACHETEVILLE YAM BOYS L-STATION
KING DALE DOU IG YOUNG MONELY LOS CITY MALL CAMP CITY REC CITY N RLD MERILL PARK GANGSTERS E JIG DAWGS STEVE
DRIVE MIXED MURDA TOWN NEW PARK WN BLUE FIN BODY SNATCHE BOYS WIZ CITY BRAIN DEAT WN CANNON CITY

FOLLYBOYS YCK E3K YCK YAM YCK
CHIEFTOWN NATEVILLE FOLLYBOYS CHIEFTOWN E3K YCK YAM
E3K NATEVILLE NATEVILLE YCK
FOLLYBOYS YAM NATEVILLE YCK YAM

WELCH
GM3 1017
1017
FACEWORLD WELCH
SIRCON GM3 DROCITY HITSQUAD BRICKSQUAD
GM3 BRICKSQUAD GM3
DROCITY

O BLOCK
300 LOWELIFE E-WOL TTE
LAMRON 600
LOWELIFE 600 300
TYM8 O BLOCK LOWELIFE TTE
TAYTOWN LAMRON 300
WIIIC 600 TTE WIIIC
300 TAYTOWN
WIIIC LOWELIFE TYM8
LAMRON DAWGPOUND
TAYTOWN LOWELIFE 300
TYM8

HOTBOYS BLO NES SCRAPVILLE SEVEN DEUC SMASHVILLE SO ICEY GUDD D SOO WOO STAIN
CITY STUBBZ WO TERROR DOME TERROR TOWN ABARI STONES TGC MANOR ROW THIRD WARD THE VILE T-LOVE T- C CITY TRIGGER TOWN
TRAP CITY TREY WARD TWELVE DEUCE UNPLUGGED THUGS WICKED CITY WILD 9 YALE BOYS COTTAGE MOB CRANKTOWN CRASHTOWN CREEPTOWN
COREY CITY CTG INSANE BLACK MOAFIA DALE GANG 70 CRAZY D-BLOCK DELLO WORLD DEUCE MOB DIPSET DIRTY WORLD DODGE CITY DRO CITY
PACTOWN TYMB D-TOWN DUB EAST END BOYS EAST SIDE EPIVILLE STONY SPOT E-WOL 5GH WARD FLIP SET G-BLOCK GEORGETOWN GHOST TOWN
GET MONEY BOYS GOLDEN GATES WENTWORTH BOYS GRIMEY VILLE GORILLA TOWN GVC HANK NATION GOTTI WORLD HOBO HOOD RICH HARV TOWN
HOYNE BOYZ ICG JUNGLE BOYS KILLER CAMP KUWAIT CITY LAKESIDE LAKE PARK LON CITY LOW LIFE MAFIA TOWN GEEK SQUAD MAUL TOWN MAY
MOB MAYBERRY LYNCHMEN MEDINA MET LIFE MURDA TOWN BONE CURSHERS BOYS TOWN BUD SQUAD BUCKTOWN BULLY BOYS BUFF
CITY CANNON CITY CASH OUT BOYS CASH MONEY BOYS CHAIN GANG CHRIS WORLD SIRCON COLES MOB CLAPVILLE CRANK TOWN COOPVILLE CREEP

GANG FACTIONS

FACTION	GANG	LOCATION
8:16	Black P Stones and Gangster Disciples	63rd to 66th and Kedzie to California
46	Gangster Disciples	46th and Cottage Grove to Woodlawn
700	Gangster Disciples	50th to 51st & Morgan to Halsted
757	Gangster Disciples	37th and Rhodes, 27th and Michigan, 27th to 37th, State St. to King Dr.
800	Black Disciples and Mickey Cobras	61st and Cottage Grove
900	Gangster Disciples	59th to 63rd on Justine
1017	Gangster Disciples	69th to 71st and Western to California
1020	Four Corner Hustlers	68th to 71st and Dorchester to Stony Island
1140	Gangster Disciples	63rd to 67th and Rockwell to Talman
1300	Traveling Vice Lords	13th and Avers to Springfield
4848	Gangster Disciples	Leland to Argyle and Marine Dr. to Broadway
5722	Conservative Vice Lords	56th to 59th and Western to Campbell
5900	Gangster Disciples	59th to 63rd on Justine
7Deuce	Gangster Disciples	71st to 73rd and Eberhart to Langley
Cooper Park	Gangster Disciples	115th to 119th and Racine to Ashland
"0667"	Gangster Disciples	65th to 69th and Cottage Grove to St Lawrence
#1800	Four Corner Hustlers	Lake to Maypole and Wood to Wolcott
071 Block	Gangster Disciples	71st to 72nd and East End
0-Block	Black Disciples	63rd to 65th and Martin Luther King Dr.
10 Town	Gangster Disciples	Altgeld Gardens Housing Complex (Block 10)
10 Trey Gangsters	Gangster Disciples	103rd and Harvard to Martin Luther King Dr.
100th and Wallace	Gangster Disciples	99th to 103rd and Eggleston to Halsted
104 & L	Latin Kings	100th to 106th and Indianapolis to Greenbay
104-L	Black Gangsters (New Breed)	104th to 105th and Wentworth
104th & Aberdeen	Traveling Vice Lords	104th to 107th and Racine to Morgan
107th & Wabash	Gangster Disciples	107th to 110th and Michigan to State
10-8	Traveling Vice Lords	107th to 111th and Halsted to Racine
10-Trey	Gangster Disciples	103rd to 105th and Halsted to Morgan
111th Street Gangster Disciples	Gangster Disciples	108th to 111th and Eggleston to Emerald
112th Street Gangster Disciples	Gangster Disciples	112th Pl and Perry to Wentworth
113th & Wentworth	Conservative Vice Lords	113th to 115th and Wentworth to Tracks
11-9	Gansgter Disciples	119th and Michigan

GANG FACTIONS

FACTION	GANG	LOCATION
11-9 Mayberg	Gangster Disciples	115th to 120th and Normal to Halsted
12 Slug	Black Disciples	25 E. 121st Place
12-Deuce	Gangster Disciples	122nd and Halsted to Racine to Ashland
12-Trey	Black Disciples	123rd and Emerald, 120th and Union
1-3 Ana Boyz	Black Gangsters (New Breed)	13th and Christiana
1400E	Gangster Disciples	71st to 75th and Kenwood to Stony Island
1-9 Breedz	Black Gangsters (New Breed)	19th and Kedzie
2 Feet Boys	Four Corner Hustlers	West End and Latrobe to Washington and Lotus
21st Boys	Traveling Vice Lords	21st and St. Louis
21st Boys	Traveling Vice Lords	Ogden to Cermak and Homan to Central Park
21st No Worst	Black Gangsters (New Breed)	21st and Spaulding
21st No Worst	Traveling Vice Lords	Ogden to Cermak & Homan to Central Park
2'4 City	Gangster Disciples	63rd to 65th and Ashland to Hermitage
2FB	Four Corner Hustlers	West End and Latrobe to Washington and Lotus
2nd City	Ambrose	62nd and Troy
300 (Lamrons)	Black Disciples	59th to 69th and Wentworth to Halsted
3-5 Boys	Latin Counts	35th St and Damen to Wood
35s	Two Six and Latin Counts	35th to 39th and Ashland to Kedzie
35's	35's	35th and Hoyne
35's	35's	35th St and California to Western
37th Aves	Black Disciples	36th to 39th and Michigan to Prairie
3rd Gang	Gangster Disciples	71st to 73rd and Morgan to Racine
3rd Ward	Conservative Vice Lords	82nd and Peoria
3rd Ward	Gangster Disciples	71st to 73rd and Winchester
3rd Ward Gangster Disciples	Gangster Disciples	70th and Wentworth to Yale
4 Block	Traveling Vice Lords	104th to 107th and Racine to Morgan
4 Duece		Gladys and Cicero
400 East	Black Disciples	67th to 71st and Michigan to State
400 East/ Slip set	Black Disciples	69th to 71st King and Rhodes
44's	Mickey Cobras	43rd to 46th and Shields
46 Terror		43rd to 46th and Drexel to Ellis
48th Side	La Raza	47th to 49th and Ashland to Racine
48th Side	La Raza	48th and Laflin

GANG FACTIONS

FACTION	GANG	LOCATION
48th Side	La Raza	48th and Racine
48th Side - "Boon Dockys"	La Raza	48th and Bishop
4-Deuces	Four Corner Hustlers	Gladys and Cicero
4Hunna	Four Corner Hustlers	Lake to Maypole and Wood to Wolcott
50 Strong	Gangster Disciples	50th to 51st and Morgan to Halsted
50 Strong	Gangster Disciples	49th to 51st and Morgan to Union
504 Hot Boys / 504 Bloodstones	Black P Stones	86th to 91st and Marquette to Escanaba
5-1 Block	Gangster Disciples	51st and Michigan
51st Insane Popes (Southside)	Insane Popes (Southside)	51st and Kilpatrick
57 Crazy	Gangster Disciples	56th to 57th and Normal to Shields
57th Ave	Gangster Disciples	57th to 58th and Prairie to Calumet
57th Crazies	Gangster Disciples	56th to 59th and Marshfield to Laflin
5900 Brick Squad	Gangster Disciples	59th and Justine and Laflin
59th St Satan Disciples	Satan Disciples	58th and Trumbull
59th St Satan Disciples	Satan Disciples	58th to 61st and Central Park to California
59th St Satan Disciples	Satan Disciples	59th and Richmond
59th St Satan Disciples	Satan Disciples	59th and Sacramento
59th St Satan Disciples	Satan Disciples	59th and Spaulding
59th St Satan Disciples	Satan Disciples	60th and Central Park
59th St Satan Disciples	Satan Disciples	59th and Mozart
5th Ward	Black Disciples	45th and St Lawrence
5th Ward	Black Disciples	46th and Ellis
5th Ward	Black Gangsters (New Breed)	Monroe and Albany
5th Ward	Conservative Vice Lords	54th and Damen to Winchester
6 Ward	Gangster Disciples	65th to 69th and Damen to Hamilton
600 (Six Hunna)	Black Disciples	60th to 63rd and Martin Luther King Dr. to State
600 Strong	Black Disciples	60th and Martin Luther King Dr.
6000 Winchester	Black P Stones	60th to 61st and Winchester to Damen
6-2 Boys	Gangster Disciples	61st to 63rd and Laflin to Ashland
6th Ward Gangster Disciples	Gangster Disciples	67th to 70th and Hamilton to Damen
7 Deuces	Gangster Disciples	71st to 75th and Ellis to Evans
70 Crazy	Gangster Disciples	71st to 75th and Seeley to Hoyne
7-2 Boys	Gangster Disciples	71st to 72nd and Campbell to Kedzie
76th Street Fours	Four Corner Hustlers	75th to 76th and Ada to Loomis

FACTION	GANG	LOCATION
7-Trey	Black Gangsters (New Breed)	73rd and Greenwood
8 Tre Mob	Gangster Disciples	82nd to 85th and Eberhart to Martin Luther King Dr.
800 EAST	Black Disciples and Mickey Cobras	61st and Cottage Grove
80s Babies	Gangster Disciples	79th to 83rd and Ashland to Leavitt
88 D-Hate	Latin Kings	88th and Exchange
8-Ball	Gangster Disciples	108th and State to Wentworth
8-Ball	Mickey Cobras	108th and Morgan
8-Ball	Mickey Cobras	106th and Union
8-Ball City	Maniac Latin Disciples	Fullerton and Pulaski
8 -Trey Music Group (8TMG)	Black P Stones	83rd to 87th and Halsted to Carpenter
8-Trey	Black P Stones	83rd to 87th and Halsted to Carpenter
90 (9-0)	Gangster Disciples	90th to 93rd and Ashland to Beverly
91st Four Corner Hustler	Four Corner Hustlers	91st to 93rd and Cottage to Dauphine
93rd Thunder	Gangster Disciples	93rd and Dobson
95th Mobb	Gangster Disciples	95th and Harvard to Lafayette
95th Street Gangster Disciples	Gangster Disciples	91st to 97th and Eggleston to Dan Ryan
96 No Limit	Latin Kings	96th and Avenue M
99 Ruthless	Latin Kings	95th to 100th and Avenue N to the Lake
9's	Gangster Disciples	119th and Lowe to Halsted
9th Ward	Gangster Disciples	69th and Talman
9th Ward Black Disciples	Black Disciples	69th and Artesian
9-Trey	Gangster Disciples	90th to 95th and Vincennes to Throop
9-Trey	Gangster Disciples	93rd and Dobson
9-Trey Tiskyville	Black P Stones	93rd to 98th & King to State
Aberdeen Bone Crushers (ABCs)	Gangster Disciples	56th to 58th Carpenter to Racine
Alley Boy City (ABC)	Four Corner Hustlers	West End and Latrobe to Washington and Lotus
Avers Boy Crazy (ABC)	Traveling Vice Lords	13th and Avers to Springfield
Aberdeen Bone Crushers (ABCs)	Gangster Disciples	56th to 58th and Aberdeen and Carpenter to Racine
Abla Homes Breeds	Black Gangsters (New Breed)	13th and Throop and Loomis
A-Block	Gangster Disciples	63rd to 66th and Artesian
A-Block	Spanish Cobras	Hirsch to Division and Western to Maplewood
All About Money (ABM)	Black Disciples	79th and St Louis
Ace Block	Black P Stones	86th to 90th and Kingston to Muskegon and 91st and Escanaba
Ace Block	Conservative Vice Lords	56th to 59th and Western to Campbell

GANG FACTIONS

FACTION	GANG	LOCATION
Ace Gang	Conservative Vice Lords	56th to 59th and Western to Campbell
A-City	Latin Kings	22nd to 22nd and Marshall to Kedzie
Ada City	Latin Kings	51st and Ada
Ada Kings	Latin Kings	51st and Ada
Ada Park	Black Disciples	109th and Loomis to Throop
Ada Park	Black Disciples	111th to 115th and Ashland to Racine
Ada Street Click	Gangster Disciples	67th to 69th and Ada
Ada World	Gangster Disciples	77th to 79th and Ada
A-Dub	Maniac Latin Disciples	Ainslie and Washtenaw
After Death	Imperial Gangsters	Austin and Diversey
Aikiville	Gangster Disciples	67th to 71st and Parnell to Wentworth
Albany Two Six	Two Six	38th and Albany
Albion & Clark	Black P Stones	Albion to Schreiber and Ashland to Wood
All About Money (ABM)	Gangster Disciples	61st to 63rd and King to Langley
All Bout Money (ABM)	Gangster Disciples	61st to 62nd and St Lawrence to Langley
All Bout Money (ABM)	Gangster Disciples	62nd to 63rd and Cottage to St. Lawrence
All Bout Money (ABM)	Gangster Disciples	67th and Dorchester
All Coty	Gangster Disciples	60th and Marshfield
All The Money (ATM)	Gangster Disciples	62nd and Marshfield
Alley Boys	Four Corner Hustlers	West End to Washington and Lotus to Pine
Allport Street	La Raza	19th to 21st and Allport to Loomis
Altgeld Garden Conservative Vice Lords	Conservative Vice Lords	133rd to 134th and Corliss to Langley
Altgeld Gardens	Black P Stones	131st and Evans
Altgeld Gardens Black P Stones	Black P Stones	132nd to 133rd and Corliss to Langley
AMB	Four Corner Hustlers	68th to 71st and Dorchester to Stony Island
Ambrose	Ambrose	61st and Richmond
Ambrose	Ambrose	62nd and Whipple
Ambrose	Ambrose	63rd and California
AMG (Avenue Money Gang)	Black Disciples	63rd to 66th and Halsted to Green
AMG (Avenue Money Gang)	Black Disciples	63rd-67th Morgan to Halsted
AMG (Avenue Money Gang)/Mack Block	Black Disciples	63rd-65th Halsted to Morgan
Ana Boys	Black Gangsters (New Breed)	Roosevelt to 14th and Kedzie to Homan
Angel City	Black P Stones	82nd and Coles
Angelo Four Corner Hustlers	Four Corner Hustlers	Adams and Laramie to Lockwood

FACTION	GANG	LOCATION
Angelo Four Corner Hustlers	Four Corner Hustlers	52st and Blackstone
Angelo Four Corner Hustlers	Four Corner Hustlers	Chicago and Hamlin
Angelo Four Corner Hustlers	Four Corner Hustlers	Fillmore and Mason
Angelo Four Corner Hustlers	Four Corner Hustlers	Fullerton to Diversey and Laramie to Central
Angelo Four Corner Hustlers	Four Corner Hustlers	Fulton and Central
Angelo Four Corner Hustlers	Four Corner Hustlers	North and Pine
Angelo Four Corner Hustlers	Four Corner Hustlers	Polk and Pulaski
Angelo Four Corner Hustlers	Four Corner Hustlers	Washington and Central
Angelo Four Corner Hustlers	Four Corner Hustlers	Washington & Long
Angelo Four Corner Hustlers	Four Corner Hustlers	Washington and Pine
Angelo Four Corner Hustlers	Four Corner Hustlers	West End and Central
Angelo Four Corner Hustlers	Four Corner Hustlers	Winsdor & Hazel
Anna Boys	Black Gangsters (New Breeds)	13th to 14th and Christiana
Annex	Vice Lords	Monroe to Adams and Wood to Honore
Anybody Killer	Gangster Disciples	72nd and Coles
AO Boys	Conservative Vice Lords	Roosevelt and Francisco and Mozart
AO Rozay	Conservative Vice Lords	Roosevelt and Francisco and Mozart
AP Kings	Latin Kings	Albion to Pratt and Western to Campbell
Apache Stones	Black P Stones	79th and Essex
Apache Stones	Black P Stones	87th to 89th and Muskegon to South Chicago
Apache Stones	Black P Stones	86th and 89th Muskegan to Kingston
Area 51	Latin Kings	Berwyn to Winnemac and Damen to Leavitt
Art Gang	Gangster Disciples	55th to 58th and Wood
Ashland Avenue	Latin Counts	35th to 39th and Ashland to Damen
Ashland Vikings	Ashland Vikings	21st and 47th
Ashland Vikings	Ashland Vikings	Altgeld and Laramie
Ashland Vikings	Ashland Vikings	Lunt and Paulina
Ashland Vikings	Ashland Vikings	Wrightwood and Laramie
A-Trey	Black P Stones	83rd and Sangamon
Avenue Money Gang (AMG)	Black Disciples	65th to 67th and Union to Halsted
Aves	Gangster Disciples	55th to 59th and King Dr to Prairie
Aztec Souls	Aztec Souls	101st and Avenue L
Aztec Souls	Aztec Souls	103rd and Avenue J
Aztec Souls	Aztec Souls	105th and Avenue L

GANG FACTIONS

FACTION	GANG	LOCATION
B.O.B	Gangster Disciples	63rd to 67th and Rockwell to Talman
B.O.N.	Four Corner Hustlers	69th and Crandon
B.O.T.	Gangster Disciples	Central and Race
Babylon City	Spanish Cobras	Belmont to Schubert and Milwaukee to Pulaski
Bad Block Brothers (BBB)	Conservative Vice Lords	79th and South Shore
Bad Block Brothers (BBB)	Conservative Vice Lords	80th to 83rd and Exchange to Burnham
Bad Boyz	Mickey Cobras	63rd to 65th and Cottage Grove to Champlain
Bad Side of Cali (BSC)	Gangster Disciples	63rd to 67th and California to Kedzie
Baldy World	Black Disciples	63rd to 67th and King Drive
BAM (By Any Means)		71st and Rhodes
Band of Thugs	Gangster Disciples	Central and Race
Bandaid Gang	Black P Stones	83rd to 87th and Morgan to Ashland
Bang Bang Gang (BBG)	Gangster Disciples	77th to 79th and Damen to Winchester
Bang Set	Gangster Disciples	901 E. 104th Street (Pullman Wheelworks Building)
Banger Gang	Four Corner Hustlers	69th to 71st and Dorchester to Stony Island
Bangout Boys	Gangster Disciples	63rd to 66th and Artesian
Bangtown	Black Disciples	107th to 108th and Perry to Wolcott
Bangtown	Gangster Disciples	108th to 110th and State
BARNONE	Black P Stones	49th Place to 51st and Racine to Ashland
BARNONE	Black P Stones	82nd and Justine
BARNONE	Gangster Disciples	131st to 134th and Corliss and Langley and St. Lawrence
BARNONE	Black P Stones	49th and Throop
BARNONE	Gangster Disciples	75th to 79th and South Shore to Exchange
BARNONE (Rockwell Boys)	Gangster Disciples	62nd to 69th and Western to Rockwell
BARNONE Crazy	Gangster Disciples	77th to 82nd and Cottage Grove to Ellis
BARNONE Gang	Traveling Vice Lords	104th to 107th and Racine to Morgan
Bash Town	Black P Stones	87th and Wabash
Bashville	Black Disciples	71st to 75th and Michigan to State
Bashville	Black P Stones	87th to 89th and Michigan to Lafayette
Bashville (BVC)	Gangster Disciples	79th and Wabash
Bay Bay Gang (BBG)	Gangster Disciples	43rd and State
BBB (Bad Black Brothers)	Conservative Vice Lords	79th and South Shore
BBB (Bad Black Brothers)	Conservative Vice Lords	80th to 83rd and Exchange to Burnham
BBG (Bang Bang Gang)	Gangster Disciples and Black P Stone Nation	77th to 79th and Damen to Winchester

GANG FACTIONS

FACTION	GANG	LOCATION
BBG (Bay Bay Gang)	Gangster Disciples	43rd and State
BC	Maniac Latin Disciples	Barry and California
BCCB (Black Currency C-Block)	Gangster Disciples	67th and Chappell
BDB (Blue Devil Boys)	Four Corner Hustlers	Ferdinand and Laramie to Lockwood
Beast Mob	Gangster Disciples	72nd to 74th and Racine to Laflin
Beek City / MAC Town	Black P Stones	52nd and Morgan
Beezle Boys	Black Disciples	63rd to 67th and King Drive
Belden City	Imperial Gangsters	Altgeld and Parkside
Belden City	Imperial Gangsters	Belden St and Monitor to Parkside
Ben Ben	Black Gangsters (New Breed)	Roosevelt to 14th and Kedzie to Homan
Bennett Boys	Gangster Disciples	79th and Bennett
BG (Bandaid Gang)	Black P. Stones	83rd to 87th and Morgan to Ashland
BGC (Black Gate / Black Gate City)	Black Disciples	54th to 56th and Calumet to Indiana
BGGS	Gangster Disciples	42nd to 45th and King Dr to Indiana
Big Money Family (BMF)	Conservative Vice Lords	Augusta to Iowa and Cicero to Lavergne
Big Money Family (BMF)	Conservative Vice Lords	Chicago Avenue and Laramie
Big Money Family (BMF)	Conservative Vice Lords	Divison and Lawndale
Big Money Family (BMF)	Conservative Vice Lords	Iowa and Springfield
Big Tyme	Latin Kings	87th to 89th and Commercial to Exchange
Big Tyme	Latin Kings	89th to 90th and Muskegon to Escanaba
Bigham	Spanish Cobras	Francis to Armitage and Milwaukee to Stave
BillVille	Gangster Disciples	63rd to 65th and Ashland to Hermitage
Bird Gang City	Gangster Disciples	67th to 70th and Hamilton to Damen
Bishops	Bishops	16th to 21st and Ashland to Damen
Bishops	Bishops	16th to 21st and Canal to Halsted
Bishops	Bishops	18th and Desplaines
Bishops	Bishops	18th and Halsted
Bishops	Bishops	18th and Wood
Bishops	Bishops	37th and Wallace
Bishops	Bishops	Cermak and 61st Ave
Black Disciples	Black Disciples	100th to 102nd and Calumet
Black Disciples	Black Disciples	107th and Edbrooke
Black Disciples	Black Disciples	108th to 110th and Wentworth to Princeton
Black Disciples	Black Disciples	110th and Wentworth

GANG FACTIONS

FACTION	GANG	LOCATION
Black Disciples	Black Disciples	111th and Vincennes
Black Disciples	Black Disciples	113th and Wabash
Black Disciples	Black Disciples	117th to 123rd and Yale to State
Black Disciples	Black Disciples	118th to 120th and Calumet to Indiana
Black Disciples	Black Disciples	126th and Union
Black Disciples	Black Disciples	12th to 13th and St. Louis to Central Park
Black Disciples	Black Disciples	59th and Elizabeth
Black Disciples	Black Disciples	59th and Hermitage
Black Disciples	Black Disciples	61st and Wabash
Black Disciples	Black Disciples	65th and Stony Island
Black Disciples	Black Disciples	65th and Wood
Black Disciples	Black Disciples	69th and Marshfield
Black Disciples	Black Disciples	70th and Lowe
Black Disciples	Black Disciples	76th to 80th and King to Eberhart
Black Disciples	Black Disciples	93rd to 95th and Bishop to Ashland
Black Disciples	Black Disciples	99th and Yale
Black Disciples	Black Disciples	Monroe and Albany
Black Flag	Four Corner Hustlers	Division to Augusta and Harding to Pulaski
Black Gangsters	Black Gangsters (New Breed)	14th and Blue Island
Black Gangsters	Black Gangsters (New Breed)	14th and Morgan
Black Gangsters	Black Gangsters (New Breed)	14th and Springfield
Black Gangsters	Black Gangsters (New Breed)	16th and Kenneth
Black Gangsters	Black Gangsters (New Breed)	16th and Kostner
Black Gangsters	Black Gangsters (New Breed)	18th and Kedzie
Black Gangsters	Black Gangsters (New Breed)	Carroll and Pulaski
Black Gangsters	Black Gangsters (New Breed)	Congress Parkway and Central Park
Black Gangsters	Black Gangsters (New Breed)	Congress Parkway and Kolmar
Black Gangsters	Black Gangsters (New Breed)	Douglas to Ogden and Albany to Kedzie
Black Gangsters	Black Gangsters (New Breed)	Fifth and Kostner
Black Gangsters	Black Gangsters (New Breed)	Fifth and Sacramento Blvd
Black Gangsters	Black Gangsters (New Breed)	Fifth and Whipple
Black Gangsters	Black Gangsters (New Breed)	Fillmore and Kilbourn
Black Gangsters	Black Gangsters (New Breed)	Grenshaw and Springfield
Black Gangsters	Black Gangsters (New Breed)	Lexington and Kostner

GANG FACTIONS

FACTION	GANG	LOCATION
Black Gangsters	Black Gangsters (New Breed)	Ogden to 21st and Sacremento to Kedzie
Black Gangsters	Black Gangsters (New Breed)	Polk and Kolmar
Black Gangsters	Black Gangsters (New Breed)	Roosevelt and Kedvale
Black Gangsters	Black Gangsters (New Breed)	Roosevelt and Spaulding
Black Gangsters	Black Gangsters (New Breed)	Roosevelt to 13th and Keeler
Black Gangsters	Black Gangsters (New Breed)	Roosevelt to 15th and Ashland to Racine
Black Gangsters	Black Gangsters (New Breed)	Taylor & Kedvale
Black Gangsters	Black Gangsters (New Breed)	Taylor and Kilbourn
Black Gangsters	Black Gangsters (New Breed)	Taylor to 16th and Racine to Ashland
Black Gangsters	Black Gangsters (New Breed)	Van Buren and Pulaski to Kildare
Black Gate	Black Disciples	54th to 56th and Calumet to Indiana
Black King Cobras	Black King Cobras	117th and Princeton Ave
Black King Cobras	Black King Cobras	59th and King Dr
Black Mob	Black P Stones	74th to 75th and Colfax to Phillips
Black Mob	Black P Stones	72nd to 76th and Kingston to Phillips
Black Mob	Four Corner Hustlers	Hirsch to Division and Cicero to Laramie
Black MOB	Gangster Disciples	72nd to 74th and Phillips to Kingston
Black MOB	Gangster Disciples	75th to 79th and Jeffery to South Shore
Black Mob Boys	Gangster Disciples	81st and Oglesby
Black Mobb	Black P Stones	87th to 89th and South Chicago to Saginaw
Black Mobb	Gangster Disciples	73rd and Marshfield to Paulina
Black P Stones	Black P Stones	105th and Halsted
Black P Stones	Black P Stones	105th and Indiana
Black P Stones	Black P Stones	105th to 107th and Edbrooke
Black P Stones	Black P Stones	111th to 112th PL and Princeton to Wentworth
Black P Stones	Black P Stones	117th and Laflin
Black P Stones	Black P Stones	122nd and Carpenter
Black P Stones	Black P Stones	128th and Lowe
Black P Stones	Black P Stones	39th to 47th and Lake Park to Ellis
Black P Stones	Black P Stones	47th and Cottage Grove
Black P Stones	Black P Stones	71st and Blackstone
Black P Stones	Black P Stones	73rd and Stony Island
Black P Stones	Black P Stones	75th and Stony Island
Black P Stones	Black P Stones	75th to 79th and Jeffrey to Yates

GANG FACTIONS

FACTION	GANG	LOCATION
Black P Stones	Black P Stones	79th and Campbell
Black P Stones	Black P Stones	79th and Homan
Black P Stones	Black P Stones	79th to 83rd and Parnell to Halsted
Black P Stones	Black P Stones	82nd and Escanaba
Black P Stones	Black P Stones	87th to 90th and Dorchester to Stony Island
Black P Stones	Black P Stones	91st and Harvard
Black P Stones	Black P Stones	97th and Cottage Grove
Black P Stones	Black P Stones	Crystal and Leavitt
Black P Stones	Black P Stones	Hollywood and Kenmore
Black P Stones	Black P Stones	Montrose to Leland & Clifton to Malden
Black P Stones	Black P Stones	Cortland to Wabansia and Humboldt
Black Peace Stones Backblock	Black P Stones	54th and Justine to Bishop
Black Side	Gangster Disciples	74th and Homan
Black Souls	Black Souls	16th and Kilbourn
Black Souls (Gangster Black Souls)	Black Souls	16th and Kostner
Black Souls (Outlaw Black Souls)	Black Souls	16th to 19th and Harding
Black Souls	Black Souls	Campbell to Francisco and Madison
Black Souls	Black Souls	Cortez and Leclaire
Black Souls	Black Souls	Fifth Ave and Sacramento
Black Souls	Black Souls	Fulton and Albany
Black Souls (Mad Black Souls)	Black Souls	Fulton and California
Black Souls (Gangster Black Souls)	Black Souls	Fulton and Cicero
Black Souls	Black Souls	Hubbard and Lamon
Black Souls (Gangster Black Souls)	Black Souls	Lake St and Walnut and Homan
Black Souls (New Life Black Souls)	Black Souls	Lexington and Albany
Black Souls (Gangster Black Souls/ Mad Black Souls)	Black Souls	Madison and Homan
Black Souls	Black Souls	Madison and Kedzie
Black Souls (Impressionist Black Souls)	Black Souls	Madison and Kostner
Black Souls	Black Souls	Madison and Sacramento
Black Souls (Gangster Black Souls)	Black Souls	Maypole and Cicero
Black Souls (Mad Black Souls)	Black Souls	Monroe and Karlov
Black Souls (Mad Black Souls/ New Life Black Souls)	Black Souls	Monroe and Pulaski

GANG FACTIONS

FACTION	GANG	LOCATION
Black Souls	Black Souls	Thomas and Leclaire
Black Souls (Mad Black Souls)	Black Souls	Walnut and Pulaski
Black Souls (New Life Black Souls)	Black Souls	Wilcox and Pulaski
Black Souls (Mad Black Souls)	Black Souls	Wilcox and Washtenaw
Black Tops	Gangster Disciples	Chicago to Divison and Larabee to Sedgwick
Black World	Gangster Disciples	47th and Drexel
Blackman World (BMW)	Traveling Vice Lords	Ogden to Cermak and Homan to Central Park
Blackstone	Gangster Disciples	79th to 89th and Stony Island to Tracks
Bleek Town	Conservative Vice Lords	Roosevelt and Francisco and Mozart
Block 1,2,3	Black P Stones	130th to 131st St. and Ellis to St. Lawrence
Block 17	Gangster Disciples	131st to 134th and Langley to St. Lawrence
Block 4	Titanic Stones	Altgeld Gardens
Block 5	Black Disciples	133rd and Corliss
Block 7	Black Disciples	133rd and Corliss
Block Heads	Black Disciples	63rd to 67th and King Drive
Blocka Squad	Black Gangsters (New Breed)	13th and Throop and Loomis
Blockheads	Black Disciples	65th and Martin Luther King Dr.
Blood Boys	Black Disciples and Gangster Disciples	63rd to 63rd and Hermitage to Honore
Blood Money	Black Disciples and Gangster Disciples	62nd to 63rd and Hermitage to Honore
Blood Money Boys (BMB)	Gangster Disciples	61st and Marshfield
Bloodstones	Black P Stones	90th to 91st and Muskegon to Commercial
Bloody Murder	Imperial Gangsters	Belden and Menard
BL's	Batos Locos	42nd to 43rd and Mozart
Blue City Liferz	Gangster Disciples	Belmont and Clifton
Blue City Outlawz	Gangster Disciples	Belmont and Clifton
Blue Devil Boys	Four Corner Hustlers	Ferdinand and Laramie to Lockwood
Blue Fin Black Disciples	Blue Fin Black Disciples	117th and Princeton Ave
Blue Fin Black Disciples	Blue Fin Black Disciples	59th and King Dr
Blue Fin Black Disciples	Blue Fin Black Disciples	62nd and Calumet
Blue Fin Black Disciples	Blue Fin Black Disciples	64th to 65th and King Dr
Blue Fin Black Disciples	Blue Fin Black Disciples	65th and Stony Island
Blue Fin Black Disciples	Blue Fin Black Disciples	69th and Marshfield
Blue Fin Black Disciples	Blue Fin Black Disciples	78th to 79 and Greenwood to Woodlawn
Blue Fin Black Disciples	Blue Fin Black Disciples	79th and Calumet

GANG FACTIONS

FACTION	GANG	LOCATION
Blue Fin Black Disciples	Blue Fin Black Disciples	82nd and Cottage Grove
Blue Fin Black Disciples	Blue Fin Black Disciples	Jackson and Damen
Blue Fin Black Disciples	Blue Fin Black Disciples	Maypole and Kilpatrick
Blue Fin Black Disciples	Blue Fin Black Disciples	Monroe and Adams
BMB (Blood Money Boys)	Gangster Disciples	60th and Marshfield
BMW (Blackman World)	Traveling Vice Lords	Ogden to Cermak and Homan to Central Park
BNC (Bar None City)	Gangster Disciples	77th to 82nd and Cottage Grove to Ellis
Bo Boys	Four Corner Hustlers	West End and Latrobe to Washington and Lotus
Bo Boys	Gangster Disciples	Roosevelt to 14th and Albany to Kedzie
Bob Gang	Gangster Disciples	63rd to 65th & Ashland to Hermitage
BOC	Gangster Disciples	63rd to 67th and Clarment and Oakley and Bell
BOCA	Gangster Disciples	63rd to 67th and Clarment and Oakley and Bell
BOCO	Gangster Disciples	63rd to 67th and Clarment and Oakley and Bell
Boco Hood	Gangster Disciples	66th and Oakley
Body Snatchers	Four Corner Hustlers	Hirsch to Ohio and Central to Austin
Body Snatchers	Four Corner Hustlers	North and Mayfield
Bogus Bogus	Gangster Disciples	67th to 71st and Western to California
Bogus Bogus	Gangster Disciples	67th to 71st Artesian to Washtenaw
Bogus Boys	Gangster Disciples	57th and Union
Bogus Boys	Gangster Disciples	68th to 71st and Jeffery to Paxton
Bogus Boys	Gangster Disciples	68th to 71st Jeffrey to Paxton
Bogus City	Latin Kings	Belmont and Central Park
Bogus Side	Conservative Vice Lords	Chicago and Lawndale
Bone Crushers	Gangster Disciples	59th to 61st and Indiana
Bony Boys	Ambrose	18th and Morgan
Boola World	Gangster Disciples	42nd to 45th and King Dr to Indiana
Boolagang Goonsquad	Gangster Disciples	42nd to 45th and King Dr to Indiana
Boon Docky's	La Raza	48th and Bishop
Born Legends (BL)	Latin Kings	51st and Homan
Boss Pimp	Gangster Disciples	87th to 95th and Skyway to Jeffery and Stony Islamd
Boss Pimps	Gangster Disciples	93rd and University
Boss Pimps (MOB)	Gangster Disciples	89th to 95th and Anthony to Yates
Boss Pimps (Renegade)	Gangster Disciples	93rd and Chappell to Clyde
Boss Pimps (Renegade)	Gangster Disciples	93rd and Merill to Paxton

FACTION	GANG	LOCATION
Boss Pimps (Renegade)	Gangster Disciples	93rd and Saginaw
Boulevard LK's	Latin Kings	22nd to 25th and Marshall Blvd
Boys Town	Gangster Disciples	79th to 81st and Vincennes to Halsted
BPS Moe Town	Black P Stones	55th to 51st and Ashland to Lowe
BPSN Crank Town	Black P Stones	62nd and Kimbark
BPSN Stony Spot	Black P Stones	62nd and Harper
Brain Dead	Black Disciples	82nd and Drexel and 87th and Cottage Grove
Brain Dead	Black Disciples	82nd and Maryland to Ingleside
Braindead	Black Disciples	80th to 83rd and Ellis to Cottage Grove
Brainerd Park GDs	Gangster Disciples	91st and Racine
Braveheart	Gangster Disciples	Irving to Waveland and Fremont to Pine
Braveheart	Gangster Disciples	Oak to Chicago Ave and Hudson to Larrabee
Breed City	Black Gangsters (New Breed)	Douglas and Christiana
Brick City	Black Disciples	58th to 60th and Martin Luther King Dr to Calument
Brick City 600	Black Disciples	59th to 60th and Prairie
Brick Flippers	Gangster Disciples	107th to 111th and Aberdeen to Throop
Brick Squad	Gangster Disciples	67th to 71st and Normal to Harvard
Bricksquad/Jojo World	Gangster Disciples	67th to 75th and Lafayette to Parnell
Brickyard Four Corner Hustlers	Four Corner Hustlers	Madison to Gladys and Hamlin to Kildare
Bridge Boys	Gangster Disciples	57th and Lasalle
Broski	Gangster Disciples	Anthony to 94th and Marquette to Colfax
Brother City	Krazy Getdown Boys	61st and Troy
Brother City	Latin Brothers	Belmont Ave and Cicero Ave
Brotherille	Black P Stones	72nd to 74nd and Carpenter to Racine
Brotherville	Black P Stones	72nd to 74th and May
Brown Jungle	Latin Jivers	Bosworth and Blackhawk
Brown Jungle	Latin Jivers	Division to Blackhawk and Ashland to Cleaver
BSC (Bad Side of Cali)	Gangster Disciples and Black P Stone Nation	63rd to 66th and Kedzie to California
BSC (Blood Stone Crazy)	Black P Stones	86th to 91st and Marquette to Escanaba
BSC (Bud Squad City)	Gangster Disciples	117th to 119th and Yale to Wentworth
BSG	Gangster Disciples	60th to 62nd and Rhodes to Cottage Grove
BTJTG (Bucktown Jtown Gangsters)	Gangster Disciples	67th to 73rd and Loomis to Ashland
B-Town	Gangster Disciples	43rd and Cottage Grove
Buck Town	Latin Dragons	88th and Buffalo

GANG FACTIONS

FACTION	GANG	LOCATION
Bucktown	Ambrose	86th and Houston
Bucktown	Ambrose	87th and Baltimore
Bucktown GDs	Gangster Disciples	67th to 73rd and Loomis to Ashland
Buff City	Black Disciples	117th to 119th and Wentworth to State
Bukk City	Spanish Vice Lords	106th to 112th and Burley to Avenue O
Bukktown	Spanish Vice Lords	106th to 112th and Burley to Avenue O
Bukktown	Spanish Vice Lords	106th to 110th and Burkley to Ave O
Bully Boys	Black Disciples and Gangster Disciples	55th and State to Michigan
Bully Boys	Gangster Disciples	55th and State to Michigan
Bunnyside	Twelfth Street Players	Roosevelt Rd and Lombard
Burnside	Gangster Disciples	92nd to 95th and St Lawrence to Cottage Grove
Burr Boys	Black Disciples	41st to 39th and Michigan to Prairie
Burr World	Gangster Disciples	37th and Indiana
Bush LK's	Latin Kings	82nd to 87th and Exchange(Baker) to Greenbay
Bush LK's	Latin Kings	83rd and Buffalo
Bush LK's	Latin Kings	84th and Burley
Bush Squad	Traveling Vice Lords	Ogden to Cermak and Homan to Central Park
BVC (Bashville)	Gangster Disciples	79th and Wabash
C & R	Unknown Vice Lords	Central and Race
C & R Boys	Unknown Vice Lords	Race to Lake Ave and Pine to Parkside
C- Block	Gangster Disciples	67th and Chappell
C.H.B.s	Gangster Disciples	93rd and Harper
C.O.B.	Gangster Disciples	70th to 74th and Claremont and Oakley and Bell
C20	Latin Kings	Clark and Winnemac
Cal Boyz	Two Two Boys	Cermak and California
Cal Two One	Latin Kings	19th to 22nd and Marshall to Fairfield
Cal Two One	Latin Kings	21st and California
Cali Boys	Traveling Vice Lords	Harrison to Arthington and Washtenaw to Albany
Camelot	Latin Counts	95th to 100th and Baltimore to Escanaba
Cameron City: Outlaws	Imperial Gangsters	North Ave and Hamlin
Cameron City: Outlaws	Imperial Gangsters	Springfield and Wabansia
Camp City	Gangster Disciples	63rd to 66th and Campbell
Camp Coolout	Latin Kings	Armitage to North and Kedzie to Kimball
Canaryville SDs	Satan Disciples	47th to 49th and Union to Halsted

FACTION	GANG	LOCATION
Cannon City	Black Disciples	108th and Morgan
Capa Boys	Black Disciples	61st to 63rd and Martin Luther King Dr. to State
Captiol Hill	Four Corner Hustlers	Lake and Central
Carpenter BDs	Black Disciples	59th to 60th and Morgan to Carpenter
Cash Money Boys (CMB)	Gangster Disciples	66th and Union
Cash Our Girls (COG)	Four Corner Hustlers	Austin Voise High School
Cash Out Boys (COB)	Gangster Disciples	61st to 62nd and St Lawrence to Langley
Cash Out Boys COB	Gangster Disciples	61st to 63rd and King to Langley
Cash Out Viking Boys	Black Disciples	57th and Carpenter
CBG (Clout Boy Gang)	Gangster Disciples	69th to 75th and Woodlawn and Kimbark
CBG (Clout Boy Gang)	Gangster Disciples	69th to 71st and Woodlawn to Kimbark
CBG (Corner Boy Gang)	Four Corner Hustlers	Lake to Maypole and Wood to Wolcott
C-Block	Spanish Cobras	Potomac to Cortez and Campbell
CCG (Coco Cornell Gang)	Four Corner Hustlers and Unknown Vice Lords	Ohio and Huron and Chicago and Avers
CeCe Land	Gangster Disciples	63rd to 65th and Ashland to Hermitage
Ced World	Four Corner Hustlers	68th to 71st and Dorchester to Stony Island
Cedblock	Black P Stones	72nd to 74nd and Carpenter to Racine
Cedgang	Black P Stones	72nd to 74nd and Carpenter to Racine
Cello	Four Corner Hustlers	Augusta to Division and Monticello
Cello World	Gangster Disciples	75th to 75th and Calumet
Central City	Gangster Disciples	75th to 78th and Sangamon to Union
Central City	Gangster Disciples	76th to 79th and Lowe to Halsted
Central Two Six	Two Six	63rd and Central
Cess World	Black Disciples	37th to 39th and Michigan to Prairie
Chain Gang	Gangster Disciples	Homan and Ohio
Chief Town	Black P Stones	60th to 63rd and Evans to Champlain
Chief Town	Latin Souls	49th and Hermitage
Chiefville	Black Disciples	67th and Ada
Chiko City	Black P Stones	86th to 91st and Marquette to Escanaba
China Joe	Black P Stones	82nd and Coles
Chi-Town Two Four	Latin Kings	24th and Drake
Chi-Town Two Four	Latin Kings	24th to 26th and Drake
Chi-Town Two Six	Two Six	23rd to 33rd and Pulaski to Hamlin
Chi-Town Two Six	Two Six	24th and Avers

GANG FACTIONS

FACTION	GANG	LOCATION
Chi-Town Two Six	Two Six	26th and Avers
Chi-Town Two Six	Two Six	27th and Avers
Chopper City	Gangster Disciples	70th to 71st and Wolcott to Damen
Chopper City	King Cobras	133rd and Ave L
Chris World	Gangster Disciples	65th to 69th and Cottage Grove to St Lawrence
Chris World Crazy	Gangster Disciples and Black Disciples	64th to 66th and Cottage to Langley
Christiana Boys	Black Gangsters (New Breeds)	13th to 14th and Christiana
Cicero Assassins	Spanish Cobras	Palmer to Armitage and Cicero to Lawler
Cicero Insane Vice Lords	Cicero Insane Vice Lords	90th and Ada
Cicero Insane Vice Lords	Cicero Insane Vice Lords	90th and Loomis
Cicero Insane Vice Lords	Cicero Insane Vice Lords	91st and Ada
Cicero Insane Vice Lords	Cicero Insane Vice Lords	91st and Loomis
Cicero Insane Vice Lords	Cicero Insane Vice Lords	92nd and Ada
Cicero Insane Vice Lords	Cicero Insane Vice Lords	92nd and Loomis
Cicero Insane Vice Lords	Cicero Insane Vice Lords	Fulton and Lavergne and Lacrosse
Cicero Insane Vice Lords	Cicero Insane Vice Lords	Iowa and Cicero
Cicero Insane Vice Lords	Cicero Insane Vice Lords	Lavergne and Iowa
Cicero Insane Vice Lords	Cicero Insane Vice Lords	Lavergne and Rice
Cicero Insane Vice Lords	Cicero Insane Vice Lords	Ohio and Cicero Ave
Cicero Insane Vice Lords	Cicero Insane Vice Lords	Superior and Cicero
Circle Boys	Gangster Disciples	39th to 43rd and Wabash to King Dr
Circle Park	Black P Stones	91st and Wabash
Circon	Gangster Disciples	71st to 76th and Kenwood to Dorchester
Cirlce Park	Gangster Disciples	87th to 92nd and State to Martin Luther King Dr.
City Knights	City Knights	47th and Rockwell
CJ City	Gangster Disciples	113th to 114th and State
Clapville	Gangster Disciples	63rd to 64th and Paulina to Wood
CLB	Crazy Latin Boys	32nd to 35th and Leavitt to Western
Cliff CVLs	Conservative Vice Lords	Chicago to Superior and Lamon to Lavergne
Clint Squad	Conservative Vice Lords	Roosevelt and Francisco and Mozart
Clybourn City (Project LK)	Latin Kings	Diversey and Clybourn
CMB (Cash Money Boys)	Gangster Disciples	69th to 71st and Racine to Green
CMB (Cash Money Brothers)	Black Gangsters (New Breed)	13th and Throop and Loomis
CNR (C&R)	Four Corner Hustlers	Central and Race to Lake St

GANG FACTIONS

FACTION	GANG	LOCATION
COB	Gangster Disciples	63rd to 67th and Clarment/Oakley/Bell
COBMG (Cashout Boys Money Gang)	Gangster Disciples	69th to 75th and Woodlawn and Kimbark
Coco Cornell Gang (CCG)	Four Corner Hustlers and Unknown Vice Lords	Ohio and Huron and Chicago and Avers
Coles Mob Gangsters	Gangster Disciples	75th to 78th and Coles
Complex	Black P Stones	76th and Racine to Loomis
Concordia	Black Disciples	130th to 131st Pl and King Dr to Daniel Dr
Concordia	Black Disciples	130th to 132nd and King to Indiana
Conservative Vice Lords	Conservative Vice Lords	104th to 106th and Eggleston to Wallace
Conservative Vice Lords	Conservative Vice Lords	107th and Champlain
Conservative Vice Lords	Conservative Vice Lords	107th and Racine
Conservative Vice Lords	Conservative Vice Lords	112th and Perry
Conservative Vice Lords	Conservative Vice Lords	117th and Normal
Conservative Vice Lords	Conservative Vice Lords	57th and Artesian
Conservative Vice Lords	Conservative Vice Lords	63rd and Wolcott
Conservative Vice Lords	Conservative Vice Lords	71st and Winchester
Conservative Vice Lords	Conservative Vice Lords	73rd and Stony Island
Conservative Vice Lords	Conservative Vice Lords	79th and Seeley
Conservative Vice Lords	Conservative Vice Lords	79th and Winchester
Conservative Vice Lords	Conservative Vice Lords	87th to 90th and Dorchester to Stony Island
Conservative Vice Lords	Conservative Vice Lords	91st and Loomis
Conservative Vice Lords	Conservative Vice Lords	Argyle and Kedzie
Conservative Vice Lords	Conservative Vice Lords	Augusta and Willard
Conservative Vice Lords	Conservative Vice Lords	Augusta Blvd and Monticello
Conservative Vice Lords	Conservative Vice Lords	Carmen and Spaulding
Conservative Vice Lords	Conservative Vice Lords	Clark St and Thorndale
Conservative Vice Lords	Conservative Vice Lords	Division and Lawndale
Conservative Vice Lords	Conservative Vice Lords	Evergreen and Homan
Conservative Vice Lords	Conservative Vice Lords	Iowa to Ferdinand and Monticello to Harding
Conservative Vice Lords	Conservative Vice Lords	Jackson Blvd and Campbell
Conservative Vice Lords	Conservative Vice Lords	Madison and Rockwell
Conservative Vice Lords	Conservative Vice Lords	North Ave and Lorel
Conservative Vice Lords	Conservative Vice Lords	North Ave and Vine
Conservative Vice Lords	Conservative Vice Lords	North to Cortland and Central to Luna
Constance Boys	Gangster Disciples	76th to 79th and Constance

GANG FACTIONS

FACTION	GANG	LOCATION
Cooper Park	Black Disciples and Gangster Disciples	115th to 119th and Racine to Ashland
Coopville	Black Disciples and Gangster Disciples	115th to 119th and Racine to Ashland
Corey City	Conservative Vice Lords	74th to 76th and Evans to Drexel
Corey City	Conservative Vice Lords	73rd to 76th and Dobson to Langley
Corey Town	Gangster Disciples	69th to 75th and Woodlawn and Kimbark
Corner Boy Gang (CBG)	Four Corner Hustlers	Lake to Maypole and Wood to Wolcott
Cottage Mob	Conservative Vice Lords	73rd to 76th and Evans to Maryland
Cottage Mob	Conservative Vice Lords	75th to 76th and Cottage to Dobson
Cottage Mob	Conservative Vice Lords	73rd to 76th and Dobson to Langley
Coulter Side	Latin Kings	22nd to 24th and St. Louis to Central Park
COVB (Cash Out Viking Boys)	Black Disciples	57th and Carpenter
CPG	Traveling Vice Lords	Grenshaw and Central Park
Crack & Crime	Latin Kings	Clark and Caltalpa
Crackland	Gangster Disciples	122nd and Halsted to Racine
Cranktown	Black P Stones	61st to 63rd and Kimbark
Cranktown	Black P Stones	61st to 65th and Stony Island to Harper
Cranktown	Black P Stones	61st to 63rd and Woodlawn to Dorchester
Crashtown GDs	Gangster Disciples	67th to 71st and Ashland to Damen
Crazy Crew	Gangster Disciples	Divison to Ogden and Larabee
Crazy Harper BPSs	Black P Stones	93rd and Harper
Crazy Latin Boys	Crazy Latin Boys	32nd to 35th and Leavitt to Western
Creep Town	Imperial Gangsters	Altgeld and Harding
Creep Town	Imperial Gangsters	Fullerton to Armitage and Kimball to Central Park
Creeptown GDs	Gangster Disciples	67th to 69th and Ashland and Wood
Cross Town	Gangster Disciples	De Sable to 38th and Wells to Princeton
Crown Town	Latin Kings	55th to 57th and California to Sacramento
Crown Town - 51 HLK's	Latin Kings	51st and Homan
Crown Town (008)	Latin Kings	51st to 55th and Kezie to St. Louis
Crown Town (009)	Latin Kings	51st to 55th and Western to Sacramento
CTG (Cuttroat Gangsters)	Gangster Disciples	78th to 81st and Ashland to Loomis
C-Town	Black P Stones	113th and Carpenter
C-Town	Black P Stones	113th and Morgan
C-Town	Black P Stones	115th and Halsted
C-Town	Four Corner Hustlers	Lake and Central

FACTION	GANG	LOCATION
Cullerton Deuces	Insane Deuces	21st and Washtenaw
Cut Throat	Conservative Vice Lords	74th to 76th and Evans to Drexel
Cuthroat	Gangster Disciples	87th to 89th and Vincennes to Loomis
Cutthroat Kutthroat	Gangster Disciples	87th to 90th and Loomis to Peoria
CVG (Crazyville Gang)	Gangster Disciples	55th to 58th and Morgan to Halsted
CWB (Chris World Bitches)	Gangster Disciples	65th to 69th and Cottage Grove to St Lawrence
C-World (Corey)	Gangster Disciples	67th to 70th and Hamilton to Damen
D Block	Black P Stones	Rogers to Howard and Clark to Ridge
D Block	Gangster Disciples	71st to 75th and Langley to Eberheart
D Block	Gangster Disciples	71st to 73rd and Eberhart to Langley
D.O.C.	Gangster Disciples	87th to 90th and Dorchester to Stony Island
D.O.D.	Black Disciples	70th to 71st and St. Lawrence to Martin Luther King Dr
Da Hollow	Satan Disciples	43rd to 48th and Ciceo Ave to Knox
Dae'mon World	Gangster Disciples	79th to 82nd and Avalon
Daevo World	Gangster Disciples	79th to 83rd and Kedzie to Western
Dale Gang	Traveling Vice Lords and Unknown Vice Lords	Athington to Flournoy and Central Park to Independence
Damen Courts	Black Disciples	Jackson and Damen
Damen Two Six	Two Six	47th to 50th and Wolcot to Hoyne
Damenville	Two Six	47th to 50th and Wolcot to Hoyne
Damenville GDs	Gangster Disciples	51st to 53rd and Damen
Damo City	Gangster Disciples	68th to 70th and Prairie to Martin Luther King
Damo City	Gangster Disciples	69th and Calumet
Danni Mob	Traveling Vice Lords	Ogden to Cermak and Homan to Central Park
Dark Crystal	Latin Jivers	Crystal and Washtenaw
Dark Side	Four Corner Hustlers	Washington and Lotus
Dark Side	Gangster Disciples	63rd to South Chicago and Vernon to Champlain
Dark Side	Gangster Disciples	67th and St Lawrence
Dark Side	Imperial Gangsters	Armitage and Spaulding
Dark Side	Imperial Gangsters	Belden and Drake
Dark Side	Imperial Gangsters	Dickens and Spaulding
Dark Side	Imperial Gangsters	Drake and Cortland
Dark Side	Imperial Gangsters	Kimball and Cortland
Dark Side Two Six	Two Six	24th to 26th and Kostner to Pulaski
Darkside	Black Disciples	72nd and Racine

GANG FACTIONS

FACTION	GANG	LOCATION
Darkside	Black Disciples	79th and Racine
Darkside	Gangster Disciples	61st to 69th and Calumet to Champlain
Darkside	Imperial Gangsters	Palmer to Armitage and Spaulding to Kimball
Darkside	Latin Kings	Drake and School
Darkside	Cicero Insane Vice Lords	Lake and Cicero
Darkside	Cicero Insane Vice Lords	Lavergne and Ferdinand
Darkside	Cicero Insane Vice Lords	West End and Lacrosse
Darkside BD's	Black Disciples	111th to 115th and Michigan to Indiana
Darkside BD's	Black Disciples	69th and Normal
Dart Gang (6217 Calumet)	Black Disciples	60th to 63rd and Martin Luther King Dr to State
Darwin City	Orchestra Albany	Logan Blvd to Armitage and Kedzie to California
Dave Gang	Four Corner Hustlers	West End to Maypole and Keeler to Karlov
D-Block	Black P Stones	107th and Indiana
D-Block	Four Corner Hustlers	103rd to 109th and Prairie to Michigan
D-Block	Gangster Disciples	71st to 73rd and Ellis to Evans
D-Block	Gangster Disciples	71st to 75th and Seely to Hoyne
D-Block	Gangster Disciples	Divison to Kingsbury and Crosby to Cleveland
D-Block	Maniac Latin Disciples	Artesian and Diversey
D-Dub	Latin Kings	Division and Wolcott
De La Wood	Saints	45th and Wood
Dearborn Homes	Mickey Cobras	28th to 29th and Federal to State
Death & Hell	Young Latin Organization Disciples	Dickens and Hamlin
Death Row	Black Disciples	100th to 101st and Michigan to State
Death Row	Black Disciples	106th to 108th and State to Wentworth
Death Row	Gangster Disciples	120th and Lafayette
Death Row	Mafia Insane Vice Lords	North Ave to Austin and Cicero
Death Row	Mafia Insane Vice Lords	North Ave to Cortland and Mayfield
Death Row	Maniac Latin Disciples	Rockwell and LeMoyne
Death Row City	Conservative Vice Lords	83rd to 86th and Muskegon to Escanaba
Death Trap Pimps	Maniac Latin Disciples	Dickens and Mobile
Death Valley	Latin Kings	Berwyn and Wolcott
Deen Mob	Gangster Disciples	56th to 58th and Aberdeen (Carpenter to Racine)
Del Mob	Gangster Disciples	45th to 48th and State to Martin Luther King
Del Viikings	Black Disciples	110th Pl to 111th St. and State to Wentworth

GANG FACTIONS

FACTION	GANG	LOCATION
Dello World	Gangster Disciples	79th to 81st and Ashland to Loomis
Demon Side	Traveling Vice Lords	Chicago Ave and Drake to Homan
Descendants of David	Black Disciples	67th to 71st and Michigan to State
Descendants of David	Black Disciples	70th to 71st and St. Lawrence to Martin Luther King Dr
Deuce Boys	Gangster Disciples	72nd to 73rd and Coles
Deuce Mo	Black P Stones	79th to 82nd and Houston to Coles
Deuce Moes	Black P Stones	79th to 82nd and Coles to Houston
Deuces	Gangster Disciples	124th and Perry
Devil Side	Imperial Gangsters	McLean and St Louis
Devil Side	Imperial Gangsters	Palmer to North and Central Park to Kimball
Devil Side	Imperial Gangsters	Wabansia and Central Park
Devil Side	Spanish Four Corner Hustlers	Addison to Belmont and Laramie to Kilpatrick
Devild Playground	Young Latin Organization Disciples	Keystone and Wabansia
Deville	Gangster Disciples	110th to 115th and Parnell to Stewart
Devils Paradise	Satan Disciples	Chicago Ave to Kinzie and Damen to Racine
Devils Point	Satan Disciples	59th and Oakley
Devilz Point	Maniac Latin Disciples	Allen and Kimball
Devilz Point	Maniac Latin Disciples	Barry and Kedzie
Diablos Children	Imperial Gangsters	Drake and Cortland
Diddy City	Black P Stones	61st and Cottage Grove
Dilly Boyz	Four Corner Hustlers	Thomas and Parkside to Mason
Dipset	Black P Stones	63rd to 65th and Blackstone to Stony Island
Dipset	Gangster Disciples	100th to 103rd and Indiana to King
Dipset	Gangster Disciples	48th and Prairie
Dipset	Gangster Disciples	65th to 67th and Wolcott to Damen
Dipset Outlaws	Gangster Disciples	57th and Wabash to State
Dirty Lo	Gangster Disciples	46th to 48th and Evans to Martin Luther King
Dirty Money on Hands (DMOH)	Black P Stones	Morse and Glenwood
Dirty Perry	Black Disciples	107th and Perry
Dirty Unknowns	Unknown Vice Lords	Chicago to Augusta and Lawler to Laramie
Dirty Us	Unknown Vice Lords	Chicago to Augusta and Lawler to Laramie
Dirty World	Gangster Disciples	55th to 57th and Normal to Princeton
Dirty World Cobras	Mickey Cobras	55th and Normal
DK St (DK Street)	Latin Eagles	Dickens and Kenneth

GANG FACTIONS

FACTION	GANG	LOCATION
DK Zone	Ambrose	35th and Laramie
DK-Town	La Raza	Harding and Wabansia
DMG (Deen Mob Gangsters)	Gangster Disciples	56th to 58th and Aberdeen (Carpenter to Racine)
DOD	Black Disciples	67th to 71st and Michigan to State
Dodge City	Mickey Cobras	55th and Normal
Dog Block	Traveling Vice Lords	104th to 107th and Racine to Morgan
Dog Pound	Black Disciples	71st to 74th and Halsted to Morgan
Dog Pound	Mickey Cobras	47th and Princeton
Dog Pound City	Black Disciples	72nd and Morgan to Racine
Dogg Pound	Four Corner Hustlers	Crystal and Lavergne
Dogpound	Black Disciples	71st to 74th and Green to Sangamon
Dome	Black P Stones	76th and Racine to Loomis
Doom	Black P Stones	76th to 80th and Wolcott to Hamilton
Doon Squad		59th to 63rd and Campbell to Washtenaw
Dorchester Boys	Gangster Disciples	69th and Dorchester
Double D Gang (50 Strong)	Gangster Disciples	50th to 51st and Morgan to Halsted
Dragon Town	Latin Dragons	83rd to 87th and Colfax to Commercial
Dragon Town	Latin Dragons	87th and Escanaba
Dragons Pitt	Insane Dragons	Augusta and Mozart
Drake Side	Latin Kings	28th to 31st and Drake
Drama City	Latin Kings	Armitage to North and Kedzie to Kimball
Drexel View	Gangster Disciples	47th and Drexel
Drizzle City	Black Disciples	61st and Martin Luther King Dr
Drizzle City	Gangster Disciples	55th to 57th and Justine to Loomis
Drizzle City	Gangster Disciples	57th to 58th and Laflin
Drizzle City	Gangster Disciples	61st and King Dr
Dro City	Gangster Disciples	63rd to 67th and Cottage Grove to Kenwood
Dro City	Gangster Disciples	63rd to 67th and Woodlawn to Cottage Grove
Dro City	Gangster Disciples	64th to 65th and Maryland to Ingleside
Dro Life	Gangster Disciples	65th to 66th and Woodlawn to Minerva
D-Row	Mafia Insane Vice Lords	Austin and Laramie
D-Town	Black Disciples	59th and Normal
D-town	Black Disciples	59th and Princeton
D-Town / Ducktown	Black P Stones	87th and Aberdeen

GANG FACTIONS

FACTION	GANG	LOCATION
D-Town / Ducktown	Black P Stones	87th and Damen to Winchester
D-Town / Ducktown	Black P Stones	87th and Racine
Dub	Gangster Disciples	121st and 125th on Racine
Dub Dub	Latin Kings	Winona and Winthrop
DUB GDs	Gangster Disciples	120th to 122nd and Normal to Parnell
Dub Zone	Gangster Disciples	120th to 122nd and Normal to Parnell
Dubside	Two Six	36th and Washtenaw
Dubtown	Gangster Disciples	63rd to 64th and Winchester
Ducktown	Black P Stones	87th to 89th and Beverly to Bishop
Duffle Bag Gang	Gangster Disciples	131st and Champlain and Langley
Duffle Gang	Black Disciples	130th to 131st and Champlain
Duke Squad Gangsters	Gangster Disciples	57th to 59th and Prairie to Calumet
Dumpstreet	Gangster Disciples	59th and Justine
Dunk World	Black Disciples and Gangster Disciples	115th to 119th and Racine to Ashland
D-Ville	Gangster Disciples	115th and Stewart to Eggleston
D-Ville	Gangster Disciples	115th to 116th and Stewart to Eggleston
D-Ville	Gangster Disciples	63rd to 65th and Ashland to Hermitage
D-Ville	Latin Dragons	83rd to 84th and Muskegon to Burnham
DVLB	Gangster Disciples	63rd to 65th and Ashland to Hermitage
E Block	Conservative Vice Lords	73rd to 76th and Dobson to Langley
E Block	Gangster Disciples	71st to 73rd and Cornell to East End
E block	Gangster Disciples	71st to 73rd Cornell to East end
E- Block GDs	Gangster Disciples	120th to 121st and Wallace to Emerald
EA	Gangster Disciples	63rd and Racine
East End Boys	Gangster Disciples	71st to 73rd and East End
East Side GDs	Gangster Disciples	71st to 75th and East End to Cornell
East Village SD's	Satan Disciples	Huron and Ashland
Eastville	Conservative Vice Lords	Crystal and Evergreen and Leavitt
Eat Bitch Eat (EBE)	Four Corner Hustlers	Hubbard to Ferdinand and Lavergne
Eberhart Boys	Gangster Disciples	63rd to 65th and Rhodes to King
EBK (Everybody Killer)	Black P Stones	51st and May
E-Block	Gangster Disciples	71st to 75th and East End to Cornell
E-Block (Central City)	Gangster Disciples	76th and Emerald
EBT (Everybody But Trap)	Gangster Disciples	63rd to 65th and Rhodes to King

GANG FACTIONS

FACTION	GANG	LOCATION
EBT	Gangster Disciples	63rd and Eberhart
EE Boys	Mafia Insane Vice Lords	81st Pl to 83rd and Houston to Exchange
EJ city	Gangster Disciples	71st and Paxton
Eleven Nine	Gangster Disciples	119th and Michigan
Eleven Thirteen Crazy (ETC)	Gangster Disciples	111th to 113th and Parnell
Emerald City	Gangster Disciples	55th to 59th and Lowe to Halsted
Emerald city	Gangster Disciples	55th to 57th and Halsted to Lowe
Emerald Mob	Black P Stones	90th to 92nd and Emerald
Epiville	Spanish Cobras	Dickens to Wabansia and Keeler to Kostner
E-Spot	Black P Stones	79th to 81st and Emerald
ETC (Eleven Thirteen Crazy)	Gangster Disciples	111th to 113th and Parnell
Ethos Ville	Gangster Disciples	65th to 69th and Cottage Grove to St Lawrence
E-Town	Gangster Disciples	69th to 74th and Union to Halsted
E-Town	Gangster Disciples	71st to 73rd and Elizabeth to Racine
ETS (Everything Shady)	Gangster Disciples	59th to 63rd and Western to Talman
Evans Mob	Gangster Disciples	75th to 76th and Evans
Evanz Mob	Gangster Disciples	82nd to 85th and Eberheart to King
Everlast Town Crazy	Black P Stones	51st to 55th and Cottage to Lake Shore Drive
Everybody But Trap (EBT)	Gangster Disciples	63rd to 65th and Rhodes to King
Evil Side	Latin Brothers	Belmont to Wellington and Kilpatrick to Knox
Evil Side	Satan Disciples	15th and Talman
Evil Side	Satan Disciples	17th and Washtenaw
Evil Side	Satan Disciples	18th and California
Evil Side	Satan Disciples	18th and Rockwell
Evil Side	Satan Disciples	Ogden to 19th and California to Western
E-Wol	Black Disciples	120th to 125th and Princeton to Halsted
Face World	Gangster Disciples	59th and Shields
Face World	Gangster Disciples	79th to 82nd and Yale to Normal
Face World (Cornell Henderson)	Gangster Disciples	69th to 71st and Western to California
Face World	Gangster Disciples	67th to 71st and Artesian to Washtenaw
Familia Stones	Familia Stones	Berteau and Albany
Familia Stones	Familia Stones	Cullom and Whipple
Familia Stones	Familia Stones	Irving Park to Leland and California to Sawyer
Familia Stones	Familia Stones	Leland and Kedzie

FACTION	GANG	LOCATION
Familia Stones	Familia Stones	Montrose and Troy
Familia Stones	Familia Stones	Sunnyside and Kedzie
Familia Stones	Familia Stones	Wilson and Sawyer
Farwell Family	Gangster Disciples	Pratt to Greenleaf and Ashland to Glenwood
Fat Shorty Gang (FSG)	Four Corner Hustlers and Unknown Vice Lords	Van Buren to Jackson and Springfield
Fatty World	Gangster Disciples	69th and Calumet
Fatz	Mickey Cobras	48 to 51st and Ellis to King
Fazoland	Black P Stones	78th to 80th and Muskegan to Exchange
FBE (Fuck Boy Entertainment)	Black Disciples	43rd to 39th and Michigan to Prairie
FBG (Fly Boy Gang)	Gangster Disciples	61st to 69th and Calumet to Champlain
Fearro City	Gangster Disciples	71st to 76th and Kenwood and Dorchester
Fearro City / Fearro World	Gangster Disciples	71st to 75th and Kenwood to Stony Island
FEB Stones	Black P Stones	73rd to 76th and Kingston to Phillips
Field Boyz	Gangster Disciples	56th and Marshfield
Fiesta Boys	Four Corner Hustlers	13th and Lawndale (Millard Park)
Fifth Ward	Gangster Disciples	68th to 69th and Damen to Hamilton
Fin Town	Conservative Vice Lords	74th to 76th and Martin Luther King Dr to Anthony
Fin Town	Conservative Vice Lords	75th and Cottage Grove
Fin Town	Conservative Vice Lords	75th and Eberhart
Fin Town	Conservative Vice Lords	75th and Ingleside
Fin Town	Conservative Vice Lords	75th to 78th and Sangamon to Union
Fin Town	Conservative Vice Lords	76th to 77th and Kingston
Finn Town	Black P Stones	87th to 90th and Halsted to Eggleston
Five Eight Homicide	Latin Kings	55th to 59th and Central Park to Pulaski
Five Eight Homicide	Latin Kings	58th and Hamlin
Flin Boyz	Gangster Disciples	57th to 58th and Laflin
Flip Set	Gangster Disciples	93rd to 95th and Langley
Flip Side	Gangster Disciples	90th to 95th and Cottage to Kenwood
Fly Boy Gang (FBG)	Gangster Disciples	61st to 69th and Calumet to Champlain
Fly Boys	Black Disciples	15th to 19th and Komensky to Pulaski
Fly Boys	Black Disciples and Black P Stone Nation	73rd and Phillips
Fly Boys	Black Gangsters (New Breed)	16th and Karlov to Komensky
Fly Boys	Black Souls	16th and Karlov to Komensky
Folly Boys	Black Peace Stones	51st to 55th and Racine to Halsted

GANG FACTIONS

FACTION	GANG	LOCATION
Forehead 4's	Four Corner Hustlers	Ohio to Kinzie and Lavergne to Lawler
Foster Park	Black P Stones	83rd to 87th and Ashland to Racine
Foster Park	Black P Stones	83rd to 87th and Morgan to Ashland
Foster Park	Black Peace Stones	81st to 87th and Aberdeen to Ashland
Four Corner Hustlers	Four Corner Hustlers	105th to 108th and Cottage to Maryland
Four Corner Hustlers	Four Corner Hustlers	106th and State
Four Corner Hustlers	Four Corner Hustlers	107th and Vernon
Four Corner Hustlers	Four Corner Hustlers	109th to 110th and Perry to Wentworth
Four Corner Hustlers	Four Corner Hustlers	123rd to 127th and Indiana to State
Four Corner Hustlers	Four Corner Hustlers	124th and Halsted
Four Corner Hustlers	Four Corner Hustlers	72nd and Bennet
Four Corner Hustlers	Four Corner Hustlers	Adams and Lotus to Lockwood
Four Corner Hustlers	Four Corner Hustlers	Augusta to Chicago and Hamlin to Avers
Four Corner Hustlers	Four Corner Hustlers	Congress and Pulaski
Four Corner Hustlers	Four Corner Hustlers	Division to Augusta and Central Park to Harding
Four Corner Hustlers	Four Corner Hustlers	Division to Chicago and Lorel to Central
Four Corner Hustlers	Four Corner Hustlers	Division to Thomas and Leamington
Four Corner Hustlers	Four Corner Hustlers	Division to Thomas and Monticello to Ridgeway
Four Corner Hustlers	Four Corner Hustlers	Hirsch to Division and Lockwood to Long
Four Corner Hustlers	Four Corner Hustlers	Jackson and Campbell
Four Corner Hustlers	Four Corner Hustlers	Lake and Austin
Four Corner Hustlers	Four Corner Hustlers	Lake and Pine
Four Corner Hustlers	Four Corner Hustlers	Madison and Rockwell
Four Corner Hustlers	Four Corner Hustlers	Monroe to Madison and Lavergne
Four Corner Hustlers	Four Corner Hustlers	Pine and Fulton
Four Corner Hustlers	Four Corner Hustlers	Quincy and Laramie to Lockwood
Four Corner Hustlers	Four Corner Hustlers	Washington to Madison and Latrobe
Four Corner Hustlers	Four Corner Hustlers	Washington to Madison and Lorel
Four Corner Hustlers	Four Corner Hustlers	Washington to Madison and Lotus
Fourth Generation Messiahs	Fourth Generation Messiahs	18th St and 58th Ave
FOXXVILLE	Gangster Disciples	63rd to 67th and Clarment and Oakley and Bell
Frank Town	Gangster Disciples	68th to 69th and Vernon to Martin Luther King Dr
Frank World	Gangster Disciples	71st to 73rd and Ashland to Wood
Fran-Psycho / Murder Town	Ambrose	63rd and Francisco

GANG FACTIONS

FACTION	GANG	LOCATION
Freaky World	Gangster Disciples	60th to 63rd and Halsted to Union
Front Street (FS)	Black Disciples	61st and Indiana
Front Street 061	Black Disciples	61st and Indiana
FTB (Free The Burr)	Black Disciples	42nd to 39th and Michigan to Prairie
Fuck City	Mickey Cobras	54th to 55th and Shields to Princeton
Fuck Your Bitch (FYB)	Gangster Disciples	61st to 69th and Calumet to Champlain
G Block	Gangster Disciples	102nd to 103rd and Princeton
G-Side	Two Six	30th and Avers
Gaiter Gang	Black Disciples	85th to 86th and Morgan to Carpenter
Gambinos	Gangster Disciples	56th and Princeton
Gambinos	Gangster Disciples	63rd and Sangamon
Gangland	Familia Stones	Addison to Berteau and Cicero to Long
Gangsta Lords	Conservative Vice Lords	Divison and Noble
Gangster City	Imperial Gangsters	Fullerton and Kimball
Gangster Disciples	Gangster Disciples	100th to 103rd and King to Cottage
Gangster Disciples	Gangster Disciples	117th to 121st and State to Calumet
Gangster Disciples	Gangster Disciples	15th to 16th and Keeler
Gangster Disciples	Gangster Disciples	16th and Sawyer
Gangster Disciples	Gangster Disciples	16th to Cermak and 50th ct to Cicero
Gangster Disciples	Gangster Disciples	18th to 19th and Keeler to Kildare
Gangster Disciples	Gangster Disciples	19th and 48th
Gangster Disciples	Gangster Disciples	19th to 22nd and Pulaski to Kostner
Gangster Disciples	Gangster Disciples	21st to 22nd and Harding to Pulaski
Gangster Disciples	Gangster Disciples	35th and Giles
Gangster Disciples	Gangster Disciples	49th to 51st and Hermitage
Gangster Disciples	Gangster Disciples	51st and James
Gangster Disciples	Gangster Disciples	51st and Prairie
Gangster Disciples	Gangster Disciples	51st to 55th and Winchester to Leavitt
Gangster Disciples	Gangster Disciples	56th to 57th and Loomis
Gangster Disciples	Gangster Disciples	56th to 58th and Elizabeth
Gangster Disciples	Gangster Disciples	56th to 58th and Halsted to Emerald
Gangster Disciples	Gangster Disciples	58th and Maplewood
Gangster Disciples	Gangster Disciples	59th to 61st and Halsted to Sangamon
Gangster Disciples	Gangster Disciples	59th to 61st and Racine to Union

GANG FACTIONS

FACTION	GANG	LOCATION
Gangster Disciples	Gangster Disciples	5th and Sacramento
Gangster Disciples	Gangster Disciples	61st and Racine
Gangster Disciples	Gangster Disciples	64th to 65th and Honore
Gangster Disciples	Gangster Disciples	65th to 66th and Lowe
Gangster Disciples	Gangster Disciples	67th and Throop
Gangster Disciples	Gangster Disciples	70th and Parnell
Gangster Disciples	Gangster Disciples	70th and Peoria
Gangster Disciples	Gangster Disciples	71st and Carpenter
Gangster Disciples	Gangster Disciples	73rd and Phillips
Gangster Disciples	Gangster Disciples	76th to 80th and Morgan to Hermitage
Gangster Disciples	Gangster Disciples	91st and Buffalo
Gangster Disciples	Gangster Disciples	93rd and Chappell to Clyde
Gangster Disciples	Gangster Disciples	93rd and Merill to Paxton
Gangster Disciples	Gangster Disciples	93rd and Saginaw
Gangster Disciples	Gangster Disciples	99th to 100th and Malta
Gangster Disciples	Gangster Disciples	99th to 103rd and Wentworth to Eggleston
Gangster Disciples	Gangster Disciples	Ainslie and St Louis
Gangster Disciples	Gangster Disciples	Divison and Karlov
Gangster Disciples	Gangster Disciples	Erie and Willard
Gangster Disciples	Gangster Disciples	Gladys to Eisenhower and Kostner to Kolmar
Gangster Disciples	Gangster Disciples	Grace and Sheffield
Gangster Disciples	Gangster Disciples	Grenshaw and Pulaski
Gangster Disciples	Gangster Disciples	Grenshaw and Western
Gangster Disciples	Gangster Disciples	Harrison and Pulaski
Gangster Disciples	Gangster Disciples	Henderson and Keeler
Gangster Disciples	Gangster Disciples	Homan and Douglas
Gangster Disciples	Gangster Disciples	Howard and Ridge
Gangster Disciples	Gangster Disciples	Huron and Willard
Gangster Disciples	Gangster Disciples	Maypole and Kedzie
Gangster Disciples	Gangster Disciples	Ohio to Franklin and Homan to Trumbull
Gangster Disciples	Gangster Disciples	Van Buren and Washtenaw
Gangster Disciples Brick Squad	Gangster Disciples	67th to 72nd and Normal to Wentworth
Gangster Disciples COV	Gangster Disciples	58th to 59th and Ashland to Green
Gangster Disciples Dell Mob	Gangster Disciples	45th to 49th and State to Martin Luther King Dr

GANG FACTIONS

FACTION	GANG	LOCATION
Gangster Lords	Gangster Disciples	Division and Noble
Gangster Lords	Vice Lords	88th to 91st and Cottage to Dauphin
Garden GDs	Gangster Disciples	131st to 134th and Langley to St. Lawrence
GBC (Goonie Boss Crazy)	Gangster Disciples	71st to 72nd and Carpenter to May
GC	Spanish Gangster Disciples	Pratt to Northshore and Ashland to Lakewood
GDG (General Doug Gang/50 Strong)	Gangster Disciples	50th to 51st and Morgan to Halsted
Geo World (SKD)	Gangster Disciples	53rd and King Drive
Georgetown	Black P Stones	103rd to 104th and Normal to Wallace
Georgetown	Gangster Disciples	87th to 89th and Vincennes to Loomis
Georgetown	Gangster Disciples	87th to 90th and Loomis to Vincennes
Germ City	Black Gangsters (New Breed)	13th and Claremont
Get Money Boys (GMB)	Black Disciples	84th to 89th and Exchange to Marquette
Get Money Boys (GMB)	Black Disciples	79th to 81st and Brandon to South Shore Dr
Get Money Boys (GMB)	Gangster Disciples	86th to 87th and Marquette to Manistee
Get Money Boys (GMB)	Mickey Cobras	74th to 75th and Chappel to Yates
Get Money Girls (GMG)	Four Corner Hustlers	Austin Voise High School
Getdown City	Krazy Getdown Boys	61st and Lawndale
GHC (Gun Head Crazy)	Combination of Gangster Disciples and Black Disciples and Black Peace Stone Nation	66th to 66th and Talman to California
Ghetto Side	Latin Kings	23rd and Homan
Ghetto Side	Two Six	28th and Kolin
Ghetto World	Four Corner Hustlers	70th to 73rd and Ridgeland to Stony Island
Ghetto World	Four Corner Hustlers	71st to 74th and Euclid to Constance
Ghost Town	Black P Stones	68th to 69th and Wolcott to Winchester
Ghost Town	Gangster Disciples	59th and Campbell
Ghost Town	Maniac Latin Disciples	Beach and Ashland
Ghost Town	Unknown Vice Lords	Congress to Monroe and Central Park to Kedzie
Ghost Town	Unknown Vice Lords	Kinzie to West End and Cicero to Kenton
Ghost Town	Insane Popes (Southside)	34th and Hoyne
Ghost Town	Latin Eagles	Irving Park and Ashland to Sheridan
GK St.	Ashland Vikings	Grand Ave and Keeler
Global Gang	Black P Stones	87th to 90th and Brandon
GMC (Getting Money Constantly)	Black Disciples	92nd and Cottage Grove
GMC (Getting Money Crew)	Gangster Disciples	60th and Marshfield

GANG FACTIONS

FACTION	GANG	LOCATION
G-Money Gang	Four Corner Hustlers	Lake to Maypole and Wood to Wolcott
Golden Gate	Gangster Disciples	131st to Riverdale and St Lawrence to Vernon
Golden Gates	Black P Stones	133rd to 134th and St. Lawrence to Vernon
Golden Gates	Gangster Disciples	131st to 133rd and St Lawrence to Vernon
Gooly Gang	Black Disciples	134th to 133rd and Prairie to Martin Luther King Dr
Goon Squad	Conservative Vice Lords	1300 N Hudson
Goon Squad	Four Corner Hustlers	67th to 70th and Clyde
Goon Squad	Gangster Disciples	71st and East End
Goon Squad	Mickey Cobras	Evergreen to Blackhawk and Cleveland to Wells
Goon Squad	Young Latin Organization Cobras	Lawndale and Diversey
Goonesville	Gangster Disciples	67th to 69th and Aberdeen
Goonie Boys	Gangster Disciples	71st to 72nd and Carpenter to May
Goontown	Gangster Disciples	103rd to 107th and Wabash to Wentworth
Gorilla Town (GT)	Gangster Disciples	115th to 117th and State to Wentworth
Gotti World	Gangster Disciples	71st to 75th and Ellis to Evans
Gotti World	Gangster Disciples	71st to 75th and Langley to Eberheart
Gotti World Roc Block	Gangster Disciples	71st to 73rd and Eberhart to Langley
Grand Champ	Gangster Disciples	71st to 73rd and Evans to Champlain
Grand City	Maniac Latin Disciples	Grand Ave to North and Hamlin to Pulaski
Granville	Black P Stones	Devon and Bell
Great Lakes	Four Corner Hustlers	Chicago to Erie and Menard to Austin
Green Briar Park	Latin Kings	Glenlake to Peterson and Talman to Washtenaw
Green Money Boys	Gangster Disciples	60th and Marshfield
Greenwood Boys	Gangster Disciples	46th and Drexel
Grim Town	Insane Popes (Southside)	62nd and Sayre
Grimey Ville (GVC)	Gangster Disciples	76th to 81st and Ashland to Loomis
Gross Park LK's	Latin Kings	Lawrence and Washtenaw
Grove Park	Black P Stones	60th to 63rd and Cottage Grove to Langley
G-Town	Gangster Disciples	87th and Vincennes
G-Town	Party People	56th to 59th and Campbell and Talman
Gucci Gang	Gangster Disciples	71st to 73rd and Cornell to East End
Gucci Ville (GVC)	Gangster Disciples	75th to 81st and Ashland to Loomis
Guillotine	Gangster Disciples	115th to 117th and State to Wentworth

FACTION	GANG	LOCATION
Gun Head	Combination of Gangster Disciples and Black Disciples and Black Peace Stone Nation	63rd to 67th and California to Kedzie
Gun Heads	Black Disciples	65th to 66th and Talman to California
Gun Heads	Black P Stones	65th to 66th and Talman to California
Gun Heads	Gangster Disciples	65th to 66th and Talman to California
Guttaville	Gangster Disciples	Ardmore to Granville and Broadway to Sheridan
Gutterville	Black Disciples	49th to 51st and King Dr to Cottage Grove
Guwop Block	Traveling Vice Lords	Ogden to Cermak and Homan to Central Park
GVC	Gangster Disciples	77th to 81st and Ashland to Loomis
G-Ville (GVC)	Gangster Disciples	75th to 81st and Ashland to Loomis
Gville 079	Gangster Disciples	75th to 81st and Ashland to Ada
H DUB	Latin Kings	Division and Wolcott
H and M (Hoes and Money)	Gangster Disciples	79th to 80th and Racine to Halsted
H/W	Insane C-Notes	Hirsch and Western
Haas Park MLDs	Maniac Latin Disciples	Altgeld to Fullerton and Washtenaw to Fairfield
Halo City	Saints	43rd to 47th and Damen to Ashland
Hamlin Park Deuces	Insane Deuces	Barry and Hoyne
Hamlin Park Deuces	Insane Deuces	Belmont to Damen
Hamlin Park Deuces	Insane Deuces	George to Roscoe and Honore to Campbell
Hamlin Park Deuces	Insane Deuces	Nelson and Damen
HANK	Gangster Disciples	69th and Calument
Hank Nation	Gangster Disciples	69th and Calumet
Hanson Park	Latin Pachucos	Grand to Fullerton and Central to Laramie
Hard Town	Gangster Disciples	118th and Wentworth to Lasalle
Harding Two Six	Two Six	30th and Harding
Harlem Boys	Four Corner Hustlers	West End to Maypole and Keeler to Karlov
Harrison Boys	Traveling Vice Lords	Harrison and Sacramento
Harrison Gents	Harrison Gents	Ashland and Walton
Harrison Gents	Harrison Gents	Augusta and Paulina
Harrison Gents	Harrison Gents	Hermitage and Cortez
Harrison Gents	Harrison Gents	Noble and Cortez
Harv Town	Gangster Disciples	116th to 118th and Harvard to Stewart
Hate City	Four Corner Hustlers	68th to 71st and Dorchester to Stony Island
HBE (Halsted Boy Entertainment)	Black Disciples	65th to 67th and Halsted

GANG FACTIONS

FACTION	GANG	LOCATION
H-Block	Gangster Disciples	63rd to 64th and Paulina to Wood
H-Block	Gangster Disciples	71st to 72nd and Honore
HD City	Black Gangsters (New Breed)	Douglas and Homan
Heart of the City (Central City)	Gangster Disciples	76th and Emerald
Heaven	Saints	45th and Hermitage
Heaven & Hell	Latin Kings	Chicago to Huron and Damen to Leavitt
Hell Zone	Satan Disciples	Cermak to 26th and California to Western
Hell Zone - Two Four Rockwell	Satan Disciples	24th and Rockwell
Hermosa Boys	Gangster Disciples	Monterey to 115th and Homewood to Hermosa
HGH (Hood Gang Hoodlum)	Black P Stones	67th and Blackstone
Hit City	Black Disciples	76th to 80th and Greenwood
Hit Squad	Black P Stones	46th and Ellis
Hit Squad	Gangster Disciples	29th and Michigan
Hit Squad	Gangster Disciples	59th to 63rd and Western to Talman
Hit Squad	Gangster Disciples	59th to 63rd and Campbell to Washtenaw
Hit Squad Breedz	Black Gangsters (New Breed)	Grenshaw and Homan
Hittas On Sight (HOS)	Gangster Disciples	71st and Aberdeen
HOBO	Gangster Disciples	42nd to 43rd and Vincennes to Langley
HOBO	Gangster Disciples	45th to 49th and Cottage Grove to King Dr
HOBO	Gangster Disciples	51st to 53rd and King Dr to Prairie
HOBO	Gangster Disciples	Jackson and California
Hollow City	Latinos Out of Control	75th to 83rd and Lawndale to Pulaski
Hollow SDs	Satan Disciples	43rd to 48th and Ciceo Ave to Knox
Holy City	Conservative Vice Lords	14th to 16th and Springfield
Holy City	Conservative Vice Lords	72nd to 74th and Ridgeland to Jeffrey
Holy City	Outlaw Lunatic Traveling Vice Lords	16th and Hamlin
Holy City	Traveling Vice Lords	14th to Ogden and Homan to Hamlin
Holy City	Unknown Vice Lords	Roosevelt to Douglas and Central Park to Millard
Holy City Breeds	Black Gangsters (New Breed)	19th and Spaulding
Homicide	Latin Kings	Lawrence and Kedzie
Homicide Boys	Homicide Boys	43rd to 45th and Troy to Albany
Homicide Town	Two Six	63rd and Homan
Homicie 5-8	Latin Kings	55th to 59th and Central Park to Pulaski
Hood Rich Boys	Four Corner Hustlers	Madison to Washington and Parkside to Lotus

FACTION	GANG	LOCATION
Horseshoe	Mickey Cobras	115th and Sangamon
HOS (Hittas on Sight)	Gangster Disciples	71st and Aberdeen
Hot Boys	Traveling Vice Lords	Douglas to 16th and Avers to Central Park
Hot Boyz	Four Corner Hustlers and Unknown Vice Lords	Ohio and Huron and Chicago and Avers
Hottie World	Gangster Disciples	61st to 62nd and St Lawrence to Langley
Hottieworld	Gangster Disciples	61st to 63rd and King to Langley
Hoyne Boys	Conservative Vice Lords	55th to 58th and Seeley to Hamilton
HSGs	Gangster Disciples	51st and Hoyne
HSK (Hitsquad)	Black Disciples	79th and Verona
H-Town Gangsters	Gangster Disciples	22nd and State
Huli World	Black Disciples	80th and Ingleside
Humboldt Park Latin Kings	Latin Kings	Beach and Spaulding
Humboldt Park Latin Kings	Latin Kings	Hirsch and Spaulding
Humboldt Park Latin Kings	Latin Kings	LeMoyne and Spaulding
Hyde Park Stones	Black P Stones	51st to 55th and Woodlawn to the Lake
HZ (Hell Zone)	Satan Disciples	24 and washtenaw and 19th and Cermak
IBB (Bishop Boys / Blood Bros)	Gangster Disciples	80th to 81st and Ashland to Loomis
Ice Cream Shop	Gangster Disciples	38th and Vincennes
ICG (Insane Cutthroat Gangsters)	Gangster Disciples	Pratt to Greenleaf and Ashland to Glenwood
ICG (Insane Cut Throat)	Gangster Disciples	Touhy to Devon and Broadway to Clark
Ill Town	Ambrose	79th and Nagle
Imperial Insane Vice Lords	Imperial Insane Vice Lords	Division to Augusta and Keystone to Keeler
Imperial Insane Vice Lords	Imperial Insane Vice Lords	Erie and Cicero
Imperial Insane Vice Lords	Imperial Insane Vice Lords	Leland and Beacon
Imperial Insane Vice Lords	Imperial Insane Vice Lords	Ohio to Chicago and Kenton to Cicero
Imperial Insane Vice Lords	Imperial Insane Vice Lords	Potomac and Lavergne
Infamous	Latin Counts	93rd and Escanaba to Muskegon
Insane Black Mafia	Black P Stones	Rogers to Howard and Clark to Ridge
Insane Campbell Boys	Insane Campbell Boys	Augusta and Campbell
Insane Cut Throat Gangsters (ICG)	Gangster Disciples	Pratt to Greenleaf and Ashland to Glenwood
Insane Deuces	Insane Deuces	19th and Rockwell
Insane Deuces	Insane Deuces	Milwaukee and Berteau
Insane Dragons	Insane Dragons	Augusta to Chicago Ave and Sacramento to Campbell
Insane Dragons	Insane Dragons	Palmer and Kilpatrick

GANG FACTIONS

FACTION	GANG	LOCATION
Insane GDs	Gangster Disciples	55th to 57th and Damen to Seeley
Insane GDs	Gangster Disciples	63rd to 65th and Damen to Hamilton (Tracks)
Insane GD's	Gangster Disciples	62nd to 63rd and Hamilton to Damen
Insane Hit Squad	Gangster Disciples	59th to 63rd and Western to Talman
Insane Majestics	Insane Majestics	31st and Laramie (Cicero, IL)
Insane Popes (Northside)	Insane Popes (Northside)	Ardmore and Central Park
Insane Popes (Northside)	Insane Popes (Northside)	Balmoral Ave and Campbell
Insane Popes (Northside)	Insane Popes (Northside)	Foster Ave and Lincoln
Insane Popes (Northside)	Insane Popes (Northside)	Gregory and Washtenaw
Insane Unknowns	Insane Unknowns	Cortez and Kostner
Insane Unknowns	Insane Unknowns	Grand to Cortez and Kostner to Pulaski
Insane Unknowns	Insane Unknowns	Hirsch and Karlov
Iowa Village	Insane Dragons	Iowa St and Western to California
Iraq	Mafia Insane Vice Lords	Trumbull and Iowa
Ishmoe City	Titanic Stones	52nd and Drexel
Ishmoe City	Titanic Stones	52nd and Ingleside
Ishmoe City	Titanic Stones	53rd and Maryland
Island Latin Kings	Latin Kings	Arthington to Roosevelt and Menard to Austin
Island Young Money	Gangster Disciples	50th and King Dr
Israelite Stones	Black P Stones	42nd and Prairie
Israelite Stones	Black P Stones	42nd to 43rd and Prairie
Israelite Stones	Black P Stones	43rd and Prairie
J Block	Black Disciples	64th and Martin Luther King Dr
J Money World	Gangster Disciples	39th to 40th and Lake Park
J Town/Bucktown	Conservative Vice Lords	68th to 71st and Justin to Ashland
Jack Boy Gang	Gangster Disciples	67th to 68th and Justine
Jack Boys	Black P Stones	51st and Marshfield
Jack Boys	Four Corner Hustlers	Division and Mason
Jack Boys	Gangster Disciples	21st and Michigan
Jack Boys	Gangster Disciples	23rd and Federal
Jack Boys	Gangster Disciples	24th and State
Jack Boys	Gangster Disciples	68th to 71st and Jeffery to Paxton
Jack Boys	Gangster Disciples	71st to 73rd and Ellis to Evans
Jack Boys	Gangster Disciples	66th and Justine

GANG FACTIONS

FACTION	GANG	LOCATION
Jack Boys	Gangster Disciples	69th to 71st and South Shore to Clyde
Jack Boys	Four Corner Hustlers	Hirsch to Potomac and Mayfield
Jamar World	Black Disciples	39th to 39th and Michigan to Prairie
Jamonie World	Gangster Disciples	39th to 40th and Lake Park
Jaro City	Gangster Disciples	61st to 65th and Champlain to Vernon
Jaro City	Gangster Disciples	62nd to 63rd and Rhodes to King
Jaro City	Gangster Disciples	61st to 63rd and King to Langley
JAY G CITY	Gangster Disciples	39th to 40th and Lake Park
JBC (Jackville Boys)	Black P Stones	52nd and Marshfield
JC	Gangster Disciples	Jackson and California
JC MLDs	Maniac Latin Disciples	Irving Park and Leavitt
Jeffery Manor Gangsters (JMG)	Gangster Disciples	95th to 103rd and Jeffery to Torrence
Jeffrey Boys	Gangster Disciples	79th and Jeffrey
Jensen Park	Conservative Vice Lords	Lawrence to Wilson and St. Louis to Hamlin
Jet Black Stones	Black P Stones	51st and Wallace
Jet Black Stones	Black P Stones	53rd and Justine
Jet Black Stones	Black P Stones	54th and Halsted
Jet Black Stones	Black P Stones	57th and Justine
Jet Black Stones - "L Station"	Black P Stones	54th and Laflin
Jig Dawg GDs	Gangster Disciples	42nd to 45th and King Dr to Indiana
Jigs Dawgs	Gangster Disciples	43rd to 47th and Calumet to Prairie
JMG	Gangster Disciples	70 to 72nd and Crandon to Jeffrey
JO BLOCK	Gangster Disciples	63rd to 67th and Clarment and Oakley and Bell
John O World	Gangster Disciples	71st to 75th and Kenwood to Stony Island
Johnny Mob	Traveling Vice Lords	13th and Avers to Springfield
Johnny World	Conservative Vice Lords	83rd to 86th and Muskegon to Escanaba
Johno World	Gangster Disciples	73rd and Dorchester
Johno World	Gangster Disciples	71st to 76th and Kenwood and Dorchester
JoJo	Gangster Disciples	67th to 71st and Parnell to Wentworth
Josh Block	Gangster Disciples	68th and Morgan
Josh Block	Gangster Disciples	69th to 75th and Woodlawn and Kimbark
J-Town GDs	Gangster Disciples	67th to 73rd and Loomis to Ashland
Juice World	Gangster Disciples	79th to 83rd and Kedzie to Western
JuJu Block	Gangster Disciples	67th to 70th and Hamilton to Damen

GANG FACTIONS

FACTION	GANG	LOCATION
June Town / J-Town	Conservative Vice Lords	55th and Winchester
June Town / J-Town	Conservative Vice Lords	59th and Winchester
June Town / J-Town	Conservative Vice Lords	60th and Winchester
Juneway Jungle	Gangster Disciples	Howard and Ashland
Juneway Jungle	Gangster Disciples	Howard and Bosworth
Juneway Jungle	Gangster Disciples	Jarvis to Juneway and Eastlake to Paulina
Juneway Jungle	Gangster Disciples	Juneway and Marshfield
Jungle	Gangster Disciples	Howard and Ashland
Jungle Blocks	Black Disciples	Adams to 13th and Leavitt to Central Park
Jungle Boys	Black Disciples	Adams to 13th and Leavitt to Central Park
Jungle Boys	Gangster Disciples	108th to 117th and Church to Vincennes
Jungle Boys	Gangster Disciples	107th to 119th and I57 to Hermosa
Jungle City	Black Disciples	Adams and Leavitt
Jungle City	Gangster Disciples	79th to 81st and Avalon to Woodlawn
K- Town	Latin Kings	Hirsh and Keeler
Kapone Town	Simon City Royals	13th and 49th and Cicero (Kapone Town)
Kay Kay	Black P Stones	72nd to 74th and Carpenter to Racine
KC (Killa City)	Simon City Royals	Kimball and Cullom
KDDG (King Dale Doug Gang/50 Strong)	Gangster Disciples	50th to 51st and Morgan to Halsted
KD's (King Drive Boys)	Gangster Disciples	53rd and King Drive
K-Dub	Latin Kings	Kimball and Wabansia
Keetah	Black Disciples	63rd to 65th and Martin Luther King Dr
Keetah Stones	Black P Stones	51st to 55th and Loomis to Ashland
Keke Land	Black Disciples	60th and Normal
Kells World		61st to 67th and California to Kedzie
Kellz City	Gangster Disciples	122nd and Halsted to Racine
Kensington Kings	Latin Kings	111th to 115th and Cottage Grove to Langley
Kensington Kings	Latin Kings	115th to 118th and Michigan to Cottage Grove (angle)
Keta World	Black Disciples	63rd to 67th and King Drive
Keta World	Black Disciples	64th Martin Luther King Dr
Keystone	Young Latin Organization Disciples	Armitage to Grand and Pulaski to Keeler
Kilbourn Park	Latin Pachucos	Addison and Kilbourn
Killa City	Maniac Latin Disciples	Keystone and Cortland
Killa Park	Imperial Gangsters	Kimball and Palmer

FACTION	GANG	LOCATION
Killa Side	Latin Jivers	Greenview and Potomac
Killa Ward / New Money Crazy	Black P Stones	81st and Marshfield
Killaward 80s babies	Gangster Disciples	76th to 83rd and Ashland to Honore
Killer Camp	Gangster Disciples	47th and Martin Luther King Dr to State
Killer Ward	Gangster Disciples	75th to 83rd and Ashland to Wood
Killer Ward	Gangster Disciples	76th to 79th and Ashland to Wood
Killer Whale	Gangster Disciples	59th and Rockwell
Killin Fieldz	Spanish Cobras	Fullerton and Kilbourn
King Cobras	King Cobras	133rd and Burley
King Dale Doug Gang (50 Strong)	Gangster Disciples	50th to 51st and Morgan to Halsted
Ko Mak	Gangster Disciples	Cermak to Ogden and Pulaski to Kenton
Koz Park	Spanish Cobras	Belmont to Schubert and Milwaukee to Pulaski
KP Boys	Unknown Vice Lords	Maypole and Kilpatrick
Krazville	Gangster Disciples	63rd and Morgan
Krazy City	Krazy Getdown Boys	69th and Rockwell
Krazy Getdown Boys	Krazy Getdown Boys	71st and California
Krazy Getdown Boys	Krazy Getdown Boys	79th to 85th and Pulaski to Cicero
K-Town	Ashland Vikings	North Ave and Keeler
K-Town	Conservative Vice Lords	16th and Kedvale to Komensky
K-Town	Gangster Disciples	14th to 15th and Pulaski to Kildare
K-Town	Latin Eagles	Armitage to Belden and Kenneth to Kildare
K-Town	Latin Eagles	Cortland to Palmer and Kostner to Kilbourn
K-Town	Maniac Latin Disciples	Fullerton to Armitage and Pulaski to Kedvale
K-Town	Two Six	26th to 32nd and Kostner to Pulaski
K-Town	Undertaker Vice Lords	16th St and Kedvale to Komensky
K-Unit	Four Corner Hustlers	West End to Maypole and Keeler to Karlov
Kutt Throat	Conservative Vice Lords	74th to 76th and Evans to Drexel
Kutthroat	Conservative Vice Lords	73rd to 76th and Dobson to Langley
Kuwait City	Black P Stones	68th to 71st and Indiana to Michigan
L&L (Lawrence and Lawndale)	Spanish Cobras	Foster to Lawrence and Avers to Lawndale
L.A. Boys	Four Corner Hustlers	Lorel and Augusta
L.L.C.P.S.M (Larry Land Crazy Princeton St. Mob)	Black Disciples	99th to 103rd and Princeton to Wentworth
L.T. Four Corner Hustlers	Four Corner Hustlers	Thomas and Laramie

GANG FACTIONS

FACTION	GANG	LOCATION
L.T. Four Corner Hustlers	Four Corner Hustlers	Thomas and Lavergne
L.T. Four Corner Hustlers	Four Corner Hustlers	Thomas and Lawler
L.T. Four Corner Hustlers	Four Corner Hustlers	Thomas and Lockwood
La Flin	Gangster Disciples	57th to 58th and Laflin
La Raza	La Raza	43rd and Whipple
La Raza	La Raza	50th and Hoyne
La Raza	La Raza	76th and Ridgeway
La Raza	La Raza	Archer to 47th and Whipple to Kedzie
La Raza	La Raza	Clark St and Estes
La Raza	La Raza	Cortez and Kostner
La Raza	La Raza	Cortland and Kedvale
La Raza	La Raza	16th to Cermak Road from Racine to Ashland Avenue
Lady CNR	Four Corner Hustlers	Central and Race
LAFA (Love Always Forever Anna)	Gangster Disciples	95th to 103rd and Jeffery to Torrence
La-Flin	Gangster Disciples	55th to 57th and Justine to Loomis
Laflin Boys	Gangster Disciples	57th to 58th and Laflin
Lake Park Gangsters	Gangster Disciples	39th to 40th and Lake Park
Lake Side (003)	Gangster Disciples	74th to 75th and Exchange to the Lake
Lake Side Gangsters	Gangster Disciples	76th to 81st and Saginaw to South Shore
Lakeside	Gangster Disciples	79th to 82nd and Marquette to Escanaba
Lakeside (004)	Gangster Disciples	79th to 82nd and Yates to Burnham
Lamron 300	Black Disciples	59th to 67th and Normal and Harvard to Lowe
Lamron BD's (300)	Black Disciples	59th to 69th and Wentworth to Halsted
Lamrons 300	Black Disciples	64th and Normal
Landlord	Gangster Disciples	55th to 59th and Halsted to Sansmon
Laramie & Congress	Four Corner Hustlers	Van Buren to Harrison and Laramie to Lockwood
Laramie Boys	Four Corner Hustlers	Van Buren to Harrison and Laramie to Lockwood
Larry Land	Gangster Disciples	99th and Princeton
Lasalle Boys	Gangster Disciples	115th and Yale
Lathrop Homes	Black P Stones	Lathrop Homes near Diversey and Hoyne
Latin Angels	Latin Angels	Roosevelt to 14th St and 50th Ave to Laramie
Latin Brothers	Latin Brothers	Barry and Knox
Latin Brothers	Latin Brothers	Belmont to George and Knox to Lavergne
Latin Brothers	Latin Brothers	Wellington and Kilpatrick

GANG FACTIONS

FACTION	GANG	LOCATION
Latin Counts	Latin Counts	71st and Albany
Latin Counts	Latin Counts	91st and Brandon
Latin Dragon	Latin Dragons	90th and Houston
Latin Dragons	Latin Dragons	132nd to 136th and Buffalo to Bradley
Latin Eagles	Latin Eagles	Armitage and Kostner
Latin Jivers	Latin Jivers	Cleaver and Potomac
Latin Kings	Latin Kings	22nd to 25th and Albany to Kedzie
Latin Kings	Latin Kings	52nd and Marshfield
Latin Kings	Latin Kings	97th and Ewing
Latin Kings	Latin Kings	Balmoral to Winnemac and Ravenswood to Damen
Latin Kings	Latin Kings	Clark and Balmoral
Latin Kings	Latin Kings	Leland and Rockwell
Latin Kings	Latin Kings	Montrose and Hazel
Latin Kings	Latin Kings	Paulina and Collum
Latin Kings	Latin Kings	Roscoe and Hoyne
Latin Kings	Latin Kings	Schiller and Leavitt
Latin Kings - 21st and Albany	Latin Kings	21st to 22nd and Marshall to Kedzie
Latin Kings - 22nd and Sawyer	Latin Kings	22nd to 24th and Sawyer
Latin Kings - 22nd and Trumbull	Latin Kings	22nd to 23rd and Trumbull to St. Louis
Latin Kings - 23rd and Homan	Latin Kings	22nd to 23rd and Homan
Latin Kings - 23rd and Spaulding	Latin Kings	23rd and Spaulding
Latin Kings - 23rd and Whipple	Latin Kings	22nd to 24th and Whipple
Latin Kings - 24th and Christiana	Latin Kings	22nd to 24th and Christiana
Latin Kings - 24th and Sawyer	Latin Kings	24th to 26th and Sawyer to Kedzia
Latin Kings - 25th and California	Latin Kings	25th to 26th and California to Sacramento
Latin Kings - 25th and Millard	Latin Kings	24th to 26th and Millard
Latin Kings - 26th and Spaulding	Latin Kings	26th to 27th and Spaulding
Latin Kings - 27th and Christiana	Latin Kings	26th to 27th and Christiana
Latin Kings - 27th and Homan	Latin Kings	26th to 28th and Homan
Latin Kings - 28th and Christiana	Latin Kings	28th to 31st and Christiana
Latin Kings -28th and Lawndale	Latin Kings	27th to 30th and Lawndale
Latin Kings - 30th and Millard	Latin Kings	30th to 31st and Central Park to Lawndale
Latin Kings - 30th and St. Louis	Latin Kings	28th to 31st and St. Louis
Latin Kings - 30th and Trumbull	Latin Kings	28th to 31st and Trumbull

GANG FACTIONS

FACTION	GANG	LOCATION
Latin Kings - 53rd and Albany	Latin Kings	51st to 55th and Sacramento to Kedzie
Latin Kings - 59th and Homan	Latin Kings	59th to 61st and Homan to Central Park
Latin Kings - 63rd and Spaulding	Latin Kings	63rd to 67th and Kedzie to Homan
Latin Kings - Ashland and Columbia	Latin Kings	Albion to Pratt and Ashland to Ravenswood
Latin Kings - Belmont and Monticello	Latin Kings	Belmont to Diversey and Central Park
Latin Kings - Belmont and Monticello	Latin Kings	Belmont to Milwaukee and Central Park to Hamlin
Latin Kings - Belmont and Monticello	Latin Kings	Roscoe to Belmont and Kimball to Hamlin
Latin Kings - Berwyn and Winthrop	Latin Kings	Balmoral to Berwyn and Sheridan to Broadway
Latin Kings - Broadway and Winona	Latin Kings	Foster to Carmen and Broadway to Lakewood
Latin Kings - Clark and Bryn Mawr	Latin Kings	Edgewater to Catalpa and Hermitage to Glenwood
Latin Kings - Kedzie and Cortez	Latin Kings	Division to Augusta and Kedzie to Homan
Latin Kings - Keystone and Cullom	Latin Kings	Montrose to Berteau and Pulaski to Kedval
Latin Kings - Lawrence and Washtenaw	Latin Kings	Argyle to Lawrence and Rockwell to the River
Latin Kings - 28th and Spaulding	Latin Kings	27th to 31st and Spaulding
Latin Kings - 59th and Whipple	Latin Kings	59th to 61st and Whipple to Kedzie
Latin Kings - Lawrence and Kedzie	Latin Kings	Foster to Leland and Kedzie to the River
Latin Kings - Rosemont and Claremont	Latin Kings	Pratt to Rosemont and Western to Rockwell
Latin Lovers - Shakespeare	Latin Lovers	Shakespeare to Armitage and Humboldt to California
Latin Pachucos	Latin Pachucos	Addison and Central Park
Latin Pachucos	Latin Pachucos	Addison and Sacramento
Latin Pachucos	Latin Pachucos	Belden and Lorel
Latin Saints	Latin Saints	45th and Wood
Latin Souls	Latin Souls	49th to 50th and Ashland to Paulina
Latin Stones	Latin Stones	82nd and Coles
Latin Stones	Latin Stones	82nd and South Shoroe Drive
Latin Stones	Latin Stones	83rd and Commercial
Latin Stones	Latin Stones	83rd and Houston
Latin Stylers	Latin Stylers	Grand to North and Cicero to Keating
Latin Stylers	Latin Stylers	North and Cicero
Latin Stylers - Blackhawk Park	Latin Stylers	Fullerton to Armitage and Knox to Laramie
Latrobe Boys	Four Corner Hustlers	West End and Latrobe to Washington and Lotus
Lavender Mob	Four Corner Hustlers and Unknown Vice Lords	Van Buren to Jackson and Springfield
Law Squad	Black Disciples	67th to 71st and Michigan to State
Law World	Gangster Disciples	60th and Marshfield

GANG FACTIONS

FACTION	GANG	LOCATION
Lawless (757)	Gangster Disciples	35th to 37th and Rhodes
Lawless Ave	Gangster Disciples	37th and Rhodes to 27th and Michigan
Lawless Gardens	Gangster Disciples	35th and Rhodes
Lawndale Gardens	Black P Stones	25th and Washtenaw
Lawndale Gardens	Conservative Vice Lords	25th St and California to Rockwell
Lawndale LK's	Latin Kings	28th and Lawndale
Lawrence City	Spanish Gangster Disciples	Lawrence Ave and Harding
LB St	Latin Brothers	Lamon and Barry Ave
L-Block	Four Corner Hustlers	North to Hirsch and Lavergne to Lockwood
L-Dub	Gangster Disciples	Leland to Argyle and Marine Dr. to Broadway
Leclaire Courts	Conservative Vice Lords	43rd and Cicero
Leclaire Courts	Conservative Vice Lords	43rd to 45th and Lavergne to Cicero
Leclaire Courts	Conservative Vice Lords	44th and Laporte
LeClaire Courts	Gangster Disciples	43rd and Lamon
Lex Boyz	Four Corner Hustlers	Lexington and Pulaski
Licksquad	Four Corner Hustlers and Vice Lords and Black Peace Stone Nation	104th and Maryland
Lil D's	Gangster Disciples	51st and Calumet
Lil Haiti	Mafia Insane Vice Lords	Trumbull and Huron to St. Louis
Lil Paris City	Gangster Disciples	71st to 75th and East End to Cornell
Little D's	Black Disciples	132nd to 134th and Ellis to Greenwood
Little Mississippi GDs	Gangster Disciples	87th to 89th and Holland Rd to Princeton
Little Paris City East Side	Gangster Disciples	71st to 73rd and Cornell to East End
LK St	Latin Kings	Lawrence and Kedzie
LME (Long Money Gang)	Black P Stones	86th to 90th and Kingston to Muskegon and 91st and Escanaba
LO City	Gangster Disciples	66th to 68th and Dorchester to Stony Island
Lo City	Gangster Disciples	Marquette and 68th and Stony Island to Dorchester
LOC City	Gangster Disciples	50th to 55 and Hermitage to Wood
LOC City	Gangster Disciples	Jarvis to Juneway and Eastlake to Paulina
LOC GDs	Gangster Disciples	52nd to 53rd and Honore
Localville	Gangster Disciples	115th to 118th and Michigan to Lafayette
Locketville	Four Corner Hustlers	68th to 71st and Dorchester to Stony Island
Locktown	Four Corner Hustlers	68th to 71st and Dorchester to Stony Island
Lon City	Black Disciples	79th and State to Cottage Grove

GANG FACTIONS

FACTION	GANG	LOCATION
Lon City	Gangster Disciples	79th and Cottage Grove to Greenwood
London Town	Black P. Stones	101st and Cottage Grove
Loomisville	Black P Stones	69th and Laflin
Looney Toons	Black Gangsters (New Breed)	12th to 15th and Ashland to Blue Island
Looneyville	Gangster Disciples	119th and Michigan
Lordsville	Conservative Vice Lords	57th and Hoyne
LOS City	Mickey Cobras	49th to 51st and Martin Luther King Dr to Cottage Grove
Los Gang	Gangster Disciples	109th Place and Perry to Wentworth
Lost World	Imperial Gangsters	Altgeld and Lavergne
Lost World	Imperial Gangsters	Deming and Leclaire
Lost World	Imperial Gangsters	Lavergne and Wrightwood
Love None	Black P Stones	52nd to 53rd and Marshfield to Paulina
Low Block	Gangster Disciples	63rd to 65th and Ashland to Hermitage
Low City	Black P Stones	67th and Blackstone
Low Life	Black Disciples	63rd to 65th and Martin Luther King Dr
Low Life	Black Disciples	64th to 66th and Lowe
Low Lyfe	Gangster Disciples	21st and State
Low Rider City	Ashland Vikings	Ashland and Walton
Lowden Homes	Gangster Disciples	91st to 97th and Eggleston to Dan Ryan
Lowe Boys	Gangster Disciples	64th and Lowe
Lowe Down	Gangster Disciples	122nd and Lowe
Lowe Life	Black Disciples	63rd to 67th and Lowe to Halsted
Lowe Town	Gangster Disciples	69th to 74th and Wallace to Union
Lowe Town Insane	Gangster Disciples	69th to 74th and Wallace to Union
Loyalty City (L's City)	Gangster Disciples	91st and Yates
LP St	Latin Pachucos	Palmer and Lorel
LPC	Gangster Disciples	71st to 75th and East End to Cornell
LPG	Gangster Disciples	39th and 40th to Lake Park
LS	Latin Kings	Lemoyne and Spaulding
LSG	Gangster Disciples	115th to 118th and Ashland to Racine
LSG	Gangster Disciples	93rd and Stony Island
LSG (New Park)	Gangster Disciples	107th to 111th and Throop to Loomis
LSG (Sircon)	Gangster Disciples	75th to 79th and Woodlawn to Stony Island
L-Station	Black P Stones	54th and Laflin

GANG FACTIONS

FACTION	GANG	LOCATION
LT Breedz	Black Gangsters (New Breed)	Thomas and Lawndale
L-Town	Black P. Stones	Chicago to Ohio and Laramie to Cental
L-Town	Four Corner Hustlers	Washington and Lockwood
L-Town	Latin Lovers	Richmond and Mclean
Luna Mob	Traveling Vice Lords	Luna and Lamoyne
Lunatic Block	Gangster Disciples	41st and Langley
M&A Boys	Four Corner Hustlers	Thomas to Iowa and Mayfield to Waller
M.O.B	Gangster Disciples	58th to 60th and State St. to Michigan
M.O.B.	Gangster Disciples	74th to 83rd (Columbus) and Central Park to Kedzie
M.O.B. City	Gangster Disciples	125th and Fairview
M.P.G.s	Gangster Disciples	114th and Church
MA (M&A)	Four Corner Hustlers	Mayfield and Augusta
M-A Boyz	Black Gangsters (New Breed)	Monroe and Albany
MAC Girls	Gangster Disciples	Hyde Park High School
MAC Town	Gangster Disciples	79th to 81st and Morgan and Aberdeen and Carpenter
Mac World	Gangster Disciples	61st to 63rd and Cottage
MacBlock	Black Disciples	64th to 65th and Halsted
Macheteville	Cicero Insane Vice Lords	94th and Throop
Macheteville	Vice Lords	90th to 91st and Ada to Loomis
Mackville	Latin Kings	Montrose and Damen to Ashland
Mad Money Gang (MMG)	Conservative Vice Lords	Roosevelt and Francisco and Mozart
Mad Town	Cullerton Deuces	21st and Washtenaw
Madville	Cullerton Deuces	21st and Washtenaw
Madville GDs	Gangster Disciples	60th to 63rd and Ashland to Paulina
Mafia Insane Vice Lords	Mafia Insane Vice Lords	41st and Princeton
Mafia Insane Vice Lords	Mafia Insane Vice Lords	41st to 43rd and Wentworth to Canal
Mafia Insane Vice Lords	Mafia Insane Vice Lords	43rd and Princeton
Mafia Insane Vice Lords	Mafia Insane Vice Lords	45th and Leclaire
Mafia Insane Vice Lords	Mafia Insane Vice Lords	82nd and Coles
Mafia Insane Vice Lords	Mafia Insane Vice Lords	94th and Loomis
Mafia Insane Vice Lords	Mafia Insane Vice Lords	Adams and Lavergne
Mafia Insane Vice Lords	Mafia Insane Vice Lords	Augusta and Monticello
Mafia Insane Vice Lords	Mafia Insane Vice Lords	Bloomingdale to Hirsch and Lockwood to Linder
Mafia Insane Vice Lords	Mafia Insane Vice Lords	Cortland to North and Central to Austin

GANG FACTIONS

FACTION	GANG	LOCATION
Mafia Insane Vice Lords	Mafia Insane Vice Lords	Division to Thomas and Pulaski to Keystone
Mafia Insane Vice Lords	Mafia Insane Vice Lords	Fulton and Hamlin
Mafia Insane Vice Lords	Mafia Insane Vice Lords	Fulton and Lacrosse
Mafia Insane Vice Lords	Mafia Insane Vice Lords	Fulton to Washington and Cicero to Lavergne
Mafia Insane Vice Lords	Mafia Insane Vice Lords	Huron and Lavergne to Leclaire
Mafia Insane Vice Lords	Mafia Insane Vice Lords	Iowa and Cicero
Mafia Insane Vice Lords	Mafia Insane Vice Lords	Lake St and Cicero
Mafia Insane Vice Lords	Mafia Insane Vice Lords	Madison and Lamon
Mafia Insane Vice Lords	Mafia Insane Vice Lords	Madison and Lotus
Mafia Insane Vice Lords	Mafia Insane Vice Lords	Madison and Mason
Mafia Insane Vice Lords	Mafia Insane Vice Lords	Madison and Menard
Mafia Insane Vice Lords	Mafia Insane Vice Lords	Madison and Waller
Mafia Insane Vice Lords	Mafia Insane Vice Lords	Madison to Jackson and Cicero to Lavergne
Mafia Insane Vice Lords	Mafia Insane Vice Lords	Madison to Monroe and Leclaire to Leamington
Mafia Insane Vice Lords	Mafia Insane Vice Lords	Monroe and Lavergne
Mafia Insane Vice Lords	Mafia Insane Vice Lords	Ohio and Cicero Ave
Mafia Insane Vice Lords	Mafia Insane Vice Lords	Potomac and Cicero
Mafia Insane Vice Lords	Mafia Insane Vice Lords	Washington and Cicero
Mafia Insane Vice Lords	Mafia Insane Vice Lords	Washington and Kilbourn
Mafia Insane Vice Lords	Mafia Insane Vice Lords	80th and Houston and 80th to 82nd and Exchange to Houston
Mafia Stones	Black P Stones	72nd to 76th and Kingston to Phillips
Mafia Town	Mafia Insane Vice Lords	40th to 43rd and Wabash to Calumet
Main City	Black Disciples	100th and State
Main City	Black Disciples	100th and Perry
Main Street / Main Block	Conservative Vice Lords	83rd to 86th and Muskegon to Escanaba
Mall	Gangster Disciples	67th to 71st and Crieger to Stony Island
Maniac Campbell Boys	Maniac Campbell Boys	Campbell and North Ave
Maniac Four Corner Hustlers	Four Corner Hustlers	68th and Clyde
Maniac Four Corner Hustlers	Four Corner Hustlers	69th and Crandon
Maniac Four Corner Hustlers	Four Corner Hustlers	69th and Dorchester
Maniac Four Corner Hustlers	Four Corner Hustlers	71st and Chappell to Clyde
Maniac Four Corner Hustlers	Four Corner Hustlers	71st and Dorchester
Maniac Four Corner Hustlers	Four Corner Hustlers	72nd to 73rd and Coles
Maniac Four Corner Hustlers	Four Corner Hustlers	73rd and Jeffery

GANG FACTIONS

FACTION	GANG	LOCATION
Maniac Four Corner Hustlers	Four Corner Hustlers	76th to 77th and Kingston
Maniac Four Corner Hustlers	Four Corner Hustlers	80th and Escanaba
Maniac Four Corner Hustlers	Four Corner Hustlers	81st and Manistee
Maniac Four Corner Hustlers	Four Corner Hustlers	Bloomingdale to North and Leclaire to Long
Maniac Gangsters	Gangster Disciples	103rd and Vernon
Maniac Geek Squad	Gangster Disciples	62nd and Campbell
Maniac Latin Disciples	Maniac Latin Disciples	14th and Ridgeland
Maniac Latin Disciples	Maniac Latin Disciples	55th to 58th and Rockwell to California
Maniac Latin Disciples	Maniac Latin Disciples	Armitage to Blmgdale and Western to California
Maniac Latin Disciples	Maniac Latin Disciples	Armitage to Cortland and Harding to Keeler
Maniac Latin Disciples	Maniac Latin Disciples	Belmont to Diversey and Kedzie to California
Maniac Latin Disciples	Maniac Latin Disciples	Belmont to Mliwaukee and Kedzie to Central Park
Maniac Latin Disciples	Maniac Latin Disciples	Belmont to Wellington and Central to Major
Maniac Latin Disciples	Maniac Latin Disciples	Diversey to Elston and Rockwell to California
Maniac Latin Disciples	Maniac Latin Disciples	Evergeen and Rockwell
Maniac Latin Disciples	Maniac Latin Disciples	Evergeen and Washtenaw
Maniac Latin Disciples	Maniac Latin Disciples	Fairfield and LeMoyne
Maniac Latin Disciples	Maniac Latin Disciples	Fullerton and Moody
Maniac Latin Disciples	Maniac Latin Disciples	Fullerton to Dickens and Austin to Narragansett
Maniac Latin Disciples	Maniac Latin Disciples	Fullerton to Palmer and Avers to Pulaski
Maniac Latin Disciples	Maniac Latin Disciples	Fullerton to Palmer and Kostner to Kenton
Maniac Latin Disciples	Maniac Latin Disciples	Grace and Albany
Maniac Latin Disciples	Maniac Latin Disciples	Hirsch and Avers
Maniac Latin Disciples	Maniac Latin Disciples	Hirsch and Hamlin
Maniac Latin Disciples	Maniac Latin Disciples	Maplewood and Hirsch
Maniac Latin Disciples	Maniac Latin Disciples	Maplewood and North
Maniac Latin Disciples	Maniac Latin Disciples	Moffat and Campbell
Maniac Latin Disciples	Maniac Latin Disciples	Roscoe and Avers
Maniac Latin Disciples	Maniac Latin Disciples	Schubert and Fairfield
Maniac Latin Disciples	Maniac Latin Disciples	Talman and LeMoyne
Maniac Latin Disciples	Maniac Latin Disciples	Washtenaw and Wabansia
Maniac Latin Disciples	Maniac Latin Disciples	Wellington to Diversey and Austin to Melvina
Maniac Side	Ambrose	18th and Morgan
Maniac Stones	Black P Stones	74th and Phillips

GANG FACTIONS

FACTION	GANG	LOCATION
Maniac Stones	Black P Stones	74th to 75th and Colfax to Phillips
Maniac Stones	Black P Stones	72nd to 76th and Kingston to Phillips
Maplewood	Latin Kings	49th to 55th and Maplewood
Maplewood MLDs	Maniac Latin Disciples	55th to 58th and Rockwell to California
Maplewood Park	Maniac Latin Disciples	Maplewood and Wabansia
Mario World	Traveling Vice Lords	104th to 107th and Racine to Morgan
Marlon World	Black Disciples	57th and Carpenter
Marshall Field Apartment Complex	Mickey Cobras	Evergreen to Blackhawk and Cleveland to Wells
Marshfield Apartments	Conservative Vice Lords	Hudson and Evergreen
Marshfield Boys (MFB)	Gangster Disciples	63rd and Marshfield
Maryland	Conservative Vice Lords	Anthony to 75th and Evans to Maryland
Maul Town	Gangster Disciples	67th to 69th and Stony Island to Ingleside
May Mob	Gangster Disciples	63rd to 65th and Racine to May
Mayberry and The Nine	Gangster Disciples	116th to 120th and Eggleston to Halsted
Mayberry Gang	Gangsster /Black Disciples	116th to 120th and Eggleston to Halsted
Mayblock	Black Peace Stones	72nd to 74th and Carpenter to Racine
MBA (Money Before Anything Vice Lords)	Unknown Vice Lords	Central and Ohio
MBA (Money Before Anything Vice Lords)	Unknown Vice Lords	Pine and Ohio
MBB (My Bad Brothers)	Gangster Disciples	118th to 119th and Parnell to Halsted
MC800	Mickey Cobras	51st to 63rd and Cottage Grove to Martin Luther King Dr and Champlain
MCG	Black Disciples	85th to 86th and Morgan to Carpenter
M-Dub	Mafia Insane Vice Lords	North Ave and Austin to Central
Meat Block 4's	Four Corner Hustlers and Unknown Vice Lords	Van Buren to Jackson and Springfield
Mecca	Black P Stones	64th to 67th and Blackstone
Medina	Black P Stones	87th and Saginaw
Memorial Park Boys	Gangster Disciples	71st to 75th and Vincennes to Lafayette
Merill Park Gangsters	Gangster Disciples	95th to 103rd and Jeffery to Yates
Merill Town Boys	Gangster Disciples	95th to 103rd and Jeffery to Yates
Merillville	Gangster Disciples	79th to 80th and Merill to Yates
Mero Block	Gangster Disciples	39th to 40th and Lake Park
Merrill Boys	Gangster Disciples	79th to 80th and Merill to Yates
Merriville	Gangster Disciples	79th to 85th and Merill
Met Boy Gangsters	Gangster Disciples	51st and Calumet

FACTION	GANG	LOCATION
Met Boys	Gangster Disciples	49th to 51st and Michigan to King
Met Boys	Gangster Disciples	48th to 51st and King Drive to Calumet
Met Life	Gangster Disciples	50th to 51st and Michigan
Met Life (6217 Calumet)	Black Disciples	60th to 63rd and Martin Luther King Dr to State
Mexico City	Latin Lovers	Milwaukee Ave and California
MFB	Four Corner Hustlers	Fulton to Madison and Mayfield to Mason
MFB (Marshfield Boys)	Gangster Disciples	60th and Marshfield
Mickey City	Mickey Cobras	61st to 63rd and Cottage Grove
Mickey Cobras	Mickey Cobras	106th and Wentworth to Eggleston
Mickey Cobras	Mickey Cobras	107th to 109th and Peoria to Beverly
Mickey Cobras	Mickey Cobras	37th to 39th and Wells to Wentworth
Mickey Cobras	Mickey Cobras	43rd to 55th and Shields to Wentworth
Mickey Cobras	Mickey Cobras	48th to 51st and King to Champlain
Mickey Cobras	Mickey Cobras	50th and Drexel
Mickey Cobras	Mickey Cobras	56th and Shields
Mickey Cobras	Mickey Cobras	62nd and Damen
Mickey Cobras	Mickey Cobras	71st and Hermitage
Mickey Cobras	Mickey Cobras	90th St and State to Indiana
Mickey Cobras	Mickey Cobras	Devon and Claremont
Midway & LK's	Latin Kings	47th to 51st and Cicero to Laramie
Mike City	Black Disciples	85th to 86th and Morgan to Carpenter
Mike City	Black Disciples	85th to 87th and Carpenter to Sangamon
Millard Mob	Traveling Vice Lords	16th and Millard
Miller Street	Gangster Disciples	19th to Cullerton and Miller
Milwaukee Kings	Milwaukee Kings	Altgeld and Meade
Mind On Business	Gangster Disciples	57th to 59th and Wabash to Michigan
Mitch World	Conservative Vice Lords	Roosevelt and Francisco and Mozart
Miter Town	Bishops	18th and Paulina
Mixed Mafia	Mafia Insane Vice Lords	Superior and Cicero
Mixed Mob	Gangster Disciples	79th to 82nd and Avalon
MMG (Money Mac Gang)	Black Disciples	64th to 66th and Lowe
MMG (Murda Mook Gang)	Gangster Disciples	75th to 79th and Wabash to Prairie
MMG (Mad Money Gang)	Conservative Vice Lords	Roosevelt and Francisco and Mozart
MOB	Black Disciples	79th and St Louis

GANG FACTIONS

FACTION	GANG	LOCATION
MOB		74th to 83rd and Columbus to Central Park
MOB (Mind On Business)	Gangster Disciples	57th to 59th and Wabash to Michigan
MOB Boss Pimps	Gangster Disciples	89th to 95th and Anthony to Yates
MOD (Money On Demand)	Gangster Disciples	64th and Seeley
Moe Block	Gangster Disciples	69th and Woodlawn
Moe Money		South Emerald Avenue
Moes	Black Peace Stones	51st to 55th and Racine to Halsted
Moetown	Black P Stones	51st and Ashland
Moetown	Black P Stones	51st and Racine and Elizabeth
Moetown	Black P Stones	51st and Sangamon and Halsted
Moetown	Black P Stones	51st and Wallace
Moetown	Black P Stones	51st to 57th and Ashland to Union
Moetown	Black P Stones	52nd and Loomis
Moetown	Black P Stones	53rd and May
Moetown	Black P Stones	53rd and Racine
Moetown	Black P Stones	53rd to 54th and Halsted
Moetown	Black P Stones	53rd to 54th and Union
Moetown	Black P Stones	54th and Laflin
Moetown	Black P Stones	55th and Ashland
Moetown	Black P Stones	55th and Carpenter
Moetown	Black P Stones	55th and Racine
Moetown	Black P Stones	57th and Justine
Mone City	Gangster Disciples	87th to 89th and Vincennes to Loomis
Money Before Anything Vice Lords (MBA)	Unknown Vice Lords	Central and Ohio
Money Before Anything Vice Lords (MBA)	Unknown Vice Lords	Pine and Ohio
Money City	Gangster Disciples	87th to 90th and Loomis to Vincennes
Money Making Group (MMG)	Four Corner Hustlers	Lake to Maypole and Wood to Wolcott
Money On Ferdinand (MOF)	Four Corner Hustlers	Hubbard to Ferdinand and Lavergne
Money Over Bitches (MOB)	Gangster Disciples	61st to 63rd and King to Langley
Money Side	Insane C-Notes	Grand Ave and Rockwell
Money Side	Insane C-Notes	Grand Ave to Ohio and California to Damen
Money Side	Insane C-Notes	Ohio and Claremont
Money Team	Traveling Vice Lords	104th to 107th and Racine to Morgan
Monk Land	Maniac Latin Disciples	Maplewood and LeMoyne

GANG FACTIONS

FACTION	GANG	LOCATION
Moo Moo Gang	Black Disciples	111th to 115th and Ashland to Racine
Moody Boys	Four Corner Hustlers	West End & Latrobe to Washington and Lotus
Moose Block	Gangster Disciples	71st to 73rd and Cornell to East End
Morgan BD's	Black Disciples	77th to 79th and Morgan to Aberdeen
Morgan Boys BD's	Black Disciples	85th to 86th and Morgan to Carpenter
Morgan LK's	Latin Kings	31st to 35th and Lituanica to Racine
Morgan LK's	Latin Kings	33rd and Morgan
Morgan Mafia	Gangster Disciples	72nd to 73rd and Morgan
Most Wanted Side	Latin Counts	16th to 18th and Loomis to Ashland
Motherland	Imperial Gangsters	Palmer and Drake
Motherland	Latin Kings	North to Division and Central Park to Kedzie
Motherland	Two Two Boys	Cermak and California
MoTown	Black P Stones	49th to 55th and Wallace to Paulina
Mozart Two Six	Two Six	Archer to 47th and California to Francisco
M-Town	Milwaukee Kings	Fullerton and Meade to Marmora
MTV (Mount Vernon)	Black Disciples	79th and Verona
Muff Mob	Black Disciples	Adams and Leavitt
Mula City	Black Disciples	80th and Ingleside
Mula Gang	Black Disciples	80th and Ingleside
Mula Gang	Gangster Disciples	75th to 79th and Wabash to Prairie
Murda Ave	Black P Stones	86th to 91st and Marquette to Escanaba
Murda Ave	Latin Kings	104th and Ave L
Murda Ave	Simon City Royals	Milwaukee Ave and Avers
Murda Town	Black P Stones	67th and Blackstone
Murda Town	Gangster Disciples	37th to 38th and Michigan to Wabash
Murda Town	Latin Kings	26th to 28th and Drake to Central Park
Murda Town	Satan Disciples	59th and Mozart
Murda Town	Two Two Boys	16th and 47th Ct
Murdafields	Satan Disciples	Ohio and Marshfield
Murder Land	Imperial Gangsters	Monticello and Leland
Murder Show	Titanic Stones	67th and Chappel
Murder Town	Gangster Disciples	37th to 39th and Wells to Wentworth
Murder Town	Gangster Disciples	67th to 69th and Carpenter to Peoria
Murder Town	La Raza	19th to 21st and Allport to Loomis

GANG FACTIONS

FACTION	GANG	LOCATION
Murder Town	Latin Kings	Winona and Winthrop
Murder Town	Party People	16th to 18th Cullerton and Racine to Peoria
Murder World	Brazers	Morse and Wayne
Murderfield	Latin Souls	49th and Marshfield
MurderTown		39th and Wentworth
Muskegon Boys	Gangster Disciples	79th and Muskegon
My Blood Borthers	Gangster Disciples	118th to 119th and Parnell to Halsted
Nate Block	Gangster Disciples	61st and Justine
Nateville	Black P Stones	103rd and Vincennes
Nateville	Black P Stones	90th and Ashland
Nateville	Black P Stones	95th and Bishop
Nateville	Black P Stones	98th and Throop
Nateville	Black P Stones	99th and Loomis
Nateville	Gangster Disciples	95th to 100th and Beverly to Vincennes
Nation Stones	Black P Stones	79th to 83rd and Halsted to Lowe
Naw Heads	Gangster Disciples	13th to Ogden and Talman to California
Neef Streets / Neef Team	Black Disciples	40th to 39th and Michigan to Prairie
New Breed	Gangster Disciples	67th to 71st and Wood to Damen
New Breed		67th to 70th and Winchester to Wood
New Breed City	Black Gangsters (New Breed)	67th and Honore
New Breed City	Black Gangsters (New Breed)	67th and Winchester
New Breed City	Black Gangsters (New Breed)	67th and Wolcott
New Homes	Black Disciples	Lake St to Madison and Damen to Western
New Homes	Black Disciples	Madison to Van Buren and Damen to Western
NEW JOC CITY	Gangster Disciples	63rd to 67th and Clarment and Oakley and Bell
New Life Black Souls	Black Souls	Madison to Wilcox and Pulaski to Karlov
New Money Crazy	Black P Stones	81st and Marshfield
New Park	Gangster Disciples	107th to 111th and Morgan to Loomis
New Town	Black Disciples	60th and Calumet
New Town	Gangster Disciples	42nd and Cottage Grove
Newtown BD's	Black Disciples	63rd to 65th and Martin Luther King Dr
Nez World	Black P Stones and Gangster Disciples	63rd to 66th and Kedzie to California
NIA (Nigga in Action)	Gangster Disciples	85th to 87th and Kedzie to California
Nickel (The Nickel)	Gangster Disciples	105th and Wentworth

GANG FACTIONS

FACTION	GANG	LOCATION
Nine 0 (9-0)	Gangster Disciples	87th to 91st and Martin Luther King Dr to Cottage Grove
Nine Trey (9-Trey)	Gangster Disciples	90th to 95th and Vincennes to Throop
Nine-0	Gangster Disciples	90th to 93rd and Ashland to Beverly
Nine-Trey (9-Trey)	Black P Stones	92nd to 95th and State to Martin Luther King Dr
Nini Ville	Gangster Disciples	60th and Marshfield
No Law	Black P Stones	60th to 63rd and Evans to Champlain
No Law	Black P Stones	62nd and Evans
No Limit	Black P Stones	84th and Colfax and 83rd to 87th and Saginaw to Essex
No Limit - No Law	Black P. Stones	77th to 79th and Jeffrey to Kingston
No Limit Stones	Black P Stones	79th and Essex
No Limit Stones	Black P Stones	83rd and Colfax
No Limit Stones	Black P Stones	83rd and Escanaba
No Love	Gangster Disciples	60th to 63rd and Halsted to Union
No Love	Spanish Gangster Disciples	Montrose to Belle Plaine and Spaulding to St. Louis
No Love	Two Six	32nd and Karlov
No Love City	Gangster Disciples	55th to 59th and Lowe to Halsted
No Love City	Latin Kings	Leland and Virginia
No Love City	Satan Disciples	47th and Campbell
No Love City	Spanish Cobras	Fullerton and Tripp
No Love GDs	Gangster Disciples	55th to 59th and Lowe to Halsted
No Love Money Gang	Simon City Royals	Augusta to Huron and Trumbull to Central Pk.
No Love Side	Two Six	28th to 33rd and Kedvale
No Love Ville	Two Six	47th and Albany
No Worse	Conservative Vice Lords	21st and Trumbull
No Worst Boys	Traveling Vice Lords	Ogden to Cermak and Homan to Central Park
Noble Sqaure	Gangster Disciples	Milwaukee and Noble
No-Heart	Ambrose	62nd to 63rd and Mozart
North Mob	Traveling Vice Lords	Roosevelt and Avers
Northpole	Gangster Disciples	Thorndale and Winthrop
Northpole	La Raza	Clark St and Estes
Nuke Side	Conservative Vice Lords	89th and Langley
Nune World	Gangster Disciples	60th and Justine
O Block	Black Disciples	64th and Martin Luther King Dr
O.A.K.	Gangster Disciples	98th and Sangamon

GANG FACTIONS

FACTION	GANG	LOCATION
O/L	Insane C-Notes	Ohio and Leavitt
Oak Boys	Gangster Disciples	35th to 39th (Oakwood) and Rhodes to Ellis
Oakdale	Gangster Disciples	95th to 96th and Halsted to Vincennes
Oakdale Park	Gangster Disciples	95th to 96th and Halsted to Vincennes
Oakk Town	Satan Disciples	18th and Oakley
Oakk Town	Satan Disciples	18th to 23rd and Western to Wolcott
Oakk Town	Satan Disciples	19th and Oakley
Oakk Town	Satan Disciples	21st and Oakley
Oakk Town	Satan Disciples	23rd and Oakley
Oakley SDs	Satan Disciples	18th and Oakley
Oakley SDs	Satan Disciples	18th to 23rd and Western to Wolcott
Oakley SDs	Satan Disciples	19th and Oakley
Oakley SDs	Satan Disciples	21st and Oakley
Oakley SDs	Satan Disciples	23rd and Oakley
Oakville	Maniac Latin Disciples	Barry and Spaulding
Oakwood Boys	Gangster Disciples	35th to 39th (Oakwood) and Rhodes to Ellis
Oakwood Boys	Gangster Disciples and Black Disciples and Black P Stones and Vice Lords	36th to 39th and Rhodes to Ellis
Obama World	Black Disciples	63rd to 65th and Cottage Grove to Drexel
Obama World	Black Disciples	63rd to 67th and King Drive
O-Block	Black Disciples	63rd to 67th and King Drive
OC City	Gangster Disciples	59th and Rockwell
OCB (Only Chasing Bands)	Gangster Disciples	69th to 75th and Woodlawn and Kimbark
O-City 81st	Mafia Insane Vice Lords	81st to 83rd and Houston to Exchange
Ogden Courts	Gangster Disciples	13th to Ogden and Talman to California
Ohio Boys	Four Corner Hustlers	Erie to Race to Menard to Austin
OJ World	Gangster Disciples	45th to 48th and State to Martin Luther King
OKC (Only Keli City)	Gangster Disciples	116th to 117th and Eggleston to Parnell
Omskiville	Maniac Latin Disciples	Belden and Kenneth
On The Block (OTB)	Gangster Disciples	68th and Sangamon
One Trey	Traveling Vice Lords	13th and Avers to Springfield
One Ways	Gangster Disciples	107th to 109th and Church
One Ways	Traveling Vice Lords	Division to Kamerling and Pulaski to Kostner
Orchestra Albany	Orchestra Albany	Belden and Albany

GANG FACTIONS

FACTION	GANG	LOCATION
Orchestra Albany	Orchestra Albany	Diversey and Harding
Orchestra Albany	Orchestra Albany	Emmett and Sawyer
Orchestra Albany	Orchestra Albany	Fullerton and Kedzie
Orchestra Albany	Orchestra Albany	Lyndale and Sacramento
Orchestra Albany	Orchestra Albany	Schubert and Kimball
Orchestra Albany	Orchestra Albany	Wellington and Hamlin
Oskeeno Gang	Traveling Vice Lords	Huron and Drake
OTF (Only The Family)	Black Disciples	60th to 63rd and Martin Luther King Dr to State
Otherside	Gangster Disciples	77th to 82nd and Cottage Grove to St Lawrence
Outlaw (014)	Gangster Disciples	Potomac to Division and Maplewood to Rockwell
Outlaw 4CH	Four Corner Hustlers	Fulton to Washington and Lockwood
Outlaw BPSN	Black P Stones	52nd to 54th and May to Aberdeen
Outlaw City	Black P Stones	83rd to 93rd and Stony Island to Jeffery
Outlaw City	Black P Stones	87th and Euclid to Jeffery
Outlaw Lunatic Traveling Vice Lords	Outlaw Lunatic Traveling Vice Lords	79th and Cicero
Outlaw Lunatic Traveling Vice Lords	Outlaw Lunatic Traveling Vice Lords	Adams and Central
Outlaw Lunatic Traveling Vice Lords	Outlaw Lunatic Traveling Vice Lords	Chicago Ave and Trumbull
Outlaw Lunatic Traveling Vice Lords	Outlaw Lunatic Traveling Vice Lords	Congress and Central
Outlaw Lunatic Traveling Vice Lords	Outlaw Lunatic Traveling Vice Lords	Gladys and Central
Outlaw Lunatic Traveling Vice Lords	Outlaw Lunatic Traveling Vice Lords	Jackson and Central
Outlaw Lunatic Traveling Vice Lords	Outlaw Lunatic Traveling Vice Lords	Monroe and Leamington
Outlaw Lunatic Traveling Vice Lords	Outlaw Lunatic Traveling Vice Lords	Van Buren and Central
Outlaw Stones	Titanic Stones	73rd to 75th and Jeffery Blvd
Outlaws	Gangster Disciples	56th to 57th and Wabash to State
Outlaws	Gangster Disciples	63rd and Ashland
Outlaws	Mickey Cobras	50th and Princeton
Outlaws	Young Latin Organization Disciples	Armitage to Palmer and Hamlin to Pulaski
Overhill Moes	Black P Stones	79th to 81st and Colfax to Yates
P Dubb	Four Corner Hustlers	Washington and Pine
Pablo City	Maniac Latin Disciples	30th and 50th Ct
Pac Town	Gangster Disciples	65th to 66th and Drexel
Paisa City	Young Latin Organization Disciples	Karlov and Wabansia
Paisa Land	Maniac Latin Disciples	Rockwell and Cortland
Palmer City	Maniac Latin Disciples	Fullerton to Armitage and Pulaski to Kedvale

GANG FACTIONS

FACTION	GANG	LOCATION
Palmer Park	Gangster Disciples	111th to 115th and Michigan to Martin Luther King Dr
Papa Stones	Black P Stones	52nd and May
Paradise	Imperial Gangsters	Lyndale and Central Park
Parkholme Two Six	Two Six	16th to Cermak and Laramie to 51st
Parkholme Two Six	Two Six	18th and 51st
Parkholme Two Six	Two Six	21st and 50th Ct
Parkside	Black Disciples	110th to 113th and Indiana
Parkside Village (PSV)	Four Corner Hustlers	Corcoran to West End and Central to Austin
Parkway Gardens	Black Disciples	63rd to 65th and Martin Luther King Dr
Parkway Gardens	Titanic Stones	65th and Martin Luther King Dr
Party People	Party People	18th to 19th and May to Racine
Party People	Party People	56th to 57th and Artesian to Western
Party Players	Party Players	65th and Spaulding
Past	Latin Kings	Pulaski and Argyle
Pat World	Four Corner Hustlers and Unknown Vice Lords	Ohio and Huron and Chicago and Avers
Patch Squad	Gangster Disciples	42nd to 45th and King Dr to Indiana
Pax Town	Gangster Disciples	69th to 71st and South Shore to Jeffrey
PBG (Pooh Bear Gang)	Gangster Disciples	Pratt to Greenleaf and Ashland to Glenwood
P-Dub	Latin Kings	Potomac and Wolcott
Pee Wee City	Maniac Latin Disciples	School and Albany
Peoria CVLs	Conservative Vice Lords	76th to 78th and Peoria to Sangamon
Pepsi Cola Girls	Gangster Disciples	131st and Champlain and Langley
Perry Ave Boys	Gangster Disciples	122nd to 124th and Perry
Pimp City	Ambrose	79th and Lavergne
Pirate Stones	Black P Stones	133rd to 134th and Martin Luther King Dr to Indiana
Pirate Stones	Black P Stones	133rd to Little Calumet River and King to Indiana
Player Town	Party Players	48th St and Wolcott
Players Alley	Twelfth Street Players	64th and Nottingham
Pluto Gang	Gangster Disciples	105th and Wabash
Pocket Town	Conservative Vice Lords	74th to 76th and Evans to Drexel
Pocket Town	Gangster Disciples	69th to 71st and Woodlawn to Kimbark
Pocket Town	Gangster Disciples	71st to 73rd and Ellis to Woodlawn
Pocket Town	Gangster Disciples	69th to 71st and Woodlawn to Kimbark
Pocket Town Gangsters (PTG)	Gangster Disciples	104th to 105th and Wentworth

GANG FACTIONS

FACTION	GANG	LOCATION
Pocket Town Gangsters (PTG)	Gangster Disciples	116th and Racine
Pocket Town Gangsters (PTG)	Gangster Disciples	119th and Justine
Pocket Town Gangsters (PTG)	Gangster Disciples	71st and Woodlawn
Pocket Town Gangsters (PTG)	Gangster Disciples	71st to 75th and Woodlawn to Kimbark and Woodlawn to S Chicago Ave
Pocket Town Gangsters (PTG)	Gangster Disciples	72nd and Ellis
Pocket Town Gangsters (PTG)	Gangster Disciples	73rd and Greenwood
Pocket Town Gangsters (PTG)	Gangster Disciples	73rd and University
Pocket Town Gangsters (PTG)	Gangster Disciples	75th and Dorchester
Pocket Town Gangsters (PTG)	Gangster Disciples	76th and Hermitage
Pocket Town Gangsters (PTG)	Gangster Disciples	93rd and Stony Island
Pooh Land	Gangster Disciples	42nd to 45th and King Dr to Indiana
Popes Alley	Insane Popes (Southside)	63rd and Oak Park
Poppy Gang	Four Corner Hustlers	Lexington and Pulaski
Pretty in Pink	Black Disciples	Dunbar High School
Princeton Park	Gangster Disciples	91st to 97th and Eggleston to Dan Ryan
Princetown	Black Disciples	108th to 110th and Wentworth to Stewart
Princetown Boys	Black Disciples	108th to 110th and Wentworth to Stewart
Project LK's	Latin Kings	Lathrop Homes
P-Street	Gangster Disciples	71st to 72nd and Parnell
Psycho Side	Saints	45th and Paulina
P-Town	Four Corner Hustlers	Polk and Pulaski
Pullman LK's	Latin Kings	113th and Langley
Purple City	Krazy Getdown Boys	79th to 83rd and Pulaski to Cicero
QMB (Quiet Money Boys)	Gangster Disciples	79th to 83rd and Kedzie to Homan
Quette Crazy	Black P Stones	79th to 87th and Marquette (2700E)
Quiet Money	Gangster Disciples	79th to 83rd and Kedzie to Homan
Quillville	Black P Stones	86th to 91st and Marquette to Escanaba
R.C.	Latin Kings	Rosemont and Claremont
R.E.C. City	Black P Stones	63rd to 66th and Kedzie to California
R.I.P. Reaper	Insane Popes (Southside)	34th and Hoyne
Racine Courts	Gangster Disciples	107th to 111th and Aberdeen to Throop
Rack City	Black P Stones	91st to 95th and Halsted to Eggleston
Rack City	Black P Stones	92nd and Union

GANG FACTIONS

FACTION	GANG	LOCATION
Rack City	Black P Stones	93rd and Halsted
Rag Town	Gangster Disciples	115th to 119th and Racine to Halsted
Rag Town: Corleons	Black Disciples	116th and Emerald
Rag Town: Corleons	Black Disciples	118th and Peoria
Ragtown	Gangster Disciples	115th to 119th and Halsted to May
Ragtown	Gangster Disciples	115th to 120th and Halsted to Morgan
RaRa	Gangster Disciples	71st to 76th and Kenwood and Dorchester
RaRa World	Gangster Disciples	71st to 75th and Kenwood to Stony Island
Rascal Life/Rascals	Conservative Vice Lords	56th to 59th and Western to Campbell
RC	Maniac Latin Disciples	Rockwell and Cortland
Real Side	Maniac Latin Disciples	Cortland to North and Campbell to California
REC City	Black P Stones and Gangster Disciples	63rd to 66th and Kedzie to California
Rec City	Black P Stones and Gangster Disciples	70th and Rockwell
Rec City		61st to 67th and California to Kedzie
Red City	Conservative Vice Lords	74th and 75th to Racine to Loomis
Red Tape	Conservative Vice Lords	Cortez to Walton and Lamon
Red Wall Street	Four Corner Hustlers	60th and Albany
Red Zone	Latin Counts	14th St and 58th Ave
Red Zone	Latin Counts	Roosevelt to 18th St and Austin to 58th Ave
Redrum City	Latin Kings	27th to 30th and Kedzie to Sawyer
Reese Money Gang (RMG)	Gangster Disciples	115th and Stewart to Eggleston
Renegade	Party People	18th to 19th and May
Renegade Stones	Black P Stones	75th to 76th and Exchange to Yates
Renegade Vice Lords	Renegade Vice Lords	79th and Houston
Renegade Vice Lords	Renegade Vice Lords	Jackson Blvd and Campbell (Rockwell Gardens)
Renegade Vice Lords	Renegade Vice Lords	Madison and Kildare
Renegade Vice Lords	Renegade Vice Lords	Madison and Rockwell (Rockwell Gardens)
Renegades	Gangster Disciples	76th to 83rd and Racine to Damen
Rey Town	Two Two Boys	Ogden to 33rd and 51st to Central Ave
Rezzy Ville	Black Disciples	63rd to 67th and King Drive
RG	Maniac Latin Disciples	Rockwell and George
Rich City	Krazy Getdown Boys	64th and Richmond
Ricky City	Gangster Disciples	68th to 69th and Vernon to MLK Dr.
Ridge Town	Black Disciples	73rd and Ridgeland

GANG FACTIONS

FACTION	GANG	LOCATION
Ridgeland	Black Disciples	72nd to 73rd and Ridgeland to East End
Ridgeland	Black Disciples	74th to 75th and East End to Stony Island
Ridgeway Boys	Latin kings	25th to 30th and Ridgeway
Rio World	Traveling Vice Lords	104th to 107th and Racine to Morgan
Risk Squad	Gangster Disciples	52nd to 53rd and Honore
Riverside Village	Black Disciples	132nd to 133rd and Prairie to King Dr
RLC (Row Life Crazy)	Gangster Disciples	65th and Minerva
RMG (Reese Money Gang)	Gangster Disciples	115th and Stewart to Eggleston
Roc Block	Gangster Disciples	71st to 75th and Ellis to Evans
Roc Island	Conservative Vice Lords	79th and Sangamon
Roc World	Gangster Disciples	108th to 111th and Eggleston to Emerald
Rock Block	Gangster Disciples	37th and Vincennes
Rock Boys	Gangster Disciples	59th and Rockwell
Rock Creek	Gangster Disciples	61st to 63rd and Cottage Grove to Woodlawn
Rock Creek	Gangster Disciples	63rd to 67th and Cottage Grove to Kenwood
Rock Island	Black P Stones	72nd to 74th and Carpenter to Racine
Rock Island	Four Corner Hustlers	73rd and Stony Island
Rock Nation	Gangster Disciples	21st to 22nd and Michigan to Indiana
Rock Nation	Gangster Disciples	27th and State
Rock Nation	Gangster Disciples	37th to DeSable and Princeton to Wentworth
Rock Nation	Gangster Disciples	37th and Rhodes to 27th and Michigan
Rock/Mac/Vic Creek (Rock Creek)	Gangster Disciples	61st and Ingleside
Rockblock	Gangster Disciples	78th to 80th and Muskegan to Exchange
Rockwell Boys	Gangster Disciples	62nd to 69th and Western to Rockwell
Ronnie World	Black P Stones	86th to 91st and Marquette to Escanaba
Rookieville (RVL)	Gangster Disciples	115th and Princeton and Wallace and Normal
Root Street MIVLS (009)	Mafia Insane Vice Lords	Root (41st) to 43rd and Shield to Wentworth
Rooville	Gangster Disciples	109th Place and Perry to Wentworth
Roseland LK's	Latin Kings	111th to 115th and Cottage Grove to Langley
Roseland LK's	Latin Kings	115th to 118th and Michigan to Cottage (angle)
Row House Boys	Gangster Disciples	46th and Evans
Row Houses	Gangster Disciples	Divison to Kingsbury and Crosby to Cleveland
Row Life Crazy	Gangster Disciples	65th and Minerva
Row Life/Saw World	Gangster Disciples	65th and Minerva

GANG FACTIONS

FACTION	GANG	LOCATION
Row Row Crazy	Gangster Disciples	55th to 58th and Normal to Princeton
Royal Family Gang	Gangster Disciples	64th and Honore
Royville	Gangster Disciples	51st to 53rd and Wood
Rozay	Conservative Vice Lords	Roosevelt and Francisco and Mozart
Rubenites	Black P Stones	55th to 58th and Ashland to Hermitage
Ruthless	Latin Kings	Lawrence to Wilson and Clark to Winchester
Ruthless	Latin Kings	Winnemac to Lawrence and Paulina to Ravenswood
Ruthless (004)	Latin Kings	95th to 100th and Avenue N to the Lake
S Dub	Insane Dragons	Walton and Sacramento
S Dubb	Gangster Disciples	71st to 74th and Ashland to Winchester
S.O.A. (Straight Off Albany)	Traveling Vice Lords	Arthington and Albany
S.O.A. (Straight Off Albany)	Traveling Vice Lords	Flournoy and Albany
S.O.A. (Straight Off Albany)	Traveling Vice Lords	Harrison and Albany
S.O.A. (Straight Off Albany)	Traveling Vice Lords	Lexington and Albany
S.O.A. (Straight Off Albany)	Traveling Vice Lords	Polk and Albany
S.O.A. (Straight Off Albany)	Traveling Vice Lords	Roosevelt and Albany
S.O.A. (Straight Off Albany)	Traveling Vice Lords	Taylor and Albany
SAC World	Gangster Disciples	67th to 70th and Hamilton to Damen
Sacramento and Wilcox	Gangster Disciples	Madison to Van Buren and California to Sacramento
Saints	Saints	45th and Honore
Saints	Saints	45th and Marshfield
Salute The General (STG/50 Strong)	Gangster Disciples	50th to 51st and Morgan to Halsted
Sam City	Gangster Disciples	63rd to 66th and Artesian
Sangamon Assassins	Gangster Disciples	56th to 60th and Green to Morgan
Satan Disciples	Satan Disciples	32nd and Lituanica
Satan Disciples	Satan Disciples	33rd and Paulina
Satan Disciples	Satan Disciples	39th to 47th and California to Western
Satan Disciples	Satan Disciples	42nd and Campbell
Satan Disciples	Satan Disciples	45th and Sawyer
Satan Disciples	Satan Disciples	50th and Oakley
Satan Disciples	Satan Disciples	71st and Central Park
Satan Disciples	Satan Disciples	81st and Tripp
Satan Disciples	Satan Disciples	Ainslie and Avers
Satan Disciples	Satan Disciples	Taylor St and Ogden to California

GANG FACTIONS

FACTION	GANG	LOCATION
Satan Disciples	Satan Disciples	18th to 19th and Wood to Damen
Savage Life	Black Disciples	64th to 66th and Lowe
Savage Squad Records	Black Disciples	62nd to 63rd and Martin Luther King Dr to State
Savage Unknowns	Unknown Vice Lords	Central and Race
Savagetown	Gangster Disciples	61st to 67th and California to Kedzie
Saw Block	Gangster Disciples	65th and Minerva
SBC (Saw Block Crazy)	Gangster Disciples	65th and Minerva
SCG (Sircon City Gangsters)	Gangster Disciples	71st to 75th and Kenwood to Stony Island
School Krazy	Latin Kings	School and Lavergne
Sco Mo	Gangster Disciples	80th and Francisco
Scoota Block	Gangster Disciples	65th to 69th and Cottage Grove to St Lawrence
Scrapville	Gangster Disciples	63rd to 67th and Rockwell to Talman
S-Dub GDs	Gangster Disciples	71st to 73rd and Ashland to Wood
S-Dubs	Gangster Disciples	71st to 73rd and Ashland to Wood
Sesame Street	Orchestra Albany	Schubert and Spaulding
Seven Deuce		71st to 74th and Artesian to Tahlman
Seven Deuces	Gangster Disciples	71st to 72nd and Rockwell
Seven Deuces	Gangster Disciples	71st to 75th and Ellis to Evans
Seven Trey	Gangster Disciples	73rd and Racine
Seven Two Boys	Gangster Disciples	71st to 72nd and Campbell to Kedzie
Seven-0's	Gangster Disciples	69th to 71st and Western to California
SGSCB (Stain Gang / Stain City)	Gangster Disciples	79th to 83rd and Kedzie to Western
Shady Boys	Black P. Stones	90th to 95th and Halsted to Eggleston
Shakespeare	Young Latin Organization Cobras	Palmer to Armitage and Central Park to Hamlin
Shank Field	Gangster Disciples	60th and Marshfield
Shannon Ville	Gangster Disciples	63rd to 65th and Ashland to Hermitage
Shawn City	Black Disciples	79th and St Louis
Shawty World	Gangster Disciples	57th to 58th and Laflin
Sheroid Squad	Black Disciples	63rd to 67th and King Drive
Sicko's	Black Gangsters (New Breeds)	15th to 19th and Christiana
Silent City	Spanish Gangster Disciples	Broadway and Cuyler
Simon City Royals	Simon City Royals	35th and Clinton
Simon City Royals	Simon City Royals	Bryn Mawr and Spaulding
Simon City Royals	Simon City Royals	Central Park and Wilson

GANG FACTIONS

FACTION	GANG	LOCATION
Simon City Royals	Simon City Royals	George and Ridgeway
Simon City Royals	Simon City Royals	Irving Park Rd and Bernard
Simon City Royals	Simon City Royals	Lawndale and Agatite
Simon City Royals	Simon City Royals	Montrose Ave and St Louis
Sin City	Black P Stones	100th to 103rd and St Lawrence to Dauphin
Sin City	Black P Stones	101st and Cottage Grove
Sin City	Young Latin Organization Cobras	Armitage to Bloomingdale and California to Humboldt
Sircon	Gangster Disciples	71st to76th and Kenwood and Dorchester
Sircon	Gangster Disciples	75th to 79th and Woodlawn to Stony Island
Sircon City	Gangster Disciples	71st to 75th and Kenwood to Stony Island
Six Deuce	Gangster Disciples	62nd and Normal
Six Deuce Boys	Gangster Disciples	61st to 63rd and Ashland to Laflin
Six Two Boys	Gangster Disciples	61st to 63rd and Laflin to Ashland
SKD	Gangster Disciples	47th to 57th and King Dr to Calumet
SKD's (South King Drive Boys)	Gangster Disciples	59th and King Drive
Skee Skee Woo	Four Corner Hustlers	Hubbard to Ferdinand and Lavergne
Skid Row	Black P Stones	100th to 103rd and Michigan to State
Skkoolyard D's	Maniac Latin Disciples	Leavitt and Cuyler
SKO	Gangster Disciples	55th to 57th and Perry to State
Slag Valley Latin Counts	Latin Counts	100th and Commercial
Slag Valley Latin Counts	Latin Counts	101st and Escanaba
Slag Valley Latin Counts	Latin Counts	95th to 103rd and Baltimore to Manistee
Slag Valley Latin Counts	Latin Counts	97th and Commercial
Slaughter Town	Black P Stones	86th to 90th and Kingston to Muskegon and 91st and Escanaba
Slim World	Gangster Disciples	79th and Wabash
Small World GDs	Gangster Disciples	71st to 73rd and Ashland to Wood
Smashville	Black Disciples	85th and Ashland to Wood
Smashville	Black Disciples	87th and Manistee
Smashville	Black P Stones	83rd and Damen
Smashville	Gangster Disciples	83rd to 85th and Ashland to Wood
Smashville	Gangster Disciples	83rd to 87th and Beverly to Ashland
Smashville (6217 Calumet)	Black Disciples	60th to 63rd and Martin Luther King Dr to State
Smoke Town	City Knights	58th and Albany
Smooth Gang	Gangster Disciples	42nd to 45th and Martin Luther King Dr to Indiana

GANG FACTIONS

FACTION	GANG	LOCATION
Snake Pitt	Spanish Cobras	Wabansia and Tripp
Sniper 4's	Four Corner Hustlers	Fulton To Washington and Latrobe to Leamington
Sniper 4's	Four Corner Hustlers	Wilcox and Adams
So Icey Crew	Gangster Disciples	40th and Vincennes
So Icey Crew	Gangster Disciples	42nd to 43rd and Cottage Grove
Solid World	Black Disciples	99th to 103rd and Princeton to Wentworth
Soo Woo	Four Corner Hustlers	Divison to Kamerling and Cicero to Lawler
Soo Woo	Gangster Disciples	37th to 38th and Cottage to Ellis
Soo Woo (007)	Black Disciples	69th and Bishop
Soulville (Gangster Black Souls)	Black Souls	Caroll and Francisco
Soulville (Gangster Black Souls)	Black Souls	Lake and Francisco
Soulville (Gangster Black Souls)	Black Souls	Madison and Francisco
Soulville (Gangster Black Souls)	Black Souls	Walnut and Francisco
Soulville (Gangster Black Souls)	Black Souls	Warren and Francisco
Soulville (Gangster Black Souls)	Black Souls	Washington and Francisco
South Commons	Gangster Disciples	26th to 31st and Michigan to King
South Cs	Black P Stones	87th to 91st and Baltimore to Avenue 0
South Deering LC's	Latin Counts	106th to 108th and Hoxie
South Deering LC's	Latin Counts	107th and Mackinaw
South End Cs	Conservative Vice Lords	47th and Cicero
South Insane C 91st	Latin Counts	91st and Commercial
South King Drive Boys (SKD's)	Black Disciples and Gangster Disciples (Met Boys/Jig Dawg)	47th to 57th and Martin Luther King Dr to Calumet
Spade Town	Insane Deuces	45th and Union
Spanish Cobras	Spanish Cobras	33rd to 35th and Artesian to Western
Spanish Cobras	Spanish Cobras	Diversey and Avers (Koz Park)
Spanish Cobras	Spanish Cobras	Division to Augusta and Western to California
Spanish Cobras	Spanish Cobras	Schubert and Central Park
Spanish Cobras	Spanish Cobras	Wolfram and Drake
Spanish Cobras	Spanish Cobras	Wrightwood and Monticello
Spanish Four Corner Hustlers	Four Corner Hustlers	Addison and Cicero
Spanish Four Corner Hustlers	Spanish Four Corner Hustlers	George to Altgeld and Lockwood to Central
Spanish Gangster Disciples	Spanish Gangster Disciples	47th and Wolcott
Spanish Gangster Disciples	Spanish Gangster Disciples	87th to 88th and Baltimore to Houston

GANG FACTIONS

FACTION	GANG	LOCATION
Spanish Gangster Disciples	Spanish Gangster Disciples	Argyle to Lawrence and Kimball to Monticello
Spanish Gangster Disciples	Spanish Gangster Disciples	Sunnyside and Kimball
Spanish Harlem	Latin Kings	24th to 26th and Spaulding
Spanish Lords	Spanish Lords	Armitage and Western
Spanish Lords	Spanish Lords	Charleston and Western
Spanish Lords	Spanish Lords	McLean and Oakley
Spanish Lords	Spanish Lords	Shakespeare and Oakley (Holstein Park)
Spanish Lords - Bucktown	Spanish Lords	Fullerton to Milwaukee and Oakley to Western
Spanish Vice Lords	Spanish Vice Lords	103rd to 109th and Torrence to Oglesby
Spanish Vice Lords	Spanish Vice Lords	104th and Hoxie
Spanish Vice Lords	Spanish Vice Lords	106th and Mackinaw
Spanish Vice Lords	Spanish Vice Lords	108th and Greenbay
Spanish Vice Lords	Spanish Vice Lords	108th and Mackinaw
Spaulding Latin Kings	Latin Kings	Beach and Spaulding
Spaulding Latin Kings	Latin Kings	Division and Spaulding
Spaulding Latin Kings	Latin Kings	Hirsch and Spaulding
Spaulding Latin Kings	Latin Kings	LeMoyne and Spaulding
Spook Town	Mickey Cobras	90th to 91st Pl and Cottage Grove
Squally Gang	Gangster Disciples	42nd to 45th and Martin Luther King Dr to Indiana
Squirt City	Gangster Disciples	60th to 63rd and King to Eberhart
SSG (Stewart Savages)	Gangster Disciples	72nd to 73rd and Stewart
St Lawrence	Gangster Disciples	62nd to 65th and Rhodes to St Lawrence
St. Stephens	Traveling Vice Lords	Adams to Van Buren and Oakley to Western
Stain City	Gangster Disciples	63rd and Damen
Stain City	Gangster Disciples	79th and Campbell
Stain City	Gangster Disciples	79th to 83rd and Kedzie to Western
Stank City	Gangster Disciples	115th to 119th and Yale to Princeton
State Boys	Black Disciples	112th to 115th and Michigan to Perry
State Boys	Four Corner Hustlers	111th to 115th and Michigan to Perry
State Boys	Gangster Disciples	113th to 114th and State
Stateway Gardens	Gangster Disciples	35th to 39th and State to Federal
Stewart Savages	Gangster Disciples	72nd to 73rd and Stewart
STG (Salute The General-50 Strong)	Gangster Disciples	50th to 51st and Morgan to Halsted
STL	Black P Stones	87th to 88th and Cottage Grove to St Lawrence

GANG FACTIONS

FACTION	GANG	LOCATION
STL (St. Lawrence Boys)	Gangster Disciples	62nd to 65th and Rhodes to St Lawrence
Stone Terrace	Black P Stones	83rd to 87th and Halsted to Parnell
Stoneville	Black P Stones	Howard and Bell and Damen
Stoneville	Black P Stones	Jarvis and Damen
Stonner Gang	Traveling Vice Lords	104th to 107th and Racine to Morgan
Stony Spot	Black P Stones	61st to 65th and Stony Island to Harper
Stonyspot	Black P Stones	62nd and Harper
Stonyspot 061	Black P Stones	61st to 63rd and Stony island to Dante
Straight Cash Nation	Gangster Disciples	26th to 31st and Michigan to King
Stubbz Squad	Black P Stones	87th to 89th and Beverly to Bishop
Sunnyside Girls	Four Corner Hustlers	Washington and Lotus
SUWU	Gangster Disciples	39th to 40th Street and Lake Park to Ellis
SUWU (007)	Black Disciples	69th and Bishop
Swift City	Milwaukee Kings	Altgeld and Marmora
Swindle Gang	Conservative Vice Lords	83rd to 86th and Muskegon to Escanaba
Sykes Gang	Gangster Disciples	71st and Aberdeen
Syndicate	Four Corner Hustlers	5th and Karlov
Syndicate	Four Corner Hustlers	5th and Pulaski
Syndicate	Four Corner Hustlers	Harrison to Taylor and Independence to Kildare
Syndicate	Four Corner Hustlers	Lexington and Karlov
T.G.C (Teeg Crazy Gang)	Renegades	104th to 105th and Wentworth
Taliban	Gangster Disciples	115th to 118th and Michigan to Lafayette
Tatioun City	Gangster Disciples	67th and Chappell
Tay City	Gangster Disciples	70th to 73rd and State to Wentworth
Tay Mobb	Four Corner Hustlers	Lake to Maypole and Wood to Wolcott
Tay Town	Black Disciples	59th to 63rd and Princeton to Normal
Tay Town (TTE)	Black Disciples	60th and Normal
Taytown	Black Disciples	59th to 62nd and Normal
TBC (Travel Boys)	4 Corner Hustlers	251 E 121st Place
T-Dubb	Maniac Latin Disciples	Cortland to North and Campbell to California
Team Get Money (TGM)	Black Disciples	Ace Tech High School
Team No Good	Black Disciples	59th to 63rd and Campbell to Washtenaw
Team Red Tape	Conservative Vice Lords	56th to 59th and Western to Campbell
Team Tim Moe	Gangster Disciples	83rd to 87th and Kedzie to California

GANG FACTIONS

FACTION	GANG	LOCATION
Ten Three	Black P Stones	103rd and Wallace
Ten Tre (10 - Trey)	Gangster Disciples	103rd to 105th and Halsted to Morgan
Ten Trey/Treyville	Gangster Disciples	103rd and Wallace
Terrence Green City	Black Disciples and Gangster Disciples	68th to 70th and Ashland to Laflin
Terror Dome	Black P Stones	75th to 79th and Wood to Damen
Terror Dome	Young Latin Organization Cobras	Dickens and Tripp
Terror Town	Black P Stones	74th and Phillips
Terror Town	Black P Stones	74th to 79th and Yates Blvd to Colfax
Terror Town	Black P Stones	75th and Colfax
Terror Town	Black P Stones	75th and Yates Blvd
Terror Town	Black P Stones	78th and Kingston
Terror Town	Black P Stones	79th and Essex
Terror Town	Black P Stones	79th and Yates Blvd
Terror Town	Gangster Disciples	51st and Wood
Terror Town	Latin Kings	25th and Troy
Terror Town	Satan Disciples	51st and Wood
Terror Town	Two Six	38th and Albany
TGC (Terrence Green City)	Black Disciples and Gangster Disciples	68th to 70th and Ashland to Laflin
The 1	Black Disciples	71st and Martin Luther King Dr
The 1	Gangster Disciples	71st and Woodlawn
The 9-1	Gangster Disciples	87th to 92nd and State to Martin Luther King Dr
The 9's	Gangster Disciples	118th and Princeton
The Ave	Black Disciples	38th to 39th and Michigan to Prairie
The Ave	Four Corner Hustlers	Chicago and Hamlin
The Ave	Gangster Disciples	39th and Martin Luther King Dr
The Ave	Imperial Insane Vice Lords	Chicago Ave and Austin
The Avenue	Conservative Vice Lords	Chicago Ave and Homan to Kedzie
The Avenue	Conservative Vice Lords	Chicago Ave and Keystone
The Avenue	Conservative Vice Lords	Chicago Ave and Keystone to Lawndale
The Avenue	Conservative Vice Lords	Chicago Ave and Lawndale
The Avenue	Conservative Vice Lords	Chicago Ave and Ridgeway
The Avenue	Conservative Vice Lords	Roosevelt and Sacramento
The Avenue	Mafia Insane Vice Lords	Chicago Ave and Cicero to Lavergne
The Back	Gangster Disciples	106th and Yates to Bensley

GANG FACTIONS

FACTION	GANG	LOCATION
The Backyard	Gangster Disciples	40th and St Lawrence
The Carter	Black Gangsters (New Breed)	Douglas and Christiana
The Deuce	Latin Kings	81st to 83rd and Houston
The Dukes	Mickey Cobras	52nd and Shields to Princeton
The Extensions	Gangster Disciples	36th and Vincennes
The Firm	Gangster Disciples	58th and Shields
The Gutter	Mickey Cobras	49th to 51st and Martin Luther King Dr to Cottage Grove
The Hole	Gangster Disciples	115th and Wallace
The Holy City	Conservative Vice Lords	16th and Central Park
The Holy City	Conservative Vice Lords	16th and Drake
The Holy City	Conservative Vice Lords	16th and Lawndale
The Holy City	Conservative Vice Lords	16th and Ridgeway
The Holy City	Conservative Vice Lords	16th St to Cermak Rd and Pulaski to Hamlin
The Holy City	Conservative Vice Lords	19th and Ridgeway
The Holy City	Conservative Vice Lords	21st and Trumbull
The Holy City	Conservative Vice Lords	Cermak and Millard
The Hornets	Conservative Vice Lords	Lake St and Wood
The Hornets	Renegade Vice Lords	Lake St and Wood (Henry Horner Homes)
The Hornetz	Four Corner Hustlers	Lake St and Wood
The Low End	Conservative Vice Lords	47th and Ellis to Drexel
The Mall	Gangster Disciples	67th to 71st and Crieger to Stony Island
The Manor	Gangster Disciples	18th and Kostner
The Naw	Gangster Disciples	13th to Ogden and Talman to California
The O (Nine-O and 9-0)	Gangster Disciples	90th to 93rd and Ashland to Beverly
The O (9-0)	Gangster Disciples	90th to 93rd and Cottage to Martin Luther King Dr
The R.O.C.	Insane C-Notes	Race and Oakley
The Rocks	Insane Dragons	Augusta and Rockwell
The Row	Four Corner Hustlers	Addison and Cicero
The Row	Gangster Disciples	119th to 122nd and State to Wentworth
The Seven	Gangster Disciples	107th to 111th and Indiana to Edgebrooke
The Square	Black Gangsters (New Breed)	18th and Karlov
The Trey	Mickey Cobras	53rd and Shields to Princeton
The Triangle	Latin Kings	Winona and Winthrop
The Valley	Black Disciples	71st and Racine

GANG FACTIONS

FACTION	GANG	LOCATION
The Vikings	Gangster Disciples	110th and State to Wentworth
The Ville	Gangster Disciples	114th to 116th and Parnell to Harvard
The Wall	Ambrose	54th Pl and Claremont
The Wall	Gangster Disciples	110th to 112th and Wallace
The Zones	Gangster Disciples	37th and Martin Luther King Dr
Therlow Ville	Gangster Disciples	39th to 40th and Lake Park
Third Ward	Gangster Disciples	71st to 73rd and Winchester
Thirsty Ville	Gangster Disciples	56th to 58th and Bishop
Tim City	Gangster Disciples	84th to 87th and Kedzie to California
Tinez City	Gangster Disciples	86th and Ingleside
Tip 17	Four Corner Hustlers	Van Buren From Lotus to Central
Titanic Stones	Black P Stones	Chicago Ave and Latrobe
Titanic Stones	Black P Stones	Drexel Sq and Cottage Grove
Titanic Stones	Black P Stones	51st to 55th and Cottage Grove to Ingleside
Titanic Stones	Titanic Stones	25th and Washtenaw (Lawndale Gardens)
Titanic Stones	Titanic Stones	61st and Cottage Grove
Titanic Stones	Titanic Stones	82nd and Baltimore
Titanic Stones	Titanic Stones	82nd and Cottage Grove
Titanic Stones	Titanic Stones	82nd and Houston
Titanic Stones	Titanic Stones	Drexel Sq and Cottage Grove
T-Love	Gangster Disciples	69th to 72nd and Loomis to Racine
T-Love	Gangster Disciples	70th to 71st and Throop
TMB (Touch Money Boys)	Gangster Disciples	45th to 46th and Vincennes to Evans
TMC (Too Much Cash)	Gangster Disciples	64th to 68th and California to Talman
TNG	Conservative Vice Lords	Walton and Lamon
TNI City	Traveling Vice Lords	Trumbull and Iowa
Tommieville	Black P Stones	61st and Evans
Tommy World	Gangster Disciples	105th and Wabash
Tommy World	Gangster Disciples	71st to 75th and Ellis to Evans
Tommy World	Gangster Disciples	71st to 73rd and Eberhart to Langley
Tone City	Black Disciples and Gangster Disciples	115th to 119th and Racine to Ashland
Tony World	Black P Stones	77th to 79th and Jeffrey to Kingston
Tookaville Gang (TVG)	Gangster Disciples	61st to 69th and Calumet to Champlain
Tookaville STL/FBG	Gangster Disciples	63rd and St Lawrence

GANG FACTIONS

FACTION	GANG	LOCATION
Toon Town	Black Disciples	63rd to 67th and King Drive
Touhy Herbert Park BDs	Black Disciples	Madison to Van Buren and Damen to Oakley
Trap City	Gangster Disciples	65th to 69th and Cottage Grove to St Lawrence
Trap City (004)	Gangster Disciples	70th to 80th and Constance
Trap City zone 7	Gangster Disciples and Black Disciples	67th to 69th and Cottage to King
Trap Life	Gangster Disciples	69th to 71st and Western to California
Trap Squad	Gangster Disciples	67th to 68th and Claremont
Trap Town Stones	Black P Stones	79th to 83rd and Halsted to Lowe
Trapp City	Satan Disciples	56th to 57th and Troy
Trapville	Latin Kings	Berwyn to Winnemac and Damen to Leavitt
Trauma Town	Maniac Campbell Boys	Lemoyne to Hirsch and Campbell to Artesian
Travelers Land	Traveling Vice Lords	Roosevelt and California
Travelers on Rice	Traveling Vice Lords	Rice and Lamon
Traveling Unknown Conservatives	Traveling Vice Lords	Chicago and Lawndale
Traveling Vice Lords	Traveling Vice Lords	107th and Normal
Traveling Vice Lords	Traveling Vice Lords	113th and Edbrooke
Traveling Vice Lords	Traveling Vice Lords	131st to 132nd and Langley to Corliss
Traveling Vice Lords	Traveling Vice Lords	15th to 16th and Christiana to Homan
Traveling Vice Lords	Traveling Vice Lords	18th and Hamlin
Traveling Vice Lords	Traveling Vice Lords	18th to 19th and Kedzie
Traveling Vice Lords	Traveling Vice Lords	91st and Colfax
Traveling Vice Lords	Traveling Vice Lords	Augusta and Kilpatrick
Traveling Vice Lords	Traveling Vice Lords	Chicago Ave and Lawndale
Traveling Vice Lords	Traveling Vice Lords	Chicago Ave and St Louis
Traveling Vice Lords	Traveling Vice Lords	Chicago Ave and Trumbull
Traveling Vice Lords	Traveling Vice Lords	Chicago to Ferdinand and Sacramento to Christiana
Traveling Vice Lords	Traveling Vice Lords	Congress and Central
Traveling Vice Lords	Traveling Vice Lords	Flournoy and Albany
Traveling Vice Lords	Traveling Vice Lords	Harrison and Central
Traveling Vice Lords	Traveling Vice Lords	Harrison to Roosevelt and Kedzie to Homan
Traveling Vice Lords	Traveling Vice Lords	Harrison to Roosevelt and Western to Washtenaw
Traveling Vice Lords	Traveling Vice Lords	Huron and St Louis
Traveling Vice Lords	Traveling Vice Lords	Huron to Ferdinand and Leamingto to Laramie
Traveling Vice Lords	Traveling Vice Lords	Leland and Magnolia

GANG FACTIONS

FACTION	GANG	LOCATION
Traveling Vice Lords	Traveling Vice Lords	Lemoyne and Cicero
Traveling Vice Lords	Traveling Vice Lords	Madison and Rockwell
Traveling Vice Lords	Traveling Vice Lords	Madison and Springfield
Traveling Vice Lords	Traveling Vice Lords	Monroe to Gladys on Central Ave
Traveling Vice Lords	Traveling Vice Lords	North to Grand and Cicero to Leclaire
Traveling Vice Lords	Traveling Vice Lords	North to Le Moyne and Luna to Central
Traveling Vice Lords	Traveling Vice Lords	Polk and California
Traveling Vice Lords	Traveling Vice Lords	Potomac to Crystal and Homan to Kedzie
Traveling Vice Lords	Traveling Vice Lords	Roosevelt to Douglas and Lawndale
Traveling Vice Lords	Traveling Vice Lords	Wabansia and Long
Tray Medina	Black P Stones	83rd and Colfax
Tre Block	Black Disciples	121st to 123rd and Michigan to State
Trey Boyz	Gangster Disciples	73rd and Dorchester
Trey Ward	Gangster Disciples	73rd and Racine
Triangle 4CH	Four Corner Hustlers	92nd to 93rd and University
Triangle GDs	Gangster Disciples	90th to 95th and Cottage to Kenwood
Triangle Park	Belizean Bloods	Evanston Border to Howard and Paulina to Clark
Tricky Ville Criminals (TVC)	Gangster Disciples	58th and Green to Sangamon
Triggatown	Black Disciples	123rd and Emerald to Union
Trigger Town	Four Corner Hustlers	Congress and Lockwood to Central
Trigger Town	Gangster Disciples	119th to 123rd and Eggleston to Halsted
Triple B's	Conservative Vice Lords	81st to 83rd and Saginaw to Exchange
Tripp City (001 of 002)	Spanish Cobras	Schubert to Fullerton and Keeler to Kenton
Tripp City (002 of 002)	Spanish Cobras	Fullerton to Dickens Keeler to Kostner
Trojans Point	Latin Brothers	Lockwood and Barry Ave
Troy Street	Latin Kings	25th to 26th and Troy
Trumbull City	Latin Kings	25th to 26th and Trumbull
TSG	Gangster Disciples	68th and Sangamon
TTE (Tay Town)	Black Disciples	60th and Normal
TTG	Gangster Disciples	79th to 83rd and Kedzie to Western
TTG (Tutu Gang)	Gangster Disciples	61st to 69th and Calumet to Champlain
TTM (Team Timmoe)	Gangster Disciples	83rd to 87th and Homan to California
Tuley Park	Black P Stones	91st and Martin Luther King Dr
Tuley Park	Gangster Disciples	87th to 91st and Martin Luther King Dr to Cottage Grove

GANG FACTIONS

FACTION	GANG	LOCATION
Tunchi World	Gangster Disciples	67th to 70th and Hamilton to Damen
Tunechi World	Black Gangsters (New Breed)	13th and Throop and Loomis
TuTu Gang	Gangster Disciples	61st to 69th and Calumet to Champlain
TVG (Tookaville Gang)	Gangster Disciples	61st to 69th and Calumet to Champlain
TW	Gangster Disciples	61st to 65th and Champlain to Vernon
Twelfth Street Players	Twelfth Street Players	18th and 61st
Twelfth Street Players	Twelfth Street Players	87th and Commercial
Twelfth Street Players	Twelfth Street Players	89th and Exchange
Twelfth Street Players	Twelfth Street Players	Roosevelt Rd to 14th and 61st ct
Twelve Deuce	Gangster Disciples	122nd to 123rd and Halsted to Ashland
Twi-Light Zone (01 of 02)	Maniac Latin Disciples	North to Crystal and Rockwell to California
Twi-Light Zone (02 of 02)	Maniac Latin Disciples	North to Hirsch and Artesian
Twin Town	Black Disciples	67th to 71st and Michigan to State
Two Feet Boys	Four Corner Hustlers	West End and Latrobe to Washington and Lotus
Two Five Keeler	Two Six	25th and Keeler
Two Four Karlov	Two Six	24th and Karlov
Two Four Rockwell	Satan Disciples	24th and Rockwell
Two Four Trumbull	Latin Kings	23rd to 25th and Trumbull to St. Louis
Two Fourz	Two Six	24th and 49th ave
Two Six	Two Six	28th to 31st and Tripp
Two Six	Two Six	24th to 26th and Springfield to Pulaski
Two Six	Two Six	26th to 28th and Karlov
Two Six	Two Six	26th to 28th and Tripp
Two Six	Two Six	27th and Keeler
Two Six	Two Six	27th and Tripp
Two Six	Two Six	27th to 30th and Komensky
Two Six	Two Six	27th to 31st and Kolin
Two Six	Two Six	28th to 33rd and Avers
Two Six	Two Six	28th to 33rd and Harding
Two Six	Two Six	28th to 33rd and Karlov
Two Six	Two Six	30th and Hamlin
Two Six	Two Six	30th and Lawndale
Two Six	Two Six	30th and Pulaski
Two Six	Two Six	35th to 39th and Western to Washtenaw

GANG FACTIONS

FACTION	GANG	LOCATION
Two Six	Two Six	35th to Archer and Washtenaw to St. Louis
Two Six	Two Six	62nd to 67th and Kedzie to Central Park
Two Six	Two Six	63rd and Hamlin
Two Six	Two Six	63rd to 67th and Mason to Kostner
Two Six	Two Six	63rd to 73rd and Central Park to Pulaski
Two Six	Two Six	79th and Lawndale
Two Six – 91st & Burley	Two Six	89th to 92nd and Buffalo to Burley
TYMB	Black Disciples	63rd to 65th and Cottage Grove to Drexel
U.P.T.s (Unplugged Thugs)	Gangster Disciples	110th to 115th and Indiana to Cottage
U-Block (Central City)	Gangster Disciples	76th and Union
Undertaker Vice Lords	Undertaker Vice Lords	Adams and Kilpatrick
Undertaker Vice Lords	Undertaker Vice Lords	Flournoy and Cicero
Undertaker Vice Lords	Undertaker Vice Lords	Jackson to Congress and Kolmar to Lavergne
Undertaker Vice Lords	Undertaker Vice Lords	Lexington to Arthington and Cicero to Lavergne
Undertaker Vice Lords	Undertaker Vice Lords	Race and Laramie
Undertaker Vice Lords	Undertaker Vice Lords	Van Buren and Cicero
Underwoods	Black P Stones	61st and Champlain
Union/Emerald Boys	Black P Stones	55th to 58th and Union to Halsted
Unit Boys	Four Corner Hustlers	West End to Maypole and Keeler to Karlov
University 4CH	Four Corner Hustlers	92nd to 93rd and University
Unknown Traveling Vice Lords	Unknown Traveling Vice Lords	Adams and Kilpatrick
Unknown Traveling Vice Lords	Unknown Traveling Vice Lords	Flournoy and Cicero
Unknown Traveling Vice Lords	Unknown Traveling Vice Lords	Gladys and Cicero
Unknown Traveling Vice Lords	Unknown Traveling Vice Lords	Ohio and Cicero Ave
Unknown Traveling Vice Lords	Unknown Traveling Vice Lords	Race and Laramie
Unknown Traveling Vice Lords	Unknown Traveling Vice Lords	Van Buren and Cicero
Unknown Traveling Vice Lords	Unknown Traveling Vice Lords	Van Buren to Harrison and Laramie to Kilpatrick
Unknown Vice Lords	Unknown Vice Lords	21st and Homan
Unknown Vice Lords	Unknown Vice Lords	73rd and Cottage Grove
Unknown Vice Lords	Unknown Vice Lords	Augusta and Central Park
Unknown Vice Lords	Unknown Vice Lords	Chicago Ave and Central Park
Unknown Vice Lords	Unknown Vice Lords	Chicago Ave and Drake
Unknown Vice Lords	Unknown Vice Lords	Chicago Ave and Homan to Kedzie
Unknown Vice Lords	Unknown Vice Lords	Chicago to Superior and Waller

GANG FACTIONS

FACTION	GANG	LOCATION
Unknown Vice Lords	Unknown Vice Lords	Erie and Cicero
Unknown Vice Lords	Unknown Vice Lords	Fifth and Homan
Unknown Vice Lords	Unknown Vice Lords	Huron and Lavergne
Unknown Vice Lords	Unknown Vice Lords	Iowa and Latrobe
Unknown Vice Lords	Unknown Vice Lords	Iowa and Sawyer
Unknown Vice Lords	Unknown Vice Lords	Jackson and Central Park
Unknown Vice Lords	Unknown Vice Lords	Jackson and Sacramento
Unknown Vice Lords	Unknown Vice Lords	Madison to Carroll and Pulaski to Kostner
Unknown Vice Lords	Unknown Vice Lords	Madison to Congress and Spaulding to Central Park
Unknown Vice Lords	Unknown Vice Lords	Monroe and Lockwood to Lotus
Unknown Vice Lords	Unknown Vice Lords	North to Hirsch and Leclaire to Leamington
Unknown Vice Lords	Unknown Vice Lords	Ohio and Lavergne
Unknown Vice Lords	Unknown Vice Lords	Polk and Kedzie
Unknown Vice Lords	Unknown Vice Lords	Potomac and Pulaski
Unknown Vice Lords	Unknown Vice Lords	Thomas to Augusta and Monticello to Lawndale
Unknown Vice Lords	Unknown Vice Lords	Washington to Madison and Kostner to Kilpatrick
UPT	Gangster Disciples	114th and Prairie
Uptop GDs	Gangster Disciples	91st to 97th and Eggleston to Dan Ryan
Uptown Gangsters	Gangster Disciples	Leland to Lawrence and Sheridan
Up-Town Green	Spanish Gangster Disciples	Broadway and Cuyler
Uptown Lords	Conservative Vice Lords	Agatite and Hazel
Uptown Lords	Conservative Vice Lords	Sunnyside and Claredon
Uptown Lords	Conservative Vice Lords	Wilson and Broadway
Uptown Lords	Conservative Vice Lords	Wilson to Montrose and Broadway to Claredon
Uptown Lords	Conservative Vice Lords	Windsor and Hazel
V Block	Black Disciples	71st and Vernon
Valley of Death	City Knights	48th and Wood
Vatican City	Insane Popes (Southside)	83rd and Homan
Vato Land	Insane Dragons	Iowa and Campbell
VBS (Van Buren & Sprinfield)	Four Corner Hustlers and Unknown Vice Lords	Van Buren to Jackson and Springfield
Venzel Block	Gangster Disciples	61st to 65th and Champlain to Vernon
Vernon BD's	Black Disciples	69th to 71st and Martin Luther King Dr to Eberhart
Vernon block/Vblock	Gangster Disciples	61st and Vernon
Vic Creek	Mickey Cobras	61st to 63rd and Cottage Grove

GANG FACTIONS

FACTION	GANG	LOCATION
Viperville	Latin Kings	Berwyn to Winnemac and Damen to Leavitt
VL City	Conservative Vice Lords	Central Ave and Monroe to Gladys
VL-City	Outlaw Lunatic Traveling Vice Lords	Quincy and Central
Vulture City	Gangster Disciples	49th to 51st and Federal to State
Wall Street	Gangster Disciples	99th to 103rd and Halsted to Eggleston
War Zone	Party People	18th to 19th and May
Ward Life	Gangster Disciples	67th to 70th and Hamilton to Damen
Warren Park LK's	Latin Kings	Albion and Western
WAWG (50 Strong)	Gangster Disciples	50th to 51st and Morgan to Halsted
WBNBC (Woods Beyond and New Breed City)	Black Gangsters (New Breeds) and Gangster Disciples	67th to 69th and Hermitage to Winchester
We All We Got (50 Strong)	Gangster Disciples	50th to 51st and Morgan to Halsted
Welch World	Gangster Disciples	39th to 41st and Federal to State
West End Body Snatchers	Four Corner Hustlers	West End to Madison and Menard to Mayfield
West End Money Gang (WMG)	Four Corner Hustlers	West End and Latrobe to Washington and Lotus
West GDs	Gangster Disciples	77th to 80th and St. Lawrence to Evans
Westgang (SKD)	Gangster Disciples	53rd and King Drive
Westside T-Stones	Black P Stones	Chicago to Ferdinand and Laramie to Central
Wheelworks	Gangster Disciples	103rd to 106th and Cottage Grove to Maryland
White Walls	Gangster Disciples	71st and Vincennes
White White (WWG)	Gangster Disciples	65th to 66th and Green
Whitey Gang	Black Disciples	63rd to 67th and King Drive
Whiz City	Black Disciples	82nd and Maryland to Ingleside
Whiz City	Black Disciples	80th to 83rd and Ellis to Cottage Grove
WIC City (Wild Insane Crazies)	Black Disciples	65th and Martin Luther King Dr.
Wicked City	Black P Stones	Lawrence to Montrose & Broadway to Clark
Wicked Town	Traveling Vice Lords	Ohio to Kinzie and Leamington to Laramie
Wickedville	Maniac Latin Disciples	31st and 49th Ave
Wicker Park Kings	Latin Kings	Potomac to Division and Wolcott to Damen
WIIC City	Black Disciples	63rd to 67th and Martin Luther King Dr
WIIC City	Black Disciples	64th and Martin Luther King Dr
Wilcox Boys	Gangster Disciples	Wilcox and Francisco
Wild 9	Gangster Disciples	59th to 63rd on Justine
Wild Bunch	Traveling Vice Lords	Huron and Trumbull

GANG FACTIONS

FACTION	GANG	LOCATION
Wild Bunch	Traveling Vice Lords	Ogden to Cermak and Homan to Central Park
Wild Insane Crazies (WIC)	Black Disciples	65th and Martin Luther King Dr
Wild Nine	Gangster Disciples	59th and Justine and Laflin
Wild Side	Ambrose	21st and Paulina
Wild Side	Gangster Disciples	111th to 119th and Princeton to Halsted
Wild Side	Maniac Latin Disciples	Altgeld to Fullerton and Washtenaw to Fairfield
Wild Side	Young Latin Organization Cobras	Dickens and Central Park
Wild West	Latin Kings	Armitage to North and Humboldt to Kedzie
Wild Wood	Satan Disciples	35th and Wood
Wildside	Latin Kings	38th and Lawndale
Wildville	Gangster Disciples	107th and Indiana
Will Gang	Mafia Insane Vice Lords	81st Pl to 83rd and Houston to Exchange
Willie P's	Four Corner Hustlers	Augusta to Iowa and Long to Pine
Willie Ville	Gangster Disciples	64th to 66th and Bishop to Justine
Willie Ville	Gangster Disciples	65th and Justine
Willy Ville	Gangster Disciples	64th to 66th and Bishop to Justine
Winchester Boys	Black P Stones	55th to 59th and Wood to Damen
Winchester Boys	Gangster Disciples	55th to 59th and Damen to Wood
Winona & Winthrop	Black P Stones	Winona to Argyle and Broadway to Sheridan
WO City	Four Corner Hustlers	68th to 71st and Dorchester to Stony Island
Wood Block	Four Corner Hustlers	Lake to Maypole and Wood to Wolcott
Wood Street	Gangster Disciples	51st to 55th and Paulina to Wolcott
Wood Street MCs	Mickey Cobras	55th to 58th and Hermitage to Wood
Woodlawn Boys	Gangster Disciples	47th and Cottage Grove
Woodlawn GDs	Gangster Disciples	46th and Drexel
Woods & Beyond	Black Gangsters (New Breeds)/Gangster Disciples	67th to 69th and Hermitage to Winchester
Wudae Gang	Black Disciples	60th and Normal
WWDC (Welch World Dub Club)	Gangster Disciples	39th to 41st and Federal to State
Yale Boys	Gangster Disciples	115th to 119th and Yale to Princeton
Yale Boys (007)	Gangster Disciples	70th to 75th and Vincennes to Stewart
Yam Boys	Gangster Disciples	79th to 83rd and May
Yatta World	Gangster Disciples	69th to 71st and South Shore to Jeffrey
YFN (Young Fucking Niggas)	Four Corner Hustlers	Madison to Washington and Leclaire
YIC (Youngsters In Charge)	Gangster Disciples	71st and Chappel and Paxton

GANG FACTIONS

FACTION	GANG	LOCATION
YIC (Youngsters In Charge)	Gangster Disciples	69th to 71st and South Shore to Jeffrey
YMHR (Young Money Hood Rich)	Black Disciples	Adams and Leavitt
YMLCMG	Black Disciples and Mickey Cobras	48th to 51st and Champlain to Ellis (51 and Cottage Grove)
YMM (Young Morgan Mafia)	Gangster Disciples	72nd to 75th and Morgan
YMOB	Gangster Disciples	74th and Homan
Young & Crazy	Young Latin Organization Cobras	Shakespeare and Central Park
Young Guns	Mickey Cobras	44th to 47th and Shields to Princeton
Young Latin Organization Cobras	Young Latin Organization Cobras	Armitage to Cortland and Central Park to Hamlin
Young Latin Organization Cobras	Young Latin Organization Cobras	Cortland and Lawndale
Young Latin Organization Cobras	Young Latin Organization Cobras	Cortland and Monticello
Young Latin Organization Cobras	Young Latin Organization Cobras	Francis and Stave
Young Latin Organization Cobras	Young Latin Organization Cobras	George and Avers
Young Latin Organization Cobras	Young Latin Organization Cobras	McLean and Lawndale
Young Latin Organization Cobras	Young Latin Organization Cobras	Schubert and Avers (Koz Park)
Young Latin Organization Disciples	Young Latin Organization Disciples	Bloomingdale to North and California to Humboldt
Young Latin Organization Disciples	Young Latin Organization Disciples	Cortland and Richmond
Young Latin Organization Disciples	Young Latin Organization Disciples	Francisco and Wabansia
Young Latin Organization Disciples	Young Latin Organization Disciples	Keystone and Lemoyne
Young Life	Gangster Disciples	72nd to 74th and Racine to Laflin
Young Money	Black Disciples	63rd to 65th and Cottage Grove to Drexel
Young Money	Black Disciples	65th and Union
Young Money	Black P Stones	50th and Drexel
Young Money 051	Mickey Cobras	51st and Cottage Grove
Young Money Hood Rich	Black Disciples	Adams and Leavitt
Young Money Los City Money Gang	Black Disciples and Mickey Cobras	48th to 51st and Champlain to Ellis (51st and Cottage Grove)
Young Money TYMB	Black Disciples	65th and Maryland
Youngins in Charge (YIC)	Gangster Disciples	71st and Paxton
Youngsters In Charge	Gangster Disciples	71st and Chappel
YTTF	Young Latin Organization Disciples	Keystone and Wabansia
Zael World	Gangster Disciples	65th to 69th and Cottage Grove to St Lawrence
Zekoworld	Mickey Cobras	48th to 51st and Ellis to Martin Luther King Dr
Zo Land	Four Corner Hustlers	68th to 71st and Dorchester to Stony Island
Zo World	Mafia Insane Vice Lords	81st Pl to 83rd and Houston to Exchange
Zone	Maniac Latin Disciples	North to Crystal and Rockwell to California

GANG FACTIONS

FACTION	GANG	LOCATION
Zone 20	Black Disciples	120th to 125th and Princeton to Halsted
Zone 7	Gangster Disciples	65th to 69th and Cottage Grove to St Lawrence
Zone 8	Gangster Disciples	67th to 68th and Claremont

FEMALE GANG MEMBERSHIP

In the face of the overwhelming violence perpetuated by and affecting young men trapped in the world of gang conflict, it is all too easy to overlook females also stranded in this unsafe, unstable environment. These girls make up less than 10% of gang members but face the highest rates of victim/offender overlap and often endure cruel, dehumanizing treatment from gang members they are attempting to appease. In order to properly address the issue of female gang membership, it is essential to understand why girls join gangs to begin with.

Reasons for Joining

Research suggests girls join gangs for many of the same reasons boys do. These motivating factors include protection from other gangs or neighborhood violence, a source of income, pre-existing social or familial connections to a gang, and a path to earning respect. This desire for respect is particularly important with females who enter

Alleged female gang member, Chicago, IL

gangs. Girls who grow up in an environment where they feel undervalued and powerless, whether familial or social, are likely to seek out ways to gain any semblance of authority and respect. Often times, this comes through gang membership. Ironically, once affiliated with a gang, girls tend to lose virtually all power.

Girls are more likely than boys to join a gang in search of a surrogate familial structure. In fact, a lack of parental supervision and monitoring has been shown to be a notable risk factor for female gang membership. In addition, female gang membership has also shown to correlate with neighborhood disorganization and low school attachment – girls who are joining gangs tend to be coming from communities without a great deal of stability, safety, and commitment, and their education is often marred by these same challenges. In addition, female gang members are likely to have endured childhood physical and/or sexual abuse. Once involved with a gang, girls often continue to suffer this type of trauma, and it becomes nearly impossible to envision any escape from this vicious cycle.

Roles

It is difficult to develop an accurate representation of the role girls play once they are actually part of a gang. Admittedly, females do make up a much smaller proportion of gang members, making it challenging to collect data. In fact, when surveyed, over 25% of police departments nationally had no data on female gang membership. Even so, Public Information Officer and Special Agent David Coulson of the Bureau of Alcohol, Tobacco, Firearms and Explosives (ATF) Chicago Field Division reports female gang members often play an essential role in the criminal activities of their organization. For many years, ATF has identified a trend of straw purchasing by women on behalf of their male counterparts in gangs. Without extensive criminal records, female gang members are used to purchase guns on behalf of the gang in which they belong. In this way, female gang members and affiliates are entirely embedded in the gang's activities, even as they are treated as inferior members within the gangs and their communities.

Female Gang Intervention and Prevention

Female gang members represent a population that is incredibly vulnerable, but also one for which there is great promise for successful intervention. Female gang members experience high rates of abuse, both at home and within their gang. Experts have shown that, in general, females are more likely than males to internalize the stress resulting from trauma such as this, many times leading to both physical and or psychological self-harming behavior. Providing services and resources to female gang members to prevent initiation into or facilitate exits from gangs would help support an entire generation of women who face this threat to their psychological and physical development. Given the proper resources, girls are more likely not only to escape gang life, but to stay clear of it permanently, shown through statistics of female prisoners with lower recidivism rates than their male counterparts.

Gakirah Barnes, 17, self-identified gang member, Chicago, IL, murdered on April 11, 2014

Alleged female gang member, Chicago, IL

Even with this information, there is a disgraceful lack of resources for young women who are at risk for gang involvement. Of the Federally funded $272 million set aside for juvenile justice programs, only $2 million goes toward supporting girls. There are many rising programs that address young men specifically, with the goal of minimizing risk factors contributing to both entry and commitment to a gang; parallel preventative programs for girls

would do well to focus on the risk factors shown to be particularly prevalent for female gang members. For example, since there is a high correlation between female gang membership and lack of parental supervision, programs providing young women with consistent, reliable mentorship may be helpful in reducing the possibility of future gang membership. Therapy and supportive services targeted toward healing survivors' experiences of sexual, physical, and emotional trauma are also sorely needed to serve the women who manage to escape gang life, many of whom have endured lifetimes of abuse.

Several organizations in Chicago do focus on the young female population either already or potentially submerged in gang lifestyle. *Working on Womanhood* and its partner program *Becoming a Man* focuses on young women who face the most significant risk factors for gang affiliation or other forms of violence. These girls participate in over 30 weeks of therapy-based small-group sessions designed to address conflict resolution, family issues, addiction, and educational achievement. Another organization, *Demoiselle 2 Femme*, provides services, education, and prevention programs to girls ages 13-19. Topics addressed by these programs include HIV / AIDS, obesity, teen pregnancy, substance abuse, violence, money management, and college access. These programs exemplifies that the capacity to provide for and support these young women does exist. In providing effective and committed programs that assist young women in obtaining the services and support they require is critical to combatting gang violence and gang culture.

Conclusion

Female gang members – and the young women threatened into joining gangs – face immense trauma, danger, and hopelessness. Through recognizing and addressing these challenges, communities and families can prevent an entire population of women who deserve support from being targeted and victimized by gangs. By taking proactive steps to provide support services for at-risk women, lives can be saved. Inaction is no longer an option as an epidemic of gang violence inflicts entire communities, schools, churches, families, and businesses.

Images retrieved from the Instagram account once belonging to Gakirah Barnes, 17, self-identified gang member, Chicago, IL, murdered on April 11, 2014.

Tagging crews differ from traditional streets gangs in many ways. Tagging crews are comprised of skateboarders, MC rappers, DJs, and break dancers. In addition, they do not engage in violent acts like retaliations, initiations, or turf wars as observed by Chicago street gangs. Taggers instead vandalize various surfaces across the Chicago metropolitan area.

Similar to gang members, taggers spray-paint their crew or their tagger name on a building's surface. Although the graffiti may look the same, the graffiti painted by taggers does not include any disrespecting symbols taunting rival gangs. Typically, a tagger's crew or name is graphically displayed in many different styles such as large bubbly letters. Generally, the letters are filled in completely using vibrant colors and/or the tagger's crew and name could be disguised using various symbols. Despite their established locations, these individuals tag across the Chicago metropolitan area, including surrounding suburbs. Taggers chose a location that will give them exposure to the public. They also choose locations which can be hard to get to, just for maximum visibility.

Tagging Crew	Meaning
AIR	24-7
CAB (312)	Always write 312
CCA	Can't Catch Aid
CMK	Chicago Must Know, Crown Me King, Crawford Mural Kids (Steel Mills)
COH	Code of Honor
DC-5	Deaf Con 5
FEDS	Freshest Even Def Style
H2O	Hell To Offer
IWM (IW)	Ill Wall Master, Inhaling Wicked Marijuana
J4F	Just For Fun
KCM	Kan't Catch Me, King's Catch Mischief
KIDS	Kids In Dope Street
LFV	Lil Fucking Village
MUL	Made U Look
SFA	Soldier Founding America
VTC	Vicious Tagging Crew, Vandals Taking Chicago, Vandals, Talk Cash
3XD (TNK, TNS, TDS)	3 X Dope (The Notorious Klan, The Native Soul, The Death Squad)

TAGGING

Examples of Chicago Tagging

SECTION II

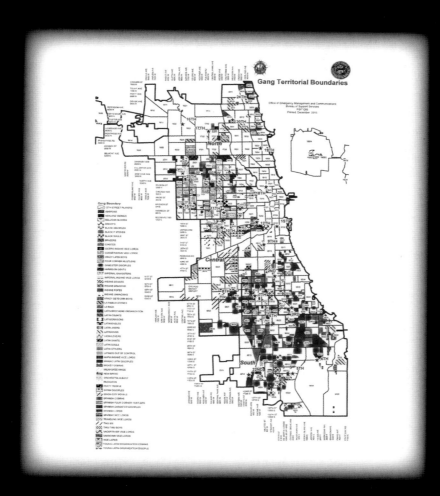

Chicago Gang Maps

chicago
crime
commission

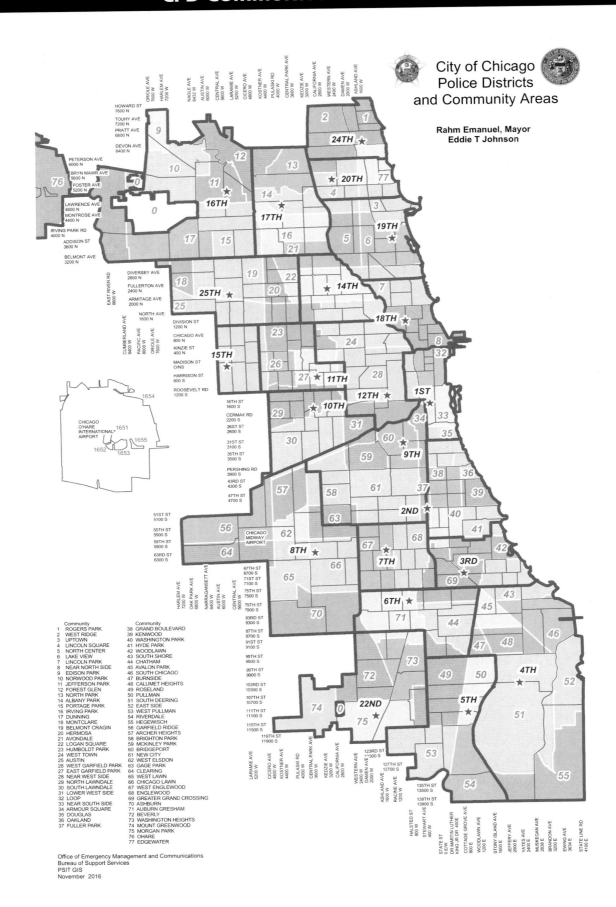

City of Chicago
Police Districts
and Community Areas

Rahm Emanuel, Mayor
Eddie T Johnson

	Community		Community
1	ROGERS PARK	38	GRAND BOULEVARD
2	WEST RIDGE	39	KENWOOD
3	UPTOWN	40	WASHINGTON PARK
4	LINCOLN SQUARE	41	HYDE PARK
5	NORTH CENTER	42	WOODLAWN
6	LAKE VIEW	43	SOUTH SHORE
7	LINCOLN PARK	44	CHATHAM
8	NEAR NORTH SIDE	45	AVALON PARK
9	EDISON PARK	46	SOUTH CHICAGO
10	NORWOOD PARK	47	BURNSIDE
11	JEFFERSON PARK	48	CALUMET HEIGHTS
12	FOREST GLEN	49	ROSELAND
13	NORTH PARK	50	PULLMAN
14	ALBANY PARK	51	SOUTH DEERING
15	PORTAGE PARK	52	EAST SIDE
16	IRVING PARK	53	WEST PULLMAN
17	DUNNING	54	RIVERDALE
18	MONTCLARE	55	HEGEWISCH
19	BELMONT CRAGIN	56	GARFIELD RIDGE
20	HERMOSA	57	ARCHER HEIGHTS
21	AVONDALE	58	BRIGHTON PARK
22	LOGAN SQUARE	59	MCKINLEY PARK
23	HUMBOLDT PARK	60	BRIDGEPORT
24	WEST TOWN	61	NEW CITY
25	AUSTIN	62	WEST ELSDON
26	WEST GARFIELD PARK	63	GAGE PARK
27	EAST GARFIELD PARK	64	CLEARING
28	NEAR WEST SIDE	65	WEST LAWN
29	NORTH LAWNDALE	66	CHICAGO LAWN
30	SOUTH LAWNDALE	67	WEST ENGLEWOOD
31	LOWER WEST SIDE	68	ENGLEWOOD
32	LOOP	69	GREATER GRAND CROSSING
33	NEAR SOUTH SIDE	70	ASHBURN
34	ARMOUR SQUARE	71	AUBURN GRESHAM
35	DOUGLAS	72	BEVERLY
36	OAKLAND	73	WASHINGTON HEIGHTS
37	FULLER PARK	74	MOUNT GREENWOOD
		75	MORGAN PARK
		76	OHARE
		77	EDGEWATER

Office of Emergency Management and Communications
Bureau of Support Services
PSIT GIS
November 2016

II – Gang Maps

KNOWN GANG MEMBERSHIP PER DISTRICT

1st District Gang Territory
Known Gang Members: 240

2nd District Gang Territory
Known Gang Members: 1,130

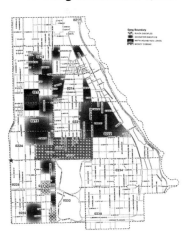

3rd District Gang Territory
Known Gang Members: 1,170

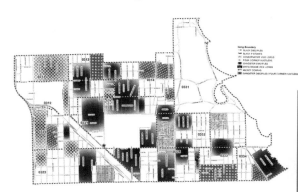

II – Gang Maps

4th District Gang Territory
Known Gang Members: 1,968

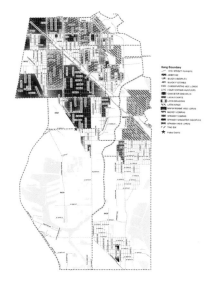

5th District Gang Territory
Known Gang Members: 1,465

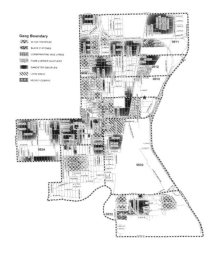

6th District Gang Territory
Known Gang Members: 1,455

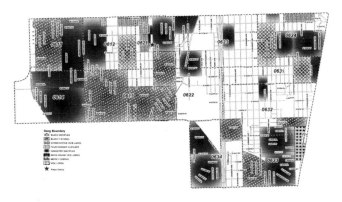

7th District Gang Territory
Known Gang Members: 1,690

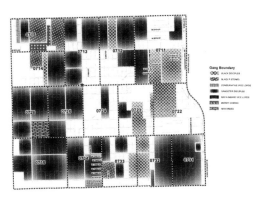

KNOWN GANG MEMBERSHIP PER DISTRICT

II – Gang Maps

8th District Gang Territory
Known Gang Members: 900

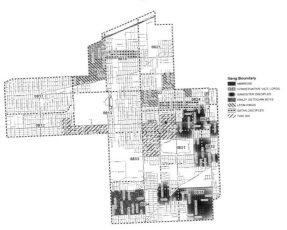

9th District Gang Territory
Known Gang Members: 2,260

10th District Gang Territory
Known Gang Members: 3,085

11th District Gang Territory
Known Gang Members: 1,640

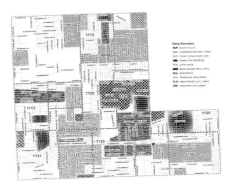

12th District Gang Territory
Known Gang Members: 550

15th District Gang Territory
Known Gang Members: 2,110

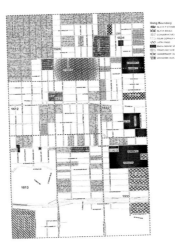

14th District Gang Territory
Known Gang Members: 675

16th District Gang Territory
Known Gang Members: 40

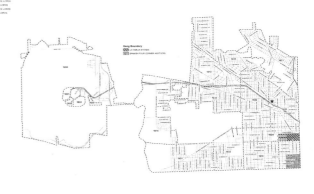

KNOWN GANG MEMBERSHIP PER DISTRICT

17th District Gang Territory
Known Gang Members: 410

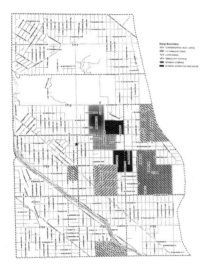

18th District Gang Territory
Known Gang Members: 75

19th District Gang Territory
Known Gang Members: 105

II – Gang Maps

20th District Gang Territory
Known Gang Members: 450

22nd District Gang Territory
Known Gang Members: 930

24th District Gang Territory
Known Gang Members: 355

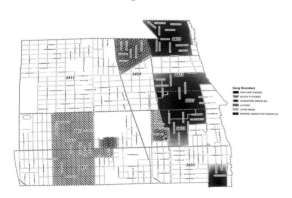

25th District Gang Territory
Known Gang Members: 1,285

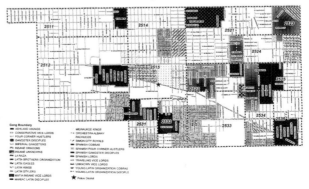

1ST DISTRICT GANG TERRITORIAL BOUNDARY

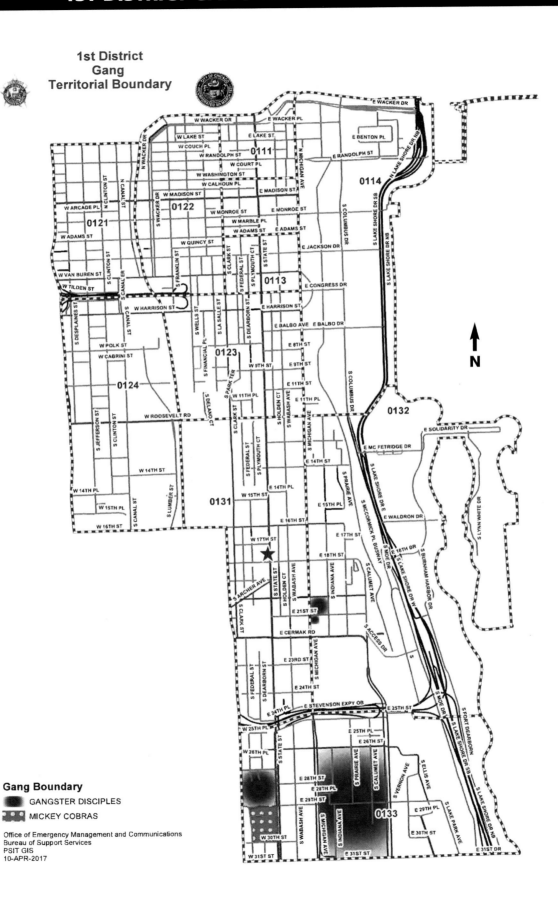

1st District Gang Territorial Boundary

Gang Boundary

GANGSTER DISCIPLES

MICKEY COBRAS

Office of Emergency Management and Communications
Bureau of Support Services
PSIT GIS
10-APR-2017

II – Gang Maps

2ND DISTRICT GANG TERRITORIAL BOUNDARY

2nd District Gang Territorial Boundary

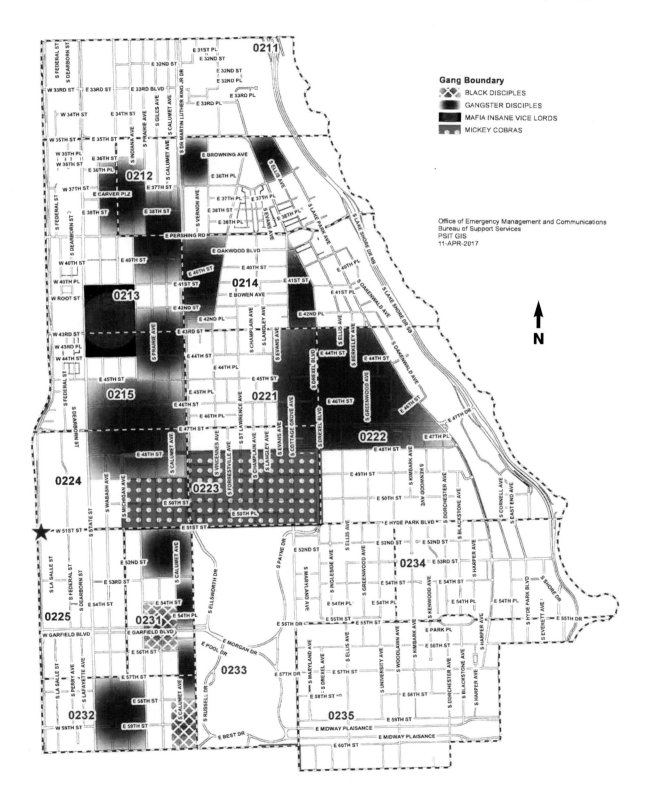

Gang Boundary
- BLACK DISCIPLES
- GANGSTER DISCIPLES
- MAFIA INSANE VICE LORDS
- MICKEY COBRAS

Office of Emergency Management and Communications
Bureau of Support Services
PSIT GIS
11-APR-2017

II – Gang Maps

3RD DISTRICT GANG TERRITORIAL BOUNDARY

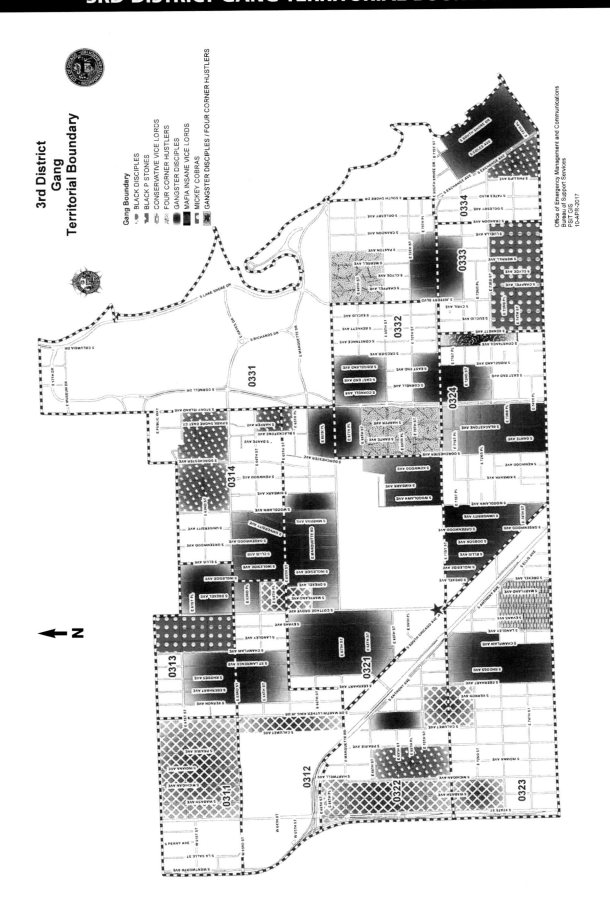

4TH DISTRICT GANG TERRITORIAL BOUNDARY

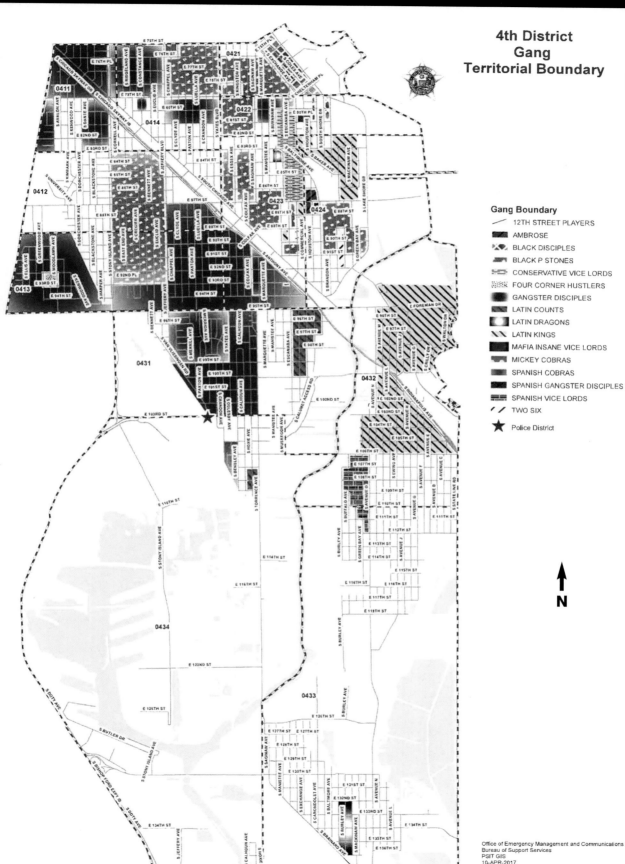

4th District Gang Territorial Boundary

II – Gang Maps

Gang Boundary

- 12TH STREET PLAYERS
- AMBROSE
- BLACK DISCIPLES
- BLACK P STONES
- CONSERVATIVE VICE LORDS
- FOUR CORNER HUSTLERS
- GANGSTER DISCIPLES
- LATIN COUNTS
- LATIN DRAGONS
- LATIN KINGS
- MAFIA INSANE VICE LORDS
- MICKEY COBRAS
- SPANISH COBRAS
- SPANISH GANGSTER DISCIPLES
- SPANISH VICE LORDS
- TWO SIX
- ★ Police District

N

Office of Emergency Management and Communications
Bureau of Support Services
PSIT GIS
10-APR-2017

5TH DISTRICT GANG TERRITORIAL BOUNDARY

**5th District
Gang Faction
Territorial Boundary**

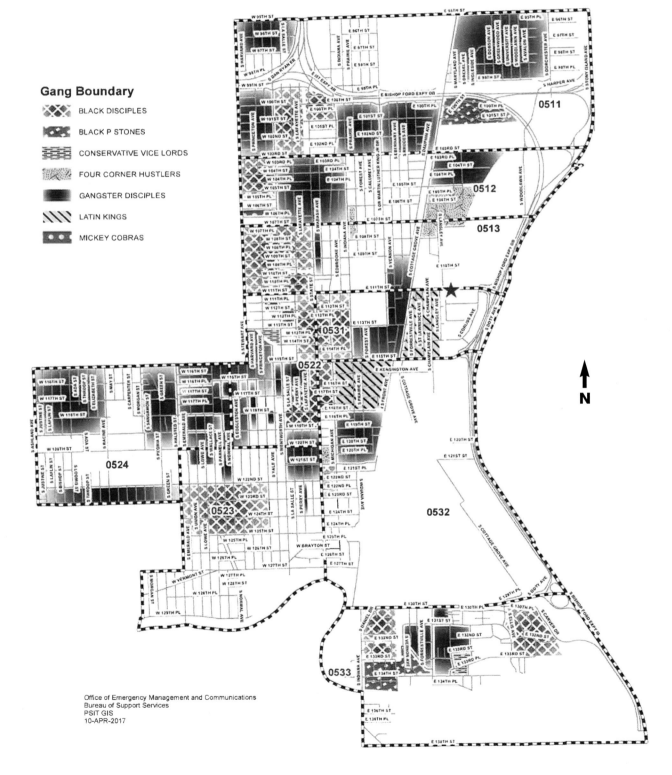

II – Gang Maps

Gang Boundary

- BLACK DISCIPLES
- BLACK P STONES
- CONSERVATIVE VICE LORDS
- FOUR CORNER HUSTLERS
- GANGSTER DISCIPLES
- LATIN KINGS
- MICKEY COBRAS

Office of Emergency Management and Communications
Bureau of Support Services
PSIT GIS
10-APR-2017

6TH DISTRICT GANG TERRITORIAL BOUNDARY

II – Gang Maps

6th District
Gang Faction
Territorial Boundary

Office of Emergency Management and Communications
Bureau of Support Services
PSIT GIS
10-APR-2017

Gang Boundary
- BLACK DISCIPLES
- BLACK P STONES
- CONSERVATIVE VICE LORDS
- FOUR CORNER HUSTLERS
- GANGSTER DISCIPLES
- MAFIA INSANE VICE LORDS
- MICKEY COBRAS
- VICE LORDS
- ★ Police District

N

7TH DISTRICT GANG TERRITORIAL BOUNDARY

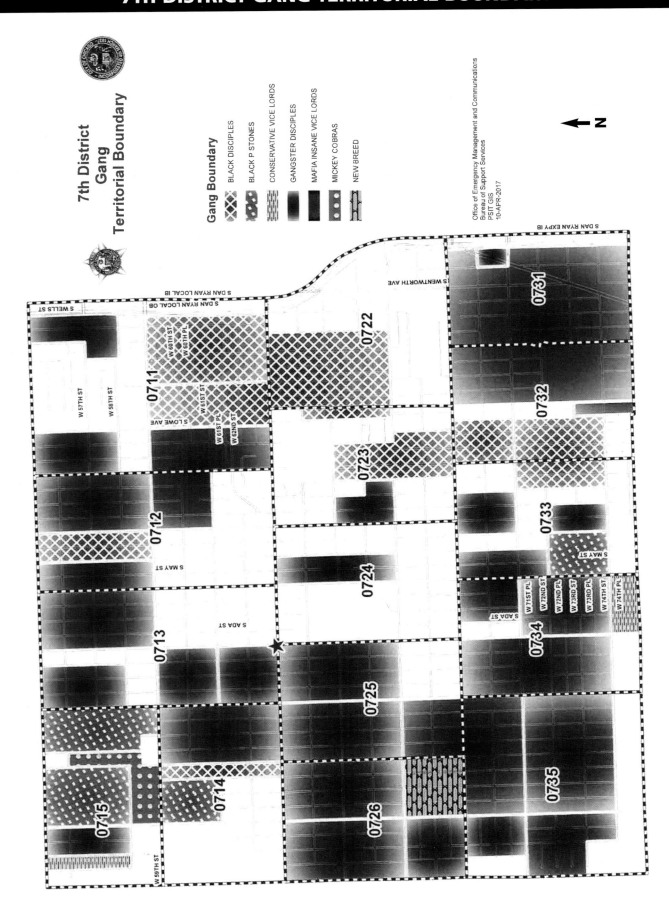

7th District Gang Territorial Boundary

Gang Boundary

- BLACK DISCIPLES
- BLACK P STONES
- CONSERVATIVE VICE LORDS
- GANGSTER DISCIPLES
- MAFIA INSANE VICE LORDS
- MICKEY COBRAS
- NEW BREED

Office of Emergency Management and Communications
Bureau of Support Services
PSIT GIS
10-APR-2017

II – Gang Maps

8TH DISTRICT GANG TERRITORIAL BOUNDARY

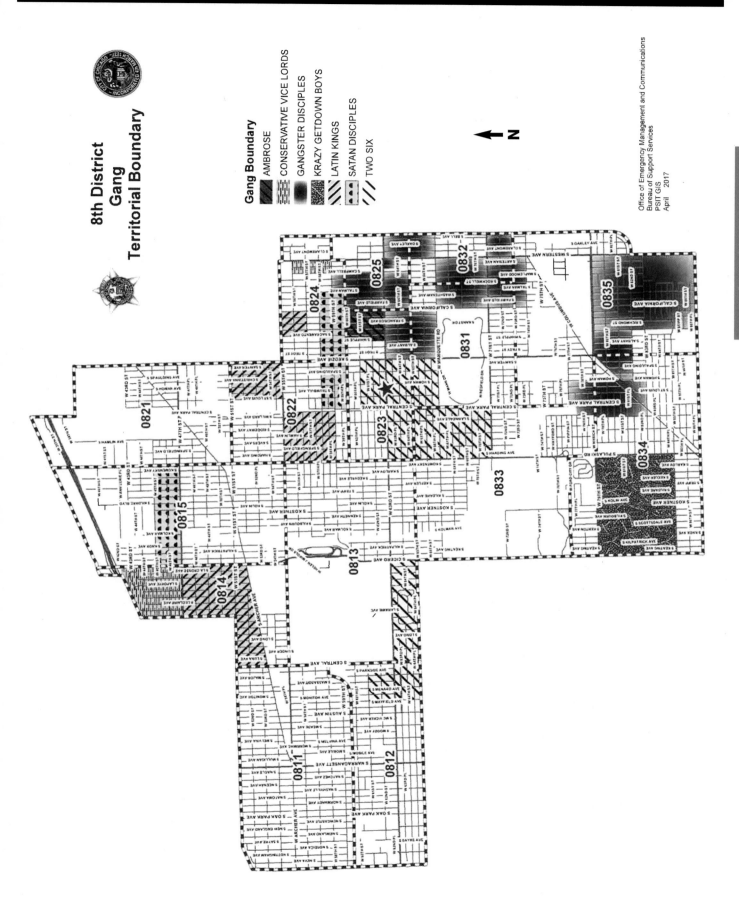

8th District
Gang
Territorial Boundary

Gang Boundary
- AMBROSE
- CONSERVATIVE VICE LORDS
- GANGSTER DISCIPLES
- KRAZY GETDOWN BOYS
- LATIN KINGS
- SATAN DISCIPLES
- TWO SIX

Office of Emergency Management and Communications
Bureau of Support Services
PSIT GIS
April 2017

II – Gang Maps

9TH DISTRICT GANG TERRITORIAL BOUNDARY

II – Gang Maps

9th District
Gang
Territorial Boundary

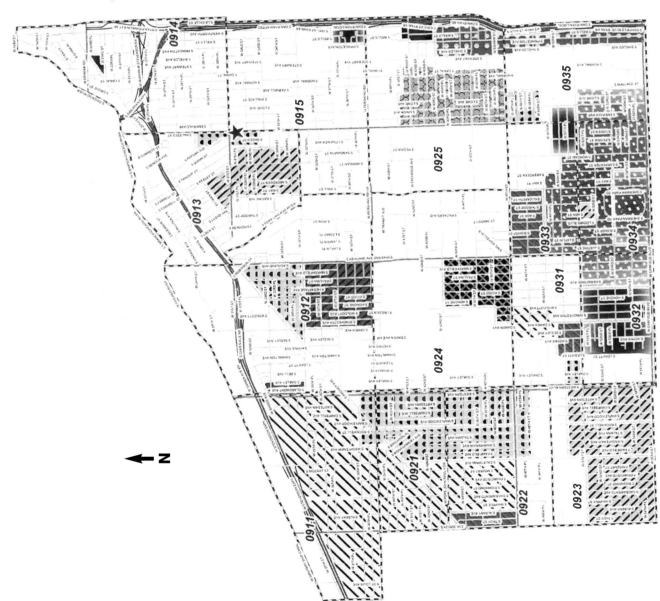

Gang Boundary

- BLACK P STONES
- CONSERVATIVE VICE LORDS
- CRAZY LATIN BOYS
- GANGSTER DISCIPLES
- INSANE DEUCES
- LA RAZA
- LATIN COUNTS
- LATIN KINGS
- LATIN SAINTS
- MAFIA INSANE VICE LORDS
- MICKEY COBRAS
- SATAN DISCIPLES
- TWO SIX
- ★ Police District

Office of Emergency Management and Communications
Bureau of Support Services
PSIT GIS
April 2017

10TH DISTRICT GANG TERRITORIAL BOUNDARY

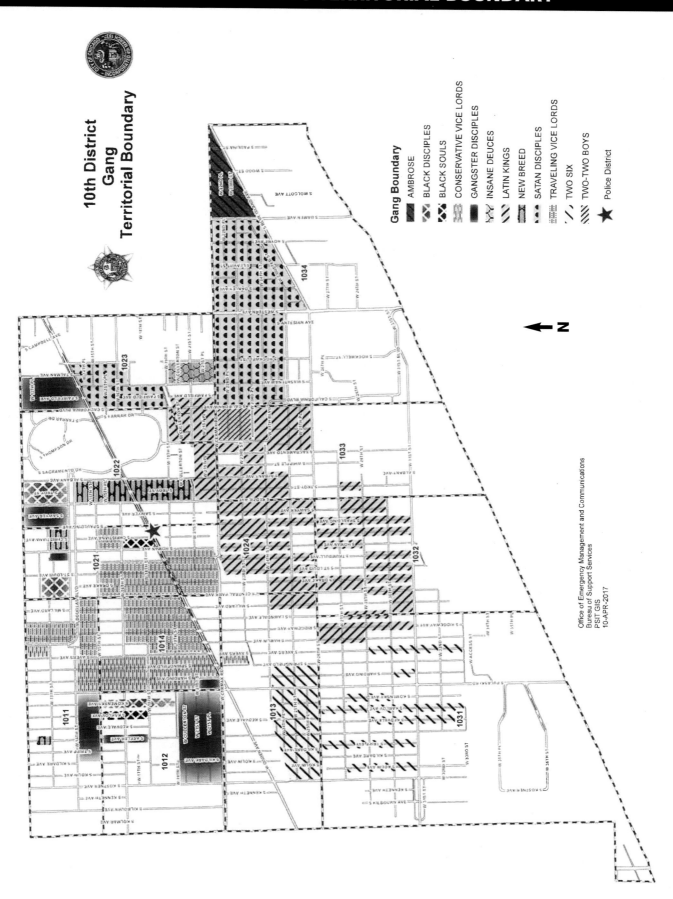

10th District Gang Territorial Boundary

Gang Boundary
- AMBROSE
- BLACK DISCIPLES
- BLACK SOULS
- CONSERVATIVE VICE LORDS
- GANGSTER DISCIPLES
- INSANE DEUCES
- LATIN KINGS
- NEW BREED
- SATAN DISCIPLES
- TRAVELING VICE LORDS
- TWO SIX
- TWO-TWO BOYS
- ★ Police District

Office of Emergency Management and Communications
Bureau of Support Services
PSIT GIS
10-APR-2017

II – Gang Maps

11TH DISTRICT GANG TERRITORIAL BOUNDARY

II – Gang Maps

11th District Gang Territorial Boundary

Gang Boundary

- BLACK SOULS
- CONSERVATIVE VICE LORDS
- FOUR CORNER HUSTLERS
- GANGSTER DISCIPLES
- LATIN KINGS
- MAFIA INSANE VICE LORDS
- NEW BREED
- TRAVELING VICE LORDS
- UNDERTAKER VICE LORDS
- UNKNOWN VICE LORDS

Office of Emergency Management and Communications
Bureau of Support Services
PSIT GIS
10-APR-2017

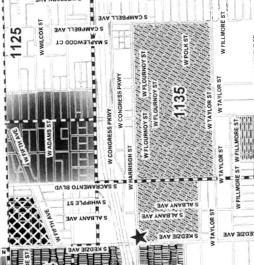

12TH DISTRICT GANG TERRITORIAL BOUNDARY

**12th District
Gang
Territorial Boundary**

Gang Boundary

- AMBROSE
- BISHOPS
- BLACK DISCIPLES
- BLACK SOULS
- C-NOTES
- FOUR CORNER HUSTLERS
- HARRISON GENTS
- INSANE DRAGONS
- LA RAZA
- LATIN COUNTS
- LATIN KINGS
- NEW BREED
- PARTY PEOPLE
- SATAN DISCIPLES
- SPANISH COBRAS
- TRAVELING VICE LORDS
- VICE LORDS

Office of Emergency Management and Communications
Bureau of Support Services
PSIT GIS
03-AUG-2017

14TH DISTRICT GANG TERRITORIAL BOUNDARY

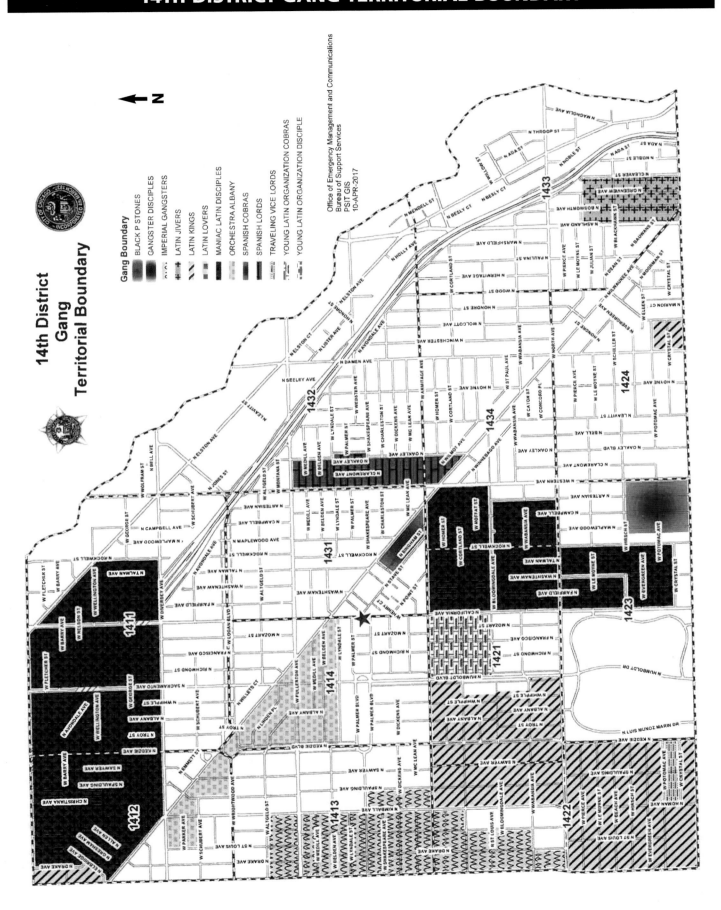

14th District
Gang
Territorial Boundary

Gang Boundary
- BLACK P STONES
- GANGSTER DISCIPLES
- IMPERIAL GANGSTERS
- LATIN JIVERS
- LATIN KINGS
- LATIN LOVERS
- MANIAC LATIN DISCIPLES
- ORCHESTRA ALBANY
- SPANISH COBRAS
- SPANISH LORDS
- TRAVELING VICE LORDS
- YOUNG LATIN ORGANIZATION COBRAS
- YOUNG LATIN ORGANIZATION DISCIPLE

Office of Emergency Management and Communications
Bureau of Support Services
PSIT GIS
10-APR-2017

15TH DISTRICT GANG TERRITORIAL BOUNDARY

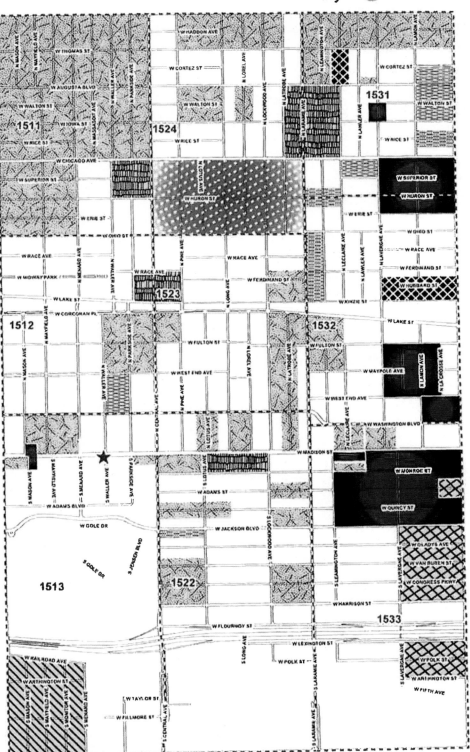

II – Gang Maps

16TH DISTRICT GANG TERRITORIAL BOUNDARY

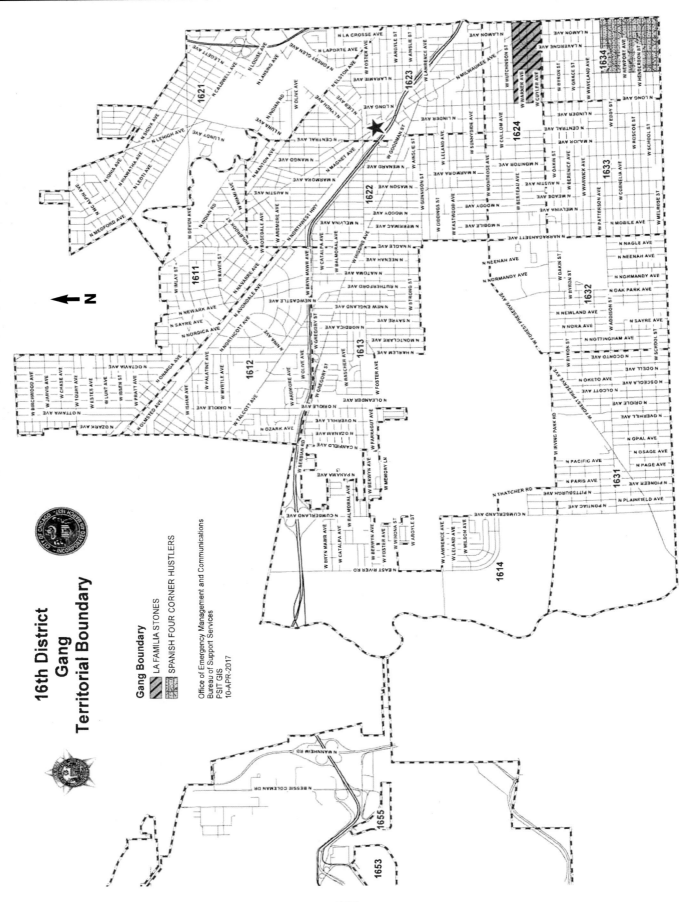

16th District Gang Territorial Boundary

Gang Boundary

LA FAMILIA STONES

SPANISH FOUR CORNER HUSTLERS

Office of Emergency Management and Communications
Bureau of Support Services
PSIT GIS
10-APR-2017

II – Gang Maps

17TH DISTRICT GANG TERRITORIAL BOUNDARY

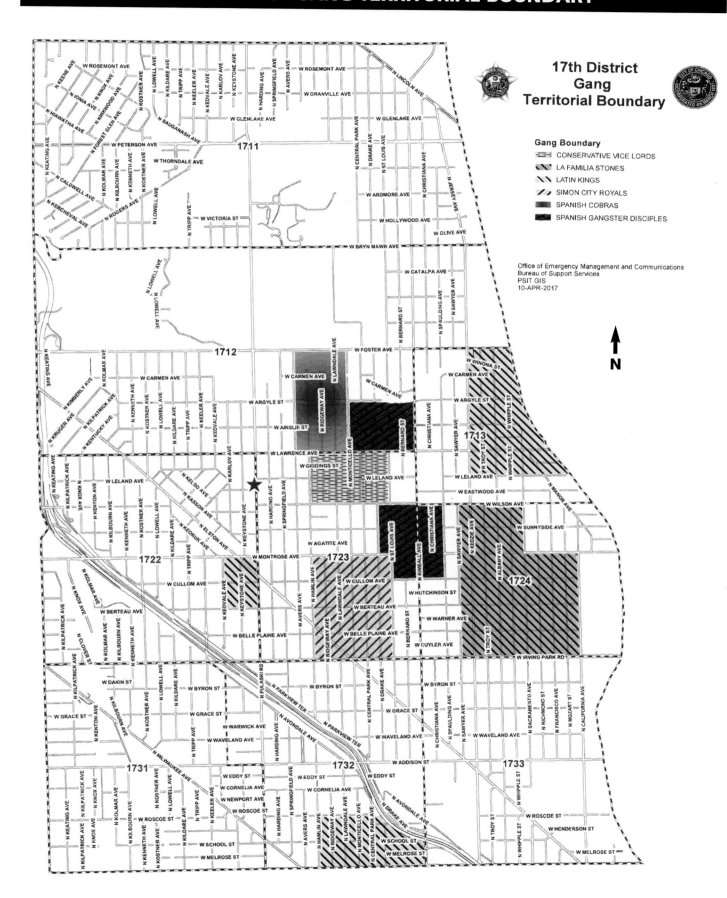

**17th District
Gang
Territorial Boundary**

Gang Boundary
- CONSERVATIVE VICE LORDS
- LA FAMILIA STONES
- LATIN KINGS
- SIMON CITY ROYALS
- SPANISH COBRAS
- SPANISH GANGSTER DISCIPLES

Office of Emergency Management and Communications
Bureau of Support Services
PSIT GIS
10-APR-2017

II – Gang Maps

18TH DISTRICT GANG TERRITORIAL BOUNDARY

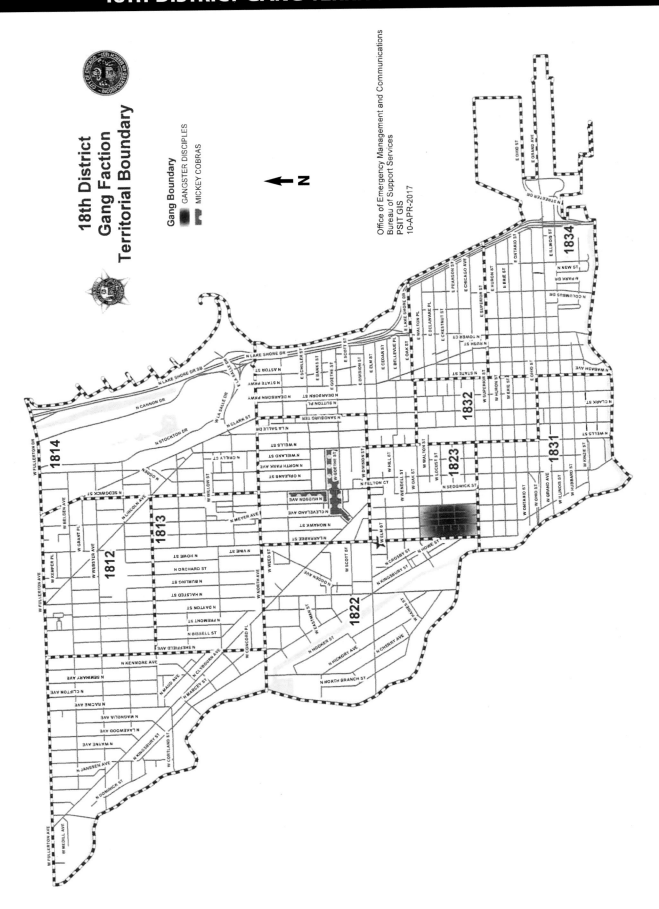

18th District
Gang Faction
Territorial Boundary

Gang Boundary
GANGSTER DISCIPLES
MICKEY COBRAS

N

Office of Emergency Management and Communications
Bureau of Support Services
PSIT GIS
10-APR-2017

19TH DISTRICT GANG TERRITORIAL BOUNDARY

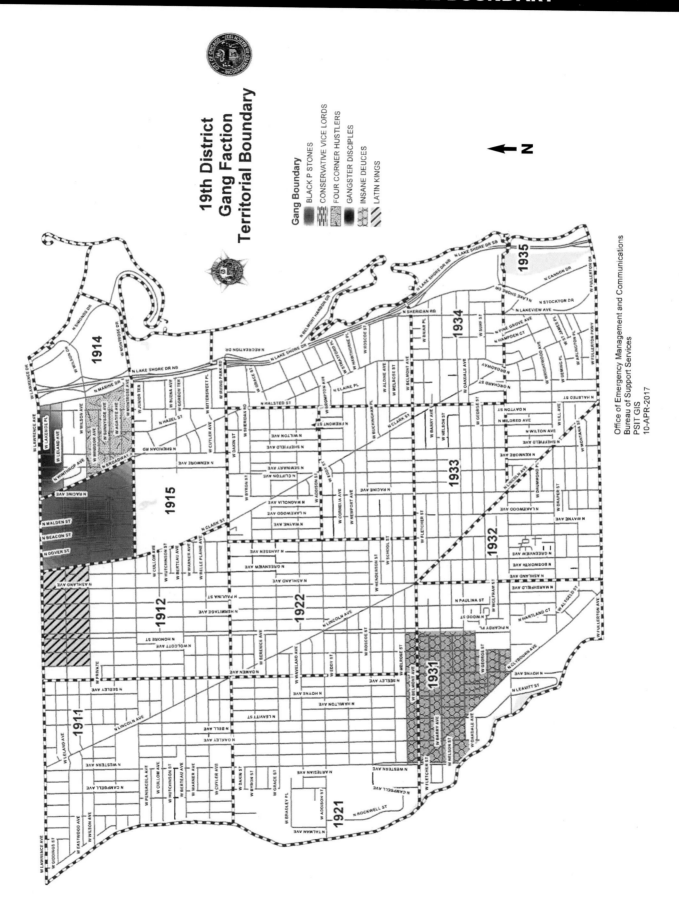

19th District
Gang Faction
Territorial Boundary

Gang Boundary
BLACK P STONES
CONSERVATIVE VICE LORDS
FOUR CORNER HUSTLERS
GANGSTER DISCIPLES
INSANE DEUCES
LATIN KINGS

N

Office of Emergency Management and Communications
Bureau of Support Services
PSIT GIS
10-APR-2017

20TH DISTRICT GANG TERRITORIAL BOUNDARY

II – Gang Maps

20th District Gang Territorial Boundary

22ND DISTRICT GANG TERRITORIAL BOUNDARY

**22nd District
Gang
Territorial Boundary**

Office of Emergency Management and Communications
Bureau of Support Services
PSIT GIS
10-APR-2017

II – Gang Maps

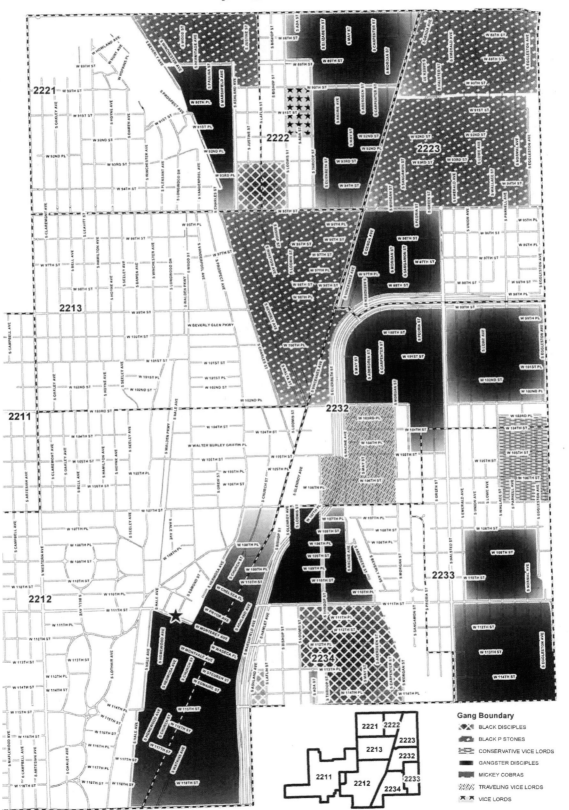

Gang Boundary

- BLACK DISCIPLES
- BLACK P STONES
- CONSERVATIVE VICE LORDS
- GANGSTER DISCIPLES
- MICKEY COBRAS
- TRAVELING VICE LORDS
- VICE LORDS

24TH DISTRICT GANG TERRITORIAL BOUNDARY

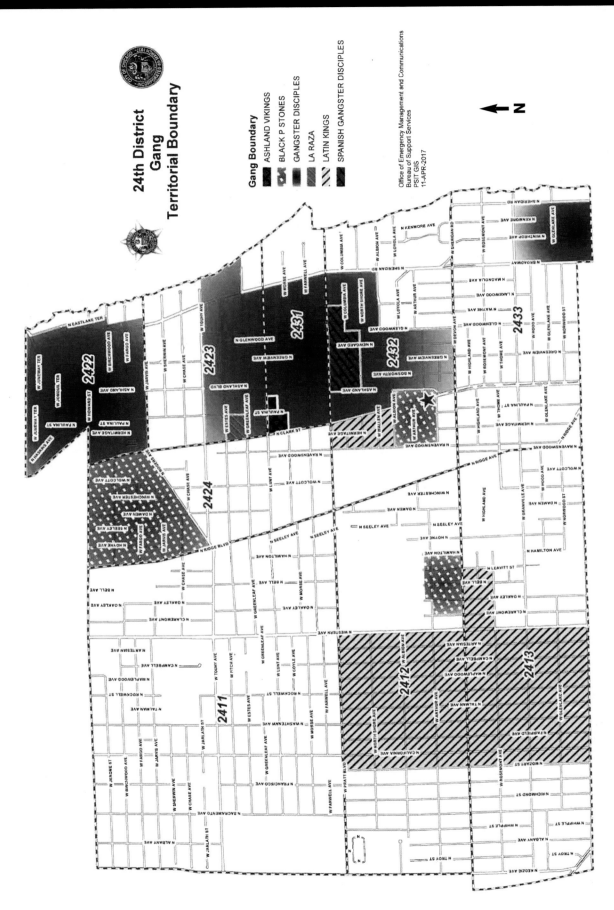

24th District Gang Territorial Boundary

Gang Boundary
- ASHLAND VIKINGS
- BLACK P STONES
- GANGSTER DISCIPLES
- LA RAZA
- LATIN KINGS
- SPANISH GANGSTER DISCIPLES

Office of Emergency Management and Communications
Bureau of Support Services
PSIT GIS
11-APR-2017

25TH DISTRICT GANG TERRITORIAL BOUNDARY

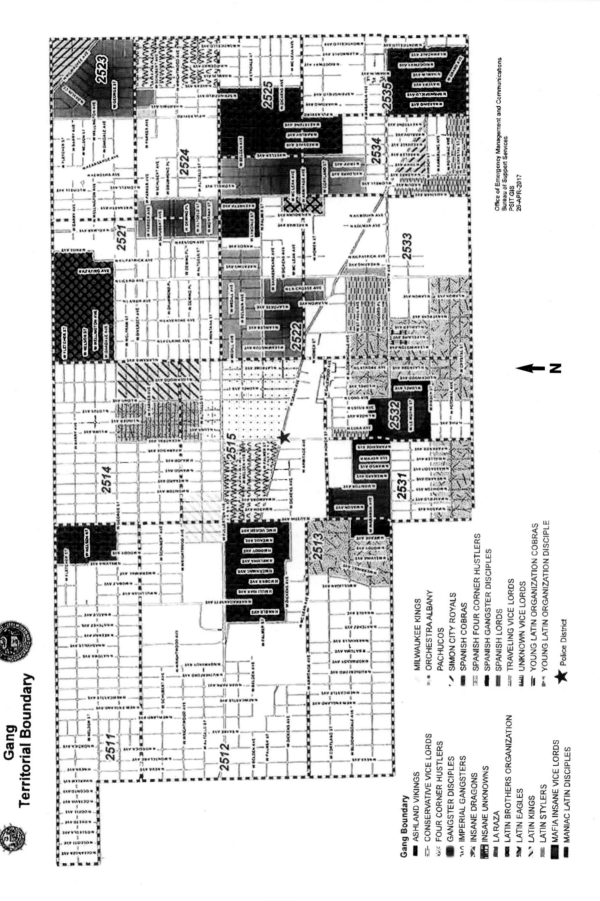

25th District
Gang
Territorial Boundary

II – Gang Maps

Office of Emergency Management and Communications
Bureau of Support Services
PSIT GIS
26-APR-2017

Gang Boundary

- ASHLAND VIKINGS
- CONSERVATIVE VICE LORDS
- FOUR CORNER HUSTLERS
- GANGSTER DISCIPLES
- IMPERIAL GANGSTERS
- INSANE DRAGONS
- INSANE UNKNOWNS
- LA RAZA
- LATIN BROTHERS ORGANIZATION
- LATIN EAGLES
- LATIN KINGS
- LATIN STYLERS
- MAFIA INSANE VICE LORDS
- MANIAC LATIN DISCIPLES

- MILWAUKEE KINGS
- ORCHESTRA ALBANY
- PACHUCOS
- SIMON CITY ROYALS
- SPANISH COBRAS
- SPANISH FOUR CORNER HUSTLERS
- SPANISH GANGSTER DISCIPLES
- SPANISH LORDS
- TRAVELING VICE LORDS
- UNKNOWN VICE LORDS
- YOUNG LATIN ORGANIZATION COBRAS
- YOUNG LATIN ORGANIZATION DISCIPLE
- ★ Police District

AREA 1 GANG TERRITORIAL BOUNDARY

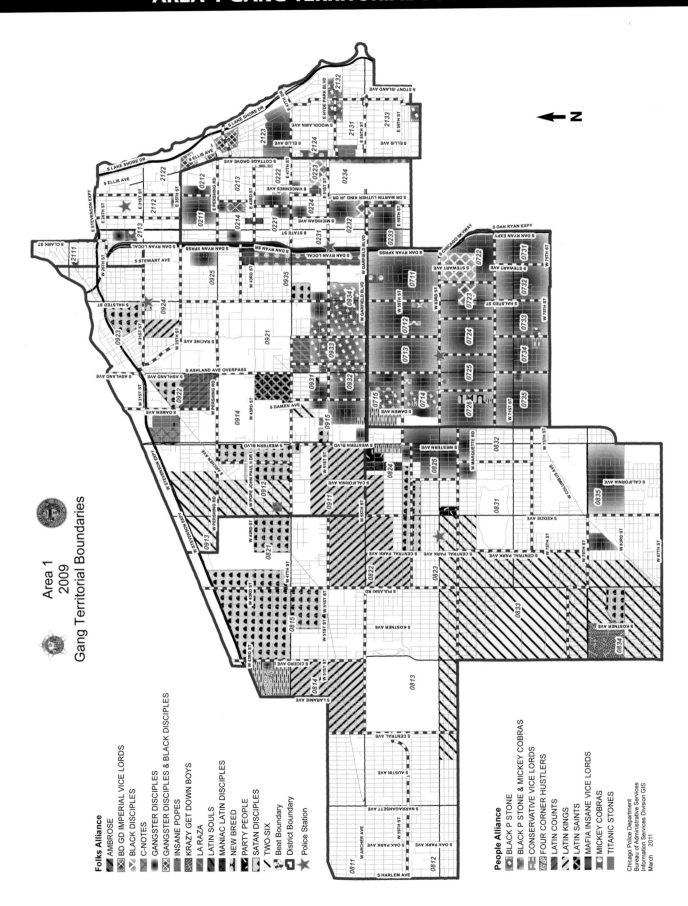

II – Gang Maps

Area 1
2009
Gang Territorial Boundaries

Folks Alliance
AMBROSE
BD GD IMPERIAL VICE LORDS
BLACK DISCIPLES
C-NOTES
GANGSTER DISCIPLES
GANGSTER DISCIPLES & BLACK DISCIPLES
INSANE POPES
KRAZY GET DOWN BOYS
LA RAZA
LATIN SOULS
MANIAC LATIN DISCIPLES
NEW BREED
PARTY PEOPLE
SATAN DISCIPLES
TWO-SIX
Beat Boundary
District Boundary
Police Station

People Alliance
BLACK P STONE
BLACK P STONE & MICKEY COBRAS
CONSERVATIVE VICE LORDS
FOUR CORNER HUSTLERS
LATIN COUNTS
LATIN KINGS
LATIN SAINTS
MAFIA INSANE VICE LORDS
MICKEY COBRAS
TITANIC STONES

Chicago Police Department
Bureau of Administrative Services
Information Services Division GIS
March   2011

AREA 2 GANG TERRITORIAL BOUNDARY

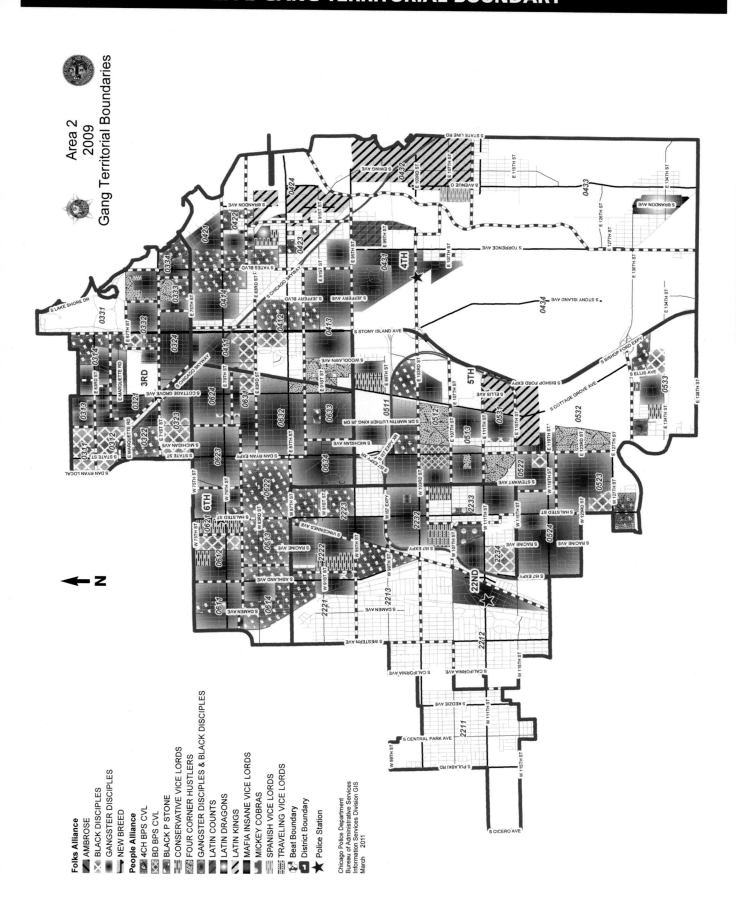

Area 2
2009
Gang Territorial Boundaries

Folks Alliance
AMBROSE
BLACK DISCIPLES
GANGSTER DISCIPLES
NEW BREED

People Alliance
4CH BPS CVL
BD BPS CVL
BLACK P STONE
CONSERVATIVE VICE LORDS
FOUR CORNER HUSTLERS
GANGSTER DISCIPLES & BLACK DISCIPLES
LATIN COUNTS
LATIN DRAGONS
LATIN KINGS
MAFIA INSANE VICE LORDS
MICKEY COBRAS
SPANISH VICE LORDS
TRAVELING VICE LORDS
Beat Boundary
District Boundary
Police Station

Chicago Police Department
Bureau of Administrative Services
Information Services Division GIS
March   2011

II – Gang Maps

AREA 3 GANG TERRITORIAL BOUNDARY

II – Gang Maps

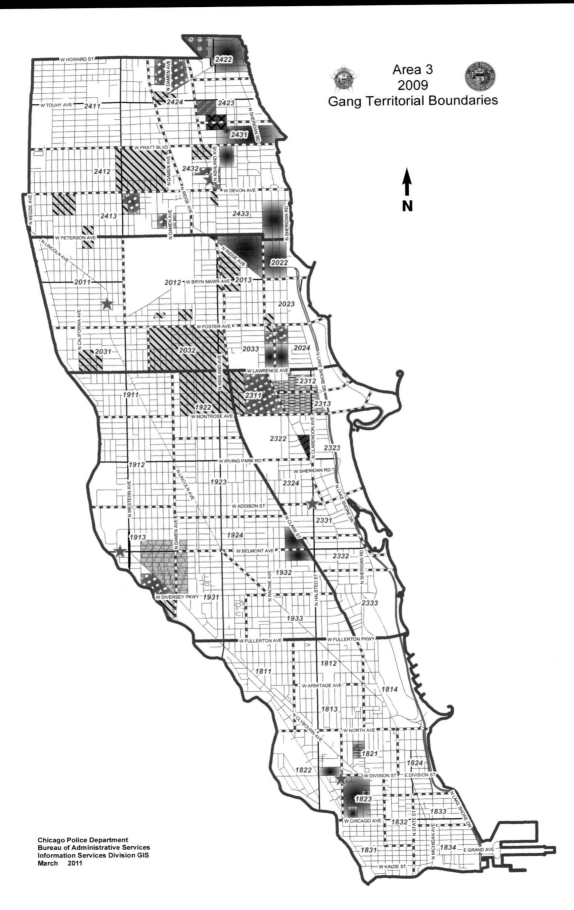

Area 3
2009
Gang Territorial Boundaries

N

Chicago Police Department
Bureau of Administrative Services
Information Services Division GIS
March   2011

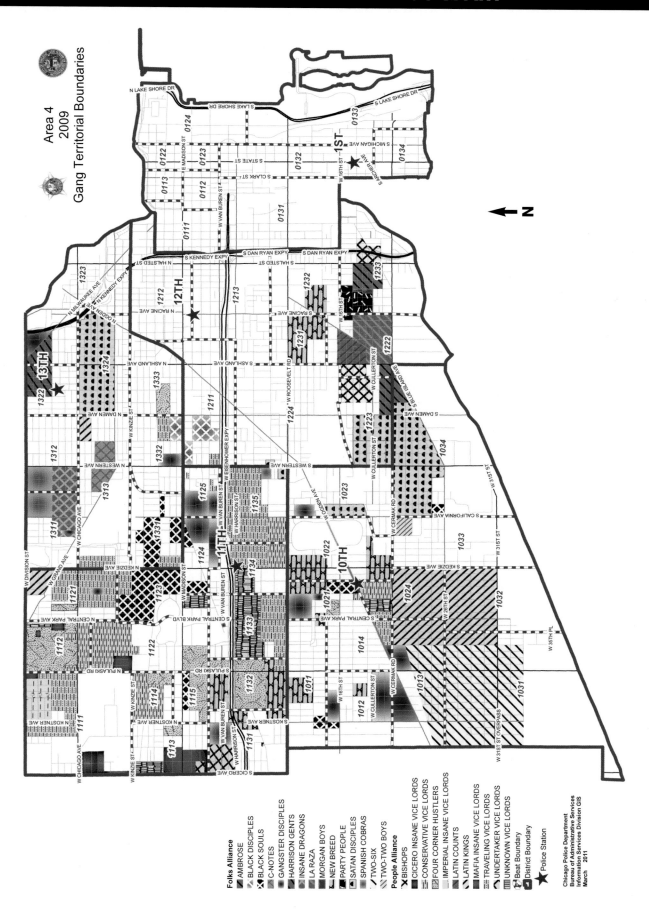

Area 4
2009
Gang Territorial Boundaries

II – Gang Maps

Folks Alliance
- AMBROSE
- BLACK DISCIPLES
- BLACK SOULS
- C-NOTES
- GANGSTER DISCIPLES
- HARRISON GENTS
- INSANE DRAGONS
- LA RAZA
- MORGAN BOYS
- NEW BREED
- PARTY PEOPLE
- SATAN DISCIPLES
- SPANISH COBRAS
- TWO-SIX
- TWO-TWO BOYS

People Alliance
- BISHOPS
- CICERO INSANE VICE LORDS
- CONSERVATIVE VICE LORDS
- FOUR CORNER HUSTLERS
- IMPERIAL INSANE VICE LORDS
- LATIN COUNTS
- LATIN KINGS
- MAFIA INSANE VICE LORDS
- TRAVELING VICE LORDS
- UNDERTAKER VICE LORDS
- UNKNOWN VICE LORDS
- Beat Boundary
- District Boundary
- Police Station

Chicago Police Department
Bureau of Administrative Services
Information Services Division GIS
March 2011

AREA 5 GANG TERRITORIAL BOUNDARY

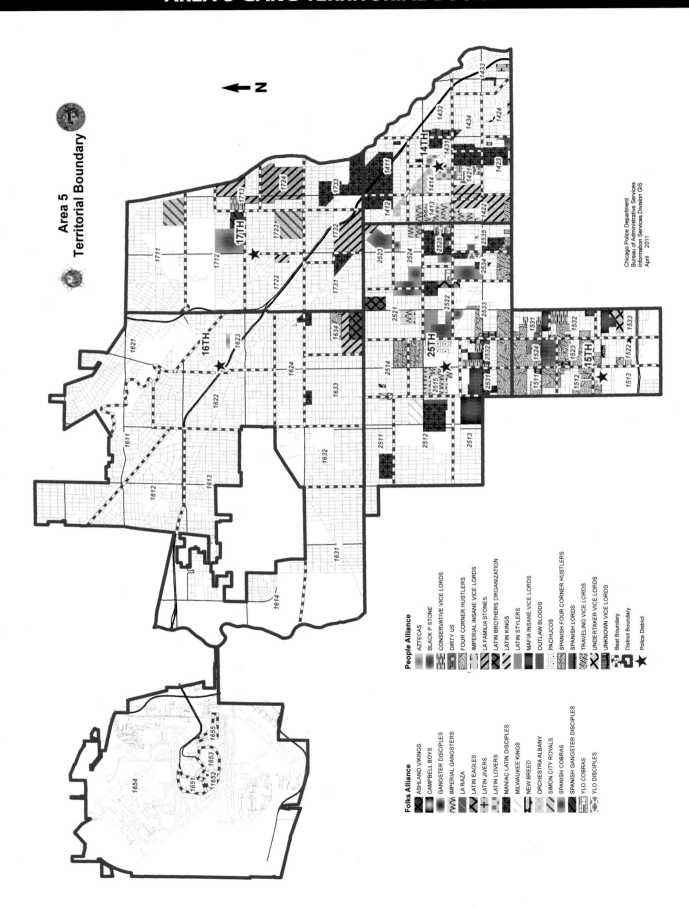

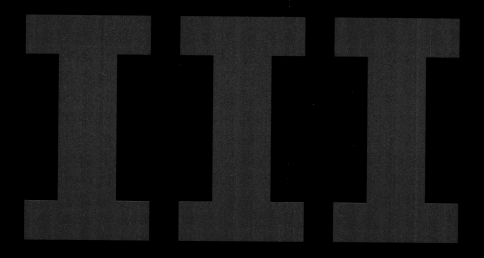

Social Media

chicago
crime
commission

Social Media Overview

Social networking and mobile applications are heavily embedded in modern street gang culture. By design, social media websites and mobile applications, such as Facebook, Instagram, Twitter, and YouTube, allow individuals to create personal networks and communicate instantaneously with others. Gang members utilize the immediacy of these sites to glorify their street gang lifestyle. Members publicly display their gang affiliations, explicitly detail their illicit activities, and freely taunt rival gangs. With the intent of becoming "viral," gang members use social networking platforms to advance their gangland personas as they upload media featuring themselves and others brandishing firearms, narcotics, and money.

Photograph of a group of alleged gang members uploaded to Twitter.

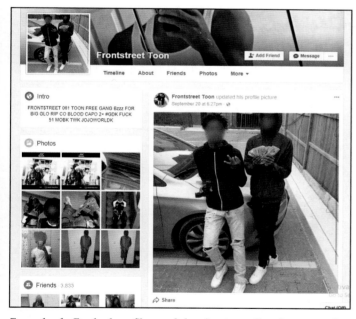

Example of a Facebook profile page belonging to an alleged gang member.

Usually, users obtain personal accounts with multiple social media sites and applications; it is common they maintain the same username across each platform. Many users encourage others to view their social media profiles. Often, some gang members may have multiple accounts for one social media platform under various aliases to preserve anonymity.

Gang members are interested in gaining instant notoriety through the constant circulation of

information via the Internet. According to Pew Research Center surveys, 51% of Americans aged 18-25 say that "to be famous" is one of the most significant goals of their generation. Therefore, they are likely to maintain minimal privacy settings for their accounts. In addition, rival gang members connect with each other via social networks to further provoke rashness which can extend to a gang member's decision to respond impulsively and/or violently. Rather than tagging buildings with graffiti, rival gang members provoke oppositions by uploading images and video clips of themselves chanting disrespectful slurs in enemy gang territory. Consequently, these exchanges cause violence to transfer to the streets.

Similar to promoting street credibility, gang members share images memorializing deceased affiliates. The images typically exhibit the deceased member's gang affiliation and/or an insulting graphic towards the alleged killer's gang or their street name. There are several social media pages dedicated to the memorialization of gang members.

III – Social Media

Drill Rap Music

Another way in which gang members utilize social media to glorify street gang culture is through "drill music." Drill music (also known as 'drill scene,' 'drill-hop,' 'drill rap,' or simply 'drill') is a sub-genre of hip hop's trap music which originated in Chicago's impoverished south and west sides. The term "drill" was coined by late Chicago rapper, Pac Man, with the meaning of retaliation against oppositions. Currently, there is no singular definition of drill as it is a slang term used to describe a range of day-to-day actions rooted in Chicago street gang culture; "hyping each other up" and committing violent and aggressive street acts are common themes. Chicago's drill rap scene became nationally recognized with the emergence of artists including Chief Keef, Lil Jojo, and Lil Durk. These artists uploaded homemade rap videos to several social media sites, including, Soundcloud, YouTube, and Myspace. Some artists use drill rap as a platform to promote the street gang lifestyle and brag of criminality. Additionally, drill rappers often explicitly "call out" oppositions with verbal "disses" and may display the rival gang's hand

Frequently, individuals in drill rap music videos are filmed brandishing firearms. The red circle indicate the firearms observed in this video.

Law enforcement can identify gang affiliations by the gang-related hand signs observed in drill rap music videos. For example, drill rapper Young Pappy is gesturing a "P" for Pooh Bear Gang.

signs upside down. Deceased drill rapper, Young Pappy, regularly rapped about targeting rival gang members; for example, in the song "Shooters", he proclaims, "Gotta a whole lotta shooters on the squad, gotta squad full of shooters. If I catch an op, I'm smoking them." Similar to a disrespectful mention of an opposition on an individual's social media profile, an insulting remark in a drill rap song can spark a cycle of retaliatory violence and gang warfare on the streets, along with the continuation of recording and posting disrespectful lyrics and videos.

Illegal Transactions

Gang members also use social media platforms to coordinate illegal transactions and disclose meetup times and locations. Members are able to instantaneously and anonymously communicate with one another with the use of mobile applications including Kik and WhatsApp. Facebook also allows registered users to create pages for private groups and events. Facebook will often remove these pages when a user's profile looks suspicious. The user can then recreate their event or group. Due to Facebook's privacy settings, these groups are virtually unsearchable by the public. Thus, gang members exploit sites to upload images

Alleged gang member advertises the sale of illegal narcotics on Facebook.

Alleged gang member advertises the sale of illegal narcotics on Instagram.

Alleged gang member advertises the sale of illegal firearms on Instagram.

Alleged gang member advertises the sale of illegal firearms on Facebook.

of narcotics and firearms to inform their followers that they have products to sell. Unlike open-air markets, these platforms allow gang members to arrange illegal transactions privately and efficiently.

Live-Streaming on Social Media

As technology continues to advance, gang members find more lucrative ways to exploit criminal activities. Recently there has been a proliferation of gang members using live video streaming services, a feature that allows them to stream their illicit activities in real time. Gang members use this feature to "brag" about their transgressions. They seek to gain instant recognition, reinforced with likes, comments, and shares by others. A publicized example took place in August 2015, Simon City when Royals gang member Jose Roman recorded a video of himself and gang leader, Thaddeus Jimenez, driving through a Chicago Northside neighborhood. The video includes Jimenez and Roman brandishing firearms. At the conclusion of the video, Jimenez is seen taunting and shooting a man twice in the legs. Another example of a violent live stream is the unintentional recording of a well-known gang member's own shooting. While jokingly talking about the store he was standing in front of, the unidentified man was approached by an unknown

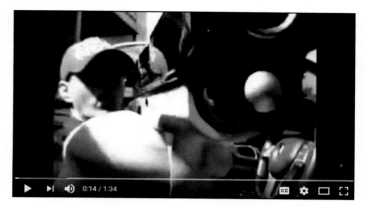

Alleged gang leader, Thaddeus Jimenez, of the Simon City Royals shoots a rival gang member in the legs on Facebook live.

gunman. The gang member's cell phone continued to stream as it fell to the ground; faced toward the sky, the unknown gunman reappears with his arms outstretched as he fires multiple times.

Tool for Law Enforcement

Despite social media acting as a new method of criminality, it helps law enforcement collect significant pieces of evidence pertinent to the successful apprehension of individual gang members involved. Through the surveillance of social media accounts, law enforcement entities have created a database categorizing street gang names, known aliases, known associates, gang hand signs, gang boundaries, and/or gang terminology.

Facebook

- Founded in 2004, Facebook is an internet website and mobile device application.

- Individuals 13 and older can be registered users.

- Pew Research Center (2016) reports 88% of Facebook users fall in the 18-29 age category.

- Individuals create user profiles in which they can connect and share what interests them with other users.

- Facebook users have the option of having a public or a private profile.

- Facebook users request other Facebook users to become 'friends.' Now, they can view each other's profiles as well as use Facebook's private messaging feature, "messenger."

- Similar to Snapchat and Instagram, Facebook messenger has a 'story' feature. Users can upload images or videos to a 24-hour lifecycle visible by all contacts.

- Users can post status updates, images, and videos.

- Users can comment, like, and share other users' posts.

- Users can tag other registered Facebook users and 'check in' to various locations and establishments in their postings.

- Facebook has a 'live' feature that allows registered users to 'go live' and stream their current activities in real time to other users.

- Facebook live has a 4-hour time limit.

- Facebook users can create groups, either private or public.

- If the group is private, it cannot be discovered through Facebook's search engine – a user must be invited to join.

- Users can create private or public events. Again, a private event cannot be searched.

Instagram

- Launched in 2010, Instagram is a picture and video sharing internet website and mobile device application.

- Unlike Facebook, Instagram users 'follow' each other. If the Instagram account is private, a user has to request to follow that particular individual.

- Registered users are able to 'like' or leave a comment on an image or video.

- Similar to Facebook, Instagram has a 'live' feature.

- Instagram has a 'story' feature similar to Snapchat. The image or video remains on the user's profile for 24 hours.

- Users can tag other Instagram users and add their geographical locations in their image and video posts.

- Instagram has an 'explore' feature that provides users with posts (based on their likes and followers) he or she might be interested in.

- Users are able to privately send graphics and messages directly to other users.

YouTube

- Launched in 2005, YouTube is a video sharing internet website and mobile device application.

- A YouTube profile can be anonymous, unlike other social media sites.

- Users can leave comments on other users' videos anonymously.

- YouTube users can post original videos.

- Similar to Instagram, YouTube users can 'subscribe' to other YouTube users.

- Users can also go "live" on YouTube.

Twitter

- Launched in 2006, Twitter is an internet website and mobile device application.

- Twitter owns Periscope and Vine (both video sharing applications). As of October 2016 Vine no longer exists.

- Twitter users can have private or public accounts.

- Like Instagram, users have to request to follow private Twitter accounts.

- Twitter users update their followers by 'tweeting.'

- Each 'tweet' is limited to 140 characters or less.

- Users may also 'tweet' pictures and videos.

- Twitter has a 'live' feature as well.

Kik

- Founded in 2009, Kik is an instant messenger application for mobile devices.

- Kik's CEO reported 300 million registered users. As of May 2016, approximately 40% are teenagers.

- Kik allows users to register without providing a telephone number, preserving user anonymity.

- This messaging application allows users to communicate with other users via one-on-one chat, group chat (up to six people) and video chat.

- Users share pictures, videos, games, etc.

WhatsApp

- Released in 2009, WhatsApp is an instant messenger mobile device application.

- WhatsApp is also available for desktop and Web use.

- As of February 2016, WhatsApp reached one billion registered users.

- To register, WhatsApp requires users to have a standard cellular mobile number.

- Using internet connection, users can send text messages, images, video and voice media messages to other users.

- Users can create group chats with up to 256 people.

- As of 2017, WhatsApp released a 'story' feature similar to Snapchat, Facebook, and Instagram.

Snapchat

- Released in 2011, Snapchat is a picture and video sharing mobile device application.

- Snapchat users can add 'friends' through users' cell phone contacts, snapchat usernames, and by scanning a user's 'snapcode.'

- Sent images and videos are viewable for 10 seconds or less.

- Users can screenshot and replay the image or video.

- Snapchat users can upload images and videos to their 'story.'

- Stories are available for viewing up to 24 hours.

- Users can also screenshot stories.

- Users can upload pictures or videos directly from their camera roll on their cell phones (before users had to take the picture on the app to send it).

OfferUp

- Founded in 2011

- Local mobile-only marketplace

- Each offer post requires at least one photograph, a description/condition, and the location of the product.

- Users can validate their credentials by uploading an image of their ID and linking their Facebook accounts through TruYou.

- To ensure public safety, all communication is limited to the application.

Alleged gang members utilize emoticons to electronically communicate in picture form via social media platforms, websites, and text messages.

Alleged Latin King gang member disrespecting rival gang members on Facebook.

Social Media and the Law: Classic Case and Overview

On a daily basis, prosecutors and law enforcement in the Chicagoland area and around Illinois are confronting social media aspects and issues in their cases. The following example is common to what is currently being confronted: Police receive a tip gang member A is preparing to attack rival gang B in the coming days. The information came from an individual who saw a Facebook Live video of gang member A detailing the attack. This tip leads law enforcement to check Facebook, Twitter, WhatsApp, and Instagram for gang member A. Law enforcement locate gang member A's social media accounts – all accounts are public with public postings.

The aforementioned tip is corroborated by these public postings, including photos, comments and videos of gang A disrespecting and declaring violence upon gang B. Police print out the postings gathered from social media and attach the information to an officer's police report. The officer takes these printed materials to a prosecutor assigned in the area. If the prosecutor takes the case, the ultimate question is: are the materials gathered from various social media platforms admissible in a trial?

Prosecutors and law enforcement alike often grapple with this tricky legal scenario as social media, virtual storage, and "the Cloud" become the new normal in investigating and prosecuting gang related criminal cases. In following the steps below and understanding the issues of your case, you can increase the chances of your social media related evidence being admitted.

The Law: Digital Evidence and Social Media as Gang Weapons

Though admissibility of social media evidence in Illinois is fraught with complication, recent accounts prove social media is increasingly used as evidence in court cases in the state. However, specific requirements must be met in order for social media evidence to be admissible in court and requires new technologies to be fully understood by the judiciary. Illinois courts, like others around the country, require a proper foundation to establish the authenticity of evidence and relevancy of the evidence. Having these areas covered and met are keys to ensuring the admissibility of social media evidence.

Digital Evidence Admissiblity Reviewed Under the Same Standards as Hard Copy Materials

In the case of *People v. Chromik*, the court analyzes what is included as electronic evidence in social media related cases. In *Chromik*, a teacher was charged with aggravated criminal sexual abuse of a minor student. On appeal, the issue whether the trial court erred in admitting a transcript of text messages between the defendant and the victim arose. The defendant principally argued there was no way for the court to authenticate such communication of a text message, no proper foundation laid, and the best evidence rule. The defendant also argued there was no way to confirm who sent the text messages and there was no way to ensure the transcript of said messages were properly transcribed. The Illinois Appellate Court ruled for the plaintiff and held the trial court did not abuse its discretion by admitting the text message transcripts as evidence. The appellate court ruled that the same standard used for hard-copy materials also apply to text message transcripts.

Authentication in Illinois

Authentication is the biggest hurdle to admitting social media evidence. Judges often struggle with the newness and nuances of social media evidence and electronically stored information (ESI). This type of evidence is stored digitally and tampering or manipulation of ESI is a question courts often face. To guard against the risks of fabrication and manipulation of social media or ESI, courts are requiring strict standards to be adhered to as outlined below.

Authentication of digital evidence and hard-copy documents in Illinois can be done in two ways: direct or circumstantial evidence. To establish the authenticity of evidence, courts look to Illinois

Rule of Evidence 901(a). The rule states the item submitted must be one its proponent claims to be. Such a threshold must be met for either digital or hard copy materials to be authenticated and potentially admitted into evidence. To establish authenticity, a witness can testify a document is what it purports to be according to the witness based on personal knowledge and is, in fact, what the witness says it is. For example, a witness can testify emails, texts, and social media accounts contained the defendant's first and last name, if the defendant used distinctive emoticons, fonts, or symbols that together can be used to authenticate the defense. In *Chromik*, the court ruled the circumstantial evidence to be authentic because the phone company and victim testified the materials were what the proponent said they were – text messages from the defendant. The phone company authenticated the date, time, and phone numbers and the victim authenticated the content was what it purported to be. Thus, the standard was met.

Seminole Social Media Cases

Enhanced Digital Evidence

Even as some courts have utilized the standards of hard copy materials to evaluate digital evidence admissibility, other courts are requiring enhanced evidence authentication. It is important to know and understand the various standards courts apply to digital evidence as the requirements take shape in Illinois.

In *Griffin v. State*, the Maryland Court of Appeals initiated the first requirements for authenticating digital evidence. In *Griffin*, the defendant was charged with murdering another individual at a bar. The prosecution introduced a MySpace profile allegedly belonging to defendant's girlfriend. The state wanted to introduce evidence from the girlfriend's MySpace page, but the page only had a photo of her embracing the defendant – no name was listed. Because of this missing detail, the court ruled the state failed to authenticate the MySpace page as that of the defendant's girlfriend and it was thrown out as evidence. The court ruled the proper measures to authenticate digital evidence are as follows:

(1) Asking purported creator if they created the profile and adding posting(s) in question

(2) Searching the computer of the alleged creator of post in question, including internet history and hard drive

(3) Obtaining information directly from social networking site linking person establishing profile

For evidence to be admissible in court, it must meet only **one** of the three criteria listed above.

In *Commonwealth v. Williams* the Massachusetts Supreme Court held a MySpace page was improperly admitted because the state failed to lay foundational evidence for who could access the page, whether the page was secure, and whether a password or code was required to access the content. Enhanced digital evidence was required by the court to properly admit the materials into evidence.

Non-Enhanced Digital Evidence

In *Tienda v. State* the Texas Criminal Court of Appeals rejected *Griffin* and ruled the authenticity of digital evidence and social media postings could be established through circumstantial evidence rather than enhanced digital evidence reliability requirements.

In *State v. Assi* the Arizona Court of Appeals ruled the state properly authenticated the defendant's MySpace page via circumstantial evidence of a witness testifying to the defendant's nickname and another witness who was familiar with the defendant's MySpace page who testified to authenticate the defendant's postings on the Myspace site. In sum, *Assi* represents a reasonableness standard that many states are following as common practice. Hence, as law enforcement and prosecutors alike handle social media related cases, they will likely confront the *Assi* standard and should prepare cases to meet a reasonableness standard.

These two cases demonstrate circumstantial evidence can establish the authenticity of social media postings. Moreover, these cases illustrate enhanced digital evidence was unnecessary given that witnesses established the evidences' authenticity through direct testimony based on direct knowledge or particular facts and circumstances – including a defendant's nickname. Regardless of what Illinois court or jurisdiction your case is in, law enforcement and prosecutors should err on the side of more versus less and following a strict versus lax standard.

Relevancy Under Rules 401 and 402

Once the hurdle of authenticity is met, courts look to relevancy. If evidence is relevant, it is generally admissible. According to the Illinois and Federal Rules of Evidence, relevant evidence is that in which "any tendency to make the existence of any fact is of consequence to the determination of the action more probable or less probable that it would be without the evidence." Relevancy is a relatively low standard to meet, so when evidence is not admitted, it is not usually because of relevancy but for another issue.

Points to Consider in Each Case

With social media and the law taking shape in Illinois, there are considerations to navigate new technological terrain. The following federal evidentiary rules should be considered in social media cases:

1. *Federal Evidence Rule 401:* the evidence must be relevant to the case at hand

2. *Evidence Rules 901-903:* the evidence to be admitted must be authentic if it is a tangible or digital document in the case

3. *Federal Rules of Evidence 803, 804, and 807:* If statements offered into evidence are assertive by its nature, the statements must meet a hearsay exception. Certain statements may also not be hearsay if they meet a hearsay exception. Such as, under Federal Rules of Evidence 801(d)(1)(A) – a declarant-witness's prior statement, 801(d)(2) – opposing party's statements or admissions.

4. *Federal Evidence Rules 1001-1008:* If the digital evidence is a writing, recording or photograph, and its contents are being offered into evidence, the requirements of the original writing rule must be met

5. *Federal Evidence Rule 105:* The probative value of the evidence must be weighed against its possible unfair prejudice on the defendant

Conclusion

Social media evidence is generally admissible in Illinois, but admissibility requirements for electronic evidence remains uncertain. It is imperative to present your evidence to the court with as much information proving authenticity as is possible. Merely "flying by the seat of your pants" is not an effective method and it is important to remember courts continue to review admissibility requirements for digital evidence just as it does for "hard copy" materials. Law enforcement and prosecutors alike must prepare cases to meet strict requirements for authenticating social evidence. This ultimately means doing a more extensive investigation at the beginning of a case. Law enforcement and prosecutors should leave enough time to understand the digital evidence being handled including: how it operates, how it is used, which authentication method is best for the case and jurisdiction, which witnesses are needed, and how to submit the necessary evidence. Putting all of these pieces together will help to ensure a successful outcome.

III – Social Media

SECTION IV

Suburban Gang Activity

chicago
crime
commission

Disclaimer:

All information in this section is taken directly from the 2016 Chicago Crime Commission Survey of Suburban Gang and Drug Activity. In 2016, the Chicago Crime Commission sent surveys to all police agencies in the six-county area including: Cook, DuPage, Kane, Lake, McHenry, and Will. In the surrounding six counties, 122 police departments responded. All information is reported exactly as it appeared on the returned surveys. If a question was left blank, the answer was recorded as unknown. For a list of the suburban police departments that responded to the survey by county, please refer to our acknowledgements. All information accessed in the Chicago Crime Commission files and archives must be credited to the original source and to the Chicago Crime Commission in all media and other use. The user of the information assumes all risk, legal and otherwise, associated in any way with use, publication, republication, or dissemination of the information.

Suburban Survey Summary of Findings

As noted in 2016, the Chicago Crime Commission developed, collected and distributed a Suburban Street Gang Survey. Of the 122 suburban police departments responding to the survey, 80 departments or 65% indicated a gang presence in their community. There appears to be an increase of gang activity in some more affluent suburbs and communities where street gang presence hasn't traditionally been observed, demonstrating activity is widespread.

The top five reported active street gangs in the suburban communities are Latin Kings, Gangster Disciples, Surenos 13, Maniac Latin Disciples, and the Vice Lords.

– As displayed on the chart on page 324, the Latin Kings are reportedly active in 82.5% of Chicago's neighboring suburban communities. The Latin Kings have a presence in each one of the six counties represented in our data. Additionally, we asked the suburban police departments to list the street gangs of most concern observed in their communities in rank order. 51% ranked the Latin Kings as either first or second of most concern.

– Gangster Disciples are reported in 43% of the responding suburban communities as having an active street gang presence.

– The Surenos 13, a prominent California street gang, hold the third largest gang presence in the six-county metropolitan area of Chicagoland. 36% of the responding suburban police departments indicated Surenos 13 as active in their community.

• The breakdown of traditional gang structures observed in the city of Chicago has emerged in the streets of the suburban communities. Many communities reporting a faction gang presence fall in Cook County (88%). One community reported, "Our department's greatest obstacle has been hybrid street gangs which have ties to other

Alleged group of Latin King gang members.
Image provided by Hanover, Park, Illinois Police Department.

Latin King graffiti.
Image provided by Streamwood, Illinois Police Department.

PERCENTAGES OF GANGS
REPORTED AS ACTIVE IN RESPONDING SUBURBS

Source: 2017 Suburban Gang and Drug Survey

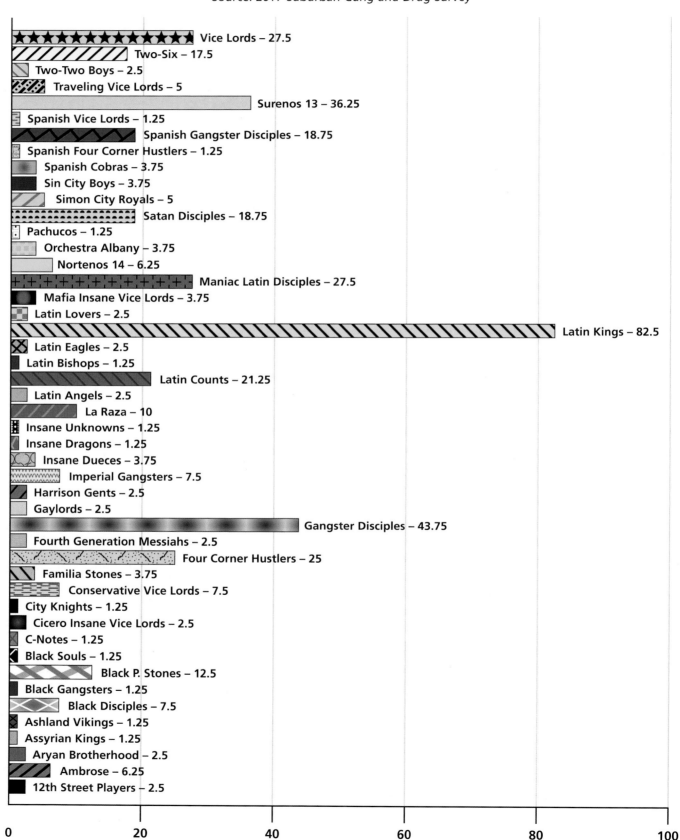

Vice Lords – 27.5
Two-Six – 17.5
Two-Two Boys – 2.5
Traveling Vice Lords – 5
Surenos 13 – 36.25
Spanish Vice Lords – 1.25
Spanish Gangster Disciples – 18.75
Spanish Four Corner Hustlers – 1.25
Spanish Cobras – 3.75
Sin City Boys – 3.75
Simon City Royals – 5
Satan Disciples – 18.75
Pachucos – 1.25
Orchestra Albany – 3.75
Nortenos 14 – 6.25
Maniac Latin Disciples – 27.5
Mafia Insane Vice Lords – 3.75
Latin Lovers – 2.5
Latin Kings – 82.5
Latin Eagles – 2.5
Latin Bishops – 1.25
Latin Counts – 21.25
Latin Angels – 2.5
La Raza – 10
Insane Unknowns – 1.25
Insane Dragons – 1.25
Insane Dueces – 3.75
Imperial Gangsters – 7.5
Harrison Gents – 2.5
Gaylords – 2.5
Gangster Disciples – 43.75
Fourth Generation Messiahs – 2.5
Four Corner Hustlers – 25
Familia Stones – 3.75
Conservative Vice Lords – 7.5
City Knights – 1.25
Cicero Insane Vice Lords – 2.5
C-Notes – 1.25
Black Souls – 1.25
Black P. Stones – 12.5
Black Gangsters – 1.25
Black Disciples – 7.5
Ashland Vikings – 1.25
Assyrian Kings – 1.25
Aryan Brotherhood – 2.5
Ambrose – 6.25
12th Street Players – 2.5

0   20   40   60   80   100

IV – Suburban Gangs

larger 'known' gangs. These hybrid street gangs have engaged in defacement/graffiti and intimidation to 'legitimize' themselves to other 'established' street gangs. Investigations of the hybrid gangs have taken longer and [have] been more difficult because their colors, signs, tagging, etc. are not well known. Law enforcement have a hard time identifying a hierarchy and often there isn't one. Individuals do their 'own' thing without having to report to anyone." Within these reporting communities, the following factions have the largest presence: Money over Bitches (MOB), Brothers Breaking Bread, About the Money (ATM), and Insane Cutthroat Gangsters. Interestingly enough, all of these are allegedly factions of the Gangster Disciples.

- Most commonly, street gangs in the suburbs are involved with the distribution of narcotics. Suburban police departments indicated drug sales occur on the street, in bars, clubs, homes, offices, convenience stores, and vehicles. In terms of narcotic seizures, the responding suburban police departments confiscated the following illegal narcotics: marijuana, cocaine, heroin, meth MDMA, crack-cocaine, and ecstasy. More notably, suburban police department have seen a rise in heroin distribution and usage. In addition, police departments reported a wide range of criminal activities such as burglary, graffiti, and theft. Several police departments are also observing theft from motor vehicles, robberies, and aggravated assault tied to gang activity. The trafficking of illegal weapons by gang members was reported not as prevalent but still apparent in the suburban communities. Many police departments indicated gang members are bringing guns into their communities via theft/burglaries, illegal purchases and straw purchases, and distribution through members of their own gang.

Approximate total number of guns confiscated in the responding suburban communities:

2012: 764

2013: 763

2014: 796

Firearm recovered by Riverwoods, Illinois Police Department

Drugs and money seized by Crystal Lake, Illinois Police Department

ILLEGAL NARCOTIC SALES

Source: 2017 Suburban Gang and Drug Survey

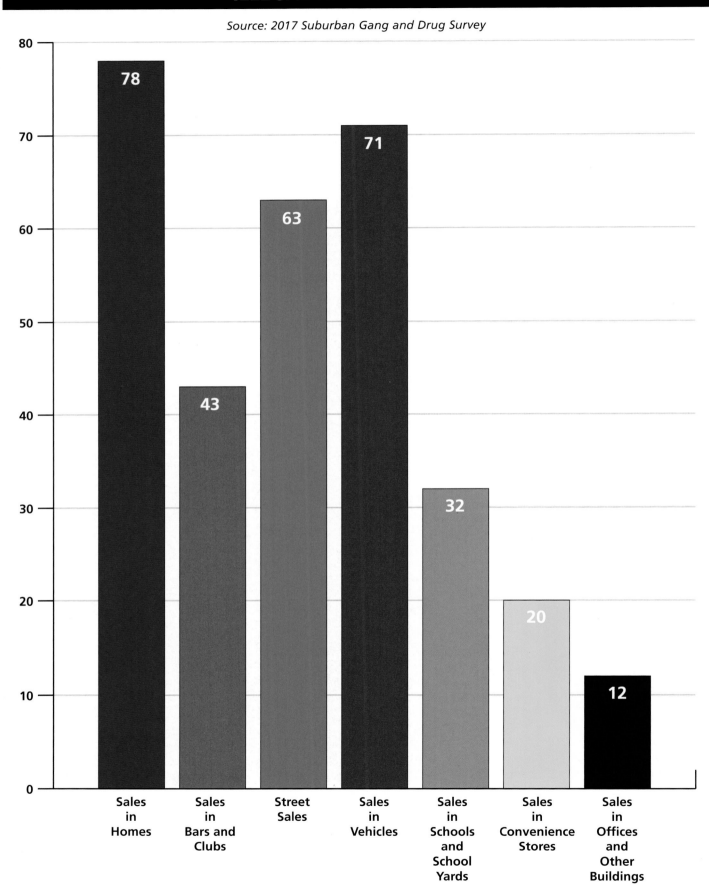

IV – Suburban Gangs

CRIMINAL ACTIVITY COMMITTED BY GANG MEMBERS

Source: 2017 Suburban Gang and Drug Survey

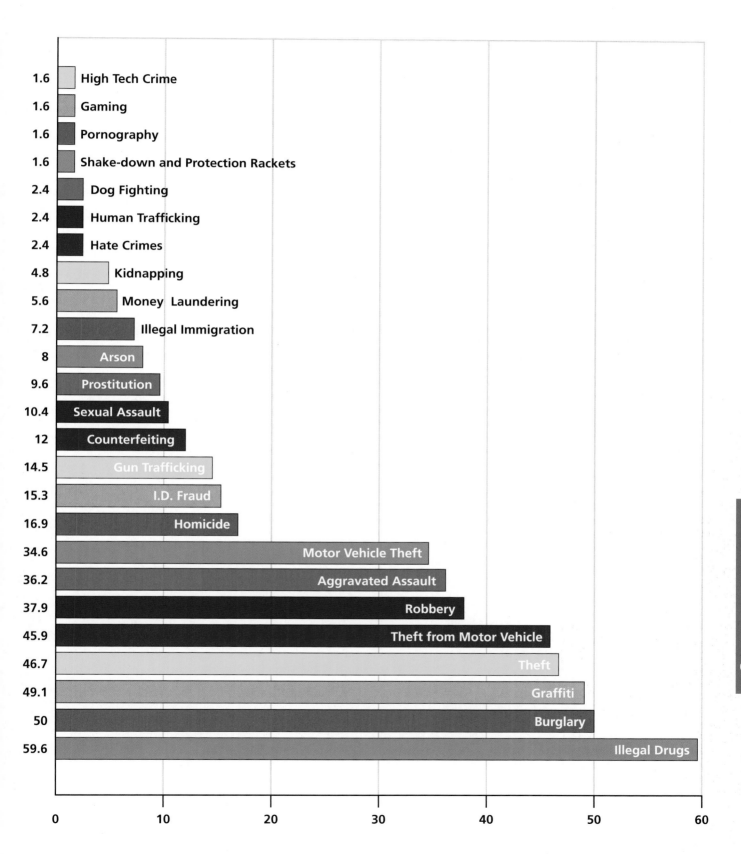

Value	Category
1.6	High Tech Crime
1.6	Gaming
1.6	Pornography
1.6	Shake-down and Protection Rackets
2.4	Dog Fighting
2.4	Human Trafficking
2.4	Hate Crimes
4.8	Kidnapping
5.6	Money Laundering
7.2	Illegal Immigration
8	Arson
9.6	Prostitution
10.4	Sexual Assault
12	Counterfeiting
14.5	Gun Trafficking
15.3	I.D. Fraud
16.9	Homicide
34.6	Motor Vehicle Theft
36.2	Aggravated Assault
37.9	Robbery
45.9	Theft from Motor Vehicle
46.7	Theft
49.1	Graffiti
50	Burglary
59.6	Illegal Drugs

IV – Suburban Gangs

• Regarding drug cartel presence in the surrounding suburban communities, 12% of responding departments reported a drug cartel presence. The southwestern suburb of Cicero reported, "On any given day, there are at least three or four outside agencies, often federal, conducting long-term narcotic investigations, many of which are tied to the major drug trafficking organizations." Similarly, a north-west suburb mentioned a case involving the Independent Cartel of Acapulco. While jointly working with HIS/ICE and DEA, this suburban police department dismantled a drug trafficking and money laundering operation, seizing approximately 1.7 million dollars in cash and several conveyances, including a semi-tractor, two trailers, a forklift, and a compact vehicle all used to facilitate the drug trafficking operations.

• Regarding gang activity in suburban schools, the major reported problems were drug distribution and possession, violent disturbances, defacing school property with gang graffiti, and through intimidation, young gang members generate fear amongst the students and teachers. In addition, suburban police departments reported older gang members using schools to recruit younger individuals to join their gang. Per the survey data, juveniles make up approximately 31% of gang populations observed in responding suburban communities.

• According to the suburban police departments, gang members are most active on the following social media sites: Facebook, Instagram, Snapchat, and Twitter. Gang members use social media to voice disparities and threats against rival gang members and law enforcement. Gang members

PERCENTAGE OF ADULT AND JUVENILE GANG MEMBERS

Source: 2017 Suburban Gang and Drug Survey

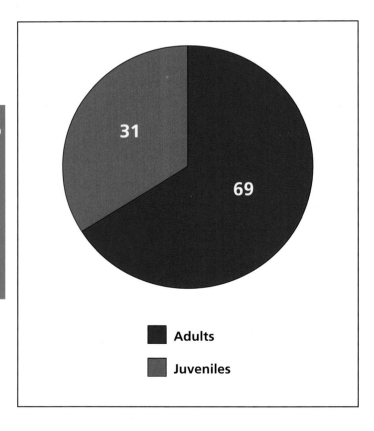

Adults
Juveniles

Latin King drawing disrespecting the Gangster Disciples, Insane Deuces La Raza, Maniac Latin Disciples, Nortenos 14, and Surenos 13 provided by Crystal Lake, Illinois Police Department

Source: 2017 Suburban Gang and Drug Survey

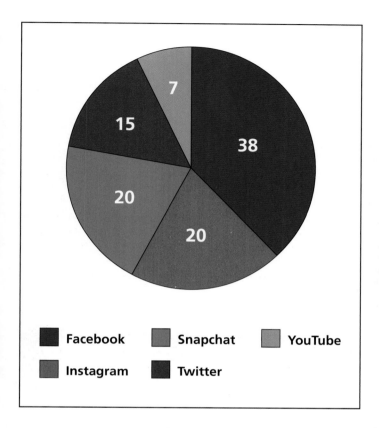

Facebook   **Snapchat**   **YouTube**

Instagram   **Twitter**

Image of alleged New Breeds gang members posted on Facebook. Image provided by Riverdale, Illinois Police Department.

actively post pictures on social media of themselves posing with firearms and drugs. These postings have in turn caused conflict to spill into streets and local schools. Cicero reported an estimated 70% of area gang conflicts develop out of social media exchanges.

• The most effective law enforcement responses to street gang matters are reflected in various policing strategies, like saturation patrols and both intelligence-led and community policing. In addition, some suburban police departments have specific gang enforcement officers or designated gang units. These policing tactics, coupled with community cooperation, allow law enforcement to take a more proactive approach to their communities' gang conflicts.

West Suburban Gang Intelligence Group

The expansion and migration of suburban street gangs present an obstacle to the successful prosecution of their criminal organizations. Due to lack of resources and manpower, suburban police departments are ill-equipped to handle the influx of gang membership and the illicit activities they engage in. To combat this issue, Cicero Police Department's gang unit partnered with Maywood Police Department's Gang unit to create the West Suburban Gang Intelligence Group (W.I.G.). W.I.G. is a "network of gang investigators, detectives, juvenile officers, patrol officers, correctional officers, special agents and states attorneys from multiple jurisdictions who congregate together to develop an intelligence network on street gangs, crews, "Persons of Interests" lists, new trends in gang conflicts, and potential gang conflicts." Through the exchange of contact cards, arrest reports, hierarchy charts or gang affiliations and "Top Ten Persons of Interests" lists, various suburban departments are

IV – Suburban Gangs

better able to identify gang affiliated individuals who may simply be passing through their community. W.I.G. meetings are open to all departments in the surrounding six counties; thus, these meetings encourage networking and intel sharing with departments who ordinarily do not interact. In addition, law enforcement officials discuss effective identification and enforcement methods that have proven successful to share with other suburban departments. Overall, W.I.G. seeks to encourage the dialogue of techniques and strategies which have worked in Cicero and Maywood to fight gangs, guns, and drugs.

Surenos 13 gang graffiti. Image provided by Mount Prospect, Illinois Police Department.

SECTION V

Cartels, Gangs and Drugs

The Drug Enforcement Administration (DEA) classifies drug cartels as large, sophisticated transnational criminal organizations (TCOs) composed of multiple drug trafficking organizations (DTOs) and cells with specific assignments such as drug transportation, security/enforcement, or money laundering (2010). DTOs are multi-faceted organizations with well-defined command-and-control structures that produce, transport, and/or distribute large quantities of one or more illicit drugs.

Drug smuggling via passenger vehicle. Image provided by the U.S. Customs and Border Protection.

TCOs supply illicit substances to DTOs and users in the United States and DTOs are the networks of groups or individuals who distribute the drugs in the US (street gang members, drug dealers, etc). According to the DEA (2017), Mexican TCOs pose the greatest threat to the United States. The DEA recognizes the following TCOs operate in the United States: the Sinaloa Cartel, Jalisco New Generation Cartel, Juarez Cartel, Gulf Cartel, Los Zetas Cartel, and Beltran-Leyva Cartel. The Knights Templar are still an active TCO in Mexico but don't maintain a strong presence in the United States.

Per a DEA drug threat assessment (2017), Mexican TCOs maintain territorial influence capable of production, cultivation, importation and exportation of illicit drugs. Mexican TCOs are in control of ports of entry (smuggling passageways) along the Southwestern Border, making the transportation of large quantities of illicit drugs into the United States accessible. Mexican TCOs are generally involved in poly-drug trafficking; dealing heroin, methamphetamine, cocaine, marijuana, and, more recently, fentanyl. While maintaining a command post in Mexico, Mexican TCOs oversee the transportation and distribution of illicit drugs to consumer markets in the United States. When operating in the United States, Mexican TCOs attempt to maintain low-profiles to avoid unwanted attention from US law enforcement.

The Sinaloa Cartel

Established during the mid-1980s, the Sinaloa Cartel is arguably one of Mexico's largest and most deeply-rooted drug-trafficking organizations. The Sinaloa Cartel is primarily based in their home state of Sinaloa but maintain operations in multiple Mexican regions mostly along the Pacific coast. According to the DEA's 2017 National Drug Threat Assessment, the Sinaloa Cartel holds the most expansive international footprint by distributing wholesale amounts of methamphetamine, marijuana, cocaine, and heroin to the United States. By using points of entry along the southwest border, the Sinaloa Cartel upholds vital distribution hubs in major cities including but not limited to, Phoenix, Los Angeles, Denver, and Chicago.

The Jalisco New Generation Cartel (CJNG)

CJNG is one of the most recently established Mexican drug cartels and one of the most powerful. Established in their home state of Jalisco, the CJNG quickly emerged in 2010 after breaking away from the Sinaloa Cartel. CJNG is a poly-drug trafficking organization dealing in wholesale amounts of primarily methamphetamine, but also cocaine, heroin, and marijuana. They access the United States along the Southwest border by way of Tijuana, Juarez, and Nuevo Laredo.

V – Gangs & Drugs

Juarez Cartel

One of the more traditional Mexican TCOs, the Juarez Cartel is based out of the Mexican state of Chihuahua, south of West Texas and New Mexico. The Juarez Cartel and endured a long-standing turf war with the Sinaloa Cartel which, at its height, was responsible for many cartel-related murders in Chihuahua. The Juarez Cartel primarily traffics marijuana and cocaine, though recently it has expanded to heroin and methamphetamine distribution in the United States. Recent law enforcement reports have indicated increased opium cultivation in the state of Chihuahua since 2013.

The Gulf Cartel

Based in the Mexican state of Tamaulipas, the Gulf Cartel primarily traffic marijuana, cocaine, and, to lesser extent, heroin and methamphetamine. The Gulf Cartel maintains territorial dominance over areas in northeastern Mexico, and smuggles the majority of its drug shipments between the Rio Grande Valley and South Padre Island in south Texas. Due to intra-cartel conflict and the arrest of key leaders, the Gulf Cartel has weakened which has led to a decline in its drug trafficking influence in the United States.

Los Zetas

Established by ex-Mexican Army Special Forces, Los Zetas formed as an independent cartel in early 2010 when it splintered from the Gulf Cartel. Immediately after the rupture, Los Zetas controlled significant territories in eastern, southern, and central Mexico. However, due to pressures from rivals and law enforcement as well as internal conflict, their control has lessened in recent years. Los Zetas smuggle the majority of their illicit drugs via border crossing points between Del Rio and Falcon Lake, Texas. Los Zetas drug exports have primarily consisted of marijuana and cocaine, though there are indications the group has recently expanded into heroin and methamphetamine distribution.

Beltran-Leyva Organization (BLO)

Upon splintering from the Sinaloa Cartel in 2008, the Beltran-Levya brothers formed the Beltran-Leyva Organization. Although all of the Beltran-Leyva brothers have been killed or arrested, they still operate independently in several regions in Mexico including the States of Guerrero, Morelos, and Sinaloa. They rely heavily on their alliances with the Gulf Cartel and Los Zetas to smuggle drugs through corridors along the southwest border. The BLO primarily traffics marijuana, cocaine, heroin, and methamphetamine trafficking and maintains distribution hubs the United States.

The Knights Templar

The Knights Templar emerged in March 2011 after breaking off from La Familia Michoacana. They are based in their home state of Michoacan but are active across central Mexico including the states of Guanajuato, Morelos, and Guerrero. The Knights Templar claimed to have started as a "self-defense" group, engaged in fighting with Mexico's larger drug cartels. They frequently display religious imagery on their public announcements. The Knights Templar are active in the cocaine and methamphetamine trade; however, because of their location in Michoacan, they have little to no control over smuggling across the border and have to negotiate with other cartels to get narcotics into the United States. In addition to drug trafficking, the Knight Templar receive income from extorting businesses in their areas of influence.

Tradecraft and the Chicago Connection

While Mexican TCOs operate primarily south of the border, they have a presence in the US and Chicago in particular. Cartel activity on the American side of the border is generally well-insulated with multiple intermediaries between leadership and the street-level dealers. TCOs like to keep a low profile in the US because they do not have the same connections with the US government as they do with the Mexican government. There is little direct cartel violence in America; the majority of cartel violence generally takes place in Mexico.

Cartel activity in the US operates much like a business, with the TCOs selling the product wholesale then having it sold by street level dealers. Depending on the cartel and their contacts in the US, law enforcement believes the TCOs might go through a middle-man who then distributes the drugs to gangs and dealers who go on to sell it at the street level. Wholesale drug distributors and logistical coordinators in the United States often have communication channels that can be traced to Mexico. However, cartels will establish a business relationship with whichever gangs are willing to buy their product, regardless of affiliation.

The Sinaloa Cartel's connection to the Flores brothers in Chicago illustrate the cartels establishing contacts within the United States. The cartel would distribute illicit drugs to the Flores brothers who would redistribute it to dealers. The Flores brothers would also take the money from the dealers and return it to the cartel. However, regarding the drug trade operations with street gangs, law enforcement believes it is fluid and constantly changing; cartels work with whoever can connect them to open drug markets. TCOs also like to compartmentalize their activities in order to limit liability. Law enforcement believes that within an organization, one group is unaware of the activities of another group. For example, individuals who work on the drug side of the operation may never interact with individuals who work on the financial side. This allows deniability if either side is ever under investigation by law enforcement.

Transnational criminal organizations also have a sophisticated transportation network. Most of the trafficking occurs on the ground, employing the use of trucks, buses, semis, etc. Cartels use vehicles with hidden compartments in passenger vehicles or comingled with various cargo in commercial trucks to smuggle drugs into the United States using ports of entry along the Southwestern border. Once the drugs are smuggled across the United States border, TCOs use warehouses or farms out in the country as stash-houses to store the narcotics until they distribute them to the street-level dealers.

Mexican cartels supply Chicago with large, wholesale supplies of methamphetamine, cocaine, marijuana, and heroin. Cartels operating in Chicago are Sinaloa, CJNG, Jalisco, and Knights Templar, with the Sinaloa being the main-stay. Because Chicago is a major marketplace, the cartels stay under the radar and do not engage in direct violence. Traditionally, cartels work with Hispanic gangs who then distribute the product to the African-American gangs. Law enforcement believes future cartel-gang relationships will result in the American gangs taking a more active role in transporting the drug shipments along the southwest border. This is to lessen the vulnerability and exposure of the TCO.

Regarding cartel finances, those handling the money almost never interact with those handling narcotics. Law enforcement believes, in some cases, the people responsible for handling the cartel's money may not be aware they are participating in any illegal activity. TCOs employ accountants so their money is properly managed. Money is placed

Identified drug smuggling tunnel. Image provided by the U.S. Customs and Border Protection.

in funnel accounts, where it is withdrawn almost as soon as it has been deposited. TCOs use multiple funnel accounts with various banks. Money going back to the cartels moves in bulk, similar to the way drugs are shipped. However, an alternative method used by TCOs is loading money onto prepaid Visa cards.

Cash businesses such as car dealerships, barber shops, and mechanics are used as fronts to launder money. Another tactic used to move money is trade-based money laundering. According to ICE, trade-based money laundering allows TCOs to move around proceeds disguised as legitimate trade. Value can be moved through this process by false-invoicing, over-invoicing and under-invoicing commodities that are imported or exported around the world. There are countries around the world such as China and Lebanon that specialize in trade-based money laundering.

Law Enforcement vs. Cartels

Law enforcement attempts to suppress cartel activity have always been a constant game of cat-and-mouse. Law enforcement officials say they are getting smarter in recognizing patterns in cartel tradecraft. However, as law enforcement evolves, so do the cartels. Law enforcement frequently comes across new concealment and smuggling methods. Advances in tactics are both high-tech and low-tech, anywhere from having their own communication networks and servers to the use of two-way radios at the US-Mexican border. Law enforcement is also employing new methods to disrupt the cartel drug trade. One approach US law enforcement is taking is working more closely with the Mexican government. Working closer together allows for better collaboration between the two countries, expediting processes such as extradition. A recent DEA report stated that the US-Mexico security partnership is strong and successful.

Drugs smuggled in carrot-like packages. Image provided by the U.S. Customs and Border Protection.

A DRUG EPIDEMIC: FENTANYL

The latest, and arguably most dangerous, product to arise from the increasingly lucrative market for drugs is fentanyl. This euphoria-inducing narcotic was initially designed for use as a prescription painkiller, but is now being used recreationally and has become extremely profitable for Mexican cartels and street gangs. Fentanyl is far more potent and lethal than its predecessors; even 2-3 milligrams of fentanyl (the equivalent of 5-7 individual grains of salt) can be deadly. Fentanyl is 30-50 times more potent than heroin and crosses the blood-brain barrier more easily, which makes it incredibly fast-acting. The rapidity of the reaction to fentanyl makes identifying symptoms of distress more difficult, and consequently significantly increases the risk of overdose death.

Lethal fentanyl traces. Image provided by Drug Enforcement Administration.

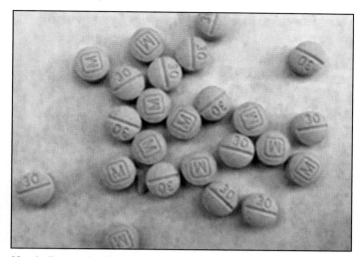
Heroin Fentanyl pills. Image provided by Drug Enforcement Administration.

Fentanyl can be either ingested or absorbed through the skin, and can be found in the form of lozenges, tablets, spray, patches, injectable formulations, pills, or powder. Increasingly, fentanyl is being fashioned into fake oxycodone pills and distributed. It is also common to see fentanyl combined with heroin. These combinations are sold in packaging with names such as Reaper, Penicillin, Lethal Injection, or (in Mexico) "diablito." The danger in these mixed compounds lies in the fact that dealers and buyers don't know precisely what they are selling or ingesting, which leads to critical underestimation of the product's potency. Many heroin dealers and producers are now lacing their products with fentanyl because it is relatively cheap and allows them to increase their profits, but the human cost of this, in terms of overdose and death, is immense.

Analogs of Fentanyl

Drug overdoses are now the leading cause of death among Americans under 50, a frightening trend in which fentanyl has likely played a part. In fact, in the past year, the amount of fentanyl recovered by American law enforcement has increased to 20 times its magnitude in 2010. In Chicago alone, fentanyl has been a factor in 571 deaths since 2014. Even more alarming, the market is now flooded with more intense, more dangerous analogs of fentanyl. The two most prevalent of these products are acrylfentanyl and carfentanyl. Acrylfentanyl is laced with heroin or cocaine, and is up to 4 times more resistant to the overdose antidote naloxone (Narcan), which makes it more likely to contribute to overdose

deaths. It was recently declared a controlled substance, which makes online purchase illegal – although that has not significantly stymied the market for it. Carfentanyl is classified as a Schedule II drug under the Controlled Substances Act, meaning that it has a high potential for abuse and addiction. Its only approved use is as a tranquilizing agent for elephants and large mammals. Carfentanyl is 100 times more potent than fentanyl, which, for reference, makes it more than 10,000 times more potent than morphine. These latest analogs are only intensifying the need for immediate increased attention to the fentanyl crisis.

The China Connection

Similarly to many other synthetic drugs, most fentanyl is produced in labs in China. The ease of sending drugs through the mail appeals especially to Chinese producers. And the fact that enough fentanyl to get nearly 50,000 people high can fit in a standard first-class envelope makes this business model an incredibly profitable one. These Chinese producers use the dark web to sell the deadly drugs which they later deliver via standard mail services. On the dark web, buyers can visit sites anonymously and make purchases using virtual currencies (such as Bitcoin), which allows a significant amount of anonymity for both sellers and buyers, and contributes to the ability to evade detection by law enforcement. In an effort to disable these distribution channels, law enforcement and legislators are working to increase oversight by the US Postal Service and improve preventative tracking of online sellers, but it is a difficult battle to fight.

In many cases, fentanyl is not simply shipped to individual buyers when it leaves China. Instead, it may be shipped into Mexico, where cartels can then transport it into the United States and distribute it through their smuggling networks. One kilogram of fentanyl can be purchased from China for less than $5,000. Then, through the use of cutting agents, a kilogram of diluted fentanyl can be sold for $80,000, leading to a total profit of over $1.6 million. With such potential for profit, street gangs have also entered the market and begun to sell fentanyl that they source either from Mexico or directly from China. Recently, the DEA announced that the Gangster Disciples are now pumping fentanyl into the market.

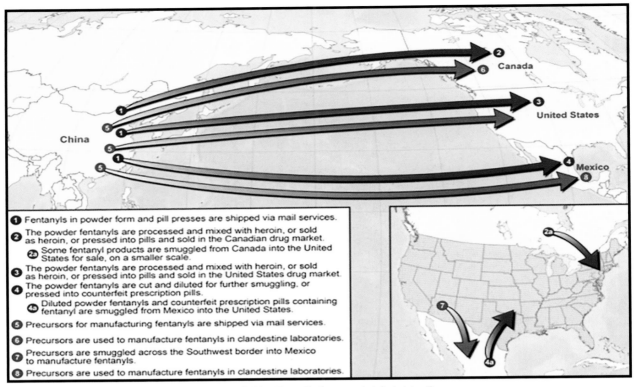

① Fentanyls in powder form and pill presses are shipped via mail services.

② The powder fentanyls are processed and mixed with heroin, or sold as heroin, or pressed into pills and sold in the Canadian drug market.

②ₐ Some fentanyl products are smuggled from Canada into the United States for sale, on a smaller scale.

③ The powder fentanyls are processed and mixed with heroin, or sold as heroin, or pressed into pills and sold in the United States drug market.

④ The powder fentanyls are cut and diluted for further smuggling, or pressed into counterfeit prescription pills.

④ₐ Diluted powder fentanyls and counterfeit prescription pills containing fentanyl are smuggled from Mexico into the United States.

⑤ Precursors for manufacturing fentanyls are shipped via mail services.

⑥ Precursors are used to manufacture fentanyls in clandestine laboratories.

⑦ Precursors are smuggled across the Southwest border into Mexico to manufacture fentanyls.

⑧ Precursors are used to manufacture fentanyls in clandestine laboratories.

Fentanyl processes for distribution. Image provided by Drug Enforcement Administration.

Handling Fentanyl

As fentanyl becomes more and more widely distributed, the risks to law enforcement are heightened. Because it is so potent, ingestion of even a very small amount (i.e. through accidental inhalation or mistaken skin contact) can be lethal. This puts first responders and law enforcement in a particularly risky position. The DEA now advises that anyone faced with an unknown substance not touch the material or its wrapping without full protective equipment.

Conclusion

The increasing presence and lethality of fentanyl makes it an urgent public health crisis, and the immense profit margins available through its sale and distribution mean that street gangs will find further ways to capitalize on the market for it. Fentanyl is in a realm of its own in its potency, ease of circulation, and extremely profitable nature, and presents an incredibly real, incredibly pressing threat to the safety of individuals and the community.

Level "A" Suits. Image provided by Drug Enforcement Administration.

Level "B" Suits. Image provided by Drug Enforcement Administration.

DRUG DESCRIPTIONS

Drug	Description	Street Names	Appearance	How it's Abused	Mental and Physical Effects	Overdose Effect	Legal Status
Heroin	Processed from morphine Extracted from poppy seed pods Grown in: Thailand, Laos, Myanmar, Afghanistan, Pakistan, Mexico, and Columbia	Big H, Black Tar, Chiva, Hell Dust, Horse, Negra, Smack, and Thunder	Sold as a brown or white powder or a black, sticky substance Often cut with other substances	Injected Smoked Sniffed/snorted High purity heroin is typically snorted or smoked	Mental effects include a surge of euphoria or a "rush," followed by a twilight state of sleep and wakefulness Physical effects include drowsiness, respiratory depression, constricted pupils, nausea, a warm flushing of the skin, dry mouth, and heavy extremities	Slow and shallow breathing, blue lips and fingernails, clammy skin, convulsion, coma, and possible death	Schedule I substance High potential for abuse Not currently accepted for medical use in the US
Hydromorphone	A legally manufactured opioid 2-8 times more powerful than morphine Obtained from friends, acquaintances, or forged prescriptions ("doctor-shopping")	D, Dillies, Dust, Footballs, Juice, and Smack	Tablets, rectal suppositories, oral solutions, and injectable formulations	Primarily ingested Tablets can be crushed and dissolved in a solution to be injected as a replacement for heroin	Produces mental effects such as euphoria, relaxation, sedation, reduced anxiety, mental clouding, mood changes, nervousness, and restlessness Physical effects include constipation, pupillary constriction, urinary retention, nausea, vomiting, respiratory depression, dizziness, impaired coordination, loss of appetite, rash, slow or rapid heartbeat, and changes in blood pressure	Severe respiratory depression, drowsiness progressing to stupor or coma, lack of skeletal muscle tone, cold and clammy skin, constricted pupils, and reduction in blood pressure and heart rate	Schedule II drug High potential for abuse Accepted medical use as a pain reliever

Source: 2017 National Drug Threat Assessment – Drug Enforcement Administration

Drug	Description	Street Names	Appearance	How it's Abused	Mental and Physical Effects	Overdose Effect	Legal Status
Methadone	A man-made narcotic Synthesized in Germany during WWII Introduced to the US in 1947	Amidone, Chocolate Chip Cookies, Fizzies, Maria, Pastora, Salvia, Street Methadone, and Wafer	Tablet, disk, oral solution, or injectable liquid	Swallowed or injected	Psychological dependence can occur over prolonged use Physical effects include sweating, itchy skin, sleepiness	Slow and shallow breathing, blue fingernails and lips, stomach spasms, clammy skin, convulsion, weak pulse, and possible death	Schedule II drug May be used legally under a doctor's supervision
Morphine	Non-synthetic narcotic One of the most effective drugs known for severe pain relief Principal constituent of opium	Dreamer, Emsel, First Line, God's Drug, Hows, M.S., Mister Blue, Morf, Morpho, and Unkie	MS-Contin, Oramorph SR, MSIR, Roxanol, Kadian, and RMS	Oral solutions, immediate and sustained release tablets and capsules, suppositories, and injectable preparations	Effects on the mind include euphoria and pain reduction Physical effects include pain relief, decreased hunger, and the inhibition of the cough reflex	Cold, clammy skin, lowered blood pressure, sleepiness, slowed breathing, slow pulse rate, coma, and possible death	Schedule II narcotic
Opium	Derived from the poppy plant Grown in the Mediterranean as early as 5,000 BC	Ah-pen-yen, Aunti, Aunti Emma, Big O, Black Pill, Chandoo, Chandu, Chinese Molasses, Chinese Tobacco, Dopium, Dover's Powder, Dream Gun, Dream Stick, Dreams, Easing Powder, Fi-do-nie, Gee, God's Medicine, Gondola, Goric, Great Tobacco, Guma, Hop/Hops, Joy Plant, Midnight Oil, Mira, O, OP, Ope, Pen Yan, Pin Gon, Pox, Skee, Toxy, Toys, When-shee, Ze, and Zero	Can be liquid, solid, or powder Most poppy straw concentrate is available as a fine brown powder	Smoked, intravenously injected, or taken as a pill Can be combined with other drugs such as marijuana and methamphetamine	Intense euphoric effects similar to a heroin high followed by relaxation and pain relief Physical effects include constipation, drying of the mucous membranes in the mouth and nose	Slow breathing, seizures, dizziness, weakness, loss of consciousness, coma, and possible death	Schedule II drug Most opioids are schedule II, III, IV, or V Some drugs derived from opium such as heroin, are schedule I substances

Drug	Description	Street Names	Appearance	How it's Abused	Mental and Physical Effects	Overdose Effect	Legal Status
Oxycodone	A semi-synthetic narcotic analgestic Synthesized from thebaine, a constituent of the poppy plants	Hillbilly Heroin, Kicker, oC, ox, Roxy, Perc, and oxy	Marketed as OxyContin in 10, 20, 40, and 80 mg capsules Immediate capsules like 5mg OxyIR Marketed in combination with aspirin such as Percodan or acetaminophen such as Roxicet	Used orally or intravenously Tablets are crushed and sniffed or dissolved in water and injected Can be placed on foil and heated until the vapors are inhalable	Mental effects include euphoria and feelings of relaxation Physical effects include pain relief, sedation, respiratory depression, constipation, papillary constriction, and cough suppression Extended use could cause liver damage	Extreme drowsiness, muscle weakness, confusion, cold and clammy skin, pinpoint pupils, shallow breathing, slow heart rate, fainting, coma, and possible death	Schedule II semi-synthetic narcotic
Amphetamines	Stimulants to speed up the body's system Originally marketed to treat nasal congestion, sleeping disorders, narcolepsy, and ADHD	Bennies, Black Beauties, Crank, Ice, Speed, and Uppers	Pills or powder Common prescriptions are Ritalin or Ritalin SR, Adderall, and Dexedrine	Generally taken orally or injected Can be smoked in the cases of "ice" (smokable methamphetamine)	Similar mental effects as cocaine except slower onset, longer duration, and remains in the nervous system longer Physical effects include increased blood pressure and pulse rates, insomnia, loss of appetite, and physical exhaustion, prolonged use could lead to psychosis that resembles schizophrenia	Agitation, increased body temperature, hallucinations, convulsions, and possible death	Schedule II stimulants High potential for abuse Pharmaceuticals are only available through prescriptions that cannot be refilled

Source: 2017 National Drug Threat Assessment – Drug Enforcement Administration

Drug	Description	Street Names	Appearance	How it's Abused	Mental and Physical Effects	Overdose Effect	Legal Status
Cocaine	Derived from coca leaves grown in Bolivia, Peru, and Columbia 90% of cocaine powder that reaches the US comes from Columbia Manufacturing takes place in remote jungles where the raw product undergoes a series of chemical transformations	Coca, Coke, Crack, Flake, Snow, and Soda Cot	Usually distributed as white crystalline powder Often diluted with other substances to stretch out the amount of product Cocaine base (crack) resembles small, irregularly shaped chunks (rocks)	Can be snorted or injected Cocaine base (crack) is smoked, sometimes with tobacco or marijuana Can be used in combination with an opiate known as "speedballing" All mucous membranes readily absorb cocaine	Cocaine's euphoric sensation depends on how fast it reaches the brain, mental effects include increased alertness and excitation, restlessness, and irritability This is usually followed by a crash resulting in depression, exhaustion, and sleepiness lasting several days Physical effects include increased heart rate and blood pressure, dilated pupils, insomnia, and loss of appetite	Cardiac arrhythmias, ischemic heart conditions, sudden cardiac arrest, convulsions, strokes, and death	Schedule II drug High potential for abuse
Khat	Native to East Africa and the Arabian Peninsula Used for its stimulant-like effects Two active ingredients: cathine and cathinone	Abyssinian Tea, African Salad, Catha, Chat, Kat, and Oat	Is a flowering green shrub	Often chewed like tobacco Can be dried and made into tea or a chewable paste Khat can even be smoked or sprinkled on food	Khat effects the mind in the ways of grandiose delusions, paranoia, nightmares, hallucinations, and hyperactivity Also causes high blood pressure and heart rate, stained teeth, gastric disorders Prolonged use can lead to physical exhaustion	Delusions, loss of appetite, difficulty breathing, and increases in both blood pressure and heart rate	Cathine is a schedule IV stimulant Cathinone is a schedule I stimulant High potential for abuse No medical use in the US

Source: 2017 National Drug Threat Assessment – Drug Enforcement Administration

Drug	Description	Street Names	Appearance	How it's Abused	Mental and Physical Effects	Overdose Effect	Legal Status
Methamphetamine	A stimulant Methods used depend on the precursor material used Traditionally has been made in the US with pseudoephedrine, ephedrine, or phenyl-propanlamine	Batu, Biker's Coffee, Black Beauties, Chalk, Chicken Feed, Crank, Crystal, Glass, Go-Fast, Hiropon, Ice, Meth, Methlies Quick, Poor Man's Cocaine, Shabu, Shards, Speed, Stove Top, Tina, Trash, Tweak, Uppers, Ventana, Vidrio, Yaba, and Yellow Bam	Regular meth comes in pill or powder Crystal meth comes in fragments of blue-white "rocks"	Meth can be swallowed, smoked, snorted, or injected	When meth is smoked, the user feel a brief, intense rush Oral ingestion or snorting produces a longer high instead of a rush Both occur from the release of high levels of dopamine into the areas of the brain that regulates pleasure Chronic meth users exhibit violent behavior, anxiety, confusion, insomnia, paranoia, aggression, visual and auditory hallucinations, mood disturbances and delusions Physical effects include increased wakefulness, increased physical activity, decreased appetite, rapid breathing and heart rate, irregular heartbeat increased blood pressure, and hyperthermia	Stroke, heart attack, or multiple organ problems caused by overheating	Schedule II stimulant High potential for abuse Only one legal meth product in the US, Desoxyn has very limited use to treat obesity and ADHA

Source: 2017 National Drug Threat Assessment – Drug Enforcement Administration

Drug	Description	Street Names	Appearance	How it's Abused	Mental and Physical Effects	Overdose Effect	Legal Status
Barbiturates 	First introduced in the 1900s Used as depressants that could range anywhere from mild sedation to coma	Barbs, Block Busters, Christmas Trees, Goof Balls, Pinks, Red Devils, Reds and Blues, and Yellow Jackets	Come in a variety of multicolored pills and tablets	Swallowed or injected when in liquid form Generally used to reduce anxiety, decrease inhibitions, and treat unwanted effects of other illicit drugs	Mild euphoria, lack of inhibition, relief of anxiety, and sleepiness Higher doses cause impairment of memory, judgment and coordination, irritability, paranoid and suicidal ideation Physical effects include the slowdown of the central nervous system and sleepiness	Shallow respiration, clammy skin, dilated pupils, weak and rapid pulse, coma, and possible death	Barbiturates range from schedule II, III, and IV depressants
Benzodiazepines 	Depressants that produce sedation, induce sleep, relieve anxiety, and muscle spasms Only available through prescription	Benzos and Downers	Common prescription drugs such as Valium, Xanax, Restoril, and Ativan	Frequently associated with adolescents and young adults Taken orally or crushed up and snorted	Mental effects include amnesia, hostility, irritability, and vivid or disturbing dreams Physical effects include the slowdown of the central nervous system and sleepiness	Shallow respiration, clammy skin, dilated pupils, weak and rapid pulse, coma, and possible death	Schedule IV depressants

Source: 2017 National Drug Threat Assessment – Drug Enforcement Administration

Drug	Description	Street Names	Appearance	How it's Abused	Mental and Physical Effects	Overdose Effect	Legal Status
GHB	Gamma-Hydroxybutyric acid Typically sold as fluid at bars or "rave" parties Has been encountered in nearly every region in the country	Easy Lay, G, Georgia Home Boy, GHB, Goop, Grievous Bodily Harm, Liquid Ecstasy, Liquid X, and Scoop	Sold as a liquid or white powder that is dissolved in water, juice, or alcohol In liquid form, GHB is clear and slightly salty in taste	Used for euphoric and calming effects Used to increase libido, passivity, and to cause amnesia Became popular in the 1990s amongst crowds at raves and night clubs Gained notoriety as a date rape drug	Mental effects include euphoria, drowsiness, decreased anxiety, confusion, and memory impairment High dose physical effects include unconsciousness, seizures, slowed heart rate, greatly slowed breathing, lower body temperature, vomiting, nausea, and coma Regular dose physical effects include insomnia, anxiety, tremors, increased heart rate and blood pressure Side effects include irritation to the skin and eyes, nausea, vomiting, incontinence, loss of consciousness, seizures, liver damage, kidney failure, and respiratory depression	A GHB overdose can lead to death	Schedule I substance Hight potential for abuse Some GHB products are listed as schedule III substances

Source: 2017 National Drug Threat Assessment – Drug Enforcement Administration

Drug	Description	Street Names	Appearance	How it's Abused	Mental and Physical Effects	Overdose Effect	Legal Status
Royphol	The trade name for flunitrazepam Produces sedative-hypnotic, anti-anxiety, and muscle relaxant effects typically used to treat insomnia Often referred to as a "date rape" drug	Circles, Forget Pill, Forget-Me-Pill, La Rocha, Lunch Money Drug, Mexican Valium, Pingus, R2, Reynolds R2, Reynolds Roach, Roach 2, Roaches, Roachies, Roapies, Robutal, Rochas Dos, Rohypnol, Roofies, Rophies, Ropies, Roples, Row-Shay, Ruffies, and Wolfies	Comes as an oblong olive green tablet with a speckled blue core that when dissolved in light-colored drinks will turn the liquid blue	Tablets can be swallowed whole or crushed and snorted or dissolved in liquid Royphol is also used to target women for sexual assault	Mental effects include drowsiness, sleep, decreased anxiety, and amnesia Physical effects include slurred speech, loss of motor skills, weakness, headache, and respiratory depression	Can cause severe sedation, unconsciousness, slow heart rate, and suppression of respiration that may result in death	Schedule IV substance Penalties for possession, trafficking, and distribution involving one gram or more are the same as those of a schedule I substance
Ecstasy/MDMA	MDMA is a synthetic chemical made in labs It acts as both a psychedelic and stimulant, producing an energizing effect, distortions in time and perception, and enhanced enjoyment of tactile experiences	Adam, Beans, Clarity, Disco Biscuit, E, Ecstasy, Go, Hug Drug, Lover's Speed, MDMA, Peace, STP, X, and XTC	Comes in a tablet, often with a logo, creating a brand name for users to seek out MDMA is also distributed in capsules, powder, and liquid forms	Tablets are mainly swallowed although occasionally crushed and snorted and occasionally smoked but rarely injected Trends such as "stacking" (taking three or more tablets at once) or "piggy-backing" (taking a series of tablets over a short period of time) are common The is also the prevalence of "candy-flipping" which is the co-abuse of MDMA and LSD	MDMA effects braincells that use serotonin to communicate with each other Mental effects of MDMA include confusion, anxiety, depression, paranoia, and sleep problems Physical effects include muscle tension, tremors, involuntary teeth clenching, muscle cramps, nausea, faintness, chills, sweating, and blurred vision	Interferes with the body's ability to regulate temperature which leads to hyperthermia, liver, kidney, and cardiovascular failure, interferes with the body's metabolism, could result in death	Schedule I drug

Source: 2017 National Drug Threat Assessment – Drug Enforcement Administration

Drug	Description	Street Names	Appearance	How it's Abused	Mental and Physical Effects	Overdose Effect	Legal Status
K2/Spice	Synthetic designer drugs that are meant to mimic the effects of THC Have been sold legally as an alternative to marijuana Sold as "herbal incense" or "potpourri" Labeled "not for human consumption" in an attempt to stifle criminal prosecution	Spice, K2, Blaze, RedX Dawn, Paradise, Demon, Black Magic, Spike, Mr. Nice Guy, Ninja, Zohai, Dream, Genie, Sence, Smoke, Skunk, Serenity, Yucatan, Fire, and Crazy Clown	Generally found in bulk powder form and is dissolved in solvents and then applied to plants There is no control mechanism to prevent contamination or regulate how much of the chemical compound is applied to the plant, making the doses unpredictable	The most common form of abuse is smoking Can also be vaporized through both disposable and reusable electronic cigarettes	Effects on the mind include acute psychotic episodes, dependence and withdrawal Physical effects include elevated heart rate and blood pressure, unconsciousness, tremors, seizures, vomiting, hallucinations, agitation, anxiety, pallor, numbness, and tingling	Overdoses can lead to death from a heart attack Acute kidney injuries have also been connected to K2/Spice use	22 synthetic cannabinoids are controlled through legislation, 75 are not May be subject to schedule I drug violation if certain criteria can be met
Ketamine	An anesthetic that has some hallucinogenic effects Referred to as the "dissociative anesthetic" because it makes patients feel detached from their pain and environment Produced commercially in the US Often seen at raves, nightclubs, and private parties, rarely seen on the street	Cat Tranquilizer, Cat Valium, Jet K, Kit Kat, Purple, Special K, Special La Coke, Super Acid, Super K, and Vitamin K	Comes in a clear liquid or a white/off white powder Powder comes in 100-200 mg glass vials, small plastic, and capsules Also seen in paper, glassine, or aluminum foils folds	Has been popular among youth as a "club drug" Commercially manufactured as a powder Cut into lines and snorted Smoked in marijuana or tobacco Sometimes combined with MDMA, amphetamine, methamphetamine, or cocaine	Produces hallucinations Distorts sight, sound, and makes user feel disconnected and not in control Lasts roughly 30-60 minutes Also causes agitation, depression, cognitive difficulties, unconsciousness, amnesia, and flashbacks several weeks after using Physical effects include involuntary rapid eye movement, dilated pupils, tear secretions, stiffening of the muscles, and sometimes nausea	Can cause unconsciousness and dangerously slow breathing	Schedule III non-narcotic substance Has acceptable medical use Some potential for abuse May lead to moderate or low physical dependence or high psychological dependence

Source: 2017 National Drug Threat Assessment – Drug Enforcement Administration

Drug	Description	Street Names	Appearance	How it's Abused	Mental and Physical Effects	Overdose Effect	Legal Status
LSD	A potent hallucinogen Produced in clandestine labs throughout the US	Acid, Blotter Acid, Dots, Mellow Yellow, and Window Pane	Sold in tablets, capsules, and occasionally in liquid form Odorless and colorless with a slightly bitter taste Added to absorbent paper and divided into squares which represents one dose	LSD is abuse orally	Users experience a change in mood during the first hour after use Users hallucinate and suffer impaired depth and time perception as well as distorted perceptions of objects, color, sound, etc. Users may suffer anxiety and depression after the "trip" Physical effects include dilated pupils, high body temperature, increased heart rate and blood pressure, sweating, loss of appetite, sleeplessness, dry mouth, and tremors	Longer, more intense "trips", psychosis, and possible death	Schedule I substance High potential for abuse No accepted use for medical treatment

Source: 2017 National Drug Threat Assessment – Drug Enforcement Administration

Drug	Description	Street Names	Appearance	How it's Abused	Mental and Physical Effects	Overdose Effect	Legal Status
Peyote/Mescaline	Peyote is a small, spineless cactus containing the active ingredient mescaline Grown in northern Mexico and the southwestern US Mescaline can be extracted from peyote or produced synthetically	Buttons, Cactus, Mesc, and Peyoto	Top of the cactus is referred to as the "crown" and consists of disc-shaped buttons that are cut off	Fresh or dried "buttons" from the "crown" are chewed or soaked in water to produce an intoxicating liquid Can also be ground into a powder and placed inside gel capsules to be swallowed Peyote can also be smoked	Illusions, hallucinations, altered perception of space and time, and altered body image Physical effects include intense nausea vomiting, dilation, increased heart rate, increased blood pressure, a rise in body temperature that causes heavy perspiration, headaches, muscle weakness, and impaired motor coordination	N/A	Schedule I substance High potential for abuse No accepted medical use
Psilocybin	A chemical that is obtained from fresh or dried mushrooms Found in Mexico, Central America, and the US	Magic Mushrooms, Mushrooms, and Shrooms	Mushrooms containing psilocybin have long, slender stems topped by caps with dark gills on the underside Fresh mushrooms have white or whitish-gray stems; the caps are dark brown around the edges and light brown or white in the center Dried mushrooms are usually rusty brown with isolated areas of off-white	Primarily ingested orally Can also be brewed in tea to mask the bitter flavor	Psilocybin effects on the mind include hallucinations and the inability to discern fantasy from reality Physical effects include nausea, vomiting, muscle weakness, and lack of coordination	Longer, more intense "trips," psychosis, and possible death	Schedule I substance High potential for abuse No accepted medical use

Source: 2017 National Drug Threat Assessment – Drug Enforcement Administration

Drug	Description	Street Names	Appearance	How it's Abused	Mental and Physical Effects	Overdose Effect	Legal Status
Marijuana **THC Concentrate** **THC Concentrate**	Psychoactive drug Contains 480 constituents, THC being the main ingredient the produces the psychoactive effect THC can also be extracted and concentrated for a stronger effect Marijuana is grown in the US, Canada, Mexico, Central America, and Asia	Aunt Mary, BC Bud, Blunts, Boom, Chronic, Dope, Gangster, Ganja, Grass, Hash, Herb, Hydro, Indo, Joint, Kif, Mary Jane, Mota, Pot, Reefer, Sinsemilla, Skunk, Smoke, Weed, and Yerba	Dry, shredded green/brown mix of flowers, stems, seeds, and leaves Typically green, brown, or gray in color and may resemble tobacco	Marijuana is usually smoked as a cigarette or in a pipe/bong Can be mixed with other drugs Marijuana can also mixed with foods or brewed as tea	Mental effects of marijuana include dizziness, tachycardia, facial flushing, merriment, happiness, and even exhilaration at high doses Disinhibition, relaxation, increased sociability, and talkativeness Enhanced sensory perception, giving rise to increased appreciation of music, art, and touch Heightened imagination leading to a subjective sense of increased creativity Time distortions Illusions, delusions, and hallucinations are rare except at high doses Impaired judgment, reduced coordination, and ataxia, which can impede driving ability or lead to an increase in risk-taking behavior Emotional lability, incongruity of affect, dysphoria, disorganized thinking, inability to converse logically, agitation, paranoia, confusion, restlessness, anxiety, drowsiness, and panic attacks may occur, especially in inexperienced users or in those who have taken a large dose Increased appetite and short-term memory impairment Physical effects include sedation, bloodshot eyes, increased heart rate, coughing, increased appetite, decreased blood pressure, nausea, dry mouth and tremor Some withdrawal symptoms include restlessness, irritability, sleep difficulties, and decreased appetite	No death from overdose of marijuana has been reported	Schedule I substance High potential for abuse Marinol is a synthetic version of THC that is prescribed to patients going through chemotherapy to control vomiting, nausea, and to stimulate appetite Marinol is a schedule III substance

Source: 2017 National Drug Threat Assessment – Drug Enforcement Administration

Drug	Description	Street Names	Appearance	How it's Abused	Mental and Physical Effects	Overdose Effect	Legal Status
Steroids	Synthetic version of the male hormone testosterone Used to promote muscle growth and physical performance Bought and sold online Also bought and sold at gyms, body building competitions, and schools from coaches, teammates, and trainers	Arnolds, Juice, Pumpers, Roids, Stackers, and Weight Gainers	Tablets, capsules, sublingual-tablets, liquid drops, gels, creams, transdermal patches, subdermal implant pellets, and water/oil-based injectable solutions	Ingested orally, injected intramuscularly, or applied to the skin Doses are between 10-100 times higher than the approved treatment doses Users typically take 2 or more anabolic steroids at the same time in a cyclic manner	Mental effects include mood and behavioral changes including mood swings, feelings of hostility, impaired judgment, and increased levels of aggression Physical effects of anabolic steroids depend on the user's age, sex, amount used, type of steroid used, and duration of use Common physical effects include early sexual development in boys, deepening of the voice in adolescent women, shrinkage of testicles and enlargement of breast tissue in men, and high cholesterol and liver damage Abusers who inject steroids at risk of contracting diseases such as HIV/AIDS or hepatitis B or C	Anabolic steroids are not associated with overdoses	Schedule III substance Only a small number of anabolic steroids are approved for medical use Steroids may be prescribed by a licensed physician for treatment of testosterone deficiency, delayed puberty, low red blood cell count, breast cancer, and tissue wasting results from AIDS
Depo-Testosterone							
Testosterone Cypionate							

Source: 2017 National Drug Threat Assessment – Drug Enforcement Administration

Drug	Description	Street Names	Appearance	How it's Abused	Mental and Physical Effects	Overdose Effect	Legal Status
Inhalants	Invisible, volatile substances found in common household products that produce chemical vapors that are inhaled for mind altering effects More than 1,000 products are very dangerous when inhaled	Gluey, Huff, Rush, and Whippets	Common household products such as glue, lighter fluid, cleaning fluids, and paint all produce chemical vapors that can be inhaled	Sniffing or snorting "Bagging" sniffing or inhaling fumes from substances sprayed or deposited in a paper bag "Huffing" from an inhalant-soaked rag stuffed in the mouth, or inhaling balloons filled with nitrous Inhalants are often used among young children; 1 in 5 kids have reported using inhalants by eighth grade	Causes damage to the brain that controls thinking, moving, seeing, and hearing Cognitive abnormalities can range from mild impairment to severe dementia Effects on the body are similar to effects of alcohol including slurred speech, dizziness, inability to coordinate movements, and euphoria Long-term abuse leads to weight loss, muscle weakness, disorientation, inattentiveness, lack of coordination, irritability, depression, and damage to the nervous system and other organs Other signs include paint or stains on body or clothing, spots or sores around the mouth, red or runny eyes or nose, chemical breath odor, drunk, dazed, or dizzy appearance, nausea, loss of appetite, anxiety, excitability, and irritability	Because the intoxication does not last long, users may prolong the process over several hours which could lead to unconsciousness or death "Sudden sniffing death" can result from a single session of inhalant; generally associated with the use of butane, propane, and chemicals in aerosols Death can result from asphyxiation from high concentration of fumes, displacing available oxygen	Inhalants are common household products Many state legislatures have tried to deter youth who by these products by placing an age restrictions to minors

Source: 2017 National Drug Threat Assessment – Drug Enforcement Administration

Drug	Description	Street Names	Appearance	How it's Abused	Mental and Physical Effects	Overdose Effect	Legal Status
Designer Cathinones	Synthetic stimulants marketed as "bath salts," "research chemicals," "plant food," "glass cleaner" and labeled "not for human consumption" Manufactured in East Asia and have been distributed wholesale throughout Europe, North America, Australia, and other parts of the world	Bliss, Blue Silk, Cloud Nine, Drone, Energy-1, Ivory Wave, Lunar Wave, Meow Meow, Ocean Burst, Pure Ivory, Purple Wave, Red Dove, Snow Leopard, Stardust, Vanilla Sky, White Dove, White Knight, White Lightening	Websites list synthetic stimulants as "plant food" or "bath salts" Come in powdered form or gelatin capsules Sold at smoke shops, head shops, convenience stores, adult book stores, and gas stations Labeled "not for human consumption"	Ingested by sniffing/snorted Can be taken orally, smoked, or put into a solution and injected	Desired effects are euphoria and alertness Mental effects include confusion, acute psychosis, agitation, combativeness, aggressive, violent, and self-destructive Physical effects include hypertension, hyperthermia, prolonged dilation of the pupil, breakdown of muscle fibers that leads to release of muscle fiber contents into the bloodstream, teeth grinding, sweating, headaches, palpitations, seizures, paranoia, hallucinations, and delusions	May result in death	Cannabimimec agents, including 15 synthetic cannabinoid compounds identified by name, 2 synthetic cathinone compounds (mephedrone and MDPV), and 9 synthetic hallucinogens known as the 2C family are now restricted by law Methylone was permanently controlled by the DEA 10 other synthetic cathinones have become subject to temporary control Synthetic cathinones may be subject to Schedule I prosecution

Source: 2017 National Drug Threat Assessment – Drug Enforcement Administration

Drug	Description	Street Names	Appearance	How it's Abused	Mental and Physical Effects	Overdose Effect	Legal Status
DXM	A cough suppressor found in more than 120 over-the-counter (OTC) cold medications Either taken alone or in combination with other drugs Can be obtained in almost any pharmacy or grocery store Powder DXM can be purchased on the internet	CCC, Dex, Poor Man's PCP, Robo, Rojo, Skittles, Triple C, and Velvet	Comes in the form of cough syrup, tablets, capsules, or powder	Abusers take various amounts based on their body weight and the effect they are attempting to achieve Some abusers ingest 250-1500 mg in a single dosage Referred to as "robo-tripping," "skittling," or "dexing" Traditionally, DXM involves drinking large volumes of OTC liquid cough medication Recently, the abuse of tablet or gel capsules has increased Newer, high-dose forms of DXM are easier to consume, easily concealable, and allows the user to continue to take DXM throughout the day DXM is also distributed illicitly or mixed with other drugs DXM is abused by individuals of all ages but is of concern for younger users	Effects on the mind are described in "plateaus" 1st plateau, 100-200 mg, mild stimulation 2nd plateau, 200-400 mg, euphoria and hallucinations 3rd plateau, 300-600 mg, distorted visual perceptions and loss of motor coordination 4th plateau, 500-1500 mg, out-of-body sensations Effects on the body include over-excitability, lethargy, loss of coordination, slurred speech, hypertension, and involuntary spasmodic movement of the eyeballs Other physical effects include liver damage, rapid heart rate, lack of coordination, vomiting, seizures, and coma	Can be treated in an emergency room Impaired senses lead to accidental death Other DXM-related deaths often come when mixing with other drugs	DXM is a legally marketed substance that is neither a controlled substance nor a regulated chemical under the Controlled Substances Act

Source: 2017 National Drug Threat Assessment – Drug Enforcement Administration

Drug	Description	Street Names	Appearance	How it's Abused	Mental and Physical Effects	Overdose Effect	Legal Status
Kratom	A tropical tree native to Southeast Asia Is a stimulant in low does and a sedative in high doses More commonly abused in the Asia Pacific region rather than the US	Kakuam, Thom, Ketum, and Biak	Leaves are crushed and then smoked, brewed with tea, or placed into gel capsules	Ingested in pill form Also may be dissolved and ingested as a tea or the leaves may be chewed	At low doses users report increased alertness, physical energy, and talkativeness At high doses users report sedative effects Several cases of psychosis have been reported resulting from use Physical effects include nausea, itching, sweating, dry mouth, constipation, increased urination, and loss of appetite Long-term use could lead to anorexia, weight loss, insomnia, dry mouth, frequent urination, and constipation	N/A	Not controlled under the Federal Controlled Substances Act There are some states the regulate or prohibit the possession and use of Kratom No legitimate medical use

Source: 2017 National Drug Threat Assessment – Drug Enforcement Administration

Drug	Description	Street Names	Appearance	How it's Abused	Mental and Physical Effects	Overdose Effect	Legal Status
Salvia Divinorum	A perennial herb in the mint family that produces hallucinogenic effects Native to the Sierra Mazleca region of Oaxaca, Mexico Can be grown outside the above region Can be grown indoors or outdoors, especially in humid semitropical climates	Maria Pastora, Sally-D, and Salvia	The plant has spade-shaped leaves the look similar to mint leaves The plants grow more than 3 feet high, have large green leaves, hollow square stems, and white flowers with purple calyces	Can be chewed, smoked, or vaporized	Psychic effects include perceptions of bright lights, vivid colors, shapes, and body movements as well disorientation Also causes fear, panic, uncontrollable laughter, a sense of overlapping realities, and hallucinations Effects on the body include loss of coordination, dizziness, and slurred speech	Overdose effects include lack of coordination, dizziness, and slurred speech	Not approved for medical use in the US Not under the Controlled Substance Act Some botanical companies and drug promotional sites have advertised Salvia as a legal alternative to other plant hallucinogens like mescaline

Source: 2017 National Drug Threat Assessment – Drug Enforcement Administration

SECTION VI

Gun Trafficking

chicago
crime
commission

GUN TRAFFICKING OVERVIEW

There is no denying the high volume of gun violence occurring in Chicago. According to the Chicago Police Department, Chicago saw a 16 percent decrease in reported homicides in 2017 compared to 2016. In 2016, the University of Chicago found 90% of recorded homicides in Chicago during 2016 were committed with a firearm. Chicago saw 3,550 shootings and 4,331 shooting victims in 2016. In addition, the University of Chicago Crime Lab found approximately 80% of the gun offenders had been previously arrested and 54% had either a current or prior gang affiliation. Roughly 64% of homicides resulted from an altercation that likely involved gangs, and approximately 50% of offenders had a prior arrest for a violent crime and approximately 40% had a prior gun-related arrest.

Guns Trafficked to Illinois

Many of the firearms used in shootings do not originate in Illinois. In a 2015 study conducted by *The Trace*, an independent, nonprofit news organization dedicated to expanding coverage of guns in the United States, the top three states

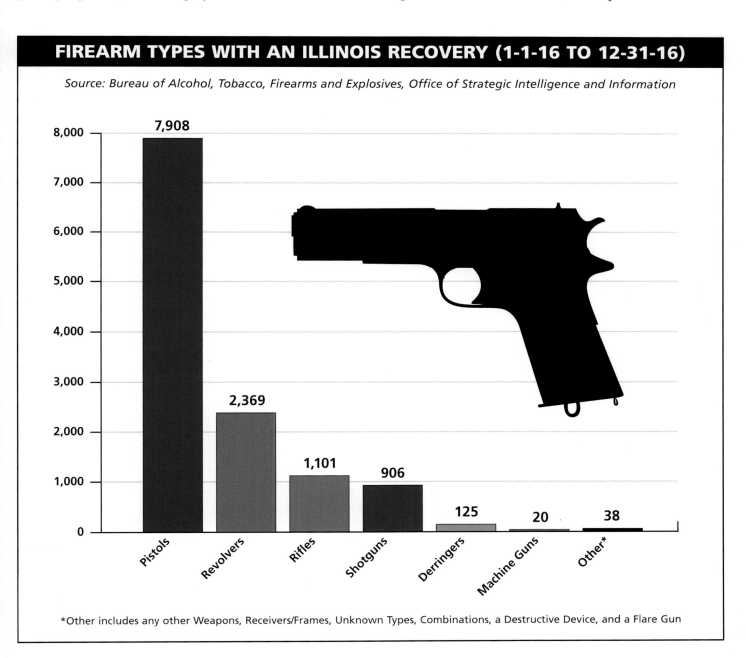

FIREARM TYPES WITH AN ILLINOIS RECOVERY (1-1-16 TO 12-31-16)

Source: Bureau of Alcohol, Tobacco, Firearms and Explosives, Office of Strategic Intelligence and Information

Pistols	7,908
Revolvers	2,369
Rifles	1,101
Shotguns	906
Derringers	125
Machine Guns	20
Other*	38

*Other includes any other Weapons, Receivers/Frames, Unknown Types, Combinations, a Destructive Device, and a Flare Gun

TOP 15 SOURCE STATES FOR FIREARMS WITH AN ILLINOIS RECOVERY (1-1-16 TO 12-31-16)

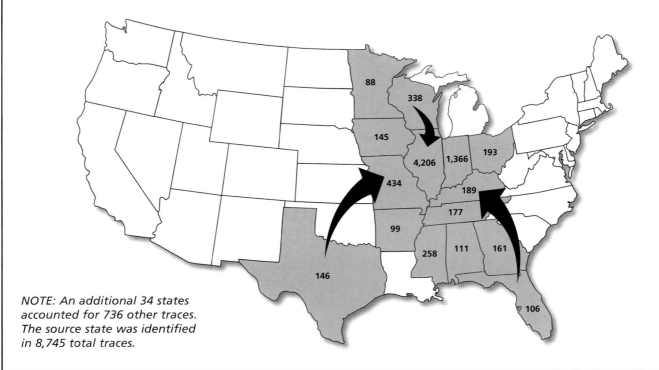

Source: Bureau of Alcohol, Tobacco, Firearms and Explosives, Office of Strategic Intelligence and Information

NOTE: An additional 34 states accounted for 736 other traces. The source state was identified in 8,745 total traces.

responsible for the influx of guns to Illinois between 2010-2014 are Indiana, Mississippi, and Wisconsin. In 2010, 2011, and 2014, Indiana topped the list with 3,269 guns be trafficked across state lines. Over the period examined, Indiana averaged 1,000 guns a year transported across state lines to Illinois.

Methods of Illegal Gun Trafficking

Many firearms purchases are made at out-of-town gun shows. Straw buyers, individuals buying guns for someone who cannot legally purchase a gun, attend gun shows and buy weapons from private sellers who do not require background checks. Buying from private sellers makes tracking guns increasingly more difficult because there is no paper trail and the transaction between buyer and seller can be completed quickly and easily. In fact, for an in-state straw buyer to sell to an intended buyer, the straw buyer simply has to write the intended buyer a bill of sale. This conflicts with federally licensed dealers who require potential buyers to have a firearm owner identification card.

Firearms are also believed to be recycled and used in other shootings. Instead of disposing of crime guns, law enforcement believes gang members sell and or give guns to other gang members post-shooting. Law enforcement has been able to link the same gun to different shootings around the city.

Firearms are also obtained through other illegal means such as robbing trainyards. For example, in 2014, 13-semi-automatic Smith and Wesson M&P 15 Sport Rifles were stolen from a freight container parked at an Englewood rail yard. While the rifles did not come with the 5.56x45mm NATO ammunition, they were equipped with high capacity 30-round magazines.

Types of Guns Used

A wide range of firearms are utilized by Chicago's street gangs. According to a 2016 report by *The Trace*, Smith & Wesson is Chicago's lead producer in guns used by gangs. Smith and Wesson holds 4 spots of CPD's 20 most commonly recovered guns. In 2014, CPD recovered 624 Smith & Wesson brand

TOP CALIBERS REPORTED ON FIREARM TRACES WITH AN ILLINOIS RECOVERY (1-1-16 TO 12-31-16)

Source: Bureau of Alcohol, Tobacco, Firearms and Explosives, Office of Strategic Intelligence and Information

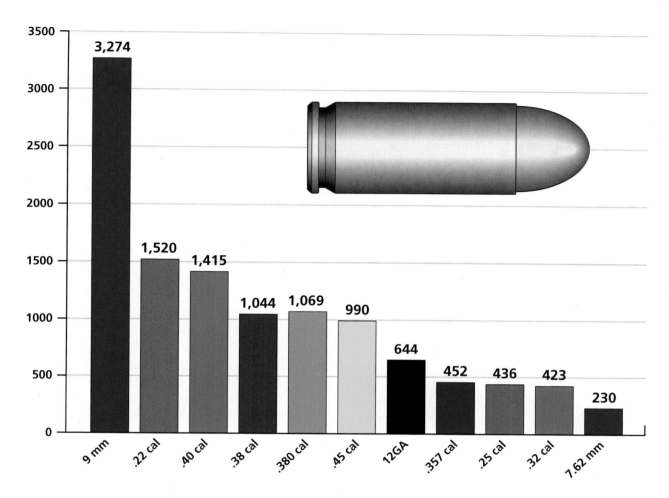

Caliber	Traces
9 mm	3,274
.22 cal	1,520
.40 cal	1,415
.38 cal	1,044
.380 cal	1,069
.45 cal	990
12GA	644
.357 cal	452
.25 cal	436
.32 cal	423
7.62 mm	230

NOTE: There were 880 additional traces that were associated with other calibers. There were 90 traces with an unknown caliber.

firearms. However, *The Trace* identifies Smith & Wesson as the United States' largest gun manufacturer and there may be a correlation between that and the prevalence of S&W weapons on the street.

The Trace reports 9mm as the caliber of choice among Chicago gang members followed closely by .40 and .45 caliber rounds. These calibers account for half the gun crimes recovered by police. .38 caliber revolvers were the gun of choice in Chicago until the 1980's, when gun manufacturers started producing affordable pistols. However, this does not imply cheap firearms are not used.

The Trace references an Ohio-based gun manufacturer, Hi-Point Firearms, as a company whose aim is to produce affordable firearms, most ranging from $162-$285. In 2005, Hi-Point's parent company, MKS Supply, drew controversy for allegedly supplying handguns to irresponsible dealers after a 17-year-old basketball player was mistaken for a gang member and killed with a 9mm Hi-Point handgun.

The use of "Saturday Night Specials," cheap handguns that often misfire or malfunction, still exist as well. Saturday Night Specials are often used for gang shootings because they are small and easily concealable. Manufacturers of these kinds of guns such as Lorcin Engineering and Raven Arms have been out of business for several years but Lorcin .380s and Raven .25s are still among some of Chicago's most seized guns. The fact that these guns are older also appeal to gang members because they are easier to acquire. According to *Some Sources of Crime Guns in Chicago: Dirty Dealers, Straw Purchasers, and Traffickers*, an article published by Cook et al, states the average gun purchased by a gang member tends to be 12.6 years old.

Combatting Illegal Gun Trafficking

While the influx of guns into the city of Chicago is an issue that should not be taken lightly, law enforcement has taken steps to identify crime guns and take them off the street. The first program of note is the Bureau of Alcohol, Tobacco, Firearms and Explosives' (ATF) National Integrated Ballistic Intelligence Network (NIBIN) Program. The NIBIN Program conducts ballistics evaluations and provides actionable investigative leads in a timely manner. Each firearm leaves a unique signature, similar to a fingerprint, on expelled cartridge casings and bullets. The NIBIN Program often links seemingly unrelated cases through ballistics evidence from multiple jurisdictions. It is also the only interstate automated ballistic imaging network in operation in the United States and is available to most major population centers in the United States.

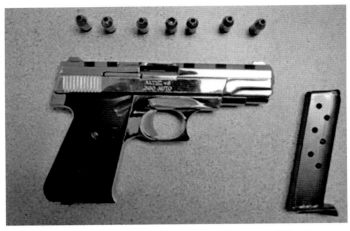

Recovered firearm. Image provided by Mount Prospect, Illinois Police Departmen.t

In 2013, the ATF partnered with the Chicago Police Department, Illinois State Police, and Northeastern Illinois Regional Crime Laboratory to implement the NIBIN Program in Illinois.

In addition to the NIBIN Program, the City of Chicago has also implemented Shotspotter, a gunfire detection system using an auditory sensor to triangulate the position of gunshots. The information is then relayed to a dispatch center where the location is forwarded to a responding officer. Districts where ShotSpotter has been implemented have seen a reduction in shootings. In March 2017, the 7th District saw 13 shootings as opposed to 23 in March of 2016. In the 11th District, shootings dropped to 11 compared to 47 in the year prior. Due to Shotspotter's recent success in districts

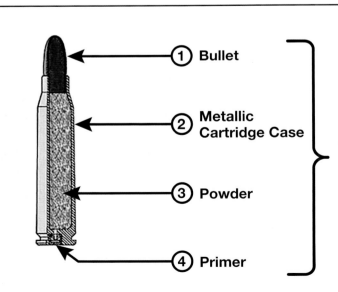

① **Bullet**

② **Metallic Cartridge Case**

③ **Powder**

④ **Primer**

A complete round of ammunition or any enumerated sub-component is ammunition as defined.

Source: Bureau of Alcohol, Tobacco, Firearms and Explosives, Office of Strategic Intelligence and Information

AGE OF POSSESSORS FOR FIREARMS WITH AN ILLINOIS RECOVERY (1-1-16 TO 12-31-16)

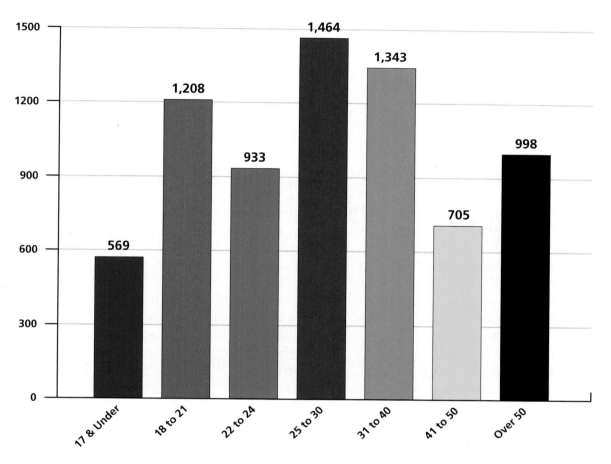

Source: Bureau of Alcohol, Tobacco, Firearms and Explosives, Office of Strategic Intelligence and Information

Chart data:
- 17 & Under: 569
- 18 to 21: 1,208
- 22 to 24: 933
- 25 to 30: 1,464
- 31 to 40: 1,343
- 41 to 50: 705
- Over 50: 998

1/1/2016 - 12/31/2016 Illinois Average Age of Possessor: 33 Years
1/1/2016 - 12/31/2016 National Average Age of Possessor: 35 Years

7 and 11, the program has been implemented in two other districts and is slated to be implemented in an additional two districts by the end of spring 2017.

Ammunition

The term "Ammunition" means ammunition or cartridge cases, primers, bullets, or propellant powder designed for use in any firearm.

The term shall not include (a) any shotgun shot or pellet not designed for use as the single, complete projectile load for one shotgun hull or casing, nor (b) any unloaded, non-metallic shotgun hull or casing not having a primer. 27 § 478.11 *(Source ATF)*

Chicago Crime Gun Strike Force logo provided by ATF Chicago. The joint city, state, and federal law enforcement task force was formed to combat gun violence.

GUIDE TO FIREARM TYPES

U.S. Dept. of Justice – Bureau of Alcohol, Tobacco, Firearms and Explosives, Office of Enforcement Programs and Services

PISTOL

A weapon originally designed, made, and intended to fire a projectile (bullet) from one or more barrels when held in one hand, and having; a chamber(s) as an integral part(s) of, or permanently aligned with, the bore(s); and a short stock designed to be gripped by one hand at an angle to and extending below the line of the bore(s).

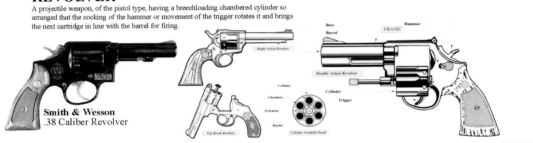

Sturm, Ruger & Co.
9mm Pistol

Multi-Barrel Pistol

Single Shot Pistol

Barrel Assembly Detail

Bore — Chamber

Barrel — Slide — FRAME — Grip

Semiautomatic Pistol

REVOLVER

A projectile weapon, of the pistol type, having a breechloading chambered cylinder so arranged that the cocking of the hammer or movement of the trigger rotates it and brings the next cartridge in line with the barrel for firing.

Smith & Wesson
.38 Caliber Revolver

Single Action Revolver

Double Action Revolver

Top Break Revolver

Cylinder Assembly Detail

Bore — Hammer — FRAME — Barrel

Cylinder — Chambers — Extractor — Rachet

Cylinder — Trigger

SHOTGUN

A weapon designed or redesigned, made or remade, and intended to be fired from the shoulder, and designed or redesigned and made or remade to use the energy of the explosive in a fixed shotgun shell to fire through a smooth bore either a number of ball shot or a single projectile for each pull of the trigger.

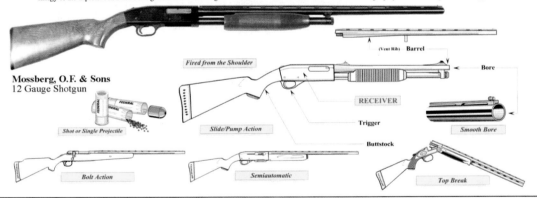

Mossberg, O.F. & Sons
12 Gauge Shotgun

Fired from the Shoulder

(Vent Rib) Barrel

Bore

RECEIVER

Trigger

Buttstock

Smooth Bore

Shot or Single Projectile

Slide/Pump Action

Bolt Action

Semiautomatic

Top Break

RIFLE

A weapon designed or redesigned, made or remade, and intended to be fired from the shoulder, and designed or redesigned and made or remade to use the energy of the explosive in a fixed metallic cartridge to fire only a single projectile through a rifled bore for each single pull of the trigger.

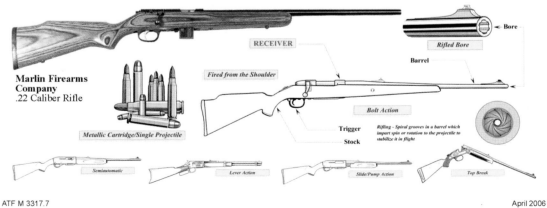

Marlin Firearms Company
.22 Caliber Rifle

Fired from the Shoulder

RECEIVER

Bore

Rifled Bore

Barrel

Bolt Action

Trigger

Stock

Rifling - Spiral grooves in a barrel which impart spin or rotation to the projectile to stabilize it in flight

Metallic Cartridge/Single Projectile

Semiautomatic

Lever Action

Slide/Pump Action

Top Break

ATF M 3317.7

April 2006

Armor Piercing Ammunition

A projectile or projectile core which may be used in a handgun and which is constructed entirely (excluding the presence of traces of other substances) from one or a combination of tungsten alloys, steel, iron, brass, bronze, beryllium copper, or depleted uranium; or

A full jacketed projectile larger than .22 caliber designed and intended for use in a handgun and whose jacket has a weight of more than 25 percent of the total weight of the projectile.

The term "armor piercing ammunition" does not include shotgun shot required by Federal or State environmental or game regulations for hunting purposes, a frangible projectile designed for target shooting, a projectile which the Attorney General finds is primarily intended to be used for sporting purposes, or any other projectile or projectile core which the Attorney General finds is intended to be used for industrial purposes, including a charge used in an oil and gas well perforating device. *(Source ATF)*

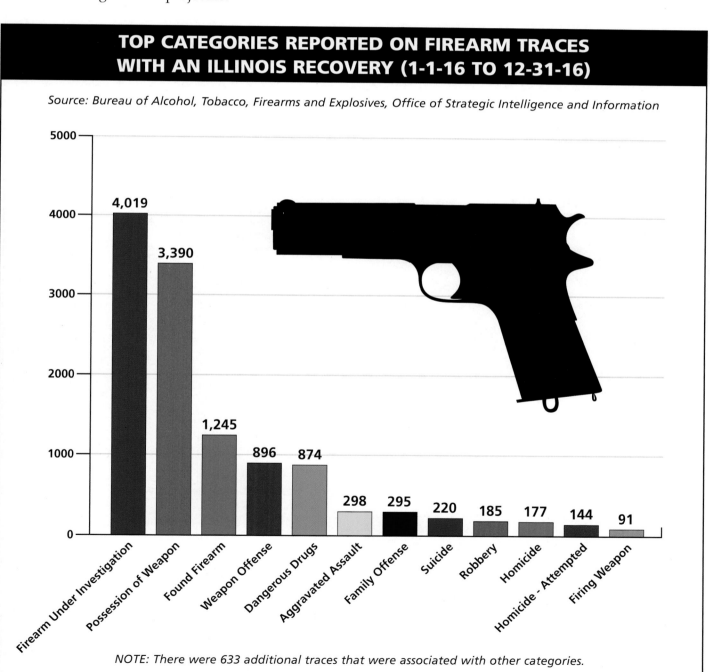

TOP CATEGORIES REPORTED ON FIREARM TRACES WITH AN ILLINOIS RECOVERY (1-1-16 TO 12-31-16)

Source: Bureau of Alcohol, Tobacco, Firearms and Explosives, Office of Strategic Intelligence and Information

Firearm Under Investigation	4,019
Possession of Weapon	3,390
Found Firearm	1,245
Weapon Offense	896
Dangerous Drugs	874
Aggravated Assault	298
Family Offense	295
Suicide	220
Robbery	185
Homicide	177
Homicide - Attempted	144
Firing Weapon	91

NOTE: There were 633 additional traces that were associated with other categories.

365

5 FAST FACTS ABOUT THE NATIONAL TRACING CENTER

1

The Country's Only Crime Gun Tracing Facility

The mission of the National Tracing Center (NTC) is to conduct firearms tracing to provide investigative leads for federal, state, local and foreign law enforcement agencies.

2

373,000+

The number of trace requests NTC received in fiscal year 2015. ATF is the sole federal agency authorized to trace firearms.

5

Goal to Complete Urgent Traces in Less Than 24 Hours

Traces classified as routine are completed within five days on average.

4

6,000+

The number of law enforcement agencies registered for eTrace, a web-based bi-lingual firearms tracing system used to assist in the tracing of U.S.-sourced firearms. Law enforcement agencies in 43 foreign countries are registered.

Provides Critical Information to Law Enforcement Agencies

Helps domestic and international law enforcement agencies solve firearms crimes; detect firearms trafficking; and track the intrastate, interstate, and international movement of crime guns.

3

Published on July 12, 2016

Instagram: @ATFHQ | Twitter: @ATFHQ |
Facebook: facebook.com/HQATF | www.atf.gov

ATF
PROTECTING THE PUBLIC
SERVING OUR NATION

SECTION VII

Directories for Assistance

Youth Programs / Educational Resources

One Summer Chicago

Contact: OneSummerChicago@cityofchicago.org

One Summer Chicago is a youth program geared at providing summer employment and internship opportunities for young adults aged 14 to 24. Partnered with community-based organizations in Chicago neighborhoods, One Summer Chicago employs 31,000 young adults. In addition, One Summer Chicago's website features web tutorials to prepare applicants for their professional futures. The webinars range from resumé building and interview tips to fraud prevention.

More Information

Website:
www.onesummerchicago.org

Social Media:
Facebook, Twitter, Instagram

Project (B.U.I.L.D.)

Contact: (773) 227-2880

Broader Urban Involvement and Leadership Development

Project BUILD is a youth intervention and prevention program designed to provide young people the necessary tools to reduce risk-taking behaviors, develop personal competencies, and strengthen their commitment to education and community engagement. Through an in-school and out-of-school curriculum, Project BUILD provides pro-social alternatives to disengage youth from participating in gang activities.

More Information

Website:
www.buildchicago.org

Social Media:
Facebook, Google+, Twitter, YouTube, Instagram

Crushers Club

Contact: (312) 221-0289

Crushers Club provides boys ages 7 to 18 with an alternative to gangs and street crimes. The boys who join Crushers Club are required to avoid gangs and maintain grades and school attendance. Youth develop crucial skills such as respect, discipline, love and ownership through the sport of boxing and mentorship.

More Information

Website:
crushersclub.org

Social Media:
Facebook, Twitter, YouTube, Instagram

Kids Off the Block

Contact: (773) 941-6864

Since 2003, Kids Off the Block has provided structured programs for youth aged 12 to 24 including tutoring/mentoring, music, sports, job readiness, General Educational Development preparation, health/fitness and nutrition and cultural arts.

More Information

Website:
kobchicago.org

Social Media:
Facebook, Twitter, YouTube, Instagram

Youth Guidance

Contact: (312) 253-4900

Becoming a Man (BAM) and Working on Womanhood (WOW)

Youth Guidance is a school-based youth program centered around cognitive-behavioral therapy (CBT). Youth Guidance works in approximately 80 Chicago Public Schools and serves roughly 8,000 middle and high school youth. In addition, Youth Guidance provides services for parents/caregivers and community members.

More Information

Website:
www.youth-guidance.org

Social Media:
Facebook, Twitter,
YouTube, LinkedIn

Boys & Girls Clubs of Chicago

Contact: (312) 235-8000

The Boys & Girls Club has 23 Chicago locations offering after-school programs for youth ages 6 to 18 including character and leadership, education and career, health and life skills, the arts, and fitness and sports.

More Information

Website:
www.bgcc.org

Social Media:
Facebook, Twitter, YouTube, Instagram

YMCA of Metro Chicago

Contact: (312) 932-1200

Youth Safety and Violence Prevention Initiative – Urban Warriors Program

As part of their Youth Safety and Violence Prevention Initiative, the YMCA of Metro Chicago has introduced the Urban Warriors Program. This program was designed based on research that has shown many similarities between gang members in the U.S. and child soldiers from around the world. Following from this, the Urban Warriors Program pairs youth from some of Chicago's most dangerous neighborhoods with military veterans who can relate to their experiences of exposure to violence. In structured sessions facilitated by the military veterans, participants process their traumatic experiences and build their skills and confidence in five thematic areas: belonging, positive identity development, cognitive restructuring, coping, and community engagement.

More Information

Website:
www.ymcachicago.org/
programs/youth-safety-and-
violence-prevention-urban-warriors

Social Media:
Facebook, Twitter, YouTube

CBT Therapy Program

Contact: (312) 747-3934

(Juvenile Detention Center)

Using a model similar to that of Becoming a Man, the Cook County Juvenile Temporary Detention Center implemented a Cognitive-Behavioral Therapy (CBT) program in an attempt to reduce recidivism rates among arrestees. CBT focuses on the act of decision-making, and teaches participants to think reflectively and overcome biases rather than respond based on automatic processes.

City Colleges of Chicago

Contact: (773) 907-4350

City Colleges of Chicago offer tuition free GED preparatory courses for adults in English and in Spanish. The GED examination fee is $30. City Colleges of Chicago also offer tuition free English as a Second Language classes.

More Information

Website:
www.ccc.edu/site/Pages/highschool.aspx

Social Media:
Facebook, Twitter, Tumblr, YouTube, Instagram

Cook County High School

Contact: (312) 814-4488
Equivalency Records Office

Cook County High School Equivalency Records Office provides adults with the necessary resources to obtain a GED. Adults seeking their GED can register at www.ged.com to locate facilities in the area that offer GED testing.

More Information

Website:
www.cookcountyged.org

Tattoo Cover-ups and Removals

Sacred Transformations

Contact: (312) 213-2505

Sacred Transformations is a nonprofit organization dedicated to helping people who are tattooed, scarred, branded and or burnt from negative experiences to transform those marks into art pieces that celebrate one's individuality. Since 2006, Eric Spruth has worked with clients to design a custom free tattoo that will become a symbol of positivity for that individual.

More information

Email address:
timeforink@gmail.com

Website:
www.sacredtransformations.org

Social Media:
Facebook, Twitter, Instagram

Ink 180

Contact: (630) 554-1404

Chris Baker started Ink 180 to offer former gang members and victims of human trafficking an opportunity to erase their past. In addition to the services he offers at his Oswego, IL facility, Chris Baker recently converted an RV into a Mobile Tattoo Removal Studio. Chris Baker travels to various Chicago neighborhoods to provide removals and cover-ups for those unable to travel to his suburban location.

More information

Email address:
chrisbaker@ink180.com

Website:
www.ink180.com

Social Media:
Facebook, Twitter, Instagram

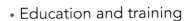

CHICAGO DEPARTMENT OF
FAMILY & SUPPORT SERVICES

BUILD • SUPPORT • EMPOWER

COMMUNITY REENTRY SUPPORT CENTERS

The City of Chicago's Community Re-Entry Support Centers provide a central location where any Chicago resident who has served time for a felony conviction can receive the support services needed to transition back into their communities and the workforce. Our services provide participants with training to move forward and succeed in life.

We offer the following services:

- Education and training
- Mentoring and support groups
- Linkage to counseling for substance use and mental health issues
- Linkage to housing assistance, emergency housing and food assistance
- Employment assistance
- Strategies for presenting criminal backgrounds to employers
- Information on sealing or expunging criminal records
- Family reunification and child-support assistance

To speak with a counselor, or to schedule an appointment at one of our Communi Re-Entry Support Centers, contact 3-1-1 or the nearest facility directly:

Howard Area Community Center
7637 North Paulina Street
Chicago, Illinois 60626
773-332-6772

Westside Health Authority
5816 West Division Street
Chicago, Illinois 60651
773-664-0612

Phalanx Family Services
837 West 119th Street
Chicago, Illinois 60643
773-291-1086 ext. 44

Teamwork Englewood
815 W. 63rd Street, 2nd Floor
Chicago, Illinois 60621
773-488-6607

Visit DFSS online at www.cityofchicago.org/fss

City of Chicago
Rahm Emanuel, Mayor

Offender Reentry Programs and Services

Safer Foundation

Contact: (312) 922-2200

Safer Foundation is a nationally recognized nonprofit organization designed to serve men and women with criminal records aged sixteen and older who live in the Chicago metropolitan area. Safer Foundation provides individuals with a case manager who works closely with them to ensure successful reentry. Case managers work with individuals throughout the entire employment process. Safer Foundation partners with companies that hire individuals with criminal records. Safer Foundation also assists young adults in obtaining their GEDs.

More information

Website:
www.saferfoundation.org

Social Media:
Facebook, Twitter, YouTube

The Salvation Army – Pathway Forward

Contact: (312) 667-2100

Pathway Forward is a by-referral reentry program for former federally incarcerated individuals. This program allows offers job readiness, recreational activities and onsite clinical counseling services.

More Information

Website:
www.safreedom.org/pathway-forward

Illinois Reentry Resource Directory

Contact: (312) 913-5796

Directory of resources categorized by IL county and service type. The directory includes a link to the specific agency's website.

More information

Website:
www.reentryillinois.net/IllinoisResourceDirectory.html

Legal Assistance

Cabrini Green Legal Aid

Contact: (312) 738-2452

Cabrini Green Legal Aid provides legal services to those who have been incarcerated or have come into contact with the Criminal Justice System. They assist individuals with criminal records relief, defense assistance, family, and housing law.

More information

Email address:
development@CGLA.net

Website:
www.cgla.net

Social Media:
Facebook, Twitter, and YouTube

Coordinated Advice & Referral

Contact: (312) 738-9200
Program for Legal Aid (CARPLS)

CARPLS provides free legal services for low-and moderate-income residents in the Cook County area.

More Information

Website: www.carpls.org

Social Media: Facebook, Twitter, Linkedin

Cook County State's Attorney's Office

Contact: (773) 674-7200
Victim/Witness Assistance Unit

Chicago Innocence Center

Contact: (312) 263-6213

Northwestern Law Medill Justice Project

Contact: (847) 491-5840

ACLU of Illinois

Contact: (312) 201-9740

Website: www.aclu-il.org

Chicago Lawyers' Committee

Contact: (312) 630-9744

Juvenile Legal Assistance

Cook County Juvenile Expungement Help Desk

Contact: (312) 229-6359

Cook County Juvenile Court Center

Contact: (312) 433-4757

Northwestern University – Bluhm Legal Clinic

Contact: (312) 503-8576

Website: www.law.northwestern.edu/legalclinic/

Chicago Legal Clinic

Contact: (773) 731-1762

Website: www.clclaw.org

Chicago Volunteer Legal Services

Contact: (312) 332-1624

Website: www.cvls.org

PHARMACEUTICAL DISPOSAL

Be Safe at Home and Help Protect the Environment

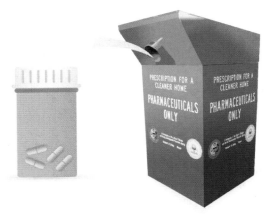

Bring unused or expired prescription and over-the counter medications to any of the Chicago Police Stations at the locations listed below. Available 24 hours a day.

1. 1718 S. STATE ST	13. 2452 W. BELMONT
2. 5101 S. WENTWORTH AVE	14. 2150 N. CALIFORNIA AVE
3. 7040 S. COTTAGE GROVE AVE	15. 5701 W. MADISON ST
4. 2255 E. 103RD ST	16. 5151 N. MILWAUKEE AVE
5. 727 E. 111TH ST	17. 4650 N. PULASKI RD
6. 7808 S. HALSTED ST	18. 1160 N. LARRABEE ST
7. 1438 W. 63RD ST	19. 850 W. ADDISON ST
8. 3420 W. 63RD ST	20. 5400 N. LINCOLN AVE
9. 3120 S. HALSTED ST	21. 1900 W. MONTEREY AVE
10. 3315 W. OGDEN AVE	22. 6464 N. CLARK ST
11. 3151 W. HARRISON ST	23. 5555 W. GRAND AVE
12. 1412 S. BLUE ISLAND	

QUESTIONS? Visit the Chicago Department of Public Health at www.cityofchicago.org/cdph

The Chicago Pharmaceutical Collection Program is a joint effort of the City of Chicago Department of Public Health (CDPH) and the Chicago Police Department. The pharmaceuticals are processed and disposed of by CDPH at the Household Chemicals and Computer Recycling Facility.

ADDITIONAL DISPOSAL OPTIONS

Bring your household chemicals, computers, and non-controlled substances to the City's **Household Chemicals & Computer Recycling Facility** located at 1150 N. North Branch St., 2 blocks east of the Kennedy Expressway at Division Street.
Visit www.cityofchicago.org/hccrf for more information.

Hours: Tuesdays, 7am—noon • Thursdays, 2pm-7pm • 1st Saturday of every month, 8am-3pm

Connect with the Chicago Department of Public Health:

Counseling and Addiction Treatment Services

Metropolitan Family Services

Contact: (312) 986-4000

Metropolitan Family Services provides services tailored to a family's needs. Metropolitan Family Services offers programs in four areas: economic stability, education, emotional wellness, and empowerment.

More Information

Email: contactus@metrofamily.org

Website: www.metrofamily.org

Social Media: Facebook, Twitter, YouTube, Flickr

Department of Human Services

Contact: (800) 843-6154
Family Community Resource Centers (FCRCs)

DHS connects individuals with the programs and services they need. DHS offers services geared at improving the health, well-being of families and individuals through partnerships within the community.

More Information

Website: www.dhs.state.il.us

Live4Lali

Contact: (844) 584-5254

Live4Lali is a care resource center for individuals who suffer from substance abuse and addiction.

More Information

Website: www.live4lali.org

Social Media: Facebook, Twitter, Instagram

Footprints to Recovery

Contact: (877) 857- 6125

Footprints to Recovery is a suburban outpatient drug treatment center.

Above and Beyond – Family Recovery Center

Contact: (773) 940-2960

Above and Beyond offers drug and alcohol treatment, life skills, and housing and employment services to clients in the Chicagoland area.

More Information

2942 W. Lake Street
Chicago, Illinois 60612

Email: info@anb.today

Website: www.anb.today

Social Media: Facebook

Employment Services

Chicago Cook Workforce Partnership

Contact: (312) 603-0200

The Chicago Cook Workforce Partnerships provides job training and assistance to all residents within Cook County, including the city of Chicago and more than 200 other municipalities. The 48 delegate agencies within this partnership are listed with their contact information on the Chicago Cook Workforce Partnership webpage. The Partnership also serves youth aged 16 to 21 years old.

More Information

Website: www.workforceboard.org

Social Media: Twitter

The Cara Program

Contact: (312) 798-3309

Since 1991, Cara has assisted Chicago residents stuck in a cycle of poverty and homelessness get back on track and secure permanent employment. Partnered with 120 Chicagoland businesses, they provide an extensive range of training, support and job placement.

More Information

Email: info@thecaraprogam.org

Website: www.thecaraprogram.org

Social Media: Facebook, Twitter, YouTube, Linkedin

Instituto del Progreso Latino

Contact: (773) 890-0055

Instituto del Progreso Latino offers services in four different areas: economic and workforce development, adult basic education, youth development, and citizenship services.

More Information

Email: info@cosachicago.org

Website: www.institutochicago.org

Social Media: Facebook, Twitter, Linkedin

Bridges to Success

Contact: (312) 733-9742

Bridges to Success provides low-income men, women, and young adults appropriate interview and workforce attire. In addition, they offer interview preparation trainings.

More Information

Website: www.thebridgetosuccess.org

Social Media: Facebook, Twitter, and Linkedin

Washington Heights Workforce Center

Contact: (773) 928-5272

Dynamic Educational Systems, Inc. (DESI) provides education, training, and job placement assistance the adults and young adults need to support themselves, their families, and the community.

More Information

Website: www.exodyne.com/desi_home.php

Jane Addams Resource Corporation (JARC)

Contact: (773) 728-9769

JARC is dedicated to serving low-income Chicago residents by providing them with the necessary skills to earn a living wage. JARC connects job seekers with permanent positions in the manufacturing sector. Recently, they have expanded their services to the DuPage County region.

More Information

Website: www.jane-addams.org

Social Media: Facebook, Twitter

Inspiration Corporation

Contact: (773) 878-0981

Inspiration Corporation provides a comprehensive range of services for Chicago resident affected by homelessness and poverty.

More Information

Website: www.inspirationcorp.org

Hotlines

Chicago Crime Commission
Anonymous Crime Reporting Hotline

Contact: (888) 393-6646

Chicago Police Department
Community Alternative Policing Strategy (CAPS)

Contact: (312) 745-5900

Chicago Public Schools

Contact: (888) 881-0606

Hotline for violence prevention

Department of Children and Family Services

Contact: (800) 252-2873

Hotline to report suspected child abuse and neglect

Cook County Crime Stoppers

Contact: (800) 535-STOP

City of Chicago Graffiti Removal

Contact: 311

Cook County State's Attorney's Office – Community Outreach

Contact: (312) 603-8710

Phone number designated for improving public safety and increasing community partnerships

....

Federal Law Enforcement Agencies

Federal Bureau of Investigation

Contact: (312) 421-6700

2111 W. Roosevelt Road, Chicago, IL 60608

Drug Enforcement Administration

Contact: (312) 353-3640

230 S. Dearborn Street, Chicago, IL 60604

Bureau of Alcohol, Tobacco, Firearms and Explosives

Contact: (312) 846-7200

525 W. Van Buren Street, Chicago, IL 60607

United States Marshals

Contact: (312) 353-4978

219 S. Dearborn Street. #2444, Chicago, IL 60604

Financial Crimes Enforcement Network (FinCEN)

Contact: (800) 767-2825

Email: FRC@fincen.gov

City of Chicago Wards

First Ward

Contact: (773) 278-0101
Website: www.ward1.org
Email: Ward01@cityofchicago.org

Second Ward

Contact: (312) 643-2299
Email: Ward02@cityofchicago.org

Third Ward

Contact: (773) 373-9273
Email: ward03@cityofchicago.org

Fourth Ward

Contact: (773) 536-8103
Email: ward04@cityofchicago.org

Fifth Ward

Contact: (773) 324-5555
Email: ward05@cityofchicago.org

Sixth Ward

Contact: (773) 635-0006
Website: www.6ward.com
Email: ward06@cityofchicago.org

Seventh Ward

Contact: (773) 731-7777
Email: ward07@cityofchicago.org

Eighth Ward

Contact: (773) 874-3300
Email: ward08@cityofchicago.org

Ninth Ward

Contact: (773) 785-1100
Website: www.ward09.com
Email: ward09@cityofchicago.org

Tenth Ward

Contact: (773) 768-8138
Email: ward10@cityofchicago.org

Eleventh Ward

Contact: (773) 254-6677
Email: ward11@cityofchicago.org

Twelfth Ward

Contact: (773) 523-8250
Email: ward12@cityofchicago.org

Thirteenth Ward

Contact: (773) 581-1313
Email: ward13@cityofchicago.org

Fourteenth Ward

Contact: (773) 471-1414
Email: ward14@cityofchicago.org

Fifteenth Ward

Contact: (773) 823-1539
Email: ward15@cityofchicago.org

Sixteenth Ward

Contact: (773) 863-0220
Email: ward16@cityofchicago.org

Seventeenth Ward

Contact: (773) 783-3672

Email: ward17@cityofchicago.org

Eighteenth Ward

Contact: (773) 284-5057

Email: ward18@cityofchicago.org

Nineteenth Ward

Contact: (773) 238-8766

Email: ward19@cityofchicago.org

Twentieth Ward

Contact: (773) 955-5610

Email: ward20@cityofchicago.org

Twenty-First Ward

Contact: (773) 881-9300

Email: ward21@cityofchicago.org

Twenty-Second Ward

Contact: (773) 762-4900

Email: ward22@cityofchicago.org

Twenty-Third Ward

Contact: (773) 582-4444

Email: ward23@cityofchicago.org

Twenty-Fourth Ward

Contact: (773) 533-2400

Email: ward24@cityofchicago.org

Twenty-Fifth Ward

Contact: (773) 523-4100

Email: ward25@cityofchicago.org

Twenty-Sixth Ward

Contact: (773) 395-0143

Email: ward26@cityofchicago.org

Twenty-Seventh Ward

Contact: (312) 432-1995

Email: ward27@cityofchicago.org

Twenty-Eighth Ward

Contact: (773) 533-0900

Email: ward28@cityofchicago.org

Twenty-Ninth Ward

Contact: (773) 237-6460

Email: ward29@cityofchicago.org

Thirtieth Ward

Contact: (773) 794-3095

Email: ward30@cityofchicago.org

Thirty-First Ward

Contact: (773) 278-0031

Email: ward31@cityofchicago.org

Thirty-Second Ward

Contact: (773) 248-1330

Email: ward32@cityofchicago.org

Thirty-Third Ward

Contact: (773) 478-8040

Email: ward33@cityofchicago.org

Thirty-Fourth Ward

Contact: (773) 928-6961

Email: ward34@cityofchicago.org

Thirty-Fifth Ward

Contact: (773) 887-3772
Email: ward35@cityofchicago.org

Thirty-Sixth Ward

Contact: (773) 745-4636
Email: ward36@cityofchicago.org

Thirty-Seventh Ward

Contact: (773) 379-0960
Email: ward37@cityofchicago.org

Thirty-Eighth Ward

Contact: (773) 283-3838
Email: ward38@cityofchicago.org

Thirty-Ninth Ward

Contact: (773) 736-5594
Email: ward39@cityofchicago.org

Fortieth Ward

Contact: (773) 769-1140
Email: ward40@cityofchicago.org

Forty-First Ward

Contact: (773) 631-2241
Email: ward41@cityofchicago.org

Forty-Second Ward

Contact: (312) 642-4242
Email: ward42@cityofchicago.org

Forty-Third Ward

Contact: (773) 348-9500
Email: ward43@cityofchicago.org

Forty-Fourth Ward

Contact: (773) 525-6034
Email: ward44@cityofchicago.org

Forty-Fifth Ward

Contact: (773) 286-4545
Email: ward45@cityofchicago.org

Forty-Sixth Ward

Contact: (773) 878-4646
Email: ward46@cityofchicago.org

Forty-Seventh Ward

Contact: (773) 868-4747
Email: ward47@cityofchicago.org

Forty-Eighth Ward

Contact: (773) 784-5277
Email: ward48@cityofchicago.org

Forty-Ninth Ward

Contact: (773) 338-5796
Email: ward49@citychicago.org

Fiftieth Ward

Contact: (773) 262-1050
Email: ward50@cityofchicago.org

VIII

SECTION

Gang Book References

chicago
crime
commission

Introduction

Córdova, T.L., & Wilson, M.D. (2016). *Lost: The Crisis of Jobless and Out Of School Teens and Young Adults In Chicago, Illinois and the U.S.* Chicago, IL: University of Illinois at Chicago Greater Cities Institute.

Hubbard, J. D., & Wyman, K. (2012). *The Chicago Crime Commission Gang Book: A Detailed Overview of Street Gangs in the Chicago Metropolitan Area.* Chicago, IL: Chicago Crime Commission.

Definitions

Gang Awareness. (2017). In *Chicago Police Department*. Retrieved May 6, 2017.

2015 National Gang Report. N.p.: National Alliance of Gang Investigators' Associations (NAGIA) and FBI Safe Streets and Gang Unit, 2015.

740 ILCS 147/10

P.A. 97-1150, eff. 1-25-13

Section 1 – Gang Profiles

Factions

Stuart, Forest. (2016, September 19). Dispatches from the Rap Wars. *Chicago Magazine*, October 2016.

65 U.S. Attorneys' Bulletin, August 2017

Cook County Sheriff's Department

Female Gang Membership

A similar version of this article first appeared as a *Police Chief online article* in 2017. Copyright held by the International Association of Chiefs of Police, Inc. Further reproduction without express permission from IACP is strictly prohibited.

National Gang Center. *National Youth Gang Survey Analysis.* Retrieved [14 June 2017] from http://www.nationalgang-center.gov/Survey-Analysis.

Hayward, R. A., & Honegger, L. (n.d.). Gender differences in juvenile gang members: An exploratory study. *Journal of Evidence-Based Social Work*, 11, 373-382.

Peterson, D., & Morgan, K. A. (2014). Sex differences and the overlap in youths' risk factors for onset of violence and gang involvement. *Journal of Crime and Justice*, 37(1), 129-154.

De La Rue, L., & Espelage, D. L. (2014). Family and abuse characteristics of gang-involved, pressured-to-join, and non-gang-involved girls. *Psychology of Violence*, 4(3), 253-265.

Coulson, David. Interview of ATF Agent by Chicago Crime Commission. Chicago, IL. July 21, 2017.

Sweeney, A. (2016, December 10). Impact of Chicago's violence on girls in toughest neighborhoods often overlooked. *Chicago Tribune*.

United States Sentencing Commission. (2016, March). *Recidivism Among Federal Offenders: A Comprehensive Overview* (K. S. Hunt, Ph.D & R. Dumville, Authors).

"Youth Guidance: Working on Womanhood." Strides for Peace. https://www.stridesforpeace.org/community-partners/youth-guidance/.

"About Demoiselle 2 Femme, NFP." Demoiselle 2 Femme. Retrieved July 24, 2017. http://demoiselle2femme.org/.

Section 3 – Social Media

Sabih Khan, Village of Skokie

Chicago Tribune Staff. (2016, October 29). Man shot during Facebook Live post in March among those killed Friday. In *Chicago Tribune*. Retrieved February 11, 2017.

Drill – Music. (n.d.). In *Hip Wiki*. Retrieved February 11, 2017.

Young Pappy (2014) Shooters [Recorded by Young Pappy] On *Savages* [MP3 file]. Chicago, IL: TFG Entertainment.

Stuart, Forest. (2016, September 19). Dispatches from the Rap Wars. *Chicago Magazine*, October 2016.

People v. Chromik, 408 Ill. App. 3d 1028 (3d Dist. 2011)

Ill. R. Evid. 901(a)

Ill. R. Evid. 401 and 403.

Kling, R. S., Hasan, K., & Gould, M. D. (2017, January). Admissibility of Social Media Evidence in Illinois. *Illinois Bar Journal*, 105(#1).

Schoen, D. I. (2011, May 17). The Authentication of Social Media Postings. In *American Bar Association*. Retrieved June 12, 2017.

Grimm, H. W., Yurwitt Bergstrom, L., & O'Toole-Loureiro, M. M. (2013). Authentication of Social Media Evidence. *American Journal of Trial Advocacy*, 36.

"Facebook" "Instagram" "Twitter" "Youtube" "Kik" "Whatsapp" "Snapchat" "Offerup" and all other product and service names, accompanying fonts, designs, and logos are the registered marks, trademarks and/or service marks of their respective owners and are used for identification purposes only. No endorsement of or sponsorship or affiliation with the Chicago Crime Commission is implied.

Section 4 – Suburban Gang Activity

Survey of Gang and Drug Activity. 2016. Chicago Crime Commission.

Section 5 – Cartels, Gangs and Drugs

2017 National Drug Threat Assessment Summary. N.p.: U.S. Department of Justice Drug Enforcement Administration, 2017.

2010 National Drug Threat Assessment. N.p.: U.S. Department of Justice Drug Enforcement Administration, 2010.

Knights Templar. (2017, June 22). In *Insight Crime*. Retrieved February 12, 2017.

2017 DEA Cartels and Gangs Threat Assessment. N.p.: U.S. Department of Justice Drug Administration, 2017.

Money Laundering. (2014, August 26). In *U.S. Immigration and Customs Enforcement*. Retrieved February 12, 2017.

Drugs of Abuse: A DEA Resource Guide 2017 Edition. N.p.: U.S. Department of Justice Drug Enforcement Administration, 2017.

DEA Targets Fentanyl: A Real Threat to Law Enforcement. N.p.: U.S. Department of Justice Drug Enforcement Administration, 2016.

"Doctors Warn About Spike in Fentanyl Deaths in Cook County." CBS Chicago. Last modified May 8, 2017. Retrieved August 31, 2017.

Katz, Josh. "Drug Deaths in America Are Rising Faster Than Ever." *New York Times*, June 5, 2017, The Upshot.

Charles, Sam. "571 Dead in Chicago Since 2014 from Fentanyl, Hero Officer One of Them." *Chicago Sun Times*, July 26, 2017.

Siemaszko, Corky. "Fentanyl Crisis: Chicago Sees Surge in Deaths From New Designer Drug." *NBC News*. Last modified May 8, 2017. Retrieved August 31, 2017.

DEA Public Affairs. "DEA Issues Carfentanil Warning to Police and Public." News release. September 22, 2016. Retrieved August 31, 2017.

NPR. "Lethal Opiates Delivered By Mail From China, Killing Addicts in the U.S." npr.org. Last modified March 11, 2017. Retrieved August 31, 2017.

Popper, Nathaniel. "Opioid Dealers Embrace the Dark Web to Send Deadly Drugs by Mail." *New York Times*, June 10, 2017.

Ahmed, Azam. "Drug That Killed Prince is Making Mexican Cartels Richer, U.S. Says." *New York Times*, June 9, 2016.

Fentanyl A Briefing Guide for First Responders. N.p.: U.S. Department of Justice Drug Administration, 2017.

Cartels, Gangs and Drugs: Sweeney, A., Meisner, J., & Bentle, K (2015, March 27). How the Flores Brothers took down El Chapo and others . In *Chicago Tribune*. Retrieved November 13, 2017.

Cartels, Gangs and Drugs: Sinaloa Cartel. (2018, January 24). In *Insight Crime*. Retrieved March 12, 2018

Section 6 – Gun Trafficking

2017 DEA Cartels and Gangs Threat Assessment. N.p.: U.S. Department of Justice Drug Administration, 2017.

Spies, M., & Fuhrman, E. (2015, November 2). Watch How Chicago Gets Flooded with Thousands of Crime Guns. In *The Trace*. Retrieved February 17, 2017.

Ernst, A. (2014, October 22). Why does Chicago have so many illegal guns?. In *Aljazeera America*. Retrieved February 18, 2017.

Tarm, M. (2017, March 3). Railroad Thefts and guns: A deadly mix in Chicago. In *Chicago Tribune*. Retrieved April 12, 2017.

Negovan, T. (2014, May 9). Assault rifles stolen from Chicago rail yard. In *WGN9*. Retrieved April 12, 2017.

Kollmorgen, S. (2016, January 6). Chicago Criminals' Favorite Gunmakers: A Visual Ranking. In *The Trace*. Retrieved April 12, 2017.

Cook, P. J., Harris, R. J., Ludwig, J., & Pollack, H. A. (2014). Some sources of crime guns in Chicago: dirty dealers, straw purchasers, and traffickers. *J. Crim. L. & Criminology*, 104, 717.

National Integrated Ballistic Information Network (NIBIN). (n.d.). In *Bureau of Alcohol, Tobacco, Firearms and Explosives*. Retrieved April 12, 2017.

Martinez, M. (2017, April 12). CPD on ShotSpotter Sensors: 'We Want to Replicate That Success'. In *CBS Chicago*. Retrieved April 19, 2017.

Types of Federal Firearms Licenses (FFLs). (n.d.). In *Bureau of Alcohol, Tobacco, Firearms and Explosives*. Retrieved April 12, 2017.

Firearms – Guides – Important & Verification of Firearms – Gun Control Act Definition – Ammunition. (n.d.). In *U.S. Department of Justice – Bureau of Alcohol, Tobacco, Firearms and Explosive, Office of Enforcement Programs and Services*. Retrieved April 12, 2017.

Chicago Police Department. (2017). *Report Covering the Week of 25-Dec-17 Through 31-Dec-17 City Wide Crime Statistics*. Retrieved from Chicago Police Department Data Portal.